Foundations First

SENTENCES AND PARAGRAPHS

WITH READINGS

Foundations First

SENTENCES AND PARAGRAPHS

WITH READINGS

Second Edition

Laurie G. Kirszner
University of the Sciences in Philadelphia

Stephen R. Mandell
Drexel University

Bedford / St. Martin's
Boston ■ New York

For Bedford/St. Martin's

Developmental Editor: Mikola De Roo
Production Editor: Bernard Onken
Senior Production Supervisor: Dennis J. Conroy
Senior Marketing Manager: Rachel Falk
Art Director: Lucy Krikorian
Text Design: Wanda Kossak
Copy Editor: Rosemary Winfield
Photo Research: Photosearch, Inc./Sherri Zuckerman
Cover Design: Lucy Krikorian
Cover Photos: left to right: Gary Conner/PhotoEdit; Tom Stewart/CORBIS; Mary Kate Denny/PhotoEdit; Gary Conner/PhotoEdit; David Lissy/eStock Photo.
Composition: Stratford Publishing Services, Inc.
Printing and Binding: R. R. Donnelley & Sons Company

President: Joan E. Feinberg
Editorial Director: Denise B. Wydra
Editor in Chief: Nancy Perry
Director of Marketing: Karen Melton Soeltz
Director of Editing, Design, and Production: Marcia Cohen
Managing Editor: Erica T. Appel

Library of Congress Control Number: 2004108138

Manufactured in the United States of America.

0 9 8 7 6 5
f e d c b

For information, write: Bedford/St. Martin's, 75 Arlington Street, Boston, MA 02116 (617-399-4000)

ISBN: 0-312-41964-3 (Instructor's Annotated Edition)
0-312-41337-8 (Student Edition with Readings)
0-312-41336-X (Student Edition)

EAN: 978-0-312-41964-6 (Instructor's Annotated Edition)
978-0-312-41337-8 (Student Edition with Readings)
978-0-312-41336-1 (Student Edition)

Acknowledgments
Acknowledgments and copyrights appear at the back of the book on pages 551–552, which constitute an extension of the copyright page.

Preface for Instructors

We believe that in college, writing comes first and that students learn writing skills most meaningfully in the context of their own writing. For this reason, *Foundations First: Sentences and Paragraphs,* like our paragraph-to-essay text *Writing First,* takes a "practice in context" approach, giving students in the context of their own writing the skills they need to become better writers.

Equally important, *Foundations First* is the only sentence-to-paragraph text to offer not just grammar and writing help but also a collection of resources to prepare developmental students for college work. By providing unique coverage of study skills, vocabulary building, ESL issues, and critical reading, *Foundations First* gives students the support and encouragement they need to build a solid foundation for success in college and beyond.

In *Foundations First,* as in the classroom and in everyday life, writing is essential. For this reason, we begin with thorough coverage of the writing process. Most chapters begin with a writing prompt, and extensive writing practice is also central to the grammar chapters of the text. Throughout the book, students learn to become better writers by applying each chapter's concepts to writing, revising, and editing their own writing.

We wrote this book for adults—our own interested, concerned, and hardworking students—and we tailored the book's approach and content to them. Instead of exercises that reinforce the idea that writing is a dull, pointless, and artificial activity, we chose fresh, contemporary examples (both student and professional) and worked hard to develop interesting exercises and writing assignments. Throughout *Foundations First* we try to talk *to* students, not *at* or *down* to them. We try to be concise without being abrupt, thorough without being repetitive, direct without being rigid, specific without being prescriptive, and flexible without being inconsistent. Our most important goal is simple: to create an engaging text that motivates students to improve their writing and that gives them the tools they need to do so.

Organization

Foundations First: Sentences and Paragraphs has a flexible organization that lets instructors teach various topics in the order that works best for their students. The book opens with a section on academic and real-world survival skills: Unit One, new to the second edition, includes four chapters that offer a broad range of practical advice to help students succeed in college and beyond. Unit Two provides a comprehensive discussion of the writing process. Units Three through Six focus on sentence skills, grammar, punctuation, mechanics, and spelling. Unit Seven, which appears only in *Foundations First with Readings,* includes eighteen essays (five by student writers), accompanied by study questions and writing prompts. Finally, an appendix, "Building Word Power," reviews the vocabulary highlighted in the text and gives students practice exercises and other opportunities for expanding their vocabulary.

For instructors wishing to emphasize the patterns of development, an Index of Rhetorical Patterns points to essays and paragraphs that exemplify particular modes. (All of the patterns are covered in Chapter 7, and the essays in Unit Seven include at least one example of each pattern.)

Features

When we wrote *Foundations First,* our goal was to create the most complete sentence-to-paragraph text available for developmental writers. In preparing the second edition, we retained all the features that instructors told us contributed to the book's accessibility and effectiveness.

A complete resource for improving student writing. With three chapters on paragraphs (including coverage of all the major patterns of development), four units on grammar, a comprehensive chapter on the essay, and numerous examples of student writing throughout the text, *Foundations First* provides comprehensive coverage of writing in a format that gives instructors maximum flexibility in planning their courses.

"Practice in Context" writing activities. A two-step exercise strand in most chapters enables students to write, revise, and edit their own work from the outset. Chapters typically begin with a ***Seeing and Writing*** activity that asks students to write a response to a visual. At the end of the chapter, a ***Revising and Editing*** activity helps students fine-tune their ***Seeing and Writing*** response, applying the skills they have learned and practiced in the chapter.

Numerous opportunities for practice and review. *Foundations First* helps students practice grammar in the context of connected-discourse exercises that mirror the kinds of material they are likely to read and write in college. ***Self-Assessment Checklists*** guide students in revising and editing their work. ***Chapter Reviews***—featuring ***Editing Practices, Collaborative Activities,*** and ***Review Checklists***—encourage students to think critically about writing. Finally, ***Answers to Odd-Numbered Exercises*** at the end of the book let students check their own work as they practice and review.

A visually appealing, easy-to-use, full-color design. Enhanced with navigation features, photos, and other visuals in every chapter, *Foundations First* helps students locate key information quickly and easily. More than two dozen visual writing prompts help students generate ideas.

Content that respects students as serious writers. The tone and level of the explanatory material and the subject matter of the exercises and examples acknowledge the diverse interests, ages, and experiences of developmental students. ***Writing Tips*** in the margins provide additional information, address common problem areas, and draw connections between chapter topics and nonacademic writing situations. Numerous examples of student writing provide realistic models for students.

Comprehensive coverage of critical reading. *Foundations First* presents reading as an integral part of the writing process, offering numerous student and professional examples throughout the text. Chapter 2, "Reading for Academic Success," introduces the basic techniques of active reading and shows students how to get the most out of their academic and professional reading. Eighteen selections (five of them by students) in Chapter 30, "Readings for Writers," provide material for writing assignments and classroom discussion.

An integrated approach to building vocabulary. In every chapter, ***Word Power*** boxes help students learn new words and use them in the context of their own writing. The appendix, "Building Word Power," gives students additional opportunities for expanding their vocabulary.

Extensive help for ESL students. Chapter 24 addresses concerns of nonnative writers. ***ESL Tips*** throughout the *Instructor's Annotated Edition* provide helpful hints to instructors.

New to This Edition

We have worked hard to make the second edition of *Foundations First* even more useful to developmental writers and their instructors. Recognizing that students often need help not just with grammar and writing but also with making a successful transition to college, we have expanded our unique coverage of study skills and related issues. Additionally, we support our "students first" philosophy with even more innovative features designed to make students' writing practice meaningful, productive, and enjoyable.

A unique unit that gives students practical strategies for college and beyond. Because students need to develop and apply hands-on problem-solving strategies in every aspect of their lives—academically, professionally, and personally—Chapter 1, "Strategies for College Success," has been expanded into a four-chapter introductory unit, "Learning Practical Success Strategies." This unit now offers a broad range of practical advice to help students succeed in all their college courses, as well as in the workplace and beyond.

- **Chapter 1, "Strategies for College Success,"** includes advice on taking notes, completing homework assignments, taking exams, and managing time efficiently.

- **Chapter 2, "Reading for College Success,"** gives students the skills they need to become active readers. It also offers strategies for reading in different situations—in college, in the workplace, and in daily life—including specific advice on reading textbooks, newspapers, Web sites, interoffice memos, and emails.
- **Chapter 3, "Using the Internet for College Success,"** shows students how to use the Internet effectively to find information for their writing assignments as well as everyday information for their own use.
- **Chapter 4, "Strategies for Workplace Success,"** gives students pragmatic advice on defining professional goals; finding job openings; researching companies; and writing effective résumés, job-application letters, and follow-up letters.

More than one hundred new grammar exercises. In response to instructors' requests, new paragraph-length ***Editing Practices*** have been added, as well as new exercises on run-ons and fragments—errors that instructors say are the most challenging for their students—and on restrictive/nonrestrictive clauses. Also included in this edition are new exercises on ESL-related grammar issues. To increase student interest, exercises throughout the book focus on everyday life, the world of work, and contemporary culture as well as on academic subjects.

Illustrations to help sharpen vocabulary skills. To provide cultural contexts for students who need additional background and to offer support for students who are visual learners, marginal photos now illustrate the ***Editing Practice*** essays at the end of each chapter.

Coverage of four additional patterns of development. In response to instructors' requests, Chapter 7, "Patterns of Paragraph Development," has been expanded to include cause and effect, process, classification, and definition. With these additions, the chapter now covers all nine patterns of development.

Expanded and improved Computer Tips. To address students' ongoing need to make effective use of the computer as they write, marginal ***Computer Tips*** have been revised and expanded to reflect the most current pedagogical strategies.

Expanded and improved cross-referencing system. For students who need additional practice with specific grammar, mechanics, and punctuation skills, the text includes new marginal cross-references to the **Exercise Central** online exercise collection. To make the book easier for ESL students to use, additional cross-references from other chapters to Chapter 24, "Grammar and Usage Issues for ESL Writers," have been added.

Ancillaries

Foundations First is accompanied by a comprehensive teaching support package that includes the following items:

Print Resources

- The *Instructor's Annotated Edition* features numerous teaching tips in the margins, including ESL tips designed especially for instructors teaching nonnative speakers. The book's annotations include answers to all the practice exercises in *Foundations First.*
- *Classroom Resources for Instructors Using FOUNDATIONS FIRST,* **Second Edition**, offers advice for teaching developmental writing as well as chapter-by-chapter pointers for using *Foundations First* in the classroom. Also included are sample course syllabi. Full chapters on collaborative learning, critical thinking, teaching ESL students, and teaching with technology address the needs of developmental writing instructors. Answers to grammar exercises in the main text are included in a separate section so that instructors can distribute these to students.
- *Teaching Developmental Writing: Background Readings,* **Second Edition**, by Susan Naomi Bernstein, contains thirty-five professional readings (thirteen new to this edition) on topics of interest to instructors. Helpful chapter introductions, informative headnotes, suggested classroom activities, pedagogical tips, and questions accompany the readings.
- *Transparency Masters to Accompany FOUNDATIONS FIRST,* **Second Edition**, includes numerous models of student writing, available as either a printed package or as files downloadable from the *Foundations First* Web site.
- *Supplemental Exercises to Accompany FOUNDATIONS FIRST,* **Second Edition**, offers additional grammar exercises (including material from the **Exercise Central** online exercise collection).
- *Diagnostic and Mastery Tests to Accompany FOUNDATIONS FIRST,* **Second Edition**, offers diagnostic and mastery tests that complement the topics covered in *Foundations First.*

New Media Resources

- *The FOUNDATIONS FIRST Web site at <bedfordstmartins.com/foundationsfirst>* features extensive support for instructors, including downloadable versions of two print ancillaries (*Classroom Resources for Instructors Using FOUNDATIONS FIRST* and *Diagnostic and Mastery Tests to Accompany FOUNDATIONS FIRST*) and downloadable forms (including all the transparency masters). For students, the Web site provides links to helpful writing sites and access to **Exercise Central**'s grammar exercise collection.
- *Exercise Central for FOUNDATIONS FIRST at <bedfordstmartins.com/foundationsfirst>* is the largest online collection of grammar exercises available. This resource is comprehensive, easy to use, and convenient for both students and instructors. Multiple exercise sets on every grammar topic, at a variety of levels, ensure that students get as much practice as they need. Customized instant feedback turns skills practice into a learning experience, and the reporting function enables both students and instructors to monitor and assess student progress.

Acknowledgments

In our work on *Foundations First,* we have benefited from the help of a great many people.

Franklin E. Horowitz of Teachers College, Columbia University, drafted an early version of Chapter 24, "Grammar and Usage Issues for ESL Writers," and his linguist's insight continues to inform that chapter. Linda Stine of Lincoln University devoted energy and vision to the preparation of *Classroom Resources for Instructors Using Foundations First.* Linda Mason Austin of McLennan Community College drew on her extensive experience to contribute Teaching Tips and ESL Tips to the *Instructor's Annotated Edition.* Susan Bernstein's work on the compilation and annotation of *Teaching Developmental Writing: Background Readings* reflects her deep commitment to scholarship and teaching. We are very grateful for their contributions.

We thank Kristen Blanco, Stephanie Hopkins, Judith Lechner, Carolyn Lengel, Carol Sullivan, Jessica Carroll, and Pamela Gerth for their contributions to the exercises and writing activities in the text, and Linda Stine for developing the PowerPoint presentation featured on the *Foundations First* Web site. We also thank Tom Greene for his help in evaluating and improving the book's Computer Tips.

Foundations First could not exist without our students, whose words appear on almost every page of the book, whether in sample sentences, paragraphs, or essays. Special thanks go to Trina Andras, Justin Brines, Charnette Carrington, Bethany Cooper, Margaret Caracappa, Jared Esposito, Hector de la Paz, Brigid Mitchell, Victoria Nasid, Chuck Newman, Thuy Nguyen, John Palcza, Sara Price, Agaja Reddy, Julia Reyes, Stacie Sasinowsky, Vanessa Scully, Kimsohn Tang, Molly Ward, David Weaver, Forrest Williams, and Mike Zink.

Instructors throughout the country have contributed suggestions and encouragement at various stages of the book's development. For their collegial support, we thank Janice Filer, Shelton State Community College; Patricia B. Handley, Bessemer State Technical College; John G. Hoover, Santa Monica College; Sharon Jaffe, Santa Monica College; Mandy Kallus, Blinn College; Tamara Kuzmenkov, Tacoma Community College; Emily Levin Lodmer, Santa Monica College; Melody Nightingale, Santa Monica College; Brit Osgood-Treston, Riverside Community College; Dee Pruitt, Florence Darlington Technical College; Rashidah Shakir, Los Angeles Trade Technical College; Joseph Smigelski, Diablo Valley College; Yolanda K. Snyder, Millersville University; Kathy Sucher, Santa Monica College; Gina L. Thompson, Mississippi Community College; and Mary McCaslin Thompson, Anoka Ramsey Community College.

At Bedford/St. Martin's, we thank founder and former president Chuck Christensen and president Joan Feinberg, who believed in this project and gave us support and encouragement from the outset. We thank Nancy Perry, editor in chief and our longtime friend, who continues to earn our respect as well as our affection. We also thank Paul Stenis, associate editor, for his diligent work in revising the book's ancillaries; Kristy Bredin and Nathan Odell, editorial assistants, for helping with numerous tasks, big and small; Erica Appel, managing editor, and Bernie Onken, project editor, for guiding the book ably through production; and Lucy Krikorian, art director, for once again overseeing a beautiful and innovative design. Thanks also go to Dennis Conroy, senior production supervisor; Karen Melton Soeltz, director of marketing; and Rachel Falk, marketing manager. Finally, we thank our editor, Mika De Roo, whose humor, attention to detail, and ability to keep the project moving made our task so much easier.

We are grateful, too, for the continued support of our families—Mark, Adam, and Rebecca Kirszner, and Demi, David, and Sarah Mandell. Finally, we are grateful for the survival and growth of the writing partnership we entered into in 1975, when we were graduate students. We had no idea then of the wonderful places our collaborative efforts would take us. Now, we know.

Laurie G. Kirszner
Stephen R. Mandell

Contents

A Student's Guide to Using Foundations First

What *Foundations First* Can Do for You

Whether you write as a student, as an employee, as a parent, or as a concerned citizen, your writing almost always has a specific purpose. When you write an essay, a memo, a letter, or a research paper, you are writing not just to complete an exercise but to give other people information or to tell them your ideas or opinions. That is why, in this book, we don't ask you simply to do grammar exercises and fill in blanks; in each chapter, we also ask you to apply the skills you are learning to a piece of your own writing.

As teachers—and former students—we know how demanding college can be and how hard it is to juggle assignments with work and family responsibilities. We also know that you don't want to waste your time or money. That is why in *Foundations First* we make information easy to find and use and provide many different features to help you become a better writer.

The following sections describe the key features of *Foundations First*. If you take the time now to familiarize yourself with these features, you will be able to use the book more effectively later on.

How *Foundations First* Makes Information Easy to Find and Use

Brief table of contents Inside the front cover is a brief table of contents that summarizes the topics covered in this book. The brief contents can help you find a particular chapter quickly.

Detailed table of contents The table of contents that starts on page xiii provides a detailed breakdown of the book's topics. Use this table of contents to find a specific part of a particular chapter.

Index The index, which appears at the back of the book starting on page 553, helps you find all the available information about a particular topic. The topics appear in alphabetical order, so, for example, if you wanted to find out how to use commas, you would find the *C* section and look up the word *comma*. (If the page number following a word is **boldfaced,** it means that on that page you can find a definition of the word.)

List of Self-Assessment Checklists On page xxviii is a list of checklists designed to help you write, revise, and edit paragraphs and even essays. Use this list to find the checklist that is most useful for the particular writing task you are working on.

A handy cross-referencing system Often, an *italicized **marginal cross-reference*** (for example, "See 2C") will point you to another section of the book. At the tops of most pages of *Foundations First,* you'll find ***quick-reference corner tabs*** consisting of green-and-blue boxes, each containing a number and a letter. This information tells you which chapter you have turned to and which section of that chapter you are looking at. Together, the cross-references and the tabs help you find information quickly. For example, if a marginal cross-reference in the text suggested, *"For more on topic sentences, see 6A,"* you could use the tabs to quickly locate section 6A.

76 **5 C**

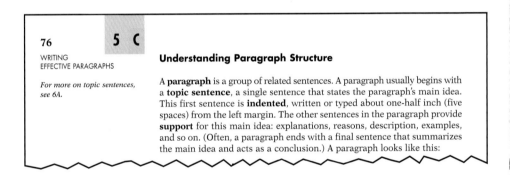

WRITING EFFECTIVE PARAGRAPHS

For more on topic sentences, see 6A.

Understanding Paragraph Structure

A **paragraph** is a group of related sentences. A paragraph usually begins with a **topic sentence**, a single sentence that states the paragraph's main idea. This first sentence is **indented**, written or typed about one-half inch (five spaces) from the left margin. The other sentences in the paragraph provide **support** for this main idea: explanations, reasons, description, examples, and so on. (Often, a paragraph ends with a final sentence that summarizes the main idea and acts as a conclusion.) A paragraph looks like this:

How *Foundations First* Can Help You Become a Better Writer

Preview boxes Each chapter starts with a list of key concepts that will be discussed in the chapter. Looking at these boxes before you skim the chapter will help you get an overview of the material that will be covered.

Seeing and Writing activities Most chapters include a two-part writing activity that helps you apply specific skills to your own writing. Each chapter starts with a ***Seeing and Writing*** exercise, accompanied by a visual, that asks you to write about a particular topic. Later, a ***Revising and Editing*** exercise guides you in fine-tuning your writing.

■ SEEING AND WRITING

If you met a person who had never been to McDonald's, what would you tell him or her about this fast-food restaurant? Look at the picture above, and then write a paragraph that answers this question.

PREVIEW

In this chapter, you will learn

- to identify a sentence's subject (9A)
- to recognize singular and plural subjects (9B)
- to identify prepositions and prepositional phrases (9C)
- to distinguish a prepositional phrase from a subject (9C)
- to identify action verbs (9D)
- to identify linking verbs (9E)
- to identify main verbs and helping verbs (9F)

Focus boxes Throughout the book, boxes with the word *Focus* in a red banner highlight useful information, identify key points, and explain difficult concepts.

FOCUS Identifying Sentence Fragments

In paragraphs and longer pieces of writing, sentence fragments sometimes appear next to complete sentences. You can often correct a sentence fragment by attaching it to a nearby sentence that includes the missing subject or verb. In the following example, a fragment appears right after a complete sentence:

COMPLETE SENTENCE — FRAGMENT

Okera majored in two subjects. English and philosophy.

To correct the fragment, attach it to the complete sentence that contains the missing subject (*Okera*) and verb (*majored*):

Okera majored in two subjects, English and philosophy.

Self-Assessment Checklists Chapters 5, 7, and 8 include Self-Assessment Checklists that give you a handy way to check your work and measure your progress. Use these checklists to help you revise your writing before you hand it in.

✓ SELF-ASSESSMENT CHECKLIST: Revising Your Paragraph

- Does your topic sentence state your main idea?
- Do you have enough material to support your main idea?
- Have you explained your ideas fully and clearly?
- Have you used enough examples and details?

Marginal notes In the margins of *Foundations First,* you'll find several kinds of notes that give you additional information in an easy-to-read format. ***Marginal cross-references*** point you to related discussions in other parts of the book. ***Writing Tips*** offer practical information and helpful hints, including definitions and examples. ***Computer Tips*** help you make effective use of your computer as you write. ***Word Power*** boxes define words that you may find useful in working with a particular writing assignment or reading selection. Finally, if you need additional practice with specific skills, ***marginal cross-references to the Exercise Central online exercises collection*** now appear in the text.

Writing Tip

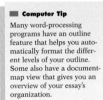

Transitional words and phrases used in narration include *first, then, next, after that, finally,* and other transitions that signal time order. See 6D.

Computer Tip

Many word-processing programs have an outline feature that helps you automatically format the different levels of your outline. Some also have a document-map view that gives you an overview of your essay's organization.

Word Power

dilemma a situation that requires a choice between two courses of action

ON THE WEB

For more practice on correcting run-ons and comma splices, visit Exercise Central at <bedfordstmartins.com/foundationsfirst>.

Review Checklists Each chapter ends with a summary of the most important information in the chapter. Use these checklists to review material for quizzes or to remind yourself of the main points in the chapter you've been studying.

✓ REVIEW CHECKLIST: Fine-Tuning Your Sentences

- You can make your sentences more interesting by varying your sentence openings. (See 12A.)
- Try to replace general words with specific ones. (See 12B.)
- Delete wordy expressions, substituting concise language where necessary. (See 12C.)
- Avoid clichés (overused expressions). (See 12D.)

Answers to Odd-Numbered Exercises Starting on page 539, you'll find answers for some of the Practice items in the book. When you need to study a topic independently, or when your instructor has you complete a Practice but not hand it in, you can consult these answers to see if you're on the right track.

How *Foundations First* Can Help You Succeed in Other Courses

In a sense, this whole book is all about succeeding in other courses. After all, as we said earlier, writing is the key to success in college. But *Foundations First* also includes sections that you may find especially useful in courses you take later on in college. We have designed these sections so you can use them either on your own or with your instructor's help.

Chapter 1, "Strategies for College Success" Here you'll find tips for making your semester (and your writing course) as successful as possible. Included are effective strategies for taking notes, completing homework assignments, doing well on exams, and managing your time efficiently.

Chapter 2, "Reading for Academic Success" This chapter will teach you the skills you need to become an active reader. It also offers specific strategies for reading in different situations—in college, in the workplace, and in daily life—and includes advice and examples on how to approach reading textbooks, newspapers, Web sites, inter-office memos, and emails.

Chapter 3, "Using the Internet for College Success" This chapter shows you how to find and evaluate Web sources—a skill that will be useful in all your courses and in your everyday life.

Chapter 4, "Strategies for Workplace Success" This step-by-step guide explains how to define your professional goals, find job openings, research companies, and market yourself by writing effective resumes, job-application letters, and follow-up letters, and by preparing for job interviews.

Appendix, "Building Word Power" This practical guide tells you how to get the most out of your dictionary. It also offers tips for building your vocabulary and gives you opportunities to practice using the words you've encountered in the Word Power boxes.

We hope *Foundations First* will help you become a better writer and student. If you have suggestions for improving this book, please send them to: Laurie Kirszner and Stephen Mandell, c/o Bedford/St. Martin's, 33 Irving Place, New York, NY 10003.

Self-Assessment Checklists for Revising and Editing Your Writing

Unit Two of *Foundations First* includes a series of Self-Assessment Checklists to help you write, revise, and edit paragraphs and essays. You can use these checklists in your writing course and in other courses that include written assignments. The page number for each checklist is included here.

Foundations First

SENTENCES AND PARAGRAPHS

WITH READINGS

UNIT ONE

Learning Practical Success Strategies

CHAPTER

1

Strategies for College Success

PREVIEW

In this chapter, you will learn

- orientation strategies (1A)
- first-week strategies (1B)
- day-to-day strategies (1C)
- note-taking strategies (1D)
- homework strategies (1E)
- exam-taking strategies (1F)
- time-management strategies (1G)
- public-speaking strategies (1H)

■ SEEING AND WRITING

How do you manage to fit everything you need to do into the limited time you have? Look at the picture above, and then write a few sentences that answer this question.

By deciding to go to college, you have decided to make some important changes in your life. In the long run, you will find that the changes will be positive, but there will be some challenges as well. One way in which your life will change is that now, perhaps more than ever, you will find yourself short of time. Life will become a balancing act as you juggle classroom time, commuting time, work time, and study time along with family responsibilities and time for yourself. The strategies discussed in this chapter can help make your life as a college student more productive and less stressful.

◆ PRACTICE 1.1

List the number of hours per day that you expect to spend on each of the following activities while you are a college student: reading, attending class, sleeping, working at a job, fulfilling family commitments, relaxing, commuting, and studying. (Be sure you have a total of twenty-four hours.) When you have finished your list, trade lists with another student, and compare your daily activities. Should any other activities be added to your list? If so, from which activities will you subtract time?

Word Power

orientation adjustment to a new environment

orient to adjust

A Orientation Strategies

Some strategies come in handy even before school begins, as you orient yourself to life as a college student. In fact, you may already have discovered some of these strategies.

- Make sure you have a college catalog, a photo ID, a student handbook, a parking permit, and any other items that entering students at your school are expected to have.
- Read your school's orientation materials (distributed as handouts or posted on the school Web site) very carefully. These materials will help familiarize you with campus buildings and offices, course offerings, faculty members, extracurricular activities, and so on.
- Be sure you know your academic adviser's name (and how to spell it), email address, office location, and office hours. Copy this information into your personal address book.
- Get a copy of your college library's orientation materials. These will tell you about the library's hours and services and explain procedures such as how to use an online catalog.
- Be sure you know where things are—not just how to find the library and the parking lot but also where you can do photocopying or buy a newspaper. You might as well learn to find your way around campus before things get too hectic.

◆ PRACTICE 1.2

Visit your school's Web site. List the three most useful pieces of information you find there. Now compare your list with those of other students in your class. Did reading their lists lead you to reevaluate your own? Do you still think the three items you listed are the most useful?

1. ______________________________

2. ______________________________

3. ______________________________

◆ PRACTICE 1.3

Working in a group of three or four students, draw a rough map of your school's campus, including the general locations of the following: the library, the financial aid office, the registrar's office, the cashier, the cafeteria, the bookstore, the computer lab, the campus police, the student health office. Now make up a quiz for another group of students, asking them to locate three additional buildings or offices on their map.

B First-Week Strategies

College can seem like a confusing place at first, but from your first day as a college student, there are steps you can take to help you get your bearings.

1. ***Make yourself at home***. Find places on campus where you can get something to eat or drink, and find a good place to study or relax before or between classes. As you explore the campus, try to locate all the things you may need—for example, pay phones, ATMs, and rest rooms.
2. ***Know where you're going and when you need to be there***. Check the building and room number for each of your classes and the days and hours the class meets. Copy this information onto the front cover of the appropriate notebook. Pay particular attention to classes with irregular schedules (for example, a class that meets from 9 a.m. to 10 a.m. on Tuesdays but from 11 a.m. to 12 noon on Thursdays).
3. ***Get to know your fellow students***. Networking with other students is an important part of the college experience. Get the name, phone number, and email address of two students in each of your classes. If you miss class, you will need to get in touch with someone to find out what material you missed.
4. ***Familiarize yourself with each course's syllabus***. At the first meeting of every course, your instructor will hand out a syllabus. (The syllabus may also be posted on the course's Web page.) A syllabus gives you three kinds of useful information:

   - Information that can help you plan a study schedule—for example, when assignments are due and when exams are scheduled
   - Practical information, such as the instructor's office number and email address and the books and supplies you need to buy
   - Information about the instructor's policies on absences, grading, class participation, and so on

   Read each syllabus carefully, ask questions about anything you don't understand, refer to all your course syllabi regularly—and do not lose them.
5. ***Buy books and supplies with care***. When you buy your books and supplies, be sure to keep the receipts, and don't write your name in your books until you are certain that you are not going to drop a course. (If you write in a book, you will not be able to return it.) If your roster of courses is not definite, you should wait a few days to buy your texts. You should, however, buy some items right away: a separate notebook and folder for each course you are taking, a college dictionary, and a pocket organizer. In addition to the books and other items required for a particular course (for example, a lab notebook, a programmable calculator, art supplies), you should buy pens and pencils in different colors, blank computer disks, paper clips or a stapler, Post-it

Word Power

networking engaging in informal communication for mutual help and support

Word Power

syllabus an outline or summary of a course's main points (the plural form is *syllabi*)

For information about how to use an organizer, see 1G.

notes, highlighter pens, and so on—and a backpack or bookbag in which to keep all these items.

FOCUS Using a Dictionary

Even though most word-processing programs have spell checkers, you still need to buy a dictionary. A college dictionary tells you how to spell words, what words mean, and how to use them.

For more on using a dictionary, see Appendix A.

6. ***Set up your notebooks***. Establish a separate notebook (or a separate section of a divided notebook) for each of your classes. (Notebooks with pocket folders can help you keep graded papers, worksheets, handouts, and class syllabi all in one place.) Copy your instructor's name, email address, phone number, and office hours and location onto the inside front cover of the notebook; write your own name, address, and phone number on the outside.

◆ PRACTICE 1.4

Set up a notebook for each course you are taking. Then exchange notebooks with another student, and review each other's notebooks.

C Day-to-Day Strategies

As you get busier and busier, you may find that it's hard to keep everything under control. Here are some strategies to help you as you move through the semester.

1. ***Find a place to study***. As a college student, you will need your own private place to work and study. Even if it's just a desk in one corner of your dorm room (or if you are living at home or off-campus, in one corner of your bedroom or at the back of your garage), you will need a place that is yours alone, a place that will be undisturbed when you leave it. (The kitchen table, which you share with roommates or family members, will not work.) This space should include everything you will need to make your work easier—quiet, good lighting, a comfortable chair, a clean work surface, storage for supplies, and so on.
2. ***Set up a bookshelf***. Keep your textbooks, dictionary, calculator, supplies, and everything else you use regularly for your coursework in one place—ideally, in your own workspace. That way, when you need something, you will know exactly where it is.
3. ***Set up a study schedule***. Identify thirty- to forty-five-minute blocks of free time before, between, and after classes. Set aside this time for review. Remember, studying should be part of your regular routine, not something you do only the night before an exam.

FOCUS Skills Check

Don't wait until you have a paper to write to discover that you don't know how to use a computer well enough. Be sure your basic word-processing skills are at the level you need for your work. If you need help, get it right away.

Computer Tip

Your school's computer lab should be the first place you turn for help with word processing, but writing lab and library staff members may also be able to help you.

4. ***Establish priorities***. It's important to understand what your priorities are. Before you can establish priorities, however, you have to know which assignments are due first, which ones can be done in steps, and which tasks or steps will be most time consuming. Then, you must decide which tasks are most pressing. (For example, studying for a test to be given the next day is more pressing than reviewing notes for a test scheduled for the following week.) Finally, you have to decide which tasks are more important than others. For example, studying for a midterm is more important than studying for a quiz, and the midterm for a course you are in danger of failing is more important than the midterm for a course in which you are doing well. Remember, you can't do everything at once; you need to know what must be done immediately and what can wait.
5. ***Check your mail***. If you have a campus mailbox or email account, check it regularly—if possible, several times a day. If you miss a message, you may miss important information about changes in assignments, canceled classes, or rescheduled quizzes.
6. ***Schedule conferences***. Try to meet with each of your instructors during the semester even if you are not required to do so. You might schedule one conference during the second or third week of school and another a week or two before a major exam or paper is due. These meetings will help you understand exactly what is expected of you, and your instructors will appreciate and respect your initiative.
7. ***Become familiar with the student services available on your campus***. College is hard work, and you can't do everything on your own. There is nothing shameful about getting help from your school's writing lab or tutoring center or from the center for students with disabilities (which serves students with learning disabilities as well as

Word Power

priorities things that deserve extra attention

FOCUS Asking for Help

Despite all your careful planning, you may still run into trouble. For example, you may miss an exam and have to make it up; you may miss several days of classes in a row and fall behind in your work; you may have trouble understanding the material in one of your courses; or a family member may get sick. Don't wait until you are overwhelmed to ask for help. If you have an ongoing personal problem or a family emergency, let your instructors know immediately.

physical challenges), the office of international students, or the counseling center, as well as from your adviser or course instructors. Think of yourself as a consumer. You are paying for your education, and you are entitled to—and should take advantage of—all the services available to students.

◆ PRACTICE 1.5

Try to figure out how and when you study best. Do you do your best studying in the morning or late at night? Alone or in a busy library? When you have answered these questions, set up a weekly study schedule. Begin by identifying your free time and deciding how you can use it most efficiently. Next, discuss your schedule with a group of three or four other students. How much time does each of you have available? How much time do you think you need? Does the group consider each student's study schedule to be realistic? If not, why not?

D Note-Taking Strategies

Learning to take notes in a college class takes practice, but taking good notes is essential for success in college. Here are some basic guidelines that will help you develop and improve your note-taking skills.

During Class

1. ***Come to class***. If you miss class, you miss notes—so come to class, and come on time. In class, sit where you can see the board and hear the instructor. Don't feel you have to keep sitting in the same place in each class every day; change your seat until you find a spot that's comfortable for you.
2. ***Date your notes***. Begin each class by writing the date at the top of the page. Instructors frequently identify material that will be on a test by dates. If you do not date your notes, you may not know what to study.
3. ***Know what to write down***. You can't possibly write down everything an instructor says. If you try, you will miss a lot of important information. Listen carefully *before* you write, and listen for cues to what's important. For example, sometimes the instructor will tell you that something is important or that a particular piece of information will be on a test. Sometimes he or she will write key terms and concepts on the board. If the instructor emphasizes an idea or underlines it on the board, you should do the same in your notes. Of course, if you have done the assigned reading before class, you will recognize important topics and know to take especially careful notes when these topics are introduced in class.
4. ***Include examples***. Try to write down an example for each general concept introduced in class—something that will help you remember what the instructor was talking about. (If you don't have time to in-

clude examples as you take notes during class, add them when you review your notes.) For instance, if your world history instructor is explaining *nationalism,* you should write down not only a definition but also an example, such as "Germany in 1848."

5. ***Write legibly, and use helpful signals***. Use dark (blue or black) ink for your note-taking, but keep a red or green pen handy to highlight important information, jot down announcements (such as a change in a test date), note gaps in your notes, or question confusing points. Do not take notes in pencil, which is hard to read and less permanent than ink.
6. ***Ask questions***. If you do not hear (or do not understand) something your instructor says, or if you need an example to help you understand something, *ask!* But don't immediately turn to another student for clarification. Instead, wait to see if the instructor explains further, or if he or she pauses to ask if anyone has a question. If you're not comfortable asking a question during class, make a note of the question and ask the instructor—or send an email—after class.

After Class

1. ***Review your notes***. After every class, try to spend ten or fifteen minutes rereading your notes, filling in gaps and examples while the material is still fresh in your mind. When you review, try giving each day's notes a title so you can remember the topic of each class. This will help you locate information when you study.
2. ***Recopy information***. When you have a break between classes or when you get home, recopy important pieces of information from your notes:

- Copy announcements (such as quiz dates) onto your calendar.
- Copy reminders (for example, a note to schedule a conference before your next paper is due) into your organizer.
- Copy questions you have to ask the instructor onto the top of the next blank page in your notes.

Before the Next Class

1. ***Reread your notes***. Leave time just before each class to skim the previous class's notes once more. This strategy will get you oriented for the class to come and remind you of anything that needs clarification or further explanation.
2. ***Ask for help***. Call a classmate if you need to fill in missing information; if you still need help, see the instructor during office hours, or come to class early so you can ask your question before class begins.

◆ PRACTICE 1.6

Compare the notes you took in one of your classes with notes taken by another student in the same class. How are your notes different? Do you think you need to make any changes in the way you take notes?

E Homework Strategies

Doing homework is an important part of learning in college. Homework gives you a chance to practice your skills and measure your progress. If you are having trouble with the homework, chances are you are having trouble with the course. Ask the instructor or teaching assistant for help *now;* don't wait until the day before the exam. Here are some tips for getting the most out of your homework:

1. ***Write down the assignment.*** Don't expect to remember an assignment; copy it down. If you are not sure exactly what you are supposed to do, check with your instructor or another student.
2. ***Do your homework, and do it on time.*** Teachers assign homework to reinforce classwork, and they expect homework to be done on a regular basis. It is easy to fall behind in college, and trying to do three—or five—nights' worth of homework in one night is not a good idea. If you do several assignments at once, you not only overload yourself, you also miss important day-to-day connections with classwork.
3. ***Be an active reader.*** Get into the habit of highlighting your textbooks and other material as you read.
4. ***Join study groups.*** A study group of three or four students can be a valuable support system for homework as well as for exams. If your schedule permits, do some homework assignments—or at least review your homework—with other students on a regular basis. In addition to learning information, you will learn different strategies for doing assignments.

For specific strategies for active reading, see Chapter 2.

◆ PRACTICE 1.7

Working in a group of three or four students, brainstorm about how a study group might benefit you. How many students should be in the group? How often should they meet? Should the group include students whose study habits are similar or different? What kind of help do you think you would need? What kind of help could you offer to other students?

F Exam-Taking Strategies

Preparation for an exam should begin well before the exam is announced. In a sense, you begin this preparation on the first day of class.

Before the Exam

1. ***Attend every class.*** Regular attendance in class—where you can listen, ask questions, and take notes—is the best possible preparation for exams. If you do have to miss a class, arrange to copy (and read)

another student's notes *before the next class* so you will be able to follow the discussion.

2. ***Keep up with the reading***. Read every assignment, and read it before the class in which it will be discussed. If you don't, you may have trouble understanding what is going on in class.
3. ***Take careful notes***. Take careful, thorough notes, but be selective. If you can, compare your notes on a regular basis with those of other students in the class; working together, you can fill in gaps or correct errors. Establishing a buddy system will also force you to review your notes regularly instead of just on the night before the exam.
4. ***Study on your own***. When an exam is announced, adjust your study schedule—and your priorities—so you have time to review everything. (This is especially important if you have more than one exam in a short period of time.) Review all your material (class notes, readings, and so on), and then review it again. Make a note of anything you don't understand, and keep track of topics you need to review. Try to predict the most likely questions, and—if you have time—practice answering them.
5. ***Study with a group***. If you can set up a study group, you should certainly do so. Studying with others can help you understand the material better. However, don't come to group sessions unprepared and expect to get everything from the other students. You must first study on your own.
6. ***Make an appointment with your instructor***. Set up an appointment with the instructor or with the course's teaching assistant a few days before the exam. Bring to this conference any specific questions you have about course content and about the format of the upcoming exam. (Be sure to review all your study material before the conference.)
7. ***Review the material one last time***. The night before the exam is not the time to begin your studying; it is the time to review. When you have finished your review, get a good night's sleep.

During the Exam

Like an athlete before a big game or a musician before an important concert, you will already have done all you could to get ready for the test by the time you walk into the exam room. Your goal now is to keep the momentum going and not do anything to undermine all your hard work.

1. ***Read through the entire exam***. Be sure you understand how much time you have, how many points each question is worth, and exactly what each question is asking you to do. Many exam questions call for just a short answer—*yes* or *no, true* or *false*. Others ask you to fill in a blank with a few words, and still others require you to select the best answer from among several choices. If you are not absolutely certain what kind of answer a particular question calls for, ask the instructor or the proctor *before* you begin to write. (Remember, on some tests there is no penalty for guessing, but on other tests it is best to answer only those questions you have time to read and consider carefully.)

FOCUS Writing Essay Exams

If you are asked to write an essay on an exam, remember that what you are really being asked to do is write a **thesis-and-support essay**. Chapter 8 of this text will tell you how to do this.

2. ***Budget your time***. Once you understand how much each section of the exam and each question are worth, plan your time and set your priorities, devoting the most time to the most important questions. If you know you tend to rush through exams, or if you find you often run out of time before you get to the end of a test, you might try putting a mark on your paper when about one-third of the allotted time has passed (for a one-hour exam, put a mark on your paper after twenty minutes) to make sure you are pacing yourself appropriately.
3. ***Reread each question***. Carefully reread each question *before* you start to answer it. Underline the **key words**—the words that give specific information about how to approach the question and how to phrase your answer.

FOCUS Key Words

Here are some helpful key words to look for on exams:

analyze	explain	suggest results, effects, outcomes
argue	give examples	summarize
compare	identify	support
contrast	illustrate	take a stand
define	recount	trace
demonstrate	suggest causes, origins, contributing factors	
describe		
evaluate		

Remember, even if everything you write is correct, your response is not acceptable if you don't answer the question. If a question asks you to *compare* two novels, *summarizing* one of them will not be acceptable.

4. ***Brainstorm to help yourself recall the material***. If you are writing a paragraph or an essay, look frequently at the question as you brainstorm. (You can write your brainstorming notes on the inside cover of the exam book.) Quickly write down all the relevant points you can think of—the textbook's points, your instructor's comments, and so on. The more you can think of now, the more you will have to choose from when you write your answer.

For more on brainstorming, see 5B.

5. ***Write down the main idea***. Looking closely at the way the question is worded and at your brainstorming notes, write a sentence that states

the main idea of your answer. If you are writing a paragraph, this sentence will be your topic sentence; if you are writing an essay, it will be your thesis statement.

For more on topic sentences, see 6A. For more on thesis statements, see 8D.

6. ***List your key points***. You don't want to waste your limited (and valuable) time writing a detailed outline, but an informal outline that lists just your key points is worth the little time it takes. An informal outline will help you plan a clear direction for your paragraph or essay.
7. ***Draft your answer***. You will spend most of your time actually writing the answers to the questions on the exam. Follow your outline, keep track of time, and consult your brainstorming notes when you need to—but stay focused on your writing.
8. ***Reread, revise, and edit***. When you have finished drafting your answer, reread it carefully to make sure that it says everything you want it to say—and that it answers the question.

G Time-Management Strategies

Learning to manage your time is important for success in college. Here are some strategies you can adopt to make this task easier:

Computer Tip

Many computers include organizer and calendar programs.

1. ***Use an organizer***. Whether you prefer a print organizer or an electronic one, you should certainly use one—and use it *consistently*. If you are most comfortable with paper and pencil, purchase a "week-on-two-pages" academic year organizer (one that begins in September, not January). The "week-on-two-pages" format (see p. 14) has two advantages: it gives you more writing room for Monday through Friday than for the weekend, and it also lets you view an entire week at once.

   Carry your organizer with you at all times. At the beginning of the semester, copy down key pieces of information from each course syllabus—for example, the date of every quiz and exam and the due date of every paper. As the semester progresses, continue to write in assignments and deadlines, and also enter information such as days when a class will be canceled or will meet in the computer lab or in the library, reminders to bring a particular book or piece of equipment to class, and appointments with instructors or other college personnel. You can also jot down reminders and schedule appointments that are not related to school—for example, changes in your work hours, a dentist appointment, or lunch with a friend. (In addition to writing notes on the pages for each date, some students like to keep a separate month-by-month "to do" list; crossing out completed items can give you a feeling of accomplishment—and make the road ahead look shorter.)

   The first sample organizer pages (p. 14) show how you can use an organizer to keep track of deadlines, appointments, and reminders. The second sample organizer pages (p. 14) include not only this information but also a study schedule, with notes about particular tasks to be done each day.
2. ***Use a calendar***. Buy a large calendar, and post it where you will see it every morning—for example, on your desk, in your car, on the refrigerator, or wherever you keep your keys and your student ID. At

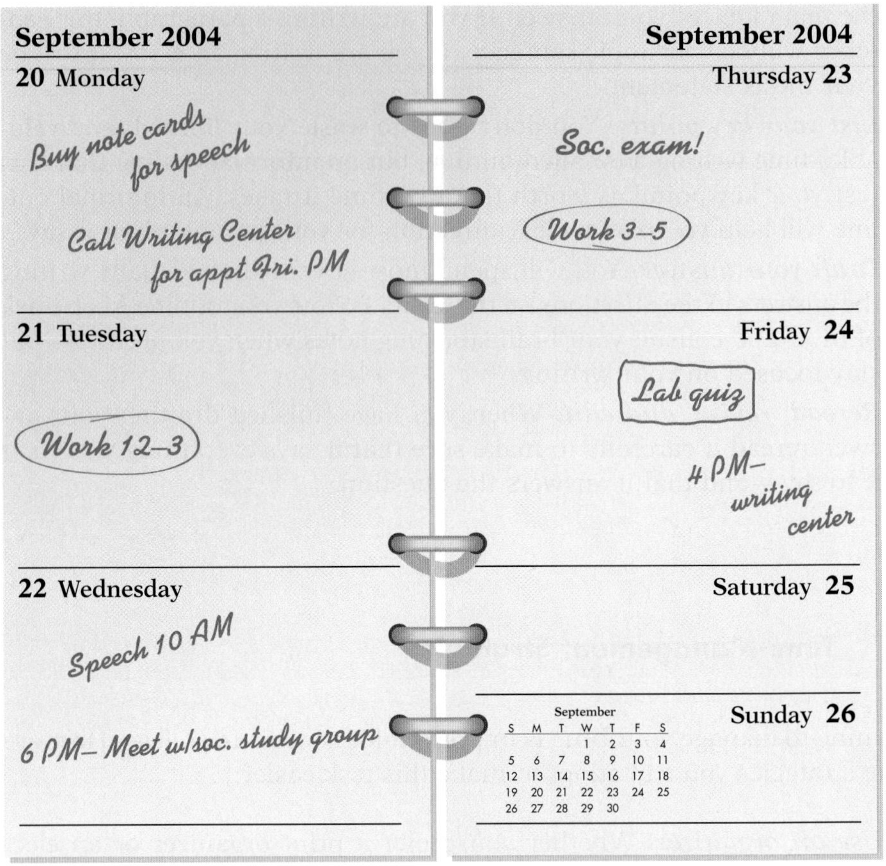

Sample Organizer Pages: Deadlines, Appointments, and Reminders Only

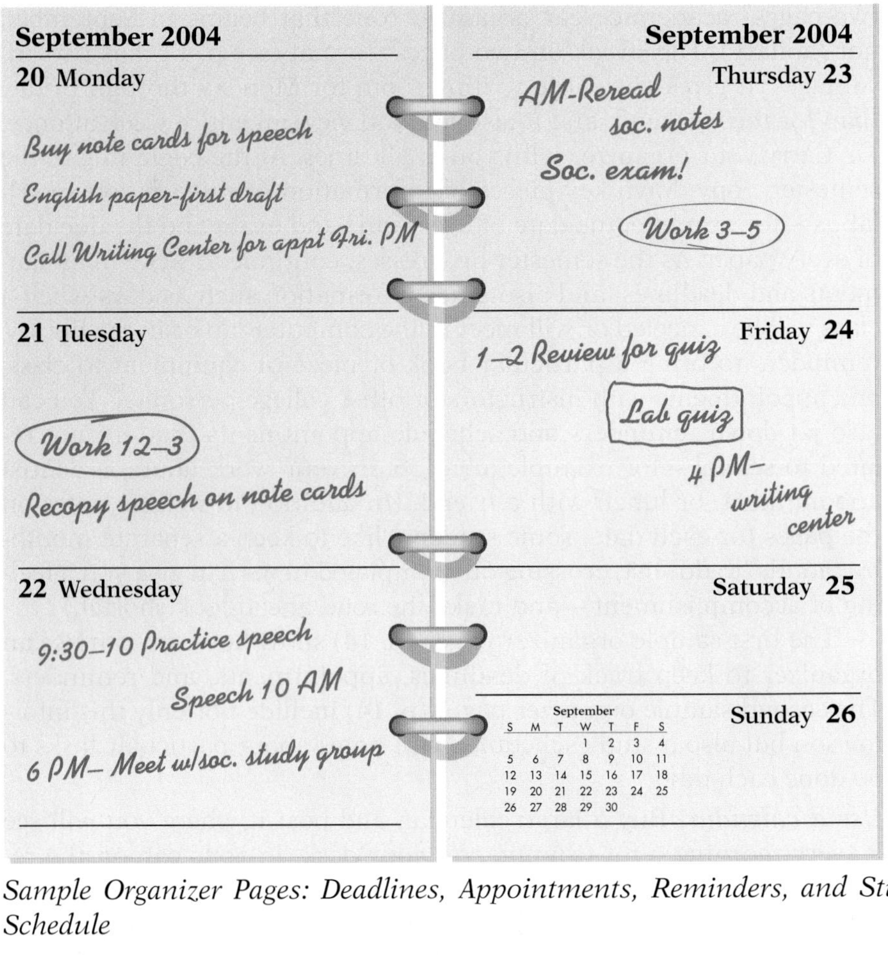

Sample Organizer Pages: Deadlines, Appointments, Reminders, and Study Schedule

the beginning of the semester, fill in important dates such as school holidays, work commitments, exam dates, and due dates for papers and projects. When you get home from school each day, update the calendar with any new information you have entered into your organizer.

3. ***Plan ahead***. If you think you will need help from a writing-lab tutor to revise a paper that is due in two weeks, don't wait until day thirteen to try to make an appointment; all the time slots may be filled by then. To be safe, make an appointment for help about a week in advance.
4. ***Learn to enjoy downtime***. One final—and very important—point to remember is that you are entitled to "waste" a little time. When you have a free minute, take time for yourself—and don't feel guilty about it.

◆ PRACTICE 1.8

Fill in the blank organizer pages below to create a schedule for your coming week. (Enter activities that are related to school as well as those that are not.) When you have finished, trade books with another student and compare your plans for the week ahead.

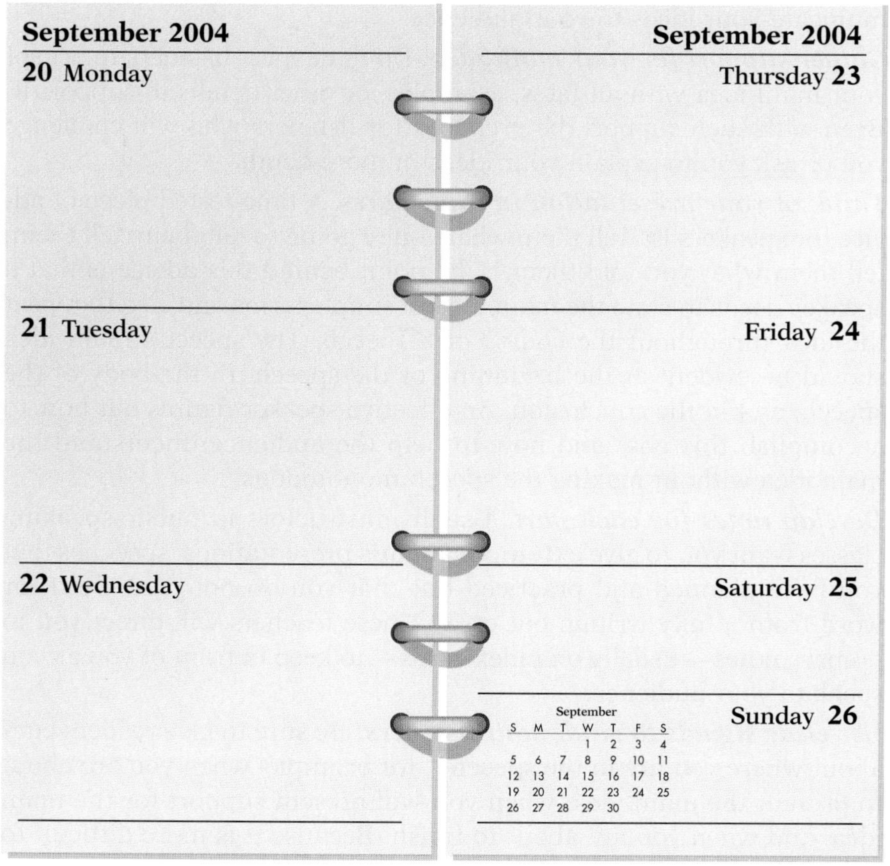

H Public-Speaking Strategies

In college classes, you may be called on to speak not only informally in one-on-one situations or in small groups, but also more formally in front of an audience. Even though many people find the thought of speaking in public terrifying, there are a number of steps you can take to make the process easier and less stressful. The following strategies can help you plan and deliver your presentation.

Before the Presentation

1. ***Know your purpose.*** When an instructor gives you a speaking assignment, be sure you know your purpose: Do you have to recount an experience, take a stand on a controversial issue, or do something else?
2. ***Know your audience.*** As with written communication, you have to figure out what listeners already know (and how they feel) about the topic of your speech. If some listeners are more knowledgeable and sophisticated than others, you have to figure out how to appeal to both groups without insulting one or confusing the other.
3. ***Identify your main idea.*** The strategies discussed in Chapter 5 can lead you to a clear statement of your speech's main idea. Keep this statement simpler and clearer than the main idea you might state in a piece of writing. Remember, readers can reread a passage they cannot understand; in an oral presentation, you have only one chance to communicate your ideas to your audience.
4. ***Gather support for your main idea.*** Do not expect listeners to accept your main idea without facts, examples, or other details to support it. Even with such support, be prepared for listeners who will challenge you or ask you to explain your ideas in more depth.
5. ***Think of your presentation in three parts.*** A time-tested piece of advice for speakers is "Tell them what you're going to tell them; tell them; tell them what you told them." The point behind this advice is that a speaker needs to state the main idea in simple terms and also to repeat the idea throughout the course of a speech. The speech's main idea should be evident at the beginning of the speech, in the body of the speech, and in the conclusion. An effective speaker figures out how to accomplish this goal and how to help the audience understand the main idea without making the speech monotonous.
6. ***Develop notes for each part.*** Usually, instructors in public-speaking classes want you to give **extemporaneous** presentations: speeches that you have planned and practiced but that you do not read word for word from a fully written-out essay. These teachers will direct you to prepare notes—usually on index cards—to keep in front of you as you speak to your audience.
7. ***Use clear signals to guide your listeners.*** Be sure to give readers cues about where you are in the speech—for example, when you are about to present the main idea, when you will present support for the main idea, and when you are about to finish. Because it is more difficult to follow a speech than a piece of writing, you will need to include more **transitions** from one idea to another than you would in your writing.

For more on transitions, see 6D.

8. ***Prepare visual aids.*** You will not always need visual aids, but sometimes—for example, when you are explaining a process or tracing causes—you may communicate your main idea and supporting points more clearly if you give the audience something to look at. If, for example, you are explaining how an abacus works, you may want to

show one to your listeners. If you are talking about a dance, you may want to have someone perform its steps during your presentation. In other cases, you may show photos, drawings, maps, posters, or even a videotape.

Alternatively, you may use presentation software such as Microsoft PowerPoint to produce graphs, charts, or lists that you can project from your computer. Or you can print these visuals on acetate sheets and, with an overhead projector, enlarge and display them on a wall or screen.

The PowerPoint slide on page 18 was prepared by a student for a presentation on how he found a job.

9. ***Integrate your visuals.*** Do not just show or read the visual to your audience; tell them more than they can see or read for themselves. For example, on a map, you might point out the route of the trip you are reporting on; for a bar graph, you might compare the raw numbers—stating, for example, how much more ice cream sells in July than in January.
10. ***Practice.*** Be sure to rehearse enough times to guarantee that you know the order of points in your presentation (including when to show visual aids) and how to move from one point to the next. You must rehearse enough so that even though you have only notes in front of you, you are confident that you can convert the words and phrases to full sentences. Leave time for a trial run with a friend, and ask for feedback on content and delivery; then take time to apply the friend's feedback

Computer Tip

Make sure the disk that contains your visuals is compatible with the presentation computer, and carry a backup copy in case your disk goes bad.

FOCUS Designing and Displaying Visual Aids

- Do not clutter your visuals with pictures (or, in the case of PowerPoint, with special effects).
- Do not use visuals that your audience cannot see clearly. Use images that are large enough for your audience to see and that will reproduce clearly.
- Do not make lettering too small. Use 40- to 50-point type for titles, 25- to 30-point type for major points, and 20- to 25-point type for other points.
- Do not include full sentences or paragraphs. Use bulleted lists (like this one) instead.
- Do not put more than three or four points on one visual.
- Do not use too many colors or too many styles of type.
- Make sure that there is a clear contrast between the background and the lettering. (See the sample PowerPoint slide on page 18.)
- Do not distract your audience by showing them the visual before you introduce it or after you finish talking about it.
- Do not talk to the visual. Look at and talk to your audience. Even if you have to point to the visual on the screen, make sure you are looking at your audience when you speak.

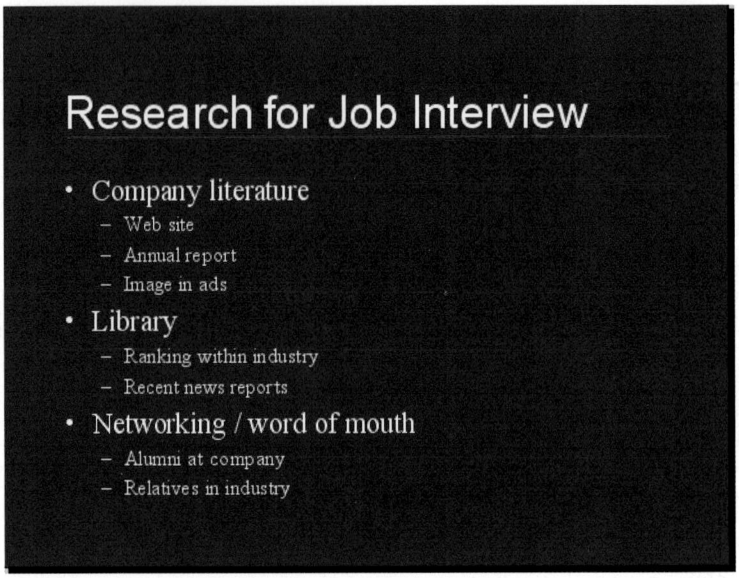

Sample PowerPoint slide

and improve your presentation. Finally, leave time to rehearse more—cutting and adding as necessary—until you know you can stay within the required time limit.

During the Presentation

1. ***Accept nervousness as part of the process.*** The trick is to convert this fear into the positive energy that will catch and hold your audience's attention.
2. ***Don't begin speaking while you are still looking at your notes.*** Look at your audience. Most speech coaches advise speakers to pick a few people in different parts of the room and to alternate eye contact among them during the speech.
3. ***Speak slowly.*** No matter how slowly you think you are speaking, chances are you can slow down further. Take your time.
4. ***Make every movement count.*** Do not pace as you speak or move your hands erratically. Stand in one spot, and gesture to emphasize a point

> **FOCUS Dealing with Anxiety**
>
> Your goal should not be to eliminate anxiety totally. The complete absence of anxiety in a speaker can lead to overconfidence, which can irritate and even bore an audience. Instead, learn to cope with anxiety by doing enough preparation so that you feel you own your speech. In other words, work on the speech to the point where you are comfortable with—but not smug about—your main idea and supporting points. You want to be so familiar with the material that you can relax enough to sound natural, not stiff.

FOCUS Group Presentations

Sometimes a public-speaking assignment will call for a group presentation that requires you to cooperate with other students. Whether you are participating in a panel discussion about college services or performing a dramatic reading of a one-act play, a group presentation involves intensive behind-the-scenes work. You must understand your own role as well as those of everyone else: Who is in charge? Who sets the pace? Who prepares and displays the visuals? Furthermore, everyone in a group situation must bear responsibility for sticking to a schedule for research and rehearsal. After rehearsals and after the actual presentation, everyone should contribute to evaluating the group effort and figuring out how to improve the next time around.

or to display a visual aid. (Arrange in advance to have someone in the audience perform certain tasks—for example, distribute handouts.) Depending on the topic and level of formality of your speech (and your instructor's guidelines), you may stand directly in front of your audience or behind a lectern.

5. ***Do not get flustered if someone asks you to speak louder.*** In addition, do not get upset if some people in your audience look bored; you might change your pace or volume to get more attention, but remember that a bored person may be overtired, preoccupied, or just a poor listener.
6. ***Do not sit down too quickly.*** Leave time for questions. Your audience may want to ask questions or challenge what you have said. If someone asks a question that you have already answered in your speech, repeat the information as briefly as possible. And do not be upset if someone begins to argue with you; an appropriate response might be "I never thought of that angle," "I don't agree because . . . ," or "I need to think about that point more."

Word Power

lectern a stand or desk with a slanted top that supports a speaker's notes

REVISING AND EDITING

Look back at your response to the Seeing and Writing exercise on page 3. Now that you have read the information in this chapter, you should have a better idea of how to manage your time in the weeks and months to come. How do you think you will fit everything in? Which of the strategies described in this chapter do you think you will find most helpful? Revise your Seeing and Writing response so that it answers these questions.

✓ REVIEW CHECKLIST: Strategies for College Success

- Some strategies come in handy even before school begins. (See 1A.)
- From your first day as a college student, there are steps you can take to help you get your bearings. (See 1B.)
- Day-to-day strategies can help you move through the semester. (See 1C.)
- Learning to take good notes is essential for success in college. (See 1D.)
- Doing homework gives you a chance to practice your skills and measure your progress. (See 1E.)
- Preparation for an exam should begin well before the exam is announced. (See 1F.)
- Learning to manage your time is important for success in college. (See 1G.)
- Knowing how to make an oral presentation can be a useful skill for college students. (See 1H.)

CHAPTER

2

Reading for Academic Success

PREVIEW

In this chapter, you will learn

- how to become an active reader (2A)
- how to preview, highlight, annotate, outline, and summarize a reading assignment (2B)
- how to read different kinds of texts (2C)

SEEING AND WRITING

When you read your textbooks, you will understand them better if you mark the pages as this student has done. Marking the pages can also be a useful strategy in other reading situations.

Word Power

highlighting marking a page to emphasize important details

annotating making explanatory notes on a page

A Becoming an Active Reader

Reading is essential in all your college courses. During your years as a college student, you will read not only textbooks but also many other books (both fiction and nonfiction), as well as newspapers, magazines, and journals (in print and online). You will also read essays, short stories, lab notes, Web sites, class handouts, and many other kinds of written material. To get the most out of your college reading, you should be prepared to take a critical stance—commenting on, questioning, evaluating, and even challenging what you read. In other words, you should be an active reader.

In practical terms, being an **active reader** means actively participating in the reading process: approaching a reading assignment with a clear understanding of your purpose and marking the text to help you understand what you are reading.

You may find it easier to understand the concept of active reading if you see how this strategy applies to "reading" a picture. Like a written text, every **visual text**—a photograph, an advertisement, a chart, or a graph; a work of fine art, such as a painting or a piece of sculpture; and even a Web site—has a message to communicate. Visual texts communicate their messages through the choice and arrangement of details.

When you approach a visual, you first note what images you actually see on the page and how they are arranged. In the following ad for Tropicana orange juice, the main idea—that the product's juicier pulp gives it fresh-squeezed taste—is presented in the heading: "We squeeze the oranges, not the pulp." This message is supported by the large central image, which emphasizes the link between the juice carton, the glass of juice, and the orange. The smaller type further supports the ad's claim, presenting specific information that explains how and why this brand of juice is fresher and tastier than others.

Tropicana advertisement

In the visual below, a painting by the American artist Winslow Homer, the images are not supported by written text, but the message is still clear. Here, the central image—the man alone in the middle of the ocean, surrounded by open space—clearly conveys the painting's emotions: fear, desperation, hopelessness. The other images—the choppy waves, the threatening sky, the sharks—reinforce and support this impression.

Winslow Homer, The Gulf Stream *(1899)*

When you "read" visuals such as these, at first you get just a general sense of what you see. But as you read more actively, you let your mind take you beyond what is represented on the page. You ask why details were selected, why they are arranged as they are, what comes to mind when you see the picture, and whether or not you find the visual effective.

For example, why is the orange in the Tropicana ad labeled "Handle with Care"? Why is it placed in front of the juice carton? Will the ad encourage consumers to purchase this brand of juice rather than another? If so, why? If not, why not? In the Winslow Homer painting, what is the man looking at? Does he see anything in the distance? How might he have come to be alone on the ocean? Does the painting frighten you? Would it have a different impact if the artist had used lighter colors? If he had added or eliminated any details?

Active reading of a written text, like active reading of a visual text, encourages you to move beyond what is on the page and to "read between the lines." In this way, it gives you a deeper understanding of the material.

B Understanding the Reading Process

The process of actively reading a written text is explained and illustrated in the pages that follow.

Determining Your Purpose

Even before you start reading, you should ask yourself some questions about your purpose—why you are reading. The answers to these questions will help you understand what kind of information you hope to get out of your reading and how you will use this information.

Questions about Your Purpose

- Will you be expected to discuss the reading selection in class?
- Will you be expected to discuss the reading selection in a one-on-one conference with your instructor?
- Will you have to write about the reading selection? If so, will you be expected to write an informal response (for example, a journal entry) or a more formal one (for example, an essay)?
- Will you be tested on what you read?

Previewing a Reading Assignment

When you **preview**, you skim a passage to get a sense of the writer's main idea and key supporting points and, if possible, the general emphasis of the passage. You can begin by focusing on the title, the first paragraph (which often contains a purpose statement or overview), and the last paragraph (which often contains a summary of the writer's points). You should also look for clues to the writer's message in the passage's **visual signals** (headings, boxes, and so on) as well as in its **verbal signals** (the words and phrases the writer uses to convey order and emphasis).

Using Visual Signals

- Look at the essay's title.
- Look at the essay's opening and closing paragraphs.
- Look at each paragraph's first sentence.
- Look at headings.
- Look at *italicized* and **boldfaced** words.
- Look at numbered lists.
- Look at bulleted lists (like this one).
- Look at visuals (graphs, charts, tables, photographs, and so on).
- Look at any information that is boxed.
- Look at any information that is in color.

Using Verbal Signals

- Look for phrases that signal emphasis ("The *primary* reason"; "The *most important* idea").
- Look for repeated words and phrases.
- Look for words that signal addition (*also, in addition, furthermore*).
- Look for words that signal time sequence (*first, after, then, next, finally*).
- Look for words that identify causes and effects (*because, as a result, for this reason*).
- Look for words that introduce examples (*for example, for instance*).
- Look for words that signal comparison (*likewise, similarly*).
- Look for words that signal contrast (*unlike, although, in contrast*).
- Look for words that signal contradiction (*however, on the contrary*).
- Look for words that signal a narrowing of the writer's focus (*in fact, specifically, in other words*).
- Look for words that signal summaries or conclusions (*to sum up, in conclusion*).

When you have finished previewing the passage, you should have a general sense of what the writer wants to communicate.

◆ PRACTICE 2.1

Following is a brief newspaper article by Nathan Black, a Colorado high school student. Preview the article in preparation for class discussion as well as for the other activities that will be assigned throughout this chapter.

As you read, try to identify the writer's main point and key supporting ideas, and write that information on the blank lines following the article.

AFTER A SHOOTING

Nathan Black

High school students in Littleton now have a new excuse to get out of class for a few extra minutes: the lockdown drill. My school had its first last year. While most students sat quietly in locked classrooms, a few teachers responded to simulated crises, like a student injury. It's one of many new features of life in Littleton since the Columbine High shootings of 1999. Most people have tried to move on, but some aspects of our lives have changed forever. 1

That reality will soon face the people of Santee, California, where two students were killed on Monday. And the shooting yesterday of a girl by a schoolmate in Pennsylvania, and the arrest this week of two boys in Twentynine Palms, California, after police found a "hit list" of their classmates, suggest that Columbine's experience will become still more common. 2

Apart from lockdown drills, there have been few changes in security procedures. The greatest change has been the increase of paranoia. For example, a few weeks after the shooting I was working on a graph assignment with a friend. We arranged the points on the graph to spell out a humorous but inappropriate message. 3

A month earlier, my friend would have said, "The teacher's going to be mad." This time he said, "If we turn this in, we'll be expelled." 4

There's the difference. The worst case I've heard of took place in Canada. A boy had written and performed, for class, a dark, vengeful monologue. After his performance, rumors swirled about hit lists, and the boy was arrested. The police said he had made death threats. No hard evidence appears to have been found in the boy's home—just the monologue. His story has now entered the larger tale of Littleton and its aftermath. 5

Only time can ease this paranoia. I wish time would hurry up about it. 6

Yet good changes have also occurred. The killings at Columbine and elsewhere have been a pitiless wake-up call to adults. Last April, 1,500 of my peers gathered at a local college to discuss education. Adults want our perspective. They may want it now because of fear, but they want it. 7

Such conversations have to continue. Violence is still happening, and as long as my school needs a lockdown drill, we need to keep asking: Why do kids kill each other and how can we stop them? There's no answer yet. But the fact that we're looking makes me feel a little less helpless. 8

Author's main point

____

____

Key supporting ideas

1. ______________________________

____

2. ______________________________

____

3. ______________________________

____

4. ______________________________

____

Highlighting a Reading Assignment

After you have previewed a passage, read it again, this time more carefully. Now your goals are to identify connections between one idea and another and to follow the writer's line of thought.

As you read, keep a pen (or a highlighter pen) in hand so you can **highlight**, using underlining and symbols to identify important information. This active reading strategy will reinforce your understanding of the writer's main ideas and key supporting points and help you see the relationships among them. (If you want to highlight material in a book that you do not own, you can photocopy the passage and then highlight it.)

The number and kinds of highlighting symbols you use when you read are up to you. All that matters is that your symbols are clear, meaningful, and easy to remember.

Highlighting Symbols

- Underline or highlight key ideas.
- Box or circle words or phrases you want to remember.
- Place a check mark (✔) or star (✶) next to an important idea.
- Place a double check mark (✔✔) or double star (✶✶) next to an especially significant idea.
- Draw lines or arrows to connect related ideas.
- Put a question mark beside a word or idea that you do not understand.
- Number the writer's key supporting points or examples.

Highlight freely, but try not to highlight too much. Remember, you will eventually be rereading every highlighted word, phrase, and sentence—and your study time is limited. Highlight only the most important, most useful information—for example, definitions, examples, and summaries.

FOCUS Knowing What to Highlight

You want to highlight what's important—but how do you *know* what's important? As a general rule, you should look for the same **visual signals** you looked for when you did your previewing. Many of the ideas you will need to highlight will probably be found in material that is visually set off from the rest of the text—opening and closing paragraphs, lists, and the like. Also, continue to look for **verbal signals**—words and phrases like *however, therefore, another reason, the most important point,* and so on—that often introduce key points. Together, these visual and verbal signals will give you clues to the writer's meaning and emphasis.

Here is how a student highlighted a passage from an introductory American history textbook. The passage focuses on the position of African Americans in society in the years immediately following World War II. Because the passage includes no visual signals apart from the section heading, the student looked carefully for verbal signals.

BLACK PROTEST AND THE POLITICS OF CIVIL RIGHTS

"I spent four years in the army to free a bunch of Frenchmen and Dutchmen," an African-American corporal declared, "and I'm hanged if I'm going to let the Alabama version of the Germans kick me around when I get home." Black men and women constituted ✓ 16 percent of military personnel in World War II, well above their 10 percent presence in the general population. African-American soldiers and civilians alike resolved that the return to peace would not be a return to the racial injustices of prewar America. Their political (?) clout had grown ✓ with the migration of 2 million African Americans to northern and western cities, where they could vote and make a difference. Even in the South, the proportion of blacks who cast ballots in local and national elections inched up from 2 percent to 12 percent in the 1940s. Pursuing civil rights through the courts and Congress, the National Association for the Advancement of Colored People (NAACP) counted half a million members.

In the postwar years, individuals broke through the color barrier, achieving several "firsts" for African Americans. Jackie Robinson integrated major league baseball when he took over second base for the Brooklyn Dodgers in 1947, braving abuse from fans and players to win the Rookie of the Year Award. In 1950, Ralph J. Bunche won the Nobel Peace Prize for his contributions to the United Nations, and Gwendolyn Brooks earned the Pulitzer Prize for poetry. A vibrant black culture, including top musicians such as Louis Armstrong, Ella Fitzgerald, and Mahalia Jackson, appealed to audiences black and white.

Still, in most respects African Americans found that little had changed. Although a number of states and cities outside the South enacted laws regarding fair employment practices in the 1940s—even as the federal government ended its wartime antidiscrimination program—African Americans struggled to hold on to the gains they had made during the war. Federal housing programs for the poor and nonpoor alike encouraged discrimination against blacks, and violence sometimes greeted those who tried to move into white areas. Postwar Detroit saw 120 incidents of arson, cross burnings, and physical attacks in neighborhoods undergoing racial transition. As African Americans migrated to northern and western cities, they found themselves crowded into what were rapidly becoming ghettos.

Things were worse in the South, where violence greeted blacks' attempts to assert their rights. White men with guns turned back Medgar Evers (who would become a key civil rights leader in the 1960s) and four other veterans who were trying to vote in Mississippi. A mob lynched Isaac Nixon for voting in Georgia, and an all-white jury acquitted the men accused of his murder. Governors, U.S. senators, and other southern politicians routinely intimidated potential voters with threats of economic retaliation and violence.

—James L. Roark et al., *The American Promise,* Second Edition

The student who highlighted this passage was preparing for a meeting of her study group. Because the class would be taking a midterm the following week, each member of the study group needed to understand the material very well. The student began her highlighting by placing check marks beside two important advances for African Americans cited in paragraph 1 and by drawing arrows to specific examples of blacks' political influence. (Although she thought she knew the meaning of the word *clout,* she circled it anyway and placed a question mark above it to remind herself to check its meaning in a dictionary.)

In paragraph 2, she boxed the names of prominent postwar African Americans and underlined their contributions, also underlining (and starring) the key phrase "'firsts' for African Americans." She then underlined and double-starred the passage's main idea—the first sentence of paragraph 3—numbering the examples in paragraphs 3 and 4 that supported this idea and drawing an arrow pointing from the main idea to the list of examples. She also underlined "Things were worse in the South" in paragraph 4 and placed a double check beside it to make it stand out.

◆ PRACTICE 2.2

Review the highlighted passage from the history textbook (pp. 28–29). How would your own highlighting of this passage be similar to or different from the sample student highlighting?

◆ PRACTICE 2.3

Reread "After a Shooting" (pp. 25–26). As you read, highlight the passage by underlining and starring main ideas, boxing and circling key words, and checkmarking important points. Also circle each unfamiliar word, and put a question mark in the margin beside it.

Annotating a Reading Assignment

As you highlight, you should also annotate what you are reading. **Annotating** a passage means making notes—of questions, reactions, reminders, and ideas for discussion or writing—in the margins or between the lines. Keeping an informal record of ideas as they occur to you will help prepare you to discuss the reading with your classmates—and, eventually, to write about it.

Asking yourself the following questions as you read will help you write useful annotations.

Questions for Annotating

- What is the writer saying?
- What is the writer's purpose—his or her reason for writing?
- What kind of audience is the writer addressing?
- Is the writer responding to another writer's ideas?
- What is the writer's main point?
- How does the writer support his or her points? With facts? Opinions? Both facts and opinions? What kinds of supporting details and examples does the writer use?

(continued on the following page)

(continued from the previous page)

- Does the writer include enough supporting details and examples?
- Do you understand the writer's vocabulary?
- Do you understand the writer's ideas?
- Do you agree with the points the writer is making?
- Do you see any connections between this reading selection and something else you have read?

The following passage reproduces the student's highlighting of the American history textbook from pages 28–29 and illustrates her annotations.

BLACK PROTEST AND THE POLITICS OF CIVIL RIGHTS

"I spent four years in the army to free a bunch of Frenchmen and Dutchmen," an African-American corporal declared, "and I'm hanged if I'm going to let the Alabama version of the Germans kick me around when I get home." Black men and women constituted ✓ 16 percent of military personnel in World War II, well above their 10 percent presence in the general population. African-American soldiers and civilians alike resolved that the return to peace would not be a return to the racial injustices of prewar America. Their po- ? ✓ litical clout had grown with the migration of 2 million African Americans to northern and western cities, where they could vote and make a difference. Even in the South, the proportion of blacks who cast ballots in local and national elections inched up from 2 percent to 12 percent in the 1940s. Pursuing civil rights through the courts and Congress, the National Association for the Advancement of Colored People (NAACP) counted half a million members.

Achievements of African Americans:

Military

Politics

In the postwar years, individuals broke through the color barrier, * achieving several "firsts" for African Americans. Jackie Robinson integrated major league baseball when he took over second base for the Brooklyn Dodgers in 1947, braving abuse from fans and players to win the Rookie of the Year Award. In 1950, Ralph J. Bunche won the Nobel Peace Prize for his contributions to the United

Sports, world politics, literature, music

Nations, and Gwendolyn Brooks earned the Pulitzer Prize for poetry. A vibrant black culture, including top musicians such as Louis Armstrong, Ella Fitzgerald, and Mahalia Jackson, appealed to audiences black and white.

Why?? (prejudice?) ** Still, in most respects African Americans found that little had changed. Although a number of states and cities outside the South enacted laws regarding fair employment practices in the 1940s—even as the federal government ended its wartime antidiscrimination program—African Americans struggled to hold on to the gains they had made during the war. Federal housing programs for

Discrimination ① the poor and nonpoor alike encouraged discrimination against blacks, and violence sometimes greeted those who tried to move

② into white areas. Postwar Detroit saw 120 incidents of arson, cross burnings, and physical attacks in neighborhoods undergoing racial *Violence* transition. As African Americans migrated to northern and western

③ cities, they found themselves crowded into what were rapidly becoming ghettos.

In South, voters intimidated ✓✓ Things were worse in the South, where violence greeted blacks'

④ attempts to assert their rights. White men with guns turned back Medgar Evers (who would become a key civil rights leader in the 1960s) and four other veterans who were trying to vote in Missis-

⑤ sippi. A mob lynched Isaac Nixon for voting in Georgia, and an all-white jury acquitted the men accused of his murder. Governors, U.S. senators, and other southern politicians routinely intimidated potential voters with threats of economic retaliation and violence.

—James L. Roark et al., *The American Promise,* Second Edition

In her annotations, this student put some of the writer's key ideas into her own words and recorded questions she hoped to discuss in her study group.

◆ PRACTICE 2.4

Reread "After a Shooting" (pp. 25–26). As you reread, refer to the Questions for Annotating (pp. 30–31), and use them to help you annotate the passage as you write your own thoughts and questions in the margins. Note where you agree or disagree with the writer, and briefly explain why.

Quickly summarize any points you think are particularly important. Take time to look up any unfamiliar words you have circled, and write brief definitions for them.

◆ PRACTICE 2.5

Trade workbooks with another student, and read over his or her highlighting and annotating of "After a Shooting." How are your written responses similar to the other student's? How are they different? Do your classmate's responses help you see anything new about the article?

Outlining a Reading Assignment

Another technique you can use to help you understand a reading assignment better is **outlining**. Unlike a **formal outline**, whichs follow fairly strict conventions, an **informal outline** is easy to make and can be a valuable reading tool: it shows you which ideas are more important than others, and it shows you how ideas are related.

To make an informal outline of a reading assignment, follow these guidelines.

> **Computer Tip**
> Many word-processing programs have an outline function that automatically formats the different levels of your outline.

FOCUS Making an Informal Outline

1. Write or type the passage's main idea across the top of a sheet of paper.
2. At the left margin, write down the most important idea of the first paragraph or section of the passage.
3. Indent the next line a few spaces, and list the examples or details that support this idea.
4. As ideas become more specific, indent further. (Ideas that have the same degree of importance are indented the same distance from the left margin.)
5. Repeat this process with each paragraph or section of the passage.

The student who highlighted and annotated the passage on pages 28–29 made the following informal outline to help her understand its content.

```
Main idea: Although African Americans had achieved
   a lot by the end of World War II, they still
   faced prejudice and violence.
African Americans as a group had made significant
   advances.
     Many had served in the military.
     Political influence was growing.
          More African Americans voted.
          NAACP membership increased.
```

```
Individual African Americans had made significant
   advances.
     Sports: Jackie Robinson
     World politics: Ralph Bunche
     Literature: Gwendolyn Brooks
     Music: Louis Armstrong, Ella Fitzgerald,
        Mahalia Jackson
Despite these advances, much remained the same for
   African Americans.
     They faced discrimination in public
        housing.
     Racial integration led to violence.
     They were pushed into ghettos.
     Southern blacks faced violence and even
        lynching if they tried to vote.
```

◆ PRACTICE 2.6

Working on your own or in a small group, make an informal outline of "After a Shooting" (pp. 25–26). Refer to your highlighting and annotations as you construct the outline. When you have finished, check to make sure your outline indicates the writer's emphasis and the relationships among his ideas.

Summarizing a Reading Assignment

Once you have highlighted and annotated a passage, you may want to try summarizing it. A **summary** retells, *in your own words,* what a passage is about. A summary condenses a passage, so it generally leaves out all but the main idea, key supporting points, and examples. A summary omits minor details and stylistic devices, and it does not include your own ideas or opinions.

FOCUS Writing a Summary

1. Review your outline.
2. Consulting your outline, restate the passage's main idea *in your own words.*
3. Consulting your outline, restate the passage's supporting points. Add connecting words and phrases between sentences where necessary.
4. Reread the original passage to make sure you haven't left out anything significant.

NOTE: To avoid accidentally using the exact language of the original, do not look at the passage while you write your summary.

The student who highlighted, annotated, and outlined the passage from the history textbook wrote the following summary.

> Although African Americans had achieved a lot by the end of World War II, they still faced prejudice and even violence. As a group, they had made significant advances, which included military service and increased participation in politics, as indicated by voting and NAACP membership. Individual African Americans had also made significant advances in sports, world politics, literature, and music. Despite these advances, however, much remained the same for African Americans after World War II. They faced discrimination even in public housing, and attempts at racial integration often led to violence. As a result, many African Americans found themselves pushed into ghettos. Conditions in the South were even worse: here, African Americans still faced the threat of violence and even lynching if they tried to vote.

◆ PRACTICE 2.7

On a separate sheet of paper, write a brief summary of "After a Shooting" (pp. 25–26). Use your outline to guide you, and remember to keep your summary short and to the point. (Your summary will probably be about one-quarter to one-third the length of the original passage.)

C Reading in College, in the Workplace, and in the Community

Although the active reading process you have just reviewed can be applied to all kinds of material, various kinds of reading often require slightly different strategies during the previewing stage. One reason for this is that different kinds of reading may have different purposes: to present information, to persuade, and so on. Another reason is that the various texts you read are aimed at different audiences, and different audiences require different signals about content and emphasis. For these reasons, you need to look for different kinds of verbal and visual signals when you preview different kinds of reading material.

Reading Textbooks

The purpose of a textbook is to present information, and when you read a textbook, your goal is to understand that information. To do this, you need to figure out which ideas are most important as well as which points support those key ideas and which examples illustrate them.

✓ CHECKLIST: Reading Textbooks

Look for the following features as you preview:

- **Boldfaced** and *italicized* words, which can indicate terms to be defined
- Boxed checklists or summaries, which may appear at the ends of sections or chapters
- Bulleted or numbered lists, which may list key reasons or examples or summarize important material
- Diagrams, charts, tables, graphs, photographs, and other visuals that illustrate the writer's points

◆ PRACTICE 2.8

The following passage from an introductory psychology textbook defines and illustrates the term *attribution*. Identify the passage's visual and verbal signals, and use them to help you identify the main idea and key supporting points. Then highlight and annotate the passage.

ATTRIBUTION
Explaining Behavior

Attribution *refers to the process of explaining people's behavior. What are the fundamental attribution error, the actor-observer discrepancy, and the self-serving bias? How do these biases shape the attributions we make?*

As you're studying in the college library, the activities of two workers catch your attention. The two men are trying to lift and move a large file cabinet. "Okay, let's lift it and tip it this way," one guy says with considerable authority. In unison, they heave and tip the file cabinet. When they do, all four file drawers come flying out, bonking the first guy on the head. As the file cabinet goes crashing to the floor, you bite your lip to keep from laughing and think to yourself, "Yeah, they're obviously a pair of 40-watt bulbs."

Why did you arrive at that conclusion? After all, it's completely possible that the workers were not dimwits. Maybe the lock on the file drawers broke. Or maybe there was some other explanation for their mishap.

Attribution is the process of inferring the cause of someone's behavior, including your own. Psychologists also use the word *attribution* to refer to the explanation you make for a particular behavior. The attributions you make have a strong influence on your thoughts and feelings about other people.

If your attribution for the file cabinet incident was that the workers were not very bright, you demonstrated a pattern that occurs consistently in explaining the behavior of other people. *We tend to spontaneously attribute the behavior of others to internal, personal characteristics, while downplaying or underestimating the effects of external, situational factors.* This bias is so common in individualistic cultures that it's called the **fundamental attribution error** (Ross, 1977). Even though it's entirely possible that situational forces are behind another person's behavior, we tend to automatically assume that the cause is an internal, personal characteristic.

The fundamental attribution error plays a role in a common explanatory pattern called **blaming the victim**. The innocent victim of a crime, disaster, or serious illness is blamed for having somehow caused the misfortune or for not having taken steps to prevent it. For example, many people blame the poor for their dire straits, the sick for bringing on their illness, and battered women and rape survivors for somehow "provoking" their attackers. Hindsight makes it seem as if the victim should have been able to predict and prevent what was going to happen (Carli & Leonard, 1989).

Along with the fundamental attribution error, a second bias contributes to unfairly blaming the victim of misfortune. People have a strong need to believe that the world is fair—that "we get what we deserve and deserve what we get." Social psychologist Melvin Lerner (1980) calls this the **just-world hypothesis**. Blaming the victim reflects the belief that, because the world is just, the victim must have done *something* to deserve his or her fate.

Why do we have a psychological need to believe in a just world? Well, if you believe the world is unfair, then no one—including you—is safe from tragic twists of fate and chance, no matter how virtuous, careful, or conscientious you may be (Thornton, 1992). Hence, blaming the victim and believing the just-world hypothesis provide a way to psychologically defend yourself against the threatening thought, "It could just as easily have been me."

—Don H. Hockenbury and Sandra K. Hockenbury, *Psychology,* Second Edition

Reading Newspapers

As a student, as an employee, and as a citizen, you read community, local, and national newspapers. Like textbooks, newspapers communicate information. In addition to relatively objective news articles, however, newspapers also contain editorials (which aim to persuade) as well as feature articles (which may be designed to entertain as well as to inform).

✓ CHECKLIST: Reading Newspapers

Look for the following features as you preview:

- ☐ The name of the section in which the article appears (news, business, lifestyle, sports, and so on)
- ☐ Headlines
- ☐ Boldfaced headings within articles

(continued on the following page)

(continued from the preceding page)

- Labels like *editorial, commentary,* or *opinion,* which indicate that an article is the writer's opinion
- Brief biographical information at the end of an opinion piece
- Phrases or sentences in boldface that emphasize key points
- The article's first sentence, which often answers the questions *who, what, why, where, when,* and *how*
- The **dateline**, which tells you the city the writer is reporting from
- Related articles that appear on the same page—for example, boxed information and **sidebars**, short articles that provide additional background on an article's people and setting
- Photographs

◆ PRACTICE 2.9

Using the checklist above as a guide, preview the following newspaper article. When you have finished, highlight and annotate the article.

Philadelphia students get a scholarship guarantee

All seniors with a financial need and proper grades will qualify.

By Susan Snyder and Kristin E. Holmes
INQUIRER STAFF WRITERS

1 Philadelphia public high school students who want to go to college—and who have the grades—will no longer be held back by lack of money.

2 What could be a dream come true for thousands of the city's 10,700 seniors was announced yesterday—a four-year, $40 million plan to pay up to $3,000 for each eligible student whose freshman-year funds fall short.

3 Mayor Street and the Philadelphia School District pledged the scholarships over the next four years for about 9,600 seniors in public schools and 1,100 more in charter schools. Most of the 4,000 city students who attend college each year require financial aid.

4 District officials could not say how many students could get the promised funds for tuition and room and board—but they estimated that lack of money keeps 2,000 to 3,000 city students from pursuing college each year.

5 "Everyone will have an opportunity to go to college," Street told students at a college-awareness rally at Temple University's Liacouras Center. The so-called "last-dollar scholarships" would cover whatever state and financial aid do not.

6 Amauris Matos-Reyes, 15, was among 2,000 high school students who cheered and applauded the announcement. Matos-Reyes, who attends Thomas A. Edison/John C. Fareira High School, sees help for students from low-income families who may not have the financial means to pay for college.

7 "This gives a chance to everybody,"

A promise of aid for college dreams

MICHAEL BRYANT / Inquirer Staff Photographer

***Bin Woo (center) and Brandon Walker (right)** of Carver High School of Engineering and Science are among the students cheering the city and school district's announcement of the four-year, $40 million plan.*

Matos-Reyes said. "It gives them hope that they can become what they want to be."

Funding for the program, called 8
CORE Philadelphia (College Opportunity Resources for Education), is subject to approval by both City Council and the School Reform Commission, which oversees the district.

The city and district will shoulder the 9
financial burden for the first four years of the program. U.S. Rep. Chaka Fattah said he was trying to create a $150 million endowment fund to cover the scholarships after 2008.

The program could grow as more 10
students realize they can afford to attend college, officials said.

Could the city and district afford it if 11
all its graduates decide to go to college?

"That's a problem we'd like to have," 12
said Debra Kahn, city education secretary.

The promise comes with a few 13
strings: Students will be eligible for up to $3,000 each only for their freshman year, and they must be accepted by one of the 14 State System of Higher Education universities, Community College of Philadelphia, or one of the four state-related institutions: Temple and Lincoln Universities, Pennsylvania State University or the University of Pittsburgh. In addition, students must have attended the city's public or charter schools for at least four consecutive years prior to graduation to be eligible.

Zuleica Diaz, a Kensington High 14
School freshman, hopes the grant will help her achieve her goal of attending Temple University and becoming a kindergarten teacher.

"I don't think [my parents] will pay 15
because it costs too much," said Diaz, 15, "but this is a chance, and I'm happy."

Matos-Reyes, who is considering a 16
career in medicine or computer engineering and design, is concerned that his college education would be a financial strain for his family.

"That's why I try my hardest in 17

CORE at a Glance

Test Scores

Average Scholastic Assessment Test score for the Philadelphia School District for 2001–02: **832**.

Average SAT score for incoming freshmen in the State System of Higher Education for fall 2002: **992**.

Costs

Tuition for the 14 State System of Higher Education schools: **$4,598**.

Room and board: **$4,290** to **$5,390**.

Students

Average number of district seniors who graduate each year: **9,600**.

Estimated number eligible for the new financial-aid program: **4,000**.

Number of seniors in charter schools this year: **1,100**.

Estimated number eligible: Not available.

For More Information

Students and families who want more information on college preparation, choices, financial resources, and other issues may call the district's office of College and Career Awareness at 215-299-7807 or go to the CORE Philadelphia Web site at www.corephilly.org.

school, so that my parents don't have to worry," Matos-Reyes said. "This helps a lot. It takes the weight a little bit off of them."

18 Fattah said the city's students would be encouraged to reach for goals that they might have thought were unattainable.

19 "The whole thrust here is to send kids a signal that college is possible. College is within your reach if you get to your senior year," he said. "Four years from today, we expect Philadelphia to lead the nation in the number of students graduating from high school and going on to college."

20 Fattah already has approached groups, such as the Bill and Melinda Gates Foundation, seeking funding. In addition, the Student Loan Marketing Association (Sallie Mae) will underwrite all administrative operating costs for the program, he said.

21 The financial help comes as national reports warn of tens of thousands of students from low-income families being kept out of college because of money. Last year, the Advisory Committee on Student Financial Assiatance reported that 170,000 top high school graduates from low- and moderate-income families could not afford to enroll in college.

22 The "average unmet need" of an urban student going off to college is $4,000, and that's after receiving aid and loans, according to the Cleveland-based National College Access Network.

23 While many communities have started college-access scholarship programs, Philadelphia's new program appears to be the most extensive, offering aid to everyone, said Tina Millano, executive director.

24 Congress created a similar program in 1999 for students in Washington, and the Washington Post reported this month that it might be paying off: Private surveys show it has spurred significant grains in college attendance. The report says no public agency has attendance figures before and after 2000, when the legislation took effect.

25 In Pennsylvania, tuition at the 14 State System of Higher Education institutions is about $4,600; room and board varies among the schools, ranging from $4,290 to $5,390.

26 Tom Gluck, a spokesman for the state system, said city applicants would have to follow normal admission procedures, which are up to each university. The system does not anticipate creating any spaces or special measures for city students.

27 "It's simply making certain that cost is not a barrier to those who are ready and interested and qualified to attend our universities," Gluck said.

28 The number of freshman positions varies each year, depending on enrollment. For fall 2002, the system received 68,786 applications; 47,311 were accepted, and 19,059 enrolled. Of those, 3,613 were Philadelphia public- and private-school students.

29 To start the scholarship fund, the school district will kick in $6 million a year for the first four years if the School Reform Commission approves. Paul Vallas, district chief executive officer, said the district would use federal funds. The city's contribution—$4 million—is subject to approval by City Council. Street said he likely would seek the funds through refinancing.

30 Councilman Michael Nutter and Councilwoman Blondell Reynolds Brown said the program sounded worthy of support. "I care very deeply about college access, and I look forward to details of the program. On its face, it certainly sounds like a great idea," Nutter said.

31 Because only the freshman year would be covered, officials acknowledged that students would have to find other funding sources for the following three years. "We want to get them started," Fattah said.

Reading Web Sites

In schools, businesses, and community life, people turn to the Web for information. However, because many Web sites have busy, crowded pages, reading one can require you to work hard to distinguish important information from not-so-important material. Some Web sites—particularly those whose **URLs** (electronic addresses) end in .com—may have a persuasive rather than an informative purpose (for example, to sell a product or to promote a political position). Those designated .edu (educational institution) or .org (nonprofit organization) are more likely—although not guaranteed—to present unbiased information.

For more on evaluating Web sites, see 3B.

✓ CHECKLIST: Reading Web Sites

Look for the following features as you preview:

- Links to other sites (underlined in blue)
- Graphics
- Color
- Headings
- Boxed material
- Page layout (placement of images and text on the page)
- Type size
- Photographs
- URL designation (.com, .org, and so on)

Computer Tip

Because text is more difficult to read on a screen than on a printed page, Web sites tend to organize information with visual signals rather than verbal signals. For this reason, well-designed professional Web sites are rich in useful visual signals.

◆ PRACTICE 2.10

The following is the home page of the U.S. Environmental Protection Agency. Preview this page, looking closely at the features listed in the checklist above. Which topics attract the most attention? Why? Do you think this page communicates its information effectively? How could its presentation be improved?

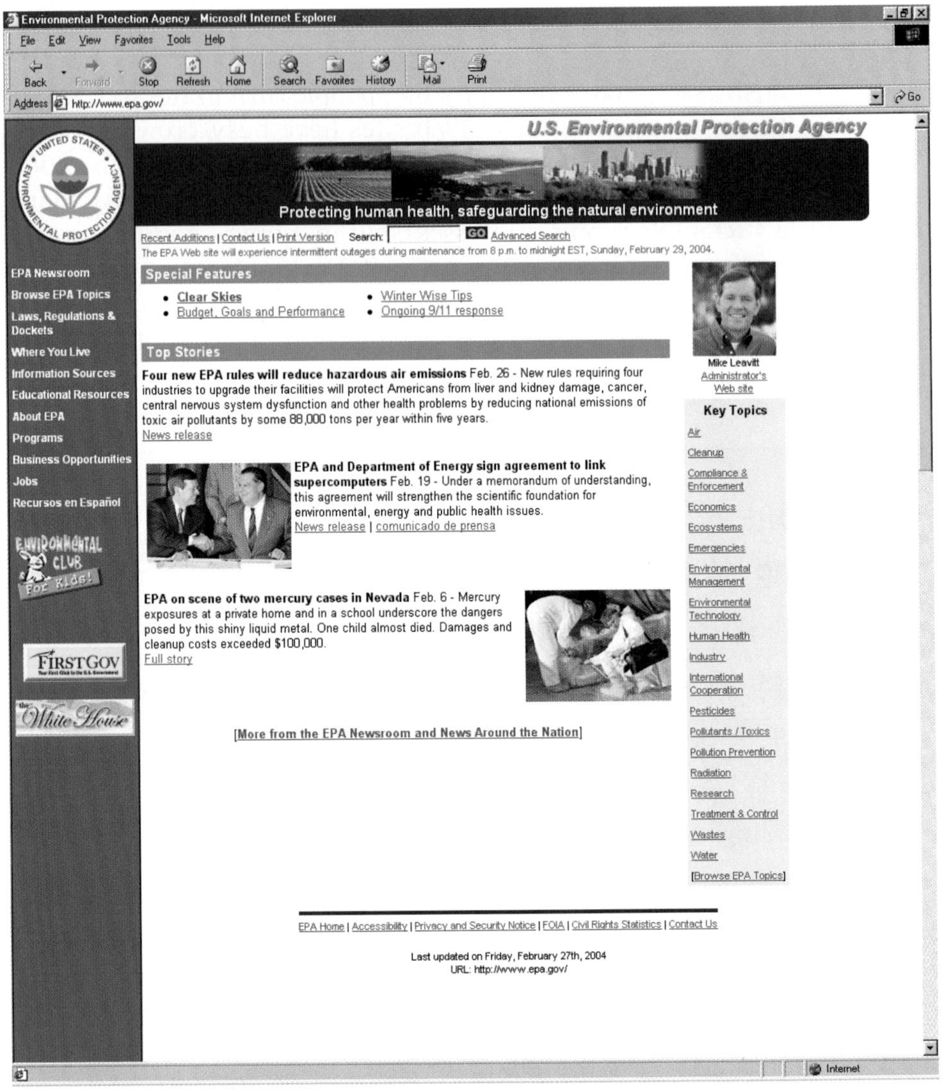

Reading on the Job

In your workplace, you will be called on to read memos, letters, emails, and reports. These documents, which may be designed to convey information or to persuade, are often addressed to a group rather than to a single person. (Note that the most important information is often presented first—in a subject line or in the first paragraph.)

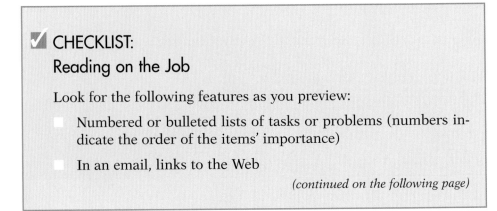

✓ CHECKLIST: Reading on the Job

Look for the following features as you preview:

- ☐ Numbered or bulleted lists of tasks or problems (numbers indicate the order of the items' importance)
- ☐ In an email, links to the Web

(continued on the following page)

(continued from the preceding page)

- In a memo or an email, the person or persons addressed
- In a memo or an email, the subject line
- In a memo or a report, headings that highlight key topics or points
- The first and last paragraphs and the first sentence of each body paragraph, which often contain key information
- Boldfaced, underlined, or italicized words

◆ PRACTICE 2.11

Preview the following samples of on-the-job writing, and answer these questions: What is each writer's purpose (that is, what does the writer want to accomplish)? What is the most important piece of information each writer wants to communicate? Then, highlight and annotate each sample, and write a *one-sentence* summary of each in your own words.

1. A memo

Memorandum

September 10, 2003
To: Hector Garzon, Executive Director
From: Marco Morales, Director, Drug and Alcohol Unit
Subject: Marta Diaz-Gold

Marta Diaz-Gold has returned to work from her maternity leave. I have assigned her a caseload that consists of our clients who have been referred from the Road to Recovery program. This means that HUD funds for substance abuse counseling that go to Road to Recovery can now be used to pay Marta's salary and that the Road to Recovery case managers can provide support for our counseling services.

Marta and I have agreed on the following:
- Regular monthly meetings with Road to Recovery case managers
- Weekly reports to me from Marta regarding progress on the Road to Recovery caseload
- Joint review of Marta's work by Miriam Cabrera and myself after six months

Marta will be meeting with the current counselor and each individual client this week so she can make a smooth transition into her new position. As of next week, she will have full responsibility for all these clients. Because the Road to Recovery clients will not comprise a full caseload, it is understood that Marta will also be getting clients on a regular rotation from our other drug and alcohol programs.

Cc: Miriam Cabrera, Human Resources Director
Marta Diaz-Gold

2. An email

To: University Faculty, Staff, and Students
Re: Emergency Closing

KYW News Radio (1060) has assumed responsibility for co-ordinating and managing the school closing program in our area. School numbers will be announced twice every hour. The University's radio identification number is **117.** The number for students attending evening classes at the University is **2117.** You may also find information about school closings on the radio station's Website at **<www.kyw1060.com>**. In addition, school closings will also be announced *by name* on WTFX-Fox TV (channel 29).

☑ REVIEW CHECKLIST: Reading for College Success

- ☐ Become an active reader. (See 2A.)
- ☐ Highlight your reading assignment. (See 2B.)
- ☐ Annotate your reading assignment. (See 2B.)
- ☐ Outline your reading assignment. (See 2B.)
- ☐ Summarize your reading assignment. (See 2B.)
- ☐ Learn how to read different kinds of texts. (See 2C.)

CHAPTER 3

Using the Internet for College Success

PREVIEW

In this chapter, you will learn

- to use the Internet to find information (3A)
- to evaluate Web sites (3B)
- to use the Internet to locate information for assignments (3C)
- to use the Internet to improve your writing (3D)
- to use the Internet to locate everyday information (3E)

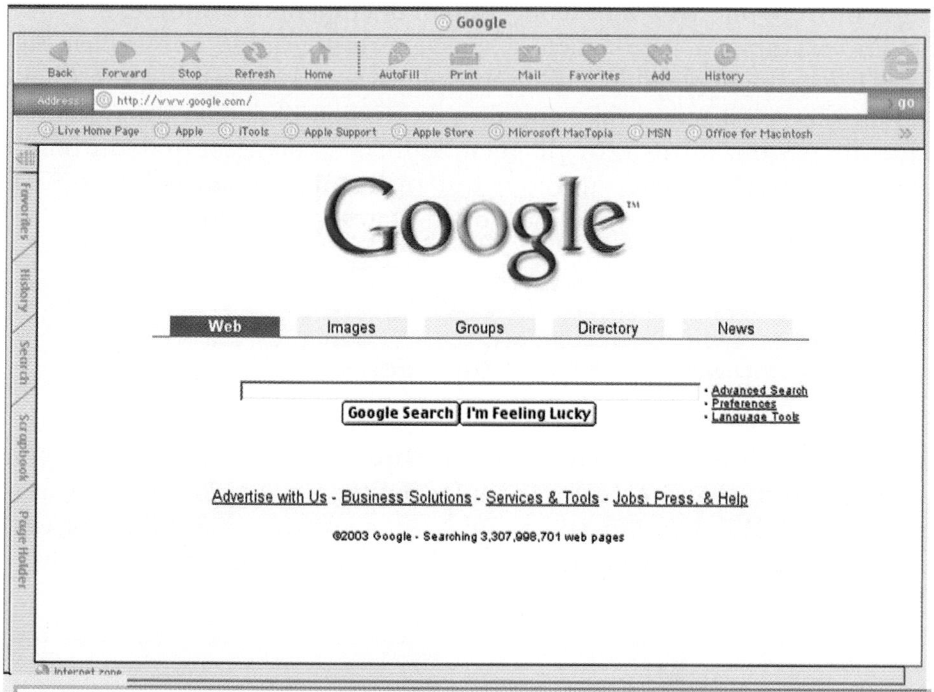

SEEING AND WRITING

Look at the picture above, the home page of Google, the most popular search engine. Then, write a paragraph telling what information you think you might be able to get by using Google. How would you go about finding this information?

Word Power

facilitate to make something easier to do

The Internet is a network of millions of computers in homes, colleges and universities, government agencies, research institutions, businesses, and libraries all over the world. The Internet can give you access to a world of information—information that can help you in school and in your everyday life. Here are some of the things you can do on the Internet:

- Send and receive messages via email
- Send and receive text files (for example, assignments), graphics, sound, animation, film clips, and live video

- Read articles and other documents about practically any subject, from asteroids to engineering to Zen Buddhism
- Send messages to electronic "bulletin boards" (set up for your classes or for other groups), and read messages sent by others
- Access your college library's home page, which enables you to use the online catalog as well as many electronic resources not available on the free Internet

When people refer to the Internet, they usually mean the **World Wide Web**. The Web, which forms an important part of the Internet, is a collection of millions of documents on every imaginable topic. The Web relies on **hypertext links**—specially highlighted words and phrases. By clicking on these links, you can move easily from one part of a document to another or from one **Web site** (collection of documents) to another.

For example, a Web article discussing immigration might have the word *Cuban* highlighted in a different color from the rest of the text. Clicking on this word might take you to a discussion of Cuban immigration. This discussion, in turn, might include links to articles, bulletin board postings, or other material about Cuban history, Cuban politics, Fidel Castro, Cuban cultural life in the United States, and so on.

A Finding Information on the Internet

To use the Internet, you need an Internet **browser**, a tool that enables you to display Web pages. The most popular browsers are Netscape Navigator and Internet Explorer. (Most new computers come with one of these browsers already installed.) The Internet Explorer home page is shown below.

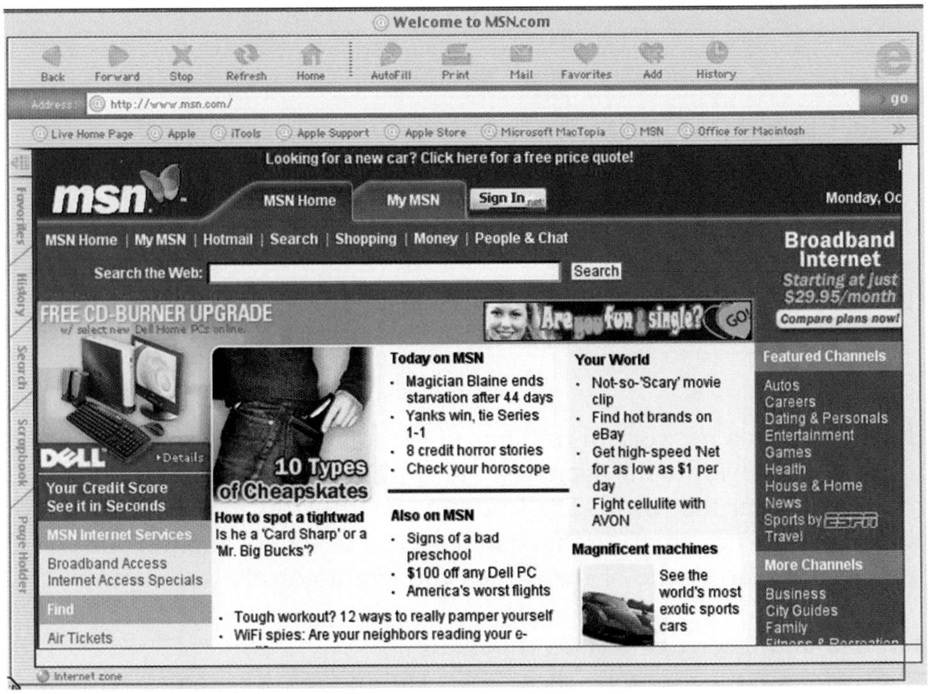

Internet Explorer Home Page

Before you can access the Internet, you have to be **online**—that is, connected to an **Internet service provider (ISP)**. Many colleges and universities provide Internet access free of charge to students. In addition, companies such as America Online provide access for a monthly fee. Once you are online, you need to connect to a **search engine**, a program that helps you find information by sorting through the millions of documents that are available on the Internet. Among the most popular search engines are AltaVista (<http://www.altavista.com>), Infoseek (<http://www.infoseek.com>), Yahoo! (<http://www.yahoo.com>), and Google (<http://www.google.com>). The opening image in this chapter shows the Google search page.

There are several ways to use a search engine to find information.

- *You can enter a Web site's URL.* All search engines have a box (the URL search field) in which you can enter a Web site's electronic address—its **uniform resource locator** or **URL**. When you click on the URL or hit your computer's Enter key, the search engine connects you to the Web site. For example, to find information about family members who entered the United States through Ellis Island, you would enter this URL: <http://www.ellisislandrecords.com>.
- *You can do a keyword search.* All search engines let you do a **keyword search**: you type a term into a box (the keyword search field), and the search engine looks for documents that contain the term, listing all the **hits** (documents containing one or both of these words) that it found. If you type in a broad term like *civil war,* you might get hundreds of thousands of hits—more than you could possibly consider. If this occurs, don't give up. Narrow your search by using a more specific term—*Battle of Gettysburg,* for example. You can focus your search even further by putting quotation marks around the term (*"Battle of Gettysburg"*). When you do this, the search engine will search only for documents that contain this phrase.

Computer Tip

It is a good idea to **bookmark** useful sites by selecting the Bookmark or Favorites option at the top of your browser screen. Once you bookmark a site, you can return to it whenever you want to.

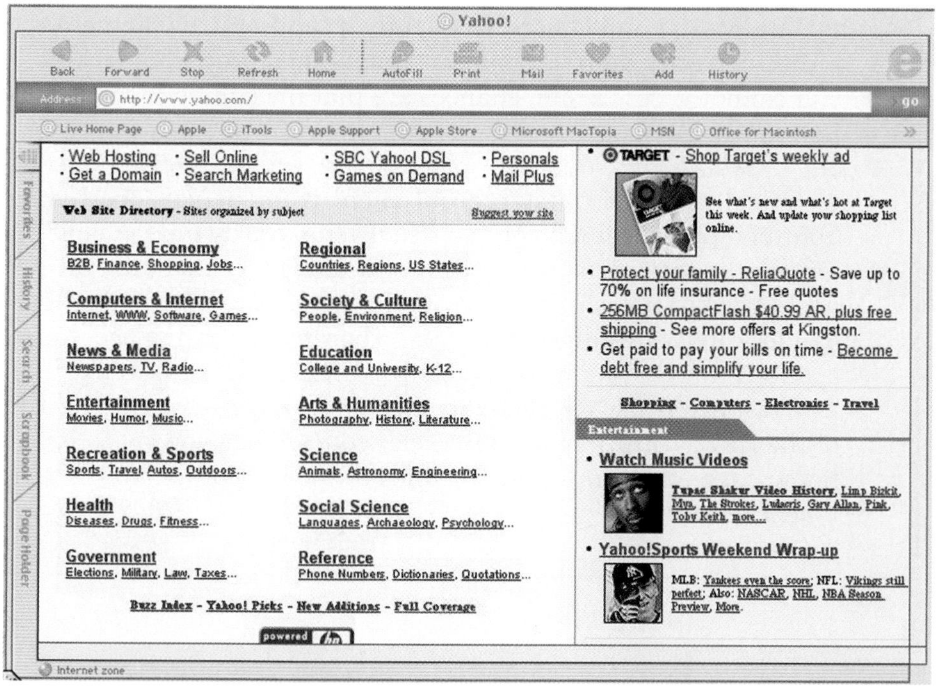

Yahoo! Subject Guide Directory

- *You can do a subject search.* Some search engines, such as Yahoo!, let you do a **subject search**. First, you choose a broad subject from a list of subjects: *The Humanities, The Arts, Entertainment, Business,* and so on. Each of these general subjects leads you to more specific subjects, until eventually you get to the subtopic that you want. For example, you could start your search on Yahoo! with the general topic *Entertainment.* Clicking on this topic would lead you to *Movies and Film* and then to *Reviews.* Finally, you would get to a list of movie reviews that might link to a review of the specific movie you are interested in. The Yahoo! subject guide directory is shown on the previous page.

FOCUS Accessing Web Sites: Troubleshooting

Sometimes your computer will tell you that a site you want to visit is unavailable or does not exist. When this occurs, consider the following possibilities before giving up and moving on to another site.

- *Check to make sure the URL is correct.* To reach a site, you have to type its URL accurately. Any error—for example, an added space or punctuation mark—will send you to the wrong site (or to no site at all).
- *Check to make sure you are connected to the Internet.* To reach a site, you have to be connected to the Internet. If you are not properly connected, your computer will indicate this.
- *Check to make sure your computer is connected to your access line.* A loose connection or an unplugged jack will make it impossible for you to access the Internet. If your computer is not connected, it will indicate that it is not receiving a signal.
- *Check to make sure the site still exists.* Web sites, especially those maintained by individuals, frequently disappear. If you entered a URL correctly, your computer is functioning properly, and you still cannot access a site, chances are that the site no longer exists.
- *Try revisiting the site later.* Sometimes Web sites experience technical problems that prevent them from being accessed. Your computer will tell you if a site is temporarily unreachable.
- *Try deleting parts of the URL.* Begin by deleting the end of the URL up to the first slash: <http://www.lib.Berkeley.edu/teachinglib/guides/internet/~~findinginfo.html~~>. Then try accessing the site again. If this doesn't work, delete the URL up to the next slash. As a last resort, try to reach the site's home page—the first part of the URL: <http://www.lib.Berkeley.edu/>. Once you get to the home page, you can follow the links to the part of the Web site that you want.

B Evaluating Web Sites

Not every Web site is a valuable source of information. In fact, anyone can put information on the Internet. For this reason, it is a good idea to approach Web sites with skepticism. In a sense, Web sites are like strangers knocking at your door: before you let them in, you need to be sure they are honest and trustworthy.

Word Power
skepticism a doubtful or questioning attitude

FOCUS Evaluating Web Sites

To decide whether to use information from a particular Web site, ask the following questions:

- *Is the site reliable?* Never rely on information by an unidentified author; always try to determine the author of material on a Web site. Also determine the author's qualifications. For example, say you are looking at a site that discusses Labrador retrievers. Is the author a breeder? A veterinarian? Someone who has had a Lab as a pet? The first two authors would probably be authorities on the subject; the third author might not be.
- *Does the site have a hidden purpose?* When you evaluate a Web site, be sure to consider its purpose. For example, a site discussing the health benefits of herbal medicine would have one purpose if it were sponsored by a university and another if it were sponsored by a company selling herbal remedies. Researchers who post information on a university site are trying to inform others about their findings. Retailers, however, put information online to sell a product; therefore, they sometimes make exaggerated claims about its usefulness.
- *Is the site up-to-date?* If a site has not been recently updated, you should question the information it contains. A discussion of foot-and-mouth disease in England, for example, would be out of date if it were written before the widespread outbreak in 2001. You would have to continue your search until you found a more current discussion.
- *Is the information on the site trustworthy?* A site should include evidence to support what it says. If it does not, consider the information to be unsupported personal opinion. Points are supported with facts, examples, statistics, and expert opinions—not rumors or third-hand opinions.
- *Does the site contain needlessly elaborate graphics?* With Web sites, substance counts more than style. When you come across a site that has slick visuals—animation, bright colors, and lots of pictures—don't be misled. Make sure that these graphic elements do not mask weak logic or uninformed opinion.

Word Power
evaluating examining something to judge its value, quality, or importance

Computer Tip
A Web site's URL can give you information about the site's purpose. For example, the abbreviation *.edu* indicates that the site is sponsored by an educational institution, *.gov* indicates a government agency, *.org* indicates a nonprofit organization, and *.com* indicates a business or personal site. Some abbreviations, such as *.uk* for United Kingdom and *.de* for Germany, indicate the Web site's country of origin.

C Using the Internet to Locate Information for Assignments

You can use the Internet to find information about the subjects you are studying. For example, if in your communication class you were discussing early television sitcoms, you could go to the Internet and find Web sites devoted to this general subject. You could also find specific sites for shows such as *I Love Lucy, The Honeymooners,* and *The Brady Bunch.* The following sites can help you access information that will be useful for many of your courses.

Academic Subjects on the Web

The Humanities

Art history
Art History Resources on the Web
<http://witcombe.sbc.edu/ARTHLinks.html>

Film
The Internet Movie Database
<http://www.imdb.com>

History
HyperHistory Online
<http://www.hyperhistory.com/online_n2/History_n2/a.html>

Literature
The On-Line Books Page
<http://digital.library.upenn.edu/books/>

Philosophy
Stanford Encyclopedia of Philosophy
<http://plato.stanford.edu>

The Natural Sciences

Biology
Biodiversity and Biological Collections Web Server
<http://biodiversity.uno.edu>

Chemistry
WWW Chemistry Resources
<http://www.chem.ucla.edu/chempointers.html>

Engineering
The Engineer's Reference
<http://www.eng-sol.com>

Mathematics
Math.com
<http://www.math.com>

Physics
Web Links: Physics around the World
<http://www.physicsweb.org/resources/>

The Social Sciences

Education
Education World®
<http://www.education-world.com/>

Political science
Political Resources on the Net
<http://www.politicalresources.net>

Psychology
PsychCrawler
<http://www.psychcrawler.com>

Sociology and social work
Social Work and Social Services Web Sites
<http://gwbweb.wustl.edu/websites.html>

FOCUS Avoiding Plagiarism

When you transfer information from Web sites into your notes, you may be tempted to "cut and paste" text without noting where the text came from. If you then copy this text into your paper, you are committing plagiarism—*and plagiarism is the theft of ideas.* Every college has rules that students must follow when using words, ideas, and visuals from books, articles, and Internet sources. Consult your school's Web site or student handbook for information on the appropriate use of such information.

D Using the Internet to Improve Your Writing

The Internet has many Web sites that can help you with your writing. Sites like the following ones include links to other useful sites.

Writing Help on the Web

The *Foundations First* site
<http://www.bedfordstmartins.com/foundationsfirst>

Help with the writing process
Principles of Composition
<http://webster.commnet.edu/grammar/composition/composition.htm>
The UVic Writer's Guide
<http://web.uvic.ca/wguide>

Help finding something to say
Paradigm Online Writing Assistant: Choosing a Subject
<http://www.powa.org/whtfrms.htm>

Help writing paragraphs
Purposes of Paragraphs
<http://www.fas.harvard.edu/~wricntr/para.html>
Writing Paragraphs
<http://www.uottawa.ca/academic/arts/writcent/hypergrammar/paragraph.html>

Advice on revision
Paradigm: Global and Local Perspectives
<http://www.powa.org/revifrms.htm>

Tips on grammar
The Online English Grammar
<http://www.edunet.com/english/grammar>
Guide to Grammar and Writing
<http://webster.commnet.edu/grammar/index.htm>

Tips on proofreading
Tips for Effective Proofreading
<http://www.ualr.edu/~owl/tipsforproofreading.html>

(continued on the next page)

(continued from the prevous page)

Proofreading
<http://www.bgsu.edu/departments/writing-lab/goproofreading.html>

Online writing centers

LEO: Literacy Education Online
<http://leo.stcloudstate.edu>

Online Writing Lab
<http://owl.english.purdue.edu>

E Using the Internet to Locate Everyday Information

The Internet can make your daily life easier. For example, you can use the Internet to access news and weather reports, download voter registration forms, get travel information, find directions, obtain consumer information, locate people, find movie reviews—or even find a job. The following sites are just a sample of the many resources available on the Internet.

Everyday Information on the Web

The Bible

The Unbound Bible
<http://www.unboundbible.org>

Book reviews

The New York Times *on the Web: Books*
<http://www.nytimes.com/books>

Calendars

Calendar Zone
<http://www.calendarzone.com>

Census data

U.S. Census Bureau Newsletter: Census and You
<http://www.census.gov/prod/www/abs/cen-you.html>

City and county data

U.S. Census Bureau: County and City Data Book
<http://www.census.gov/statab/www/ccdb.html>

Computers

Free Online Dictionary of Computing
<http://www.foldoc.doc.ic.ac.uk/foldoc/index.html>

Dictionaries

yourDictionary.com™
<http://www.yourdictionary.com>

Employment

America's Job Bank
<http://www.ajb.dni.us/>

Encyclopedias

Britannica.com®
<http://www.britannica.com>

Genealogy

Lineages
<http://www.lineages.com>

(continued on the next page)

(continued from the prevous page)

Insurance company ratings
A. M. Best Insurance Information
<http://ambest.com/insurance>

Law and legal information
American Law Sources Online
<http://www.lawsource.com/also/>

Maps and directions
MapBlast!
<http://www.mapblast.com/myblast/index.mb>

Movie reviews
The Internet Movie Database
<http://www.imdb.com>

Newspapers
Newspapers.Com
<http://www.newspapers.com>

Telephone directories
AnyWho
<http://www.tollfree.att.net>
Switchboard.com
<http://www.switchboard.com>

Weather forecasts and information
National Weather Service Home Page
<http://www.nws.noaa.gov>

◆ PRACTICE 3.1

At home or in your school's computer lab, practice entering five of the URLs listed on pages 50–53. Make sure you enter the URLs exactly as they appear on the page. If entering a URL does not take you to the appropriate Web site, check to make sure that you entered the URL correctly. (If the site is no longer active, choose another URL from the list.)

◆ PRACTICE 3.2

Working in a group of four students, select one of the Web sites listed on pages 50–53. At home or in your school's computer lab, access the site, and make a list of three things you like and three things you dislike about it. Then exchange lists with another student in your group. On what do you agree? On what do you disagree?

◆ PRACTICE 3.3

Access the following Web site, which focuses on evaluating Web resources: *<http://www2.widener.edu/Wolfgram-Memorial-Library/webevaluation/webeval.htm>*. Do you think this site is useful? Why or why not? Write a few sentences explaining your answer.

◆ PRACTICE 3.4

Working in a group of three or four students, access two or three of the Web sites listed on pages 50–53. Choose one site, and evaluate it according to the guidelines listed on page 49. Present your group's findings to the class.

◆ PRACTICE 3.5

Use one of the search engines mentioned on page 47 to locate a Web site that focuses on a topic you know a lot about—for example, your hometown, a famous person, or a sport. Evaluate the site according to the guidelines listed on page 49.

■ REVISING AND EDITING

Look back at your response to the Seeing and Writing exercise on page 45. Having read this chapter, you should now know how to use Google to find information. Revise your Seeing and Writing response so that it tells someone not familiar with Google how to locate a specific piece of information.

✓ REVIEW CHECKLIST: Internet Strategies for College Success

- Use a search engine to find information on the Internet. (See 3A.)
- Evaluate Web sites to decide whether to use information from them. (See 3B.)
- Use the Internet to locate information for assignments. (See 3C.)
- Use the Internet to improve your writing. (See 3D.)
- Use the Internet to locate everyday information. (See 3E.)

CHAPTER

4

Strategies for Workplace Success

PREVIEW

In this chapter, you will learn

- how to define your goals (4A)
- how to learn about job openings (4B)
- how to research companies and organizations (4C)
- how to market yourself (4D)
- how to write a résumé, application letter, and follow-up letter (4D)
- how to prepare for an interview (4D and 4E)

SEEING AND WRITING

Look at the picture above. Then write a paragraph telling how you would go about finding a job. Where would you look? How would you apply? How would you prepare for a job interview?

Word Power

anticipate to consider something before it happens and make necessary changes

demeanor a person's manner, appearance, or behavior

Seeking a job—whether to earn money while you are in school or to pursue a career after you have finished school—requires that you understand your goals, look for job leads in the right places, learn about companies and organizations that might employ you, and—most important—learn how to market yourself.

A Defining Your Goals

Before you look for a job, you should determine how much time you can devote to work and what you hope to gain from the experience.

1. ***Determine how much time you have.*** How many hours do you think you need to work? How many hours a week *can* you work while still in school? Are those hours distributed throughout the week, or are they all grouped in one or two days—for example, Saturday and Sunday? Can you work during conventional business hours, or will you need to work evenings? In addition to conventional full-time jobs demanding a minimum of thirty-five hours per week, part-time jobs and special short-term assignments are increasingly available as employers replace expensive staff with more affordable freelance workers.
2. ***Consider unpaid work.*** If you can afford to fill a low-paying or unpaid internship, you can gain the experience you need to get a paying position later on. In addition to exploring established internships, you can create your own internship by offering to work at an organization without pay so that you can gain experience. In either case, you should take your internship seriously—showing up regularly (and on time), volunteering for unglamorous tasks, and seeking out contacts with whom you can network.

FOCUS Finding Part-time and Short-term Jobs

- Think carefully about balancing school and part-time work. Do not let work get in the way of school assignments or pull down your grades.
- Be honest from the outset with a potential employer. For a part-time job, be clear about the maximum number of hours you can work each week. For a summer or other short-term job, indicate when you will be returning to school.
- Consider industries that often look for people who want to work eight to twenty hours a week and who do not need employment benefits. These industries include publishing, public relations, and event planning for sports, performing arts, and trade organizations. Many small offices look for college students—especially those who are computer literate—to help with paperwork and administrative duties one or two days a week.

B Learning about Job Openings

Once you define your goals, you should look for a job in a systematic way. The strategies below will help you get the most out of your search.

1. ***Check your college placement office.*** Placement offices generally list both part-time and full-time jobs as well as short-term and temporary positions. Sometimes these lists are available only in the office; sometimes they are accessible online. In addition to placement offices, individual academic departments may use real or virtual bulletin boards to list job openings for students.

2. ***Scan newspaper and Web listings.*** Many people find jobs through classified advertisements in newspapers or on Web sites, so you may want to check them out. Commercial Web sites called *job boards* also post listings and invite job seekers to post their résumés for employers to scan. Here are three of the most popular job boards:

For sample résumés, see 4E.

- America's Job Bank: <http://www.ajb.dni.us>
- Monster Board: <http://www.monster.com>
- The Job Resource: <http://wwwthejobresource.com>

3. ***Network.*** Networking is a powerful tool for learning about job openings and for learning the values and priorities of employers. Basically, **networking** involves telling instructors, friends, and relatives about your goals and qualifications and finding out who may have helpful information for you.
4. ***Keep your eyes open.*** Many jobs are never advertised. Some small businesses, for example, rely on word of mouth, signs put in store windows, or flyers posted on campus or community bulletin boards. If you are looking for work, you need to be on the alert for job possibilities at all times.

C Researching Companies and Organizations

Once you have found a job lead, take the time to find out as much as you can about the position. This information will help you decide whether the job is right for you, and it will also come in handy later when you go for an interview.

1. ***Explore company Web sites.*** Even though Web sites exist to enhance companies' images, they can be useful to you. First, they tell you how a company or organization sees itself. Second, they usually identify key personnel. Third, they often contain news releases that can keep you up-to-date about new projects or possible plans for expansion.
2. ***Use library resources.*** In your campus library, in the library section of your college placement service, or in a local public library, you can find books and electronic resources that can help you with your job search. Ask a librarian which books he or she recommends. Also, ask about electronic services such as *Career Search.* These resources will help you to find answers to questions about the organization that an interviewer or a network acquaintance might ask you. The library is also the place where, by using one or more electronic databases, you can locate and read magazine, journal, and newspaper articles about the organizations of interest to you.
3. ***Expand your network.*** Once you have identified companies and organizations that appeal to you and that may be hiring, use the resources in your college placement office or the alumni office to find out if graduates of your school already work there. Sometimes these graduates will be willing to share information that can help you learn if a company is right for you—or if it will be hiring in the near future.

D Marketing Yourself

Once you have found a job you want to apply for, you have to get ready to market yourself to a prospective employer. You do this by preparing an effective résumé and writing a convincing job letter. Remember, the purpose of both the résumé and the job letter is to get you an interview. For this reason, you should include details that will make you stand out from all the others who might be applying for the same job.

Computer Tip

Although an eye-catching format is desirable for a paper résumé, many electronic job boards ask for a plain, text-only format that is suitable for electronic scanning or pasting into emails. Learn how to save your current résumé in multiple formats.

1. ***Prepare your résumé.*** Here is one of the most surprising facts about job searching: the résumé that you spend hours perfecting usually gets no more than a one-minute review. To increase your résumé's chance of generating interest, you need to include everything an employer expects to see. Beyond the essential contact information, a résumé should include most of the following items:

   - **Objective** or **Goal** to help a screener who may have several positions to fill
   - **Education** and **Experience** to demonstrate qualifications (under *Experience,* be sure to include internships and volunteer work, summer and campus jobs, temporary work, entrepreneurial undertakings, and extracurricular positions)
   - **Special Skills** to illustrate how you are different from others who are applying for the job (under *Special Skills,* be sure to include proficiency in languages other than English as well as specific computer expertise)
   - **Activities, Achievements, Honors, Leadership,** and **Interests** to highlight exceptional accomplishments
   - **References** to support what you have written about yourself

   Your school placement office can tell you which of the above items to include. The placement office will also have the latest information on résumé formats, including the formats required for submitting a résumé electronically. (Some word-processing programs contain templates that you can use to format your résumé.) Be prepared to update your résumé on a regular basis as your experiences and preferences change.
2. ***Prepare a cover letter.*** Don't simply repeat in the cover letter what your résumé already says. Instead, use the cover letter to make yourself stand out from the crowd by showing what you know about the organization's needs, identifying how you can benefit the organization, and requesting an interview. If possible, address your letter to a specific individual rather than to a general audience such as "Dear Sir or Madam." The company's Web site, the job ad or posting, or your networking contacts can help you identify the person to whom you should write. (Remember that when you post a résumé online, you usually do not include a cover letter.)
3. ***Prepare for an interview.*** During the job interview, you will meet with an interviewer, answer his or her questions, and ask questions of your

own. Interviews take place in person or by phone; they may occur on campus or in an employer's office. The interviewer wants to see if you are suited for the job and if you can think on your feet. Go into an interview prepared to answer standard questions.

FOCUS Interviews: Frequently Asked Questions

- Tell me about yourself.
- Where do you see yourself in five years?
- How do you respond to criticism?
- What accomplishment are you most proud of? How did you solve problems along the way to the accomplishment?
- Are you a team player? Are you more a leader or a follower?
- What have you learned about handling conflict?
- What is your greatest strength? What is your greatest weakness?
- Why did you choose your school? What did you like about it? What did you not like?
- Why isn't your GPA higher?
- What do you know about our organization?
- Are you willing to relocate or travel?

At the interview, dress neatly and conservatively, make eye contact, smile comfortably, demonstrate common-sense behavior (arrive on time, do not smoke, and so on), and be honest about your qualifications—but do not undersell yourself.

Speak slowly, answer the interviewer's questions fully, and illustrate your points with specific examples from your previous job experiences. If the interviewer asks you a difficult question, take time to think of an answer; don't just say the first thing that comes to your mind. Above all, show yourself to be the kind of person who would be an asset to the company. At the end of the interview, thank the interviewer for taking his or her time to talk with you.

4. ***Write the follow-up letter.*** A strong follow-up letter—one that is both respectful and enthusiastic—will make a favorable impression on a potential employer. If you want to expand on or adjust an answer that you gave in the interview, this is your chance.

For a sample follow-up letter, see 4E.

E Sample Job-Application Materials

An important part of applying for a job is the process of assembling an effective résumé and writing letters of application and follow-up letters. The following examples were written by a student who was applying for a full-time position in the field of hotel management.

Rolando J. Matta

UNTIL JUNE 1, 2003	AFTER JUNE 1, 2003
321 Topland Avenue	6543 Lincoln Street, 6D
Johnson City, NY 13790	Chicago, IL 60666
607-737-1111	312-787-5555
rjmatta@fhcc.edu	rjmatta@hotmail.com

OBJECTIVE Associate innkeeper position in the Chicago area

EDUCATION Fox Hollow Community College,
Johnson City, NY 13790
Major: Hospitality Management
Expected date of graduation: June 2003
GPA of 3.4 on a 4.0 scale

Omit if under 3.0; explain grades if asked

Major courses (partial list)
Hotel and Restaurant Accounting
Hotel-Restaurant Organization and Management
Food Purchasing
Principles of Food Preparation
Executive Housekeeping
Hotel Front-Office Operations
Hospitality Law

Use boldface and bullets to highlight data

EXPERIENCE **Hospitality Internship,**
May 2002 to August 2002
Grande Hotel, New York, NY

- Rotated through Front Desk, Housekeeping, and Room Service departments in hands-on and supervisory positions
- Participated in weekly question-and-answer sessions with key managers
- Reported on satisfaction of American Bar Association conventioneers
- Researched cost savings on alternative gifts for returning guests

Assistant to Meetings Supervisor,
August 2001 to May 2002
VIP Executive Suites, Binghamton, NY

- Coordinated and reviewed setup and breakdown of furniture and refreshments for all meeting rooms
- Communicated with Audiovisual Department
- Reviewed all billing against contracts
- Scheduled appointments for prospective clients with supervisor

OTHER SKILLS Proficiency with MS Office, the Internet; good communication with computer technicians; bilingual (English/Spanish)

ACTIVITIES Travel in Latin America; summer cooking classes in New York

REFERENCES Available on request

Or give names, titles, and telephone numbers here

Sample Résumé

321 Topland Avenue
Johnson City, NY 13790
607-737-1111
rjmatta@fhcc.edu

April 1, 2003

Ms. Jennifer T. White
Manager
Rotunda Hotel and Sports Club
88990 Airport Highway
Chicago, IL 60677

Dear Ms. White:

Mr. Luigi Cuenca of the Grande Hotel in New York, where I worked last summer, tells me that you will be interviewing candidates for management assistants. I believe my experience at the Grande Hotel and elsewhere has prepared me for the challenge of working at the Rotunda.

Try writing to a specific person rather than sending a blind mailing

Since your hotel is at O'Hare Airport, I know that many of your guests stay at the Rotunda because of last-minute flight cancellations due to weather. For this reason, my experience in responding to frustrated travelers will be of use to you. In addition, I have been reading about services that boutique hotels in Europe and Australia offer to business travelers. I would like to have the opportunity of implementing some of these services for business travelers in the States.

Tell what you know about the organization and what you can bring to it

I have enclosed my résumé, and I look forward to talking with you at your convenience. I will be available for an interview anytime after my final exams on May 30.

Politely indicate what comes next

Sincerely,

Rolando J. Matta

Rolando J. Matta

Remember to sign above your typed name

Sample Cover Letter

321 Topland Avenue
Johnson City, NY 13790
607-737-1111
rjmatta@fhcc.edu

June 10, 2003

Ms. Jennifer T. White
Manager
Rotunda Hotel and Sports Club
88990 Airport Highway
Chicago, IL 60677

Dear Ms. White:

Thank the interviewer

Thank you for meeting with me earlier today. I appreciated the opportunity to speak with you. I especially enjoyed hearing how your facility is similar to and different from the Grande Hotel in New York City.

Provide supplementary information

The Web site for the boutique hotel in Sydney that we discussed is <http://www.medusa.com.au>. On this Web site you will find photos of the wall units that each room contains. These units not only make an attractive appearance, but they also save space in the closet and in the mini-kitchen.

State enthusiasm directly and briefly

I am extremely interested in joining your staff and feel certain that I could contribute much to your organization.

Sincerely,

Rolando J. Matta

Rolando J. Matta

Sample Letter after an Interview

FOCUS Coping with Application Forms

Large organizations often require job applicants to fill out an application form even though they are carrying carefully prepared résumés. Usually, these forms ask for information not provided on the résumé—for example, a Social Security number, the telephone number of someone to call in case of an emergency, or the reasons for leaving former jobs. Arrive prepared to fill in those blanks. Sometimes the human resources office will allow an applicant to attach his or her résumé to the form after he or she has filled it out.

◆ PRACTICE 4.1

Make a list of what you want to get from a job. Other than money, what do you hope for?

◆ PRACTICE 4.2

Go to your college placement office, a job board on the Web, and a newspaper's help wanted section, and find a job from each source for which you could apply. What do you like about each job? What qualifications do you have for each of these three jobs?

◆ PRACTICE 4.3

Choose one of the jobs you found for Practice 4.2. Then prepare a résumé and a job-application letter that you could send to the prospective employer.

◆ PRACTICE 4.4

Working in a group of three students, distribute the job ad, the résumé, and the application letter that you put together for Practice 4.3. Critique each other's job materials, making sure that both the résumé and the letter of application specifically address the job mentioned in the ad.

◆ PRACTICE 4.5

Prepare short, focused answers to each of the frequently asked interview questions listed in the Focus box on page 59. In a group of five students, share your answers. As a group, choose the most effective answer for each question.

REVISING AND EDITING

Look back at your response to the Seeing and Writing exercise on page 55. Now that you have read the information in this chapter, you should have a better idea of how to find a job. What specific strategies would you use? How would you market yourself? In what ways would you prepare for an interview? Revise your Seeing and Writing response so that it answers these questions.

✓ REVIEW CHECKLIST: Strategies for Success in the Workplace

- Define your goals. (See 4A.)
- Look for a job in a systematic way. (See 4B.)
- Once you have located specific job openings, research the companies and organizations. (See 4C.)
- Market yourself to your prospective employer by preparing an effective résumé, writing a convincing job letter, preparing for your interview, and writing a follow-up letter. (See 4D and 4E.)

UNIT TWO

Writing Effective Paragraphs

CHAPTER

5

Writing a Paragraph

PREVIEW

In this chapter, you will learn

- to focus on your assignment, purpose, and audience (5A)
- to use invention strategies (5B)
- to select and arrange ideas (5C)
- to draft a paragraph (5D)
- to revise and edit a paragraph (5E)

SEEING AND WRITING

Why did you decide to go to college? Look at the picture above, and think about this question carefully before you read the pages that follow. This is the topic you will be writing about as you move through this chapter.

Word Power

self-esteem pride in oneself; self-respect

It's no secret that writing is essential in most of the courses you will take in college. Whether you write a lab report or an English paper, a midterm or a final, your ability to organize your ideas and express them in writing will affect how well you do. In other words, succeeding at writing is the first step toward succeeding in college. Even more important, writing is a key to success outside the classroom. On the job and in everyday life, if you can express yourself clearly and effectively, you will stand a better chance of achieving your goals and influencing the world around you.

This chapter will guide you through the process of writing a **paragraph**, a group of related sentences working together to develop one main idea. Because paragraphs play an important part in almost all the writing you do, learning to write a paragraph is central to becoming an effective writer.

A Focusing on Your Assignment, Purpose, and Audience

In college, a writing task almost always begins with an assignment. Before you begin to write, stop to ask yourself some questions about this **assignment** (*what* you are expected to write) as well as about your **purpose** (*why* you are writing) and your **audience** (*for whom* you are writing). If you answer these questions now, you will save yourself a lot of time later.

Questions about Assignment, Purpose, and Audience

Assignment

- What is your assignment?
- Do you have a word or page limit?
- When is your assignment due?
- Will you do your writing at home or in class?
- Will you work on your own or with other students?
- Will your instructor return your work so you can revise it?

Purpose

- Are you expected to express your feelings—for example, to tell how you feel about a story in the newspaper?
- Are you expected to give information—for example, to answer an exam question?
- Are you expected to take a position on a controversial issue?

Audience

- Who will read your paper—just your instructor or other students, too?
- Do you have an audience beyond the classroom—for example, your supervisor at work or the readers of your school newspaper?
- How much will your readers already know about your topic?
- Will your readers expect you to use a formal or an informal style? (For example, are you writing a research paper or a personal essay?)

◆ PRACTICE 5.1

Each of the following writing tasks has a different audience and purpose. On the lines following each task, write a few notes about how you would approach the task. (The Questions about Assignment, Purpose, and Audience above can help you decide on the best approach.) When you have finished, discuss your responses with the class or in a group of three or four students.

1. For the other students in your writing class, describe the best or worst class you have ever had.

 ____

 ____

 ____

 ____

2. Write a short letter to your school newspaper in which you try to convince readers that a certain course should no longer be offered at your school.

 ____

 ____

 ____

 ____

3. Write a letter applying for a job. Explain how the courses you have taken will help you in that job.

 ____

 ____

 ____

 ____

 ____

B Using Invention Strategies

Once you understand your assignment, purpose, and audience, you can begin to find ideas to write about. This process of finding material to write about is called **invention**. Invention is different for every writer. You may be the kind of person who likes a structured way to find ideas, or you may prefer a looser, more relaxed way to find things to write about. As you gain more experience as a writer, you will learn which of the four invention strategies discussed in the pages that follow (*freewriting, brainstorming, clustering,* and *journal writing*) work best for you.

Julia Reyes, a student in an introductory writing course, was given the following assignment:

ASSIGNMENT Is it better to go to college right after high school or to wait? Write a paragraph in which you answer this question.

Before she could begin her paragraph, Julia needed to find ideas to write about. She used all four invention strategies to find ideas. The pages that follow explain these four strategies and show how Julia used them.

Word Power

dilemma a situation that requires a choice between two courses of action

■ **Computer Tip**

Try doing "invisible free-writing" by turning off your monitor and writing without looking at the screen. When you have finished, turn on the monitor to see what you have written.

Freewriting

When you **freewrite**, you write whatever comes into your head, and you write for a set period of time without stopping. Grammar and spelling are not important; what is important is to get your ideas down on paper. So even if your words don't seem to be going anywhere, keep on writing. Sometimes you freewrite to find a topic. Most often, however, you free-write on a specific topic that your instructor gives you. This strategy is called **focused freewriting**.

When you finish freewriting, read what you have written. As you read, try to find an idea you think you might be able to write more about. Underline this idea, and then freewrite again, using the underlined idea as a starting point.

Here is Julia's focused freewriting on the topic "Is it better to go to college right after high school or to wait?"

Which is better? To start college right away? To wait? I waited, but last year was such a waste of time. Such a waste. Every job I had was stupid. Telemarketing — the worst worst job. Why didn't I just quit the first day? (Money.) Waitressing was a dumb job. Everybody had an attitude. The customer was always right, blah blah. Another waste of time. Why didn't I just go right to college? I needed money. And I was sick of school. School was hard. I wasn't good at it. But work was boring. But now I hate how all my friends are a year ahead of me. So I guess it's better not to wait.

Freewriting

◆ PRACTICE 5.2

Read Julia's freewriting. What ideas do you think she should write more about? Write your suggestions on the following lines.

____

____

____

____

____

◆ PRACTICE 5.3

Freewrite about the topic "Why did you decide to go to college?" On a blank sheet of lined paper (or on your computer), write for at least five minutes without stopping. If you can't think of anything to write, just write the last word over and over again until something else comes to mind.

◆ PRACTICE 5.4

Reread the freewriting you did for Practice 5.3. Which sentence expresses the most interesting idea? Use this sentence as a starting point for a focused freewriting exercise.

Brainstorming

When you **brainstorm**, you write down all the ideas you can think of about your topic. Brainstorming is different from freewriting, and it looks different on the page. Instead of writing on the lines, you write all over the page. You can star, check, box, or underline words, and you can ask questions, make lists, and draw arrows to connect ideas.

Here is Julia's brainstorming on the topic "Is it better to go to college right after high school or to wait?"

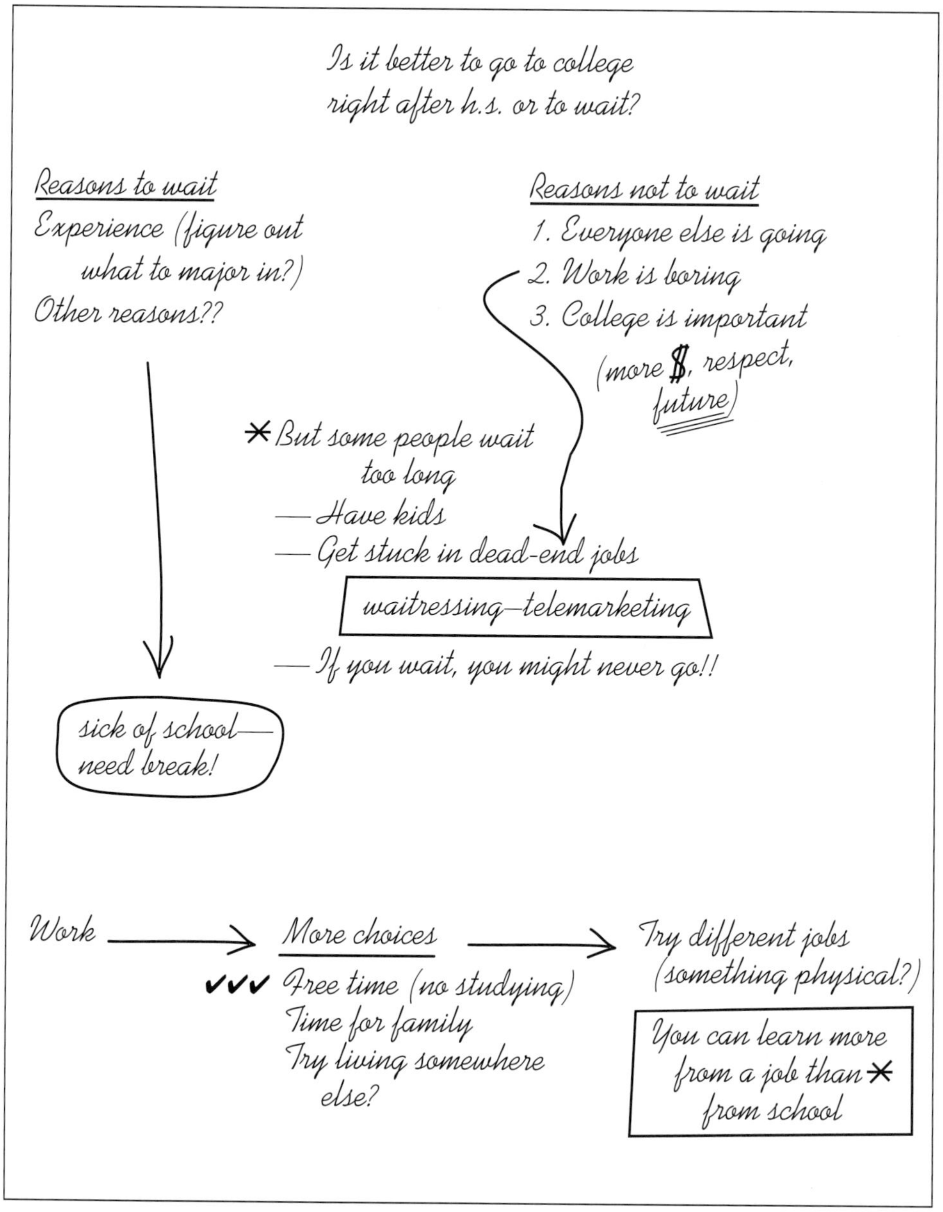

Brainstorming

◆ PRACTICE 5.5

Read Julia's brainstorming notes. How is her brainstorming similar to her freewriting (p. 70)? How is it different? Which ideas do you think she should write more about? Which ones should she cross out? Write your suggestions on the following lines.

____

____

____

____

____

____

◆ PRACTICE 5.6

Practice brainstorming on the topic "Why did you decide to go to college?" Write on a sheet of *unlined* paper. Write quickly, without worrying about being neat or using complete sentences. Experiment with writing on different parts of the page, making lists, drawing arrows to connect related ideas, and starring important ideas. When you have finished, look over what you have written. Which ideas seem most interesting? Did you come up with any new ideas in your brainstorming that you did not think of in your freewriting?

◆ PRACTICE 5.7

Brainstorm with three or four other students on the topic of why you decided to attend college. First, choose one person to write down ideas on a sheet of paper or on a section of the board. Then discuss the topic informally. After about fifteen minutes, review all the ideas that have been listed. Has the group come up with any ideas that you can use in your writing? Be sure to keep a list of these ideas so that you can use them later on.

Clustering

> **Writing Tip**
> If you can find an empty classroom, try using the board for clustering.

If you like to use brainstorming, you will probably also be comfortable with **clustering**, which is sometimes called *mapping*. When you cluster, you begin by writing your general topic in the center of a sheet of paper. Then you draw lines from the general topic to related ideas, moving from the center to the corners of the page. (These lines will look like spokes of a wheel or branches of a tree.) Your ideas will get more and more specific as you move from the center to the edges of the page.

When you finish clustering, you can cluster again on a new sheet of paper, this time beginning with a specific idea that you thought of the first time.

Here is Julia's clustering on the topic "Is it better to go to college right after high school or to wait?"

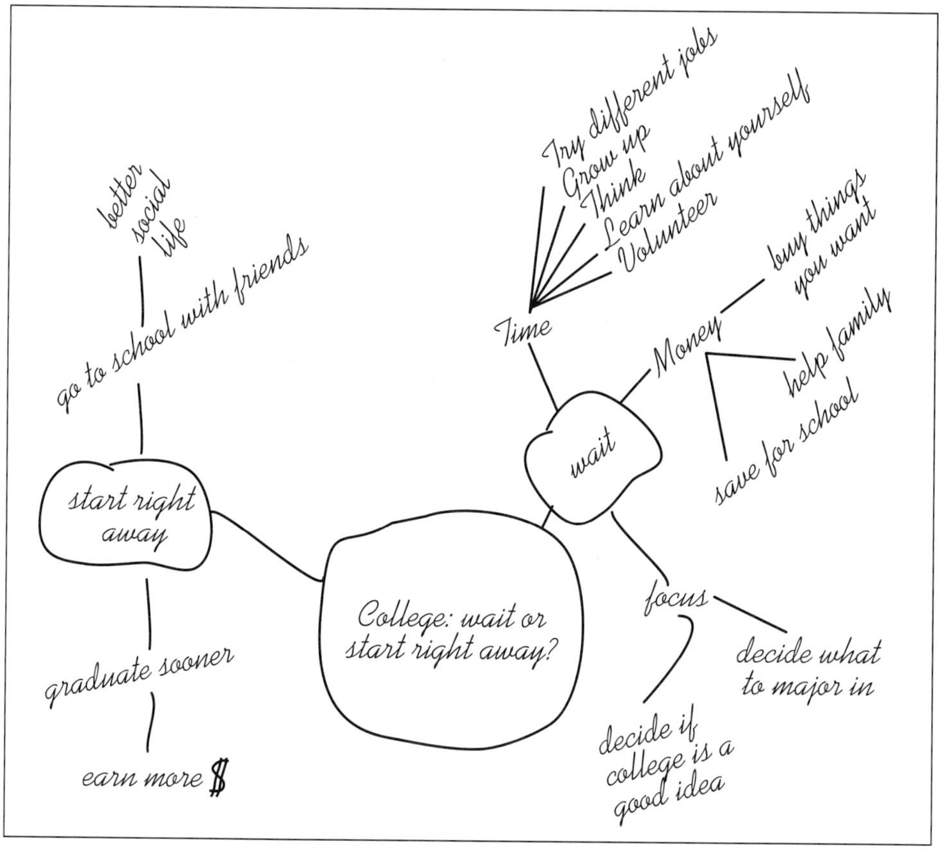

Clustering

◆ PRACTICE 5.8

How is Julia's clustering similar to her brainstorming on the same subject (p. 71)? How is it different? Which branch of her cluster diagram do you think Julia should focus on? Why? Should she add any other branches? Write your suggestions on the following lines. Then discuss them with the class or in a small group.

____

____

____

____

____

____

____

◆ PRACTICE 5.9

Practice clustering on the topic "Why did you decide to go to college?" Begin by writing this topic in the center of a sheet of unlined paper. Circle the topic, and then draw branches to connect specific ideas and examples, moving toward the edges of the page. When you have finished, look over what you have written. Which ideas are the most interesting? Which ones do you think you can write more about? Have you come up with any new ideas that your freewriting and brainstorming did not suggest?

Journal Writing

A **journal** is a place to write down your thoughts. It is also a place to jot down ideas that you might be able to write more about and a place to think on paper about your assignments. In your journal, you can do problem solving, try out sentences, keep track of details and examples, and keep a record of interesting things you read or observe.

Once you have started writing regularly in your journal, go back every week or so and reread what you have written. You may find ideas for an assignment you are working on—or just learn more about yourself.

> **Computer Tip**
> Try keeping a journal on your computer by making entries at set times every day—when you check your email, for example.

> **Computer Tip**
> If you work on several different computers, look into keeping an online Web journal that you can update from anywhere.

FOCUS Journals

Here are some subjects you can write about in a journal:

- *Your schoolwork* Writing regularly about the topics you are studying in school is one way to become a better student. In a journal, you can explore ideas for writing assignments in your courses. You can also think about what you are learning, ask questions about topics you are having trouble understanding, and examine new ideas.
- *Your job* You can write about the day-to-day triumphs and frustrations of your job. For example, you can write down conversations with coworkers, or you can list problems and remind yourself how you solved them. Rereading your journal may help you understand your strengths and weaknesses as an employee.
- *Your ideas about your community and your world* As you learn more about the social and political world around you, you can explore your reactions to new ideas. For example, you may read an interesting story in the newspaper or see something on television or on the Internet that challenges your beliefs. Even if you are not ready to talk to others about what you are thinking, you can still "talk" to your journal.
- *Your impressions of what you observe* Many writers carry their journals with them and record interesting, unusual, or funny things they notice as they go about their daily business. If you get into the habit of writing down your observations and reactions, you may be able to use them later in your writing.

(continued on the following page)

(continued from the previous page)

- *Personal thoughts* Although you may not feel comfortable writing about your personal thoughts and experiences—especially if your instructor will read your journal—you should try to be as honest as you can. Writing about relationships with family and friends, personal problems, and hopes and dreams can help you get to know (and understand) yourself better.

Here is Julia's journal entry on the topic "Is it better to go to college right after high school or to wait?"

This is a hard topic for me to write about. When I finished high school, I never wanted to go to school again. High school was hard. I worked hard, but teachers always said I could do better. Studying was boring. I couldn't concentrate. I never seemed to get things right on homework or on tests. Things seemed easier for everyone else. Sometimes I hated school. So I decided I'd work and not go to college right away, or maybe ever. But after a year, here I am. I'm still not sure why. School always felt hard. Work was boring, but it was easy. For the first time, I could do everything right. I got raises and promotions and better hours because I was a good worker. I wasn't judged by how I did on some dumb test. For once, I had some self-esteem. So why am I here? Good question.

Journal Entry

◆ PRACTICE 5.10

Buy a notebook to use as a journal. Make an appointment with yourself to write for fifteen minutes or so—during lunch, for example, or right before you go to bed—every day. Then write your first journal entry. Being as honest with yourself as possible, try to explain why you really decided to go to college.

Writing Tip

If at any stage in the writing process you run out of ideas, return to the invention strategies you found most helpful, and use them to help you come up with more material.

C Selecting and Arranging Ideas

When you think you have enough material to write about, the next step is to find a main idea to develop. Then you choose details to support this main idea, and you organize those details into a paragraph.

For more on topic sentences, see 6A.

Understanding Paragraph Structure

A **paragraph** is a group of related sentences. A paragraph usually begins with a **topic sentence**, a single sentence that states the paragraph's main idea. This first sentence is **indented**, written or typed about one-half inch (five spaces) from the left margin. The other sentences in the paragraph provide **support** for this main idea: explanations, reasons, description, examples, and so on. (Often, a paragraph ends with a final sentence that summarizes the main idea and acts as a conclusion.) A paragraph looks like this:

Paragraph

> The **topic sentence** states the main idea of the paragraph. **Support** develops the main idea with explanations, reasons, description, examples, and so on. The **closing sentence** summarizes the paragraph's main idea.

Stating Your Topic Sentence

Writing Tip

If your topic is in the form of a question, your topic sentence should answer that question.

To find a main idea for your paragraph, read through all your notes—your freewriting, brainstorming, clustering, and journal entries. Look for the central point or idea that these notes can best support. The phrase or sentence that states this main idea and gives your paragraph its focus will become your topic sentence.

Julia thought most of her notes supported the idea that it was better to wait instead of starting college right after high school. She stated this idea in a sentence.

TOPIC SENTENCE `I think it's better to wait a few years instead of beginning college right after high school.`

Choosing Supporting Material

After you identify your main idea, review your notes again. This time, you are looking for specific details, facts, and examples to support your topic sentence. Write or type the topic sentence at the top of a sheet of paper. As you review your notes and continue to think about your topic, list all the supporting points you think you might be able to use in your paragraph.

Julia chose the following points from her notes to support her paragraph's topic sentence.

TOPIC SENTENCE (MAIN IDEA) `I think it's better to wait a few years instead of beginning college right after high school.`

- `Time to think`
- `Work experience`
- `Chance to earn money`

- Chance to develop self-esteem
- Time to grow up
- Chance to decide if college is right for you

Ordering Supporting Material

Once you have made a list of supporting points, arrange them in the order in which you think you will discuss them. Julia arranged her supporting points in the following list.

TOPIC SENTENCE I think it's better to wait a few years instead of beginning college right after high school.

1. Waiting gives people time to earn money.
2. Waiting gives people time to think about life and grow up.
3. Waiting helps people decide if college is right for them.
4. Waiting gives people a chance to develop self-esteem.

◆ PRACTICE 5.11

In Practices 5.3, 5.6, 5.9, and 5.10, you practiced freewriting, brainstorming, clustering, and journal writing. Now you are ready to select and arrange ideas for a paragraph about why you decided to go to college. Begin by looking over all the work you have done, and then think some more about your topic. What main idea does all your material seem to support? On the following lines, write a topic sentence that expresses this idea.

____

____

____

____

Now reread your invention exercises, and list below all the points you can use to support your topic sentence. You can also list any new points you think of.

____

____

____

____

____

____

Reread the points you listed above. Does each point support your topic sentence? Cross out any points that do not. On the following lines, arrange the remaining points in the order in which you plan to write about them.

1. ______________________________

2. ______________________________

3. ______________________________

4. ______________________________

D Drafting Your Paragraph

Computer Tip

Try typing your paragraph directly into the computer. It may feel strange at first, but once it becomes familiar, you may find that it is more efficient than typing from a handwritten copy.

So far, you have found a main idea for your paragraph, written a topic sentence, listed supporting points, and arranged them in the order in which you will write about them. Now you are ready to write a first draft.

Begin drafting your paragraph by stating your topic sentence. Then, referring to your list of supporting points, write down your ideas without worrying about correct sentence structure, word choice, spelling, or punctuation. If you think of an idea that is not on your list, write it down. (Don't worry about where it fits or whether you will keep it.)

You can type your first draft, or you can write it by hand. (Julia wrote hers by hand because it was an in-class assignment.) Remember, though, that your first draft is a rough draft that you will revise. If you plan to revise on your handwritten draft, make things easy for yourself by leaving wide margins and skipping lines so you have room to add ideas. If you type your draft, use large type and triple-spacing between lines.

When you have finished your rough draft, don't start correcting it right away. Take a break, and then return to your draft and read it.

Here is a draft of Julia's paragraph on the topic "Is it better to go to college right after high school or to wait?"

Waiting

I think it's better to wait a few years instead of beginning college right after high school. Many people start college right after high school just because that's what everybody else is doing.

(continued on the following page)

(continued from the previous page)

But that's not always the right way to go. Different things are right for different people. There are other possible choices. Taking a few years off can be a better choice. During this time, people can work and earn money. They also have time to think and grow up. Waiting can even help people decide if college is right for them. Finally, waiting gives them a chance to develop self-esteem. For all these reasons, waiting a year or two between high school and college is a good idea.

Draft

◆ PRACTICE 5.12

Read Julia's draft paragraph. What do you think she should change in her draft? What should she add? What should she take out? Write your suggestions on the following lines. Then, discuss your suggestions with the class or in a small group.

◆ **PRACTICE 5.13**

Using the material you came up with for Practice 5.11, draft a paragraph on the topic of why you decided to go to college. Be sure to state your main idea in the topic sentence and support it with specific points. Leave wide margins; if you like, skip lines. (If you type your draft, triple-space.) When you have finished, give your paragraph a title.

E Revising Your Paragraph

Revision means much more than correcting a few commas or crossing out one word and putting another one in its place. Often it means moving sentences around, adding words and phrases, and even changing the topic sentence. To get the most out of revision, begin by carefully rereading your draft—first aloud, then to yourself. Then consider each of the questions on the checklist that follows.

✓ SELF-ASSESSMENT CHECKLIST: Revising Your Paragraph

- Does your topic sentence state your main idea?
- Do you have enough material to support your main idea?
- Have you explained your ideas fully and clearly?
- Have you used enough examples and details?
- Are all your examples and details necessary?
- Does every sentence say what you mean?
- Does the order of your sentences make sense?
- Is every word necessary?
- Have you used the right words?
- Does your paragraph have a closing sentence that summarizes your main idea and acts as a conclusion?

After Julia drafted the paragraph on pages 78–79 in class, she typed it, triple-spacing to leave room for handwritten changes. Then, she used the Self-Assessment Checklist above to help her revise her paragraph.

Waiting

For students who are not getting much out of school, it is often
~~I think it's~~ better to wait a few years instead of beginning college right after high school. Many people

(continued on the following page)

(continued from the previous page)

start college right ~~after high school~~ *away* just because ~~that's~~ *that is* what everybody else is doing. ~~But that's~~ *However, that is* not always the right ~~way to go~~ *thing to do.* ~~Different things are right for different people. There are other possible choices.~~ Taking a few years off can *often* be a better choice. During this time, people can work and earn money *for college. Working at different jobs can help them decide on a career.* ~~They also have~~ *Taking a year or two off also gives people* time to think and grow up. Waiting can even help people decide if college is *really* right for them. ~~Finally~~ *Most important of all,* waiting gives them a chance to develop self-esteem. *I was a poor student in high school. School always felt hard. When I took a year off, everything changed. In high school, I always saw all the things I couldn't do. At work, I learned what I could do. Now, I think I can succeed.* For ~~all these reasons,~~ *me,* waiting a year ~~or two~~ between high school and college ~~is~~ *was* a good idea*, and I think it can be a good idea for other students, too.*

Revised Draft

When she revised her paragraph, Julia crossed out sentences, added sentences, and changed the way she worded her ideas. Her biggest change was to add an explanation of how taking a year off had helped her. (Note that she revised her topic sentence to reflect the broader perspective her personal experience gave her.) Here is the final version of her revised paragraph.

Waiting

For students who are not getting much out of school, it is often better to wait a few years instead of beginning college right after high school. Many people start college right away just because that is what everybody else is doing. However, that is not always the right thing to do. Taking a few years off can often be a better choice. During this time, people can work and earn money for college. Working at different jobs can help them decide on a career. Taking a year or two off also gives people time to think and grow up. Waiting can even help people decide if college is really right for them. Most important of all, waiting gives them a chance to develop self-esteem. I was a poor student in high school. School always felt hard. When I took a year off, everything changed. In high school, I always saw all the things I couldn't do. At work, I learned what I could do. Now, I think I can succeed. For me, waiting a year between high school and college was a good idea, and I think it can be a good idea for other students, too.

For information on editing, see 8G.

FOCUS Editing

Don't confuse revision with editing, which comes *after* revision. When you **edit**, you check for correct grammar, punctuation, and spelling. Then you proofread your writing carefully for typing errors that a computer spell checker may not identify.

Remember, editing is a vital last step in the writing process. Readers may not take your ideas seriously if there are grammatical or spelling errors in your writing.

◆ PRACTICE 5.14

Read the final version of Julia's revised paragraph (pp. 81–82), and compare it with her draft (pp. 78–79). What specific changes did she make? Which do you think are her best changes? Why? Answer these questions on the following lines. Then, with the class or in a small group, discuss your reaction to the revised paragraph.

____

____

____

____

____

____

◆ PRACTICE 5.15

Use the Self-Assessment Checklist on page 80 to help evaluate the paragraph you drafted for Practice 5.13. What can you add to support your topic sentence more fully? Should anything be crossed out because it doesn't support your topic sentence? Can anything be stated more clearly? On the following lines, list some of the changes you might make in your draft.

____

____

____

____

REVISING AND EDITING

Revise the draft paragraph that you wrote in this chapter. Begin by crossing out unnecessary material and any material you want to rewrite, and then add new and rewritten material. After you finish your revision, edit the paragraph, checking grammar, punctuation, and spelling—and look carefully for typing errors. When you are satisfied with your paragraph, print out a clean copy.

Computer Tip

Your computer's grammar checker and spell checker can spot many potential problems, but don't assume that they can find everything. It's still up to you to find errors and to know what is wrong and how to fix it.

✓ REVIEW CHECKLIST: Writing a Paragraph

- Before you start to write, consider your assignment, purpose, and audience. (See 5A.)
- Use invention strategies—freewriting, brainstorming, clustering, and journal writing—to find ideas. (See 5B.)
- Select ideas from your notes, and arrange them in a logical order. (See 5C.)
- Write a first draft. (See 5D.)
- Revise your draft. (See 5E.)
- Edit your draft. (See 5E.)

CHAPTER

6 Fine-Tuning Your Paragraph

PREVIEW

In this chapter, you will learn

- to write effective topic sentences (6A)
- to write unified paragraphs (6B)
- to write well-developed paragraphs (6C)
- to write coherent paragraphs (6D)

Word Power

spectacle a public performance or exhibition; an unusual sight

SEEING AND WRITING

Look at the picture above. Then write a paragraph about an event that you wanted to attend but could not. What was special about the event? What caused you to miss it?

A Writing Effective Topic Sentences

Every paragraph that you write should include a **topic sentence**—a sentence that states the paragraph's main idea. Your topic sentence is the sentence that the other sentences in the paragraph explain, support, or discuss. For this reason, it is usually the most general sentence in the paragraph. In the following paragraph, the topic sentence is the first sentence.

One of my most satisfying experiences occurred when I volunteered at the day-care center at the Whosoever Gospel Mission. Most of the people who live at the mission are recovering addicts or alcoholics. Some are just down on their luck. Many residents have small children who must be cared for while their parents are in recovery. These children need a lot of attention, and anyone who gives it to them is rewarded with love and affection. During the summer that I worked at the mission, I grew very attached to the children. I played with them, read to them, and hugged them anytime I could. Although I was sad to leave the mission in September, I was happy that I could make a difference in the children's lives.

Victoria Nasid (student)

FOCUS Writing Effective Topic Sentences

Although a topic sentence can appear anywhere in a paragraph, it is a good idea to place the topic sentence at the beginning of your paragraph. This placement will tell readers immediately what they should expect to read in your paragraph. It will also keep you on track as you write.

Here are two important things to remember as you write your topic sentences:

1. ***An effective topic sentence should clearly state the paragraph's main idea. It should not state your topic or announce what you plan to write about.***

EFFECTIVE TOPIC SENTENCE	One of my most satisfying experiences occurred when I volunteered at the day-care center at the Whosoever Gospel Mission.
TOPIC	A satisfying experience
ANNOUNCEMENT	In this paragraph, I will write about a satisfying experience.

2. ***An effective topic sentence should present an idea that you can discuss in a single paragraph.*** If your topic sentence is too broad, you will not be able to discuss it in just a paragraph. If it is too narrow, you will not be able to say much about it.

EFFECTIVE TOPIC SENTENCE	The construction of a Giant supermarket in my neighborhood is a bad idea because it will force many small stores out of business.
TOPIC SENTENCE TOO BROAD	Building a supermarket in my neighborhood will destroy our community.
TOPIC SENTENCE TOO NARROW	If a Giant supermarket is built in my neighborhood, White's market may have to close.

◆ PRACTICE 6.1

Underline the topic sentence in each of the following paragraphs. Keep in mind that the topic sentence will not always be the first sentence of the paragraph.

Example

How did the Himalayas, the world's tallest mountains, come to exist? They were created the same way the Andes mountains were—by forces that are also responsible for earthquakes in California. The earth's surface is divided into several large masses called plates. The plates are in constant, gradual motion. When two plates push against each other, mountains form. When they slide against each other suddenly, the result is an earthquake. Scientists call such interactions plate tectonics. Many of the world's geographic features have been created by plate tectonics.

1. Having my tonsils removed when I was six was a dramatic event. My overnight stay in the hospital was exciting and strange. I wasn't used to being away from home. The idea of having the operation made me a little nervous, but the nurses explained everything to me. Afterward, my throat was sore for several days. Generous doses of ice cream helped make my recovery bearable.

2. Not long ago, all public schools were run by local governments. Parents relied on government officials to meet their children's needs. Today, however, many public schools seem to be doing a poor job. Charter schools are changing the way public education works. Charter schools are funded with public money but are run by private groups. They tend to be small and specialized. Some teach moral values as well as reading and math. Supporters believe charter schools will grow in popularity over time.

3. Sunlight travels through space in waves. It contains all the colors of the spectrum, from red to deep blue. When sunlight enters the earth's atmosphere, the light waves run into dust particles. Red light waves, which are long, move around the particles without much trouble. Shorter blue light waves, on the other hand, crash into the particles and are scattered. Those scattered waves reach our eyes from every direction, crowding out other colors. The sky appears to be blue because light waves of different colors react to dust particles in different ways.

◆ PRACTICE 6.2

Read the following items. Put a check mark next to each one that you think would make an effective topic sentence for a paragraph.

Examples

Reviewing a car's service record. ____

Buying a used car requires careful research. _✓_

1. Domestic cats and lions and tigers. ____
2. Domestic cats resemble lions and tigers in several ways. ____
3. Fresh water, a limited resource, is in short supply in some western states. ____
4. In this paragraph, I will discuss renting an apartment. ____
5. Instead of tearing down old factories in the waterfront district, the city should convert them into high-tech office buildings. ____

◆ PRACTICE 6.3

The following topic sentences are either too broad or too narrow. On the line after each sentence, write *Too broad* if the sentence is too broad and *Too narrow* if the sentence is too narrow. Then rewrite each sentence—making it more specific or more general—so that it could be an effective topic sentence for a paragraph.

Examples

Global warming is a serious issue.

Too broad. Possible rewrite: Global warming could cause dramatic changes to our environment.

Many supermarkets sell more salsa than ketchup.

Too narrow. Possible rewrite: Ethnic foods have become very popular with American consumers.

1. Required courses are a bad idea.

____

____

2. Many jobs require computer skills.

____

____

3. Cigarette smoking is a public nuisance.

____

____

4. Many laws are not properly enforced.

____

____

5. One candidate for mayor has more campaign funds than the other.

____

____

◆ PRACTICE 6.4

The following paragraphs do not have topic sentences. Think of a topic sentence that sums up each paragraph's main idea, and write it on the lines above the paragraph.

Example

Possible answer: The risk of heart disease can be lowered in several ways.

One major cause of heart disease is a diet high in fat and cholesterol. Reducing fat and cholesterol, therefore, can reduce the risk of illness. Another way to reduce the risk is to exercise regularly. A third technique for avoiding heart disease is to balance work and recreation.

1. ____

____

The first night, we set up camp and cooked dinner over the fire. I hadn't seen so many stars in years. On Saturday, we hiked five miles to a nearby lookout point. It was so clear that we could see parts of three states. On the way back, we took turns naming different trees and flowers. I slept like a log after all that exercise. Sunday was overcast, so we stayed near the camp and sang songs. It seemed a shame to pack up and come home.

2. ____

____

Taking a warm bath or drinking a cup of hot herbal tea is relaxing for some people. Others prefer to ease tension by doing some form of exercise, such as walking or running. Another soothing activity is meditation, which can be done almost anywhere. But the easiest way to relax is simply to take a series of slow, deep breaths.

3. ____

____

In some cultures, personal space is shared constantly. Men hug each other, women hold hands, and strangers kiss. In other cultures, it is considered impolite to touch someone, even to shake hands. Individuals have different ideas about personal space as well. Some people are comfortable only when they are in physical contact with other people. Others prefer to keep an imaginary bubble around themselves, avoiding contact at all costs.

B Writing Unified Paragraphs

A paragraph is **unified** when all of its sentences focus on the single main idea stated in the topic sentence. A paragraph lacks unity when its sentences wander away from the main idea.

When you write, it is easy to lose sight of your main idea and write sentences that go off in all different directions. You can correct this problem by rereading the topic sentence and crossing out or rewriting any sentences that do not support it.

> **Writing Tip**
> Underline the topic sentence of your paragraph before you start to revise.

Paragraph Not Unified

Although applying for a loan can be confusing, the process is not all that difficult. The first step is to determine which bank has the lowest interest rate. There are a lot of banks in my neighborhood, but none of them is very friendly. The last time I went into one, I waited for twenty minutes before anyone bothered to wait on me. Once you have chosen a bank, you have to go to the bank in person and apply, and if the bank isn't friendly, you don't want to go there. This is a real problem when you apply for a loan. If you have any questions about the application, you won't be able to get anyone to answer them. After you have submitted the application comes the hard part—waiting for approval.

This paragraph is not unified. After telling readers that applying for a loan is not difficult, the writer wanders from his main idea to complain about how unfriendly the banks in his neighborhood are. For this reason, most of the sentences in the paragraph do not support the topic sentence.

The revised paragraph that follows is unified. When the writer reread his paragraph, he deleted the sentences that had nothing to do with the topic sentence. He then added sentences that supported his main idea. The result is a paragraph that supports its main idea: that applying for a loan is easy.

Paragraph Unified

Although applying for a loan can be confusing, the process is not all that difficult. The first step is to determine which bank has the lowest interest rate. Although a half-percent difference in rates may not seem like much, over the course of a four-year loan, the savings can really add up. Once you have chosen a bank, you have to go to the bank in person and apply. Make sure you tell the loan officer exactly what rate you are applying for. Then take the application home and fill it out, being careful not to omit any important information. If you have any problems with your credit, explain them on the application or in a separate letter. Then take the application back to the bank, and ask any questions that you might have. (Do not sign the application until all your questions have been answered.) After you have submitted the application comes the only hard part—waiting for approval.

Hector de la Paz (student)

◆ PRACTICE 6.5

Read the following paragraphs. Write *unified* after the paragraphs that are unified and *not unified* after the ones that are not unified.

Example

Pet ownership is a big responsibility. Thousands of families adopt dogs and cats every month. Other family activities include taking vacations and playing sports together. In fact, families who spend time together tend to be happier and communicate more. Most people give little thought to the animals' needs for a proper diet, exercise, company, and veterinary care. In fact, few people realize how much time and money they will spend taking care of their pets. not unified

1. Drivers must be careful to avoid road rage incidents. Road rage occurs when a driver loses control over his or her emotions in a stressful situation. Driving in bad weather can be very stressful. A car does not handle as easily on snowy or icy roads as it does on dry ones. Snow tires can make winter driving safer. Even with snow tires, though, driving on slippery roads requires concentration. Road rage can lead to property damage and even injury. Therefore, drivers should always keep their emotions under control. ______________

2. Music can either help or hurt a person's ability to recall information. For example, students who study while listening to loud dance music tend to remember less than those who study in quiet settings. The reason for this is that dance music has a strong rhythm, which tends to distract a person from the material being studied. Classical music, on the other hand, may help improve memory. Research shows that some people remember information more clearly if they listen to quiet classical music while studying. Understanding the link between music and memory can help students make wise choices about listening to music while studying. ______________

3. Georgia O'Keeffe was a bold and influential painter. Her most famous paintings are of flowers and of scenes from the Southwest. Many tourists visit the Southwest to enjoy its beautiful deserts. Taos, New Mexico, is an especially busy tourist spot. O'Keeffe developed a unique painting style. She created dramatic images that went against the artistic fashion of her times. In fact, her rich use of color has inspired many artists. Quite a few artists today work in video and collage as well as in paint. O'Keeffe's work is on display in many of the world's leading museums. ______________

◆ PRACTICE 6.6

Reread the paragraphs in Practice 6.5 that you decided were not unified. Now, cross out the sentences in each paragraph that do not belong.

Example

Pet ownership is a big responsibility. Thousands of families adopt dogs and cats every month. ~~Other family activities include taking vacations and playing sports together. In fact, families who spend time together tend to be happier and communicate more.~~ Most people give little thought to the animals' needs for a proper diet, exercise, company, and veterinary care. In fact, few people realize how much time and money they will spend taking care of their pets.

1. Drivers must be careful to avoid road rage incidents. Road rage occurs when a driver loses control over his or her emotions in a stressful situation. Driving in bad weather can be very stressful. A car does not handle as easily on snowy or icy roads as it does on dry ones. Snow tires can make winter driving safer. Even with snow tires, though, driving on slippery roads requires concentration. Road rage can lead to property damage and even injury. Therefore, drivers should always keep their emotions under control.

2. Music can either help or hurt a person's ability to recall information. For example, students who study while listening to loud dance music tend to remember less than those who study in quiet settings. The reason for this is that dance music has a strong rhythm, which tends to distract a person from the material being studied. Classical music, on the other hand, may help improve memory. Research shows that some people remember information more clearly if they listen to quiet classical music while studying. Understanding the link between music and memory can help students make wise choices about listening to music while studying.

3. Georgia O'Keeffe was a bold and influential painter. Her most famous paintings are of flowers and of scenes from the Southwest. Many tourists visit the Southwest to enjoy its beautiful deserts. Taos, New Mexico, is an especially busy tourist spot. O'Keeffe developed a unique painting style. She created dramatic images that went against the artistic fashion of her times. In fact, her rich use of color has inspired many artists. Quite a few artists today work in video and collage as well as in paint. O'Keeffe's work is on display in many of the world's leading museums.

C Writing Well-Developed Paragraphs

A paragraph is **well developed** when it includes the details, facts, and examples needed to support the topic sentence. Without this material, readers will have difficulty following your discussion. As you write, imagine your readers asking, "What do you mean?" or "What support do you have for this statement?" Be sure your paragraph answers these questions.

How do you determine how much support you need? The answer to this question depends on how complicated the idea in your topic sentence is. Remember that the purpose of support is to make the meaning of the statement you are making in the topic sentence clear. If your topic sentence is relatively straightforward—for example, "My school's registration process is a nightmare"—two or three well-chosen examples will probably be enough. If, however, your statement is more complicated—for example, "The plan that the mayor has presented for building a new stadium is flawed"—you will have to present more support.

Writing Tip

A long paragraph is not necessarily well developed, and a short paragraph is not necessarily undeveloped. Remember, a well-developed paragraph supports the topic sentence with specific details (facts and examples).

FOCUS Developing Paragraphs with Specific Details

Specific details can make a paragraph convincing. For example, in a paragraph on a history test, you could say that many soldiers were killed during the American Civil War. Your paragraph would be far more effective, however, if you said that over 500,000 soldiers were killed during the Civil War—more than in all the other wars in U.S. history combined.

Computer Tip

Type your topic sentence and each sentence that follows it on its own line. Use a different color text or highlighting to distinguish all the details (facts and examples) in your paragraph. By looking at the different blocks of color, you will easily be able to evaluate the amount and kind of support you have.

When you are checking your paragraphs to make sure they are well developed, look for unsupported general statements. If you find any, add the details, facts, and examples you need to support these statements. The following paragraph is not well developed.

Undeveloped Paragraph

Computerized special effects now bring to the screen things that never could have been shown before. Modern digital technology has created effects that would have been too expensive or too difficult to create in the studio. It is almost certain that in the future, special effects will become even more realistic. They may even blur the line between what the audience believes to be real and what actually is real.

The paragraph above consists of one topic sentence and three general statements. It does not, however, give readers specific information about how computerized special effects have changed the film industry (which is what the topic sentence promises). In the following revised paragraph, notice how the writer added details (facts and examples) that help readers understand the point made by the topic sentence.

Well-Developed Paragraph

Computerized special effects now bring to the screen scenes that never could have been shown before. Modern digital technology has created effects that would have been too expensive or too difficult to create in the studio. With the help of computerized special effects, films can show disasters and re-create the past. For example, in the movie *Titanic,* computerized special effects showed the *Titanic* splitting in half as it sank. Real actors were combined with digitally generated figures to show people falling to their deaths from the upended ship. In *Gladiator,* computerized special effects were used to re-create the ancient city of Rome. In addition, the film was able to show gladiators fighting in a digital re-creation of the Colosseum as it might have appeared two thousand years ago. It is almost certain that in the future, special effects will become even more realistic. They may even blur the line between what the audience believes to be real and what actually is real.

Andrew McGillin (student)

◆ PRACTICE 6.7

Some of the following paragraphs are well developed; others are not. On the line after each paragraph, write *well developed* if the paragraph is well developed and *not well developed* if it is not.

Examples

Genealogy is the study of a family's lineage, or history. Genealogy is an interesting and important field. Some family histories are easier to trace than others. Professional genealogists use both traditional and modern techniques to trace a person's lineage. Many people who research their family histories make surprising discoveries. Everyone should trace his or her family's history at some point. *not well developed*

Consumer items such as televisions, clothing, and electronics are selling well. One reason they are in such high demand is the growth of the national economy in recent decades. As a result of economic expansion, many people are earning more money than they once did. In addition, families with two incomes are more common than ever. Some couples who spend most of their time working reward themselves by shopping. *well developed*

1. Caffeinated drinks are very popular, but caffeine has negative effects on some people. Beverages that do not contain caffeine are healthier than those that do. Decaffeinated soda, coffee, and tea are possible options. Herbal tea and juices are other caffeine-free drinks. The best drink of all, though, is plain water. ____________________

2. Last Saturday, the marching band gave an excellent performance at the football game. The musicians were all quite talented and performed with great energy, especially when they played a John Philip Sousa march. The drummers, in particular, were really lively. Their performance during halftime was especially exciting, inspiring fans in the stands to give them a standing ovation. The director should be congratulated for his work with the band. ____________________

3. Shad are fascinating fish. In some ways, they behave like salmon, yet in other ways, they are unique. The behavior of shad is interesting to different groups of people. Their anatomy, too, is of interest. Information about each fish's history is revealed in its anatomy. For generations, people have been intrigued by shad and their behavior. ____________________

◆ PRACTICE 6.8

The following paragraphs are not well developed. On the lines below each paragraph, write three questions or suggestions that might help the writer develop his or her ideas more fully.

Example

Adam Sandler is a wonderful comedian. Some of his movies are absolutely hilarious. He is especially good at using funny voices to express his emotions. I never get tired of watching Adam Sandler's movies. I have seen *The Wedding Singer* and *The Waterboy* several times each.

1. *Describe the voices Adam Sandler uses.*
2. *Give an example of a part he has played in one of the movies mentioned.*
3. *Tell about the funny way he talks in this movie.*

1. For me, having a regular study routine is important. I need to do the same things at the same times. If I have important school work to do, I stick to my routine. As long as I follow my schedule, everything works out all right.

1. __________
2. __________
3. __________

2. Religion is a deeply personal issue. Attitudes toward religion vary from person to person. One person I know considers religion an essential part of life. Another feels just the opposite. Because of such differences, it is impossible to generalize about religious attitudes.

1. __________
2. __________
3. __________

◆ PRACTICE 6.9

Choose one of the paragraphs from Practice 6.8. Reread it, and review your suggestions for improving it. Then rewrite the paragraph, adding any details (facts and examples) you think are needed to make it well developed.

D Writing Coherent Paragraphs

A paragraph is **coherent** when all its sentences are arranged in a definite order. Readers should be able to see the connections between ideas and should not have to guess why one sentence follows another. You can make a paragraph coherent by arranging details in a logical order and by choosing transitional words and phrases to show the connections between sentences.

In general, you can arrange the ideas in a paragraph in three ways: in *time order,* in *spatial order,* or in *logical order*.

Time Order

When you use **time order**, you arrange events in the order in which they occurred. News reports, historical accounts, and process explanations are usually arranged like this.

The following paragraph presents events in time order.

> No other American writer achieved as great a reputation on the basis of a single book as Ralph Ellison did. Ellison was born in 1914 in Oklahoma City, Oklahoma, and grew up in the segregated South. In 1936, he came to New York City to earn money to pay his tuition at Tuskegee Institute, where he was a senior majoring in music. After becoming friends with many writers who were part of the Harlem Renaissance—a flowering of art, music, and literature among African Americans—he decided to remain in New York. During this period, Richard Wright, author of *Native Son* and *Black Boy,* encouraged Ellison to write his first short story. In the years that followed, Ellison published two collections of essays and some short fiction. Eventually, in 1952, he wrote *Invisible Man,* the novel that established him as a major twentieth-century writer.
>
> Mike Burdin (student)

Word Power

renaissance a rebirth or revival

This paragraph moves in time order, tracing events from Ellison's childhood in the South to his arrival in New York to the publication of *Invisible Man.* Notice that throughout the paragraph, the writer uses transitional words and phrases that signal time order—*in 1936, after, during this period, in the years that followed,* and *eventually*— to help make the paragraph coherent.

Some Transitional Words and Phrases That Signal Time Order

after	eventually	now	today
afterward	finally	since	when
at first	first . . . next	soon	while
before	later	still	dates (for example, "in 1920")
earlier	meanwhile	then	

◆ PRACTICE 6.10

Read the following paragraphs, whose sentences are organized in time order. Underline the transitional words and phrases that make each paragraph coherent.

Example

Writing a research paper requires several steps. First, you must choose a topic to write about. The topic should be broad enough to allow for an interesting discussion but narrow enough to cover in a few pages. Next, begin researching your topic. Reference sources, books, articles, and Web sites are all good places to look for information. While you are gathering material, you might adjust your topic on the basis of what you are learning about it. When you have finished collecting information, it is time to plan your paper by drafting an outline. Then it is time to write and to revise. Finally, you will want to add a bibliography or works-cited page and proofread your paper.

1. A job interview is most likely to go well when you are prepared for it. The first step is to determine your strengths. Do you have the right level of education for the job? Are you experienced in the field? What special skills do you have? The next step is to research the company and the kind of business it does. If you have a thorough knowledge of the company, you will make a good impression and be able to answer many questions. Finally, decide what points you want to emphasize in the interview. Although the interviewer will guide the conversation, you should be ready to offer your own thoughts as well.

2. Filmmaker Spike Lee has had a successful career making unusual movies. Before he started making movies professionally, he was a film student at New York University. In 1986, he released his first feature film, *She's Gotta Have It.* Critics praised this low-budget movie for its strong characters and clever dialogue. Then, Lee went on to make such acclaimed movies as *Do the Right Thing, Jungle Fever, Malcolm X,* and *Bamboozled.* What many people do not realize is that Lee also writes, produces, directs, and acts in many of his films. To this day, he uses his movies to explore ideas about race and class in American society.

◆ PRACTICE 6.11

Arrange the following sentences into a coherent paragraph. Be sure you are able to explain why you arranged the sentences the way you did.

____ 1. During colonial times, public voice votes were common.

____ 2. Soon individual voters may be able to cast ballots on the Internet.

____ 3. Voting machines, which ensured privacy and accuracy, were common by the early 1900s.

____ 4. Then voting became a private matter with the use of secret paper ballots around the time of the Revolutionary War.

_____ 5. Until the late 1800s, political parties printed and distributed their own ballots.

_____ 6. Voting methods in the United States have changed dramatically in the past 250 years.

_____ 7. In recent decades, voting officials have used computers to count votes.

Spatial Order

When you use **spatial order**, you present details in the order in which they are seen—from top to bottom, from right to left, from near to far, and so on. Spatial order is used most often in paragraphs that describe something—for example, in a lab report describing a piece of equipment or in an art history paper describing a painting.

The following paragraph uses spatial order.

> When I was fourteen, my family and I traveled to Michigan to visit the town where my great-grandmother had lived. Somerset was hardly a town; in fact, it seemed to be just a collection of farms and cow pastures. Scattered among the fields were about twenty buildings. One of them was my great-grandmother's old brick farmhouse that was sold after she died. Next to the house were a rusting silo and a faded barn. In front of the house was a long wooden porch that needed painting. On the porch were a potted plant, two white wooden rocking chairs, and a swing. The house was locked, so all we could do was walk around it and look. The lace curtains that my great-grandmother had made before she died still hung in each window. In back of the house was a small cemetery that contained eight graves. There, off in the corner, on the oldest-looking stone, was the name "Azariel Smith"—the name of my great-grandmother's father.
>
> Molly Ward (student)

This writer uses spatial order as she describes her great-grandmother's farmhouse. She moves from far to near, beginning by describing the fields around the farmhouse and then moving closer to the house itself. Eventually, she moves behind the farmhouse to the cemetery and then to a specific grave. Notice how transitional words and phrases that signal spatial order—*next to, in front, on the porch, in back,* and *off in the corner*—add to the paragraph's coherence.

Some Transitional Words and Phrases That Signal Spatial Order

above	beside	near	on the top
along	here	next to	outside
behind	in back	on the bottom	over
below	in front	on the left	there
beneath	inside	on the right	under

◆ PRACTICE 6.12

Read the following paragraphs, whose details are arranged in spatial order. Underline the transitional words and phrases that make each paragraph coherent.

Example
My childhood home was a typical one-story house. The front door opened into a small foyer. Above the foyer and to the right was a carpeted living room shaped like the letter *L*. The short part of the *L* served as our dining room. Behind the living room was the kitchen. A hallway led from the kitchen to a bathroom on the right and then to two bedrooms. Below the bedrooms was a playroom. At the other end of the first floor, beneath the living room, was a garage.

1. Visitors to the White House in Washington, D.C., tour rooms that are decorated in a variety of styles and that serve a variety of functions. For example, in front of the Visitors' Entrance is the Library, furnished in the style of the Federal period (1800–1820). To the left of the Library is the Vermeil Room, decorated in gold and silver and used occasionally as a women's lounge. To the right and front of the Library is the East Room, traditionally used for large gatherings, such as concerts and press conferences. Next to the East Room is the Green Room, a drawing room decorated in delicate shades of green. Beside the Green Room is the Blue Room, an oval-shaped room used as a reception area. From the Blue Room, visitors enter the Red Room, decorated in the French Empire style. These and other public rooms give visitors a sense of the beauty and history of the White House.

2. My favorite restaurant in New York is in an old firehouse in Greenwich Village. It is located just east of Bleecker Street. In front, where horse-drawn carriages used to enter and leave the building, there is now a large bay window. To the right of the window is the door. Inside, the firehouse is long and narrow, with a bar on the left and a fireplace on the right. Clustered around the fireplace are a few chairs and loveseats. The interior is lighted by candles and gaslights. Small trees covered in tiny white lights are placed along the staircase and in the corners. But the most striking feature of all is the color: it's decorated entirely in rich, romantic red.

◆ PRACTICE 6.13

Arrange the following sentences into a coherent paragraph. Be sure you are able to explain why you arranged the sentences the way you did.

_____ 1. Next to the video gallery is a display of celebrity portraits.

_____ 2. For example, museum officials have installed a brightly colored fountain on the main lawn in front of the museum.

_____ 3. In a small gallery to the left of the entrance hall, videotapes made by artists play on three monitors.

_____ 4. The Middletown Museum of Art has added several displays designed to attract younger visitors.

_____ 5. Inside the main doors is a large entrance hall, above which hang a dozen large, spinning mobiles.

_____ 6. Officials hope young people will wander behind and above the entrance hall toward the rest of the museum's art exhibits.

_____ 7. A series of small animal sculptures leads from the fountain back toward the main doors.

Logical Order

When you use **logical order**, you present ideas in a sequence that indicates why one idea logically follows another. For example, a paragraph may move from general to specific or from specific to general. In addition, writers may start with the least important idea and end with the most important one, or they may begin with the most important idea and then go on to the less important ones.

The following paragraph presents ideas in logical order.

> As someone who is both a parent and a student, I have had to develop strategies for coping. First, I try to do my studying at night, after I have put my son to bed. I want to give my son all the attention that he deserves, so after I pick him up from day care, I play with him, read to him, and watch a half hour of TV with him. When I am sure he is asleep, I begin doing my schoolwork. Second, I try to use every spare moment that I have during the day. If I have an hour between classes, I go to the computer lab and do some work. While I eat lunch, I get some of my reading out of the way. When I ride home from work on the bus, I review my class notes. Finally, and most important, I always keep my priorities in mind. My first priority is my son, my second priority is my schoolwork, and my last priority is keeping my apartment clean. If I have studying to do, or if I have promised to take my son to the movies, I will skip housecleaning or doing the wash. Naturally, my apartment can get messy, and occasionally I run out of clean clothes, but that is all right as long as I am able to give my son the attention he deserves.
>
> Vanessa Scully (student)

The writer of this paragraph moves from her least important to her most important point. Notice how transitional words and phrases that signal logical order—*first, second,* and *finally*—add to the paragraph's coherence.

Some Transitional Words and Phrases That Signal Logical Order

also	for instance	not only . . . but also
consequently	furthermore	one . . . another
equally important	in addition	similarly
finally	in fact	the least important
first . . . second . . . third	last	the most important
for example	moreover	therefore

◆ PRACTICE 6.14

Read the following paragraphs, whose sentences are organized in logical order. Underline the transitional words and phrases that make each paragraph coherent.

Example

Among the many reasons to support school sports, the most important is the education students get on the playing field. Students in a sports program such as baseball or field hockey learn teamwork, self-confidence, and the value of physical fitness. They also feel a sense of belonging that athletes on a team enjoy. In addition, schools often benefit financially from the sales of tickets to sporting events. Attending a football game may help provide students with new textbooks and other materials. The least important reason to support school sports is the chance that a school athlete could go on to become a famous sports figure. Such success is extremely rare, and most young people should be encouraged to pursue other, more practical careers.

1. The negative effects of illegal drug use are as serious now as they have ever been. First, illegal drug users risk arrest every time they buy, sell, or use drugs. Drug enforcement has become more aggressive over time, and jail sentences are often long. Moreover, drug use is associated with problems such as crime and unemployment. Drug users are more likely to be involved in crimes or to experience periods of unemployment than are people who do not use drugs. But the most important risk to drug users is the physical and mental damage that drugs can cause. Such damage can be life threatening and is often irreversible.

2. I have made some important decisions lately. For example, last year I decided to move from my home in rural Connecticut to an apartment in New York City. This move has had many benefits. For instance, being in the city gave me more career opportunities. It also helped me to meet many more people than I could have in my small Connecticut town. Furthermore, I found plenty of interesting things to do with my time. My new interests include Thai food and modern dance. In fact, I find the cultural mix in the city interesting and exciting.

◆ PRACTICE 6.15

Arrange the following sentences into a coherent paragraph. Be sure you are able to explain why you arranged the sentences the way you did.

____ 1. Rankin became, therefore, one of the first women in the world elected to a governing body.

____ 2. Jeanette Rankin had one of the most unusual political careers in American history.

____ 3. As a result of this vote, Rankin lost her bid for election to the Senate in 1918, but she remained active in peace issues.

____ 4. Although this constitutional amendment passed the House, it was defeated in the Senate and not enacted until 1919.

_____ 5. First, she was elected to Congress in 1916, four years before American women had the right to vote.

_____ 6. While in Congress, Rankin helped draft a constitutional amendment to give women the right to vote.

_____ 7. Reelected to Congress in 1940, Rankin cast her vote against U.S. entry into World War II.

_____ 8. Another action Rankin is remembered for is her vote against U.S. entry into World War I.

_____ 9. Finally, Rankin is remembered as someone who stood by her principles, regardless of the cost to her career.

_____ 10. By doing so, Rankin became the only member of Congress to vote against U.S. entry into both world wars.

REVISING AND EDITING

Look back at your response to the Seeing and Writing exercise on page 84. First, make sure your paragraph has an effective topic sentence. Then, revise the paragraph so that it is unified, well developed, and coherent.

CHAPTER REVIEW

◆ EDITING PRACTICE

Read the following paragraphs, and evaluate each one in terms of its unity, development, and coherence. First, underline the topic sentence. Next, cross out any sentences that do not support the topic sentence. Then, add transitional words and phrases where needed. Finally, discuss in class what additional details, facts, and examples might be added to each paragraph.

1. At a young age, pirate Anne Bonny traded a life of wealth and privilege for one of adventure and crime. In 1716, she ran away from home to marry a sailor. Sailors passed through the place where she lived, on the East Coast of the United States, on a regular basis. Later, through her husband, she met a pirate named Calico Jack Rackham. Bonny soon left her husband to join Rackham's crew. She developed a reputation as a fierce

Anne Bonny and Mary Read

fighter. In 1720, Bonny met another female pirate named Mary Read. They were captured by authorities. Bonny, who was pregnant, was not sentenced to death because executing a woman criminal who was pregnant was against the law. Read received a death sentence. Before it could be carried out, she died of a fever in prison. No one knows what finally became of Bonny.

WUSA players Mia Hamm (right) and Stephanie Mugneret-Beghl

2. The Women's United Soccer Association (WUSA) was founded in February 2000 to promote women's professional soccer worldwide. There were eight teams made up of women from the World Cup championship team and five top-notch Chinese players. The Chinese women play a different style of soccer than the Americans. The teams were located in major cities, such as Atlanta, Boston, San Diego, San Jose, Washington, New York, Philadelphia, and Raleigh/Durham. The women began attracting corporate sponsors. They created team logos in preparation for their first season. Corporate sponsors provide a lot of money for sports teams. That first year, the games were carried on television by TNT, CNN/Sports Illustrated, and China Central Television.

3. The number of all-volunteer fire departments has declined for a number of reasons. People have less time than they used to for volunteer activities. Most volunteer fire departments were founded when two-parent, single-income families were the rule. That model is far less common than it once was. Many people have come to expect payment for the work they do. The ideal of community service for its own sake is held by fewer and fewer people. American families are more mobile than they have ever been. Long commutes and frequent moves often mean that people are not strongly connected to their neighborhoods. They are less likely to volunteer time and risk their personal safety for the good of the community.

◆ COLLABORATIVE ACTIVITIES

1. Working in a group, list some reasons why many students find it difficult to perform well in college, and arrange these reasons from least important to most important. Then create a topic sentence that states

the main idea suggested by the reasons. Finally, write your own draft of a paragraph in which you discuss why some students have difficulty in college.

2. Think of a place you know well. Write a paragraph that describes the place so that readers will be able to imagine it almost as clearly as you can. Decide on a specific spatial order—outside to inside, left to right, front to back, or another arrangement that makes sense to you. Use that spatial order to organize the details in your draft paragraph. When you have finished, trade paragraphs with another student. See if you can sketch the place described in your partner's paragraph. If you cannot, offer suggestions that could improve his or her description.
3. Bring to class a paragraph from a newspaper or a magazine. Working in a group of three students, find the main idea of each paragraph, and underline the paragraph's topic sentence. Then decide whether each paragraph is unified, well developed, and coherent. If it is not, work together to make it more effective.

☑ REVIEW CHECKLIST: Fine-Tuning Your Paragraph

- ☐ Every paragraph you write should include a topic sentence that states the paragraph's main idea. (See 6A.)
- ☐ A paragraph is unified when it focuses on a single main idea, which is usually stated in the topic sentence. (See 6B.)
- ☐ A paragraph is well developed when it contains enough details (facts and examples) to support the main idea. (See 6C.)
- ☐ A paragraph is coherent when its sentences are arranged in a definite order and it includes all necessary transitional words and phrases. (See 6D.)

CHAPTER

7 Patterns of Paragraph Development

PREVIEW

In this chapter, you will learn to write the following kinds of paragraphs:

- exemplification (7A)
- narration (7B)
- description (7C)
- process (7D)
- cause and effect (7E)
- comparison and contrast (7F)
- classification (7G)
- definition (7H)
- argument (7I)

SEEING AND WRITING

What skills do you have that would help you survive if you were stranded on a deserted island? Why would these skills be helpful? Look at the picture above, and then write a paragraph that answers these questions.

Word Power

maroon to put ashore on a deserted island

improvise to make do with the tools or resources at hand

As you write paragraphs, you will discover that you present ideas in patterns that reflect the ways in which your mind works. Recognizing these patterns and understanding how they help you communicate your ideas will make you a stronger, more self-confident writer. In this chapter, you will learn about nine ways of developing paragraphs—*exemplification, narration, description, process, cause and effect, comparison and contrast, classification, definition,* and *argument.*

A Exemplification

An **example** is a specific illustration of a general idea. An **exemplification paragraph** explains or clarifies a general statement or idea—the topic sentence—with one or more specific examples. (Giving one or more examples is often the best way to support the general statement you make in your topic stenence.) Personal experiences, class discussions, observations, conversations, and reading (for example, material from newspapers, magazines, or the Internet) can all be good sources of examples.

How many examples you need depends on your topic sentence. A complicated, far-reaching statement might require many examples to convince readers that it is reasonable. A simple, more straightforward statement would require fewer examples.

The following paragraph uses examples to make the point that the English language sometimes makes no sense.

> Sometimes you have to believe that all English speakers should be committed to an asylum for the verbally insane. In what other language do people drive in a parkway and park in a driveway? In what other language do people recite at a play and play at a recital? In what other language do privates eat in the general mess and generals eat in the private mess? In what other language do men get hernias and women get hysterectomies? In what other language do people ship by truck and send cargo by ship? In what other language can your nose run and your feet smell?
>
> Richard Lederer, "English Is a Crazy Language"

Notice that the author of the paragraph above uses a number of short examples, one after the other, to make his point. Each example supports the statement that Lederer makes in his topic sentence: that sometimes you have to think speakers of English are insane.

> ● **Writing Tip**
> Transitional words and phrases that are used in exemplification include *for instance, for example,* and *one reason . . . another reason.*

✓ SELF-ASSESSMENT CHECKLIST: Writing an Exemplification Paragraph

- ☐ Does your topic sentence clearly express what you have written in the rest of the paragraph?
- ☐ Do all your examples support your topic sentence?
- ☐ Have you used enough examples?
- ☐ Have you used appropriate transitional words and phrases?

> ● **Writing Tip**
> Many everyday writing tasks require exemplification. For example, in a memo to your employer, you might give examples of how your department could save money.

◆ PRACTICE 7.1

Read this exemplification paragraph, and answer the questions that follow it.

Squash is a delicious vegetable that comes in many different shapes, sizes, flavors, and colors, but few people are aware of its tremendous variety. Most consumers have encountered the popular types of squash: pumpkin, butternut, acorn, and spaghetti. There are many less popular but equally appealing varieties, however. For example, stripetti squash is yellow with green stripes, has stringy flesh much like the spaghetti squash, and is crisp with a taste somewhat like corn. Another relative unknown, Hubbard squash, is a huge variety, weighing at least ten pounds. It has blue skin and orange flesh, and the flavor, unlike some other types of squash, is not sugary. A few other varieties of squash are also not very well known. Sweet dumplings, for instance, are a small squash with dark green and white striped skin. Their flavor is rich, buttery, and very sweet. Kabochas, another unusual variety of squash, look a lot like a butternut squash and also have a sweet flavor. They have dark green or dark orange skin, sometimes with white stripes. You can experiment with these different kinds of squash by using them as filling in ravioli; making them into soup; stuffing, sautéing, or baking them; or making them into pies. Now that you have learned about the many kinds of squash, explore a few new varieties.

1. Underline the topic sentence of the paragraph.
2. List the specific examples the writer uses to support the topic sentence. The first example has been listed for you.

   Stripetti, yellow and green, tastes like corn
   ____
   ____
   ____

3. Circle the transitional words and phrases that the writer uses to connect ideas in the paragraph.

◆ PRACTICE 7.2

Following are four topic sentences for exemplification paragraphs. After each sentence, list three examples that could support the main idea. For example, if you were writing about the poor quality of food in your school cafeteria, you could give examples of mystery meat, weak coffee, and stale bread.

1. Many of the skills learned by our grandparents are not needed in today's high-tech world.

   ____
   ____
   ____

2. People who want to get their news from the Internet have a variety of options.

   ____
   ____
   ____

3. I have always been very unlucky (or lucky) in love.

___

___

___

4. Although many people criticize television shows as mindless, there are important exceptions.

___

___

___

◆ PRACTICE 7.3

Choose one of the following topics (or one of your own choice) as the subject of an exemplification paragraph. Then, on a separate sheet of paper, list as many examples as you can for the topic you have chosen. Use the invention strategies discussed in 5B to help you think of examples.

- Why the Internet is important to you
- The importance of family in your life
- What is memorable about a favorite movie
- The benefits of a healthy diet
- How not to act on a first date
- How your school could be improved
- The accomplishments of a historical figure
- Violence in movies
- The demands of being a parent
- Drivers who are a menace
- Annoying trends on your college campus
- Exercise for busy people
- Books that have influenced you
- The best jobs for a recent college graduate
- Ways to organize your day
- The consequences of procrastinating (putting things off)

◆ PRACTICE 7.4

On a separate sheet of paper, write an exemplification paragraph on the topic you chose in Practice 7.3. When you have finished, use the Self-Assessment Checklist on page 105 to help you revise your paragraph.

◆ PRACTICE 7.5

On a separate sheet of paper, write a final, edited draft of your exemplification paragraph.

B Narration

Narration means telling a story. Most of the time, a **narrative paragraph** tells a story to make a point—for example, that an experience you had as a child changed you, that the life of Helen Keller is inspiring, or that the Battle of Gettysburg was the turning point of the Civil War. The topic sentence states this idea, and the rest of the paragraph develops it, with events and details arranged in time order.

Effective narrative paragraphs should include details that advance the story and avoid asides that could confuse readers. In addition, effective narrative paragraphs present events in a definite time order, usually the order in which the events occurred. In the following narrative paragraph, the writer tells about the poverty she experienced as a child.

> **Word Power**
> **dilapidated** in a state of disrepair or ruin

> Like rural Southern gypsies, we moved from one dilapidated Southern farmhouse to another in a constant search for a decent place to live. Sometimes we moved when the rent increased beyond the 30 or 40 dollars my mother could afford. Or the house burned down, not an unusual occurrence in substandard housing. One year, when we were gathered together for Thanksgiving dinner, a stranger walked in without knocking and announced that we were being evicted. The house had been sold without our knowledge and the new owner wanted to start remodeling immediately. We tried to finish our meal with an attitude of thanksgiving while he worked around us with his tape measure.
>
> Melanie Scheller, "On the Meaning of Plumbing and Poverty"

> **Writing Tip**
> Transitional words and phrases used in narration include *first, then, next, after that, finally,* and other transitions that signal time order. See 6D.

Notice that the details in the paragraph above follow a time sequence: first one thing happens, then another thing happens, and so on. The transitional words and phrases in the paragraph—*sometimes* and *one year*—help make this structure clear.

> **Writing Tip**
> Many everyday writing tasks require narration. For example, in a letter to your HMO, you might summarize the history of your claim.

✓ SELF-ASSESSMENT CHECKLIST: Writing a Narrative Paragraph

- ☐ Does your narrative paragraph make a point?
- ☐ Is your topic sentence specific enough?
- ☐ Does your narrative move clearly from an earlier time to a later time?
- ☐ Have you used appropriate transitional words and phrases?

◆ PRACTICE 7.6

Read this narrative paragraph, and answer the questions that follow it.

I've lived in the same house my entire life, and when I was eight years old, I helped to build part of it. Our house was too small, so one summer my father decided to build two new bedrooms for my older brother and me. I remember clearly how we all worked together on the project. Even though I was only eight years old, I was very proud of how I helped carry the heavy concrete blocks that formed the foundation of what would be my new bedroom. After the foundation was built, we had to lay down the wooden floor. I watched with fascination as my father fitted together the planks of pine that he had carefully finished with a deep brown stain. Next, he framed the walls and, with my mother's help, put up wallboard. After that came the ceiling and, finally, the roof. At each stage, my father would give me and my brother a small job to do so that we would feel as if we were constructing along with him. Most often, my brother and I were limited to hammering nails, but we felt that this was a major accomplishment. I was too small to do some of the jobs my brother was permitted to help on, but I felt I was contributing just the same. The whole family spent many happy weekends outside, hammering and sawing, listening to music and telling jokes. After many months, we finished the project, an occasion we celebrated with uncles, aunts, cousins, and grandparents.

1. Underline the topic sentence of the paragraph.
2. List the major events of the narrative. The first event has been listed for you.

   When I was eight, my father decided to add two new bedrooms to our house.

   ____

   ____

   ____

   ____

   ____

3. Circle the transitional words and phrases that the writer uses to link events in time.

◆ PRACTICE 7.7

Following are four topic sentences for narrative paragraphs. After each topic sentence, list four events you could include in a narrative paragraph to support the main idea. For example, if you were telling about a dinner that turned out to be a disaster, you could tell about how the meat burned, the vegetables were overcooked, the cake fell, and the guests arrived late.

1. The day started out normally enough, but, before it was over, all our lives had changed forever.

   ____

   ____

   ____

   ____

2. When I was young, my grandmother would tell me stories about her childhood.

____

____

____

____

3. I'll never forget my first college roommate, a person I grew to hate.

____

____

____

____

4. It was a difficult decision for me to make.

____

____

____

____

◆ PRACTICE 7.8

Choose one of the following topics (or one of your own choice) as the subject of a narrative paragraph. Then, on a separate sheet of paper, list as many events and details as you can for the topic you have chosen. Use the invention strategies discussed in 5B to help you think of events and details.

A fairy tale
Your proudest moment
Overcoming an obstacle
A family legend
A great adventure
A fortunate accident
Your first day at school
An important choice
Your most embarrassing moment
Your favorite holiday memory
A terrifying event
Taking a risk
An incredible coincidence
A new experience
A humorous incident
A great loss
A lesson learned

◆ PRACTICE 7.9

On a separate sheet of paper, write a narrative paragraph on the topic you chose in Practice 7.8. When you have finished, use the Self-Assessment Checklist on page 108 to help you revise your paragraph.

◆ PRACTICE 7.10

On a separate sheet of paper, write a final, edited draft of your narrative paragraph.

C Description

When you write a **description**, you express what your five senses experience. In a **descriptive paragraph**, you paint a word picture of a person, an object, or a place. To convey your ideas to your readers, you use language to create a vivid impression of what you have seen, heard, smelled, tasted, or touched.

When you write a descriptive paragraph, you try to communicate a single **dominant impression**—a particular mood or quality—in your topic sentence. For example, if you were describing your younger sister's room and wanted to leave readers with the impression that it was a cluttered, messy place, your topic sentence would convey that idea: *My sister's room looks like a place that has just been burglarized.* All the other sentences in the paragraph would include details to support this dominant impression.

In the following paragraph, writer Jeanne Wakatsuki Houston, a second-generation Japanese American who along with her family was imprisoned in Manzanar internment camp in 1942, describes the pictures on a page of her high school yearbook.

> All the class pictures are there, from the seventh grade through twelfth, with individual head shots of seniors, their names followed by the names of the high schools they would have graduated from on the outside: Theodore Roosevelt, Thomas Jefferson, Herbert Hoover, Sacred Heart. You see pretty girls on bicycles, chicken yards full of fat pullets, patients back-tilted in dental chairs, lines of laundry, and finally, two large blowups, the first of a high tower with a searchlight, against a Sierra backdrop, the next, a two-page endsheet showing a wide path that curves among rows of elm trees. White stones border the path. Two dogs are following an old woman in gardening clothes as she strolls along. She is in the middle distance, small beneath the snowy peaks. It is winter. All the elms are bare. The scene is both stark and comforting. The path leads toward one edge of the camp, but the wire is out of sight, or out of focus. The tiny woman seems very much at ease. She and her tiny dogs seem almost swallowed by the landscape, or floating in it.
>
> Jeanne Wakatsuki Houston, "Manzanar, U.S.A."

Here the writer uses vivid language and specific details to convey an unsettling dominant impression: that the innocence of the students' high school yearbook pictures is overshadowed by the picture of a guard tower and the suggestion of barbed wire. The specific details that support this dominant impression are arranged in spatial order, and transitional words and phrases—*the first* and *the next*—reinforce this organization.

Writing Tip

Transitional words and phrases used in description include *in front, in back, next to, near, beyond,* and other transitions that signal spatial order. See 6D.

Word Power

stark bare; harsh; grim

FOCUS Description

Good descriptions rely on language that is specific and original. Vague, overused words such as *good, nice, bad,* and *beautiful* do not help readers see what you are describing. When you write a descriptive paragraph, try to use specific words and phrases that make your writing come alive.

VAGUE The dogs are following a woman.

SPECIFIC Two dogs are following an old woman in gardening clothes as she strolls along.

SELF-ASSESSMENT CHECKLIST: Writing a Descriptive Paragraph

- Does your topic sentence communicate the paragraph's dominant impression?
- Do all your details support the dominant impression?
- Have you used language that is both specific and original?
- Have you used appropriate transitional words and phrases?

Writing Tip

Many everyday writing tasks require description. For example, in a job-application letter, you might describe a piece of equipment you have worked with.

◆ PRACTICE 7.11

Read this descriptive paragraph, and answer the questions that follow it.

When I first moved to New York City, it seemed huge and dirty. In the winter especially, it felt as if the entire city was lonely and gray. As I walked to work every day, the glass and steel buildings towered over the street and seemed to look down at me. The concrete sidewalks were cold and gritty under my feet. Everything seemed gray—the massive bridges, the crowded subways, even the sky. The city teemed with people huddled in their dark coats and hats and scarves, pale from lack of sun. They didn't seem to notice the garbage on the street, the foul odors in the air, or even the people around them. I thought I'd never adjust, but eventually I began to get used to New York.

1. Underline the topic sentence of the paragraph.

2. In a few words, summarize the dominant impression the writer gives of the subject, New York City.

____

____

3. What are some of the details the writer uses to create this dominant impression? The first detail has been listed for you.

    Towering buildings

◆ PRACTICE 7.12

Following are four topic sentences for descriptive paragraphs. After each topic sentence, list three details that could help convey the dominant impression. For example, to describe an interesting person, you could tell what the person looked like, how he or she behaved, and what he or she said.

1. It was a long hike, but when we finally got to the top of the mountain, the view was incredible.

2. Every community has one house that all the kids swear is haunted.

3. In every living situation, there is one person who is an unbelievable slob.

4. I'll never forget the first time I met her (him).

◆ PRACTICE 7.13

Choose one of the following topics (or one of your own choice) as the subject of a descriptive paragraph. Then, on a separate sheet of paper, list as many details as you can for the topic you have chosen. Use the invention strategies discussed in 5B to help you think of details.

A childhood hideout
Your first pet
A beautiful view
A memorable gift
A musical or other performance
The place you feel the most comfortable
Your favorite article of clothing
An essential household appliance
The face of a loved one
A place you never want to go to again
Your most treasured possession
Your dream car (or the car you already have)
A frightening sight
Your dream house
The best meal you've ever eaten

◆ PRACTICE 7.14

On a separate sheet of paper, write a descriptive paragraph on the topic you chose in Practice 7.13. When you have finished, use the Self-Assessment Checklist on page 112 to help you revise your paragraph.

◆ PRACTICE 7.15

On a separate sheet of paper, write a final, edited draft of your descriptive paragraph.

D Process

When you describe a **process**, you explain how something happens. In a **process paragraph**, you explain how something works or how something is done. The topic sentence of your paragraph should identify the process and communicate the point you want to make about it (for example, "Sewing on a button is easy" or "By following a few simple steps, you can find a job that is right for you"). The rest of the paragraph should discuss the steps in the process—one at a time and in the order in which they occur.

In general, there are two kinds of process paragraphs: *process explanations* and *instructions*. In a **process explanation**, your purpose is simply to help readers understand a process, not perform it—for example, how a cell phone works or why the sky is blue.

The following paragraph is a process explanation.

> A white-dwarf star is formed in three stages. In the first stage, the white dwarf is a cloud of hydrogen gas that has become a star. In stage two, the star burns up its hydrogen and becomes a red giant. Then, after the star has consumed all its hydrogen, it begins to shrink and cool. In the final stage, the surface of this compressed star becomes so hot that it becomes a white dwarf. Even though a white dwarf is small, it is very dense: a piece the size of a pack of gum would weigh more than four thousand pounds.
>
> Feroz Ahmed (student)

The topic sentence identifies the paragraph above as a process explanation, and the rest of the paragraph presents the steps in strict chronological order. Throughout the paragraph, transitional words and phrases—*In the first stage, In stage two,* and *In the final stage*—clearly identify the individual steps in the process.

The other kind of process paragraph gives readers **instructions**. The purpose of instructions is to give readers the information they need to actually perform a task or an activity—for example, to fill out a job application, operate a piece of equipment, or help someone who is choking.

In the following paragraph, a volunteer firefighter explains how to operate a home fire extinguisher.

> Even though many people have fire extinguishers in their homes, most do not know how use them. A fire extinguisher is a metal cylinder filled with water or some other material that will put out a fire. Before you attempt to use a fire extinguisher, check the gauge to see if the extinguisher is pressurized. If it is, the extinguisher is ready for use. Next, pull out the safety pin that is located just below the operating lever at the top of the cylinder. When you do this, you open a valve that allows the material in the extinguisher to flow up through the nozzle. Then point the nozzle of the extinguisher at the base of the fire and squeeze the operating lever. This allows the compressed gas in the cylinder to push the fire suppressant out of the nozzle. As you spray, move the stream in a sweeping motion, making sure to aim at the fuel, not the fire. Finally, continue spraying until the fire is completely out. By following these simple steps, you should be able to deal with most small fire emergencies that occur in your home.
>
> Jeff Jones (student)

Writing Tip

Transitional words and phrases used in process include *first, second, next, then, at the same time,* and *finally.*

In his topic sentence, the writer identifies the process he is going to describe and indicates that he is writing a set of instructions. To make sure that readers can follow his instructions, he includes transitions that indicate the exact order in which each step is to be performed (*Before, Next, Then, Finally*). Because the writer expects readers to follow his instructions, he addresses readers directly, using commands to tell them what to do (*check the gauge . . . , pull the valve*). Notice that the writer ends his paragraph with a sentence that emphasizes the importance of the process.

Writing Tip

Many everyday writing tasks require you to explain a process. For example, in a memo to your employer, you might point out how a change in the way you perform a particular activity could save the company both time and money.

✓ SELF-ASSESSMENT CHECKLIST: Writing a Process Paragraph

- Does the topic sentence identify the process?
- Does the topic sentence indicate that you are either giving instructions or explaining how something works?
- Do you present all the steps of the process in the order in which they occur?
- Have you included the transitions that readers need to follow the process?

◆ PRACTICE 7.16

Read this process paragraph, and answer the questions that follow it.

In October 2003, engineers, scientists, and National Park Service employees worked together to move a 2,000-pound bell. The Liberty Bell, a symbol of freedom and justice around the world, was moved from a small pavilion on Market Street in Philadelphia to a larger home in the new Constitution Center. But because the bell is so fragile, it took months of careful planning before the experts felt ready to undertake the task. Not only did the experts carry out a trial run, but they also took special precautions to make sure the bell would not be damaged as it was being moved. First, a Vermont company, with help from the National Science Foundation, designed small sensors to attach to the bell. During the move, these sensors would sound an alarm on a nearby computer if the bell experienced stress. Next, experts x-rayed the bell to determine what impurities the metal contained and what the various thicknesses were. After they made sure the bell was ready, the experts loaded it onto a specially designed cart for the 200-yard trip to its new home. The actual trip—over a distance of about two football fields—took four hours to complete.

1. Underline the topic sentence of the paragraph.

2. List the words that tell you that the writer is moving on to another step in the process. The first word has been listed for you.

   First ____

   ____

   ____

   ____

3. How many steps did it take to move the bell?

   ____

4. List the steps on the lines below.

   ____

   ____

   ____

   ____

   ____

◆ PRACTICE 7.17

Following are four topic sentences for process paragraphs. List three steps or stages that might occur in each process.

1. Registering for college courses can be a frustrating process.

____

____

____

2. Balancing a checkbook is not as complicated as it may seem.

____

____

____

3. Parallel parking is not difficult if you follow a few simple steps.

____

____

____

4. Purchasing products online can save you time and money.

____

____

____

◆ PRACTICE 7.18

Choose one of the topics below as the subject of a process paragraph. Make sure to note whether the topic requires you to give your readers instructions or simply information.

Setting the table for a holiday meal	Studying for a test
Writing a letter of complaint	Taking care of a pet
Tying a tie	Living on a budget
Planning the perfect party	Meeting people
Deciding which gym to join	Programming a VCR
Succeeding at a job interview	Dressing well
	Dealing with disappointment

◆ PRACTICE 7.19

On a separate sheet of paper, write a process paragraph on the topic you chose in Practice 7.18. When you have finished, use the Self-Assessment Checklist on page 115 to help you revise your paragraph.

◆ PRACTICE 7.20

On a separate sheet of paper, write a final, edited draft of your process paragraph.

E CAUSE AND EFFECT

A **cause** makes a particular effect happen. An **effect** is the situation that results from a cause. You write **cause-and-effect paragraphs** to explain why something happened or is happening or to show how one thing affects something else. For example, has the increased use of seat belts in cars led to a decline in accident-related deaths? Are the polar ice caps melting because of global warming?

The main problem you may have in planning a cause-and-effect paragraph is making sure that a **causal relationship** exists—that one event actually caused another. Another problem is making sure you consider all the possible causes, not just the most obvious ones. As you write, be careful that you do not make one cause or effect seem more important than it really is.

A cause-and-effect paragraph can focus on causes or on effects. The topic sentence of a cause-and-effect paragraph usually tells readers whether the paragraph will focus on causes or on effects.

The following paragraph focuses on causes.

> For a number of reasons, Americans are gaining weight at a frightening rate. First, the diet of many Americans is not healthy. We eat a great deal of fried foods that are high in salt and unsaturated fat. Also, many Americans do not take time to eat breakfast. Many of us eat on the run, grabbing a pastry or a doughnut on the way to work. Again, these foods are high in fat. Another reason that Americans are gaining so much weight is that we eat out so much. In many two-income families, dinner involves taking out meals from a fast-food restaurant. These meals are usually high in fat and salt. Finally, and perhaps most important, many Americans do not exercise. Most of us are couch potatoes who watch television for hours and get up only to go to the bathroom or to get a snack. The effects of this unhealthy lifestyle are easy to predict. Unless we begin eating better and exercising more, many of us will have severe weight-related problems in the future.
>
> Jen Kinzer (student)

The topic sentence of the paragraph above indicates that the writer will focus on identifying causes. The rest of the paragraph examines each cause, one at a time. After first discussing the less important causes, the writer ends with the most important——the lack of exercise. Throughout the paragraph, transitional words and phrases signal the writer's movement from one cause to another (*First, Also, Another, Finally,* and *perhaps most important*).

The paragraph below focuses on effects.

> **Writing Tip**
> Transitional words and phrases used in cause-and-effect paragraphs include *the first cause, the second cause, one result, another result, because,* and *since.*

> A number of research studies done when television was a relatively new medium demonstrated that television interfered with family activities and the formation of family relationships. One survey showed that seventy-eight percent of the respondents indicated no conversation taking place during viewing except at specified times such as commercials. The study noted: "The television atmosphere in most households is one of quiet absorption on the part of the family members who are

present. The nature of the family social life during a program could be described as 'parallel' rather than interactive, and the set does seem to dominate family life when it is on." Thirty-six percent of the respondents in another study indicated that television viewing was the only family activity participated in during the week.

Marie Winn, "Television: The Plug-In Drug"

The topic sentence of the paragraph above identifies the cause of the problem (television watching) the paragraph will discuss. The paragraph then goes on to discuss two effects of television watching on family activities. Transitional words and phrases signal the writer's movement from one effect to another (*One survey showed, in another survey*).

FOCUS Cause and Effect

Be careful not to confuse the words *affect* and *effect*. *Affect* is a verb meaning "to influence." *Effect* is usually a noun meaning "result."

Writing Tip

Many everyday writing tasks require you to identify causes and effects. For example, in a letter of complaint, you could explain how a defective product caused you a great deal of inconvenience.

SELF-ASSESSMENT CHECKLIST: Writing a Cause-and-Effect Paragraph

- Does the paragraph focus on causes or on effects?
- Does the topic sentence indicate the focus of the paragraph?
- Are the causes or effects clearly identified?
- Do transitional words and phrases signal a shift from one cause or effect to another?

◆ PRACTICE 7.21

Read this cause-and-effect paragraph, and answer the questions that follow it.

Some students wonder whether a college degree is really worth the money they are spending for tuition. Having a college degree has substantial effects on a person's income over a lifetime. Studies show people who graduate from college earn more money than people who do not. According to the U.S. Department of Labor, someone with a bachelor's degree earns 55 percent more than someone with a high school diploma. Moreover, a person with a master's degree earns 98 percent more than someone with a high school diploma. Even more dramatic is that those with doctoral degrees earn 161 percent over someone with a high school diploma. Even people who graduate from a two-year college or institution typically earn $4,000 a year more than their high school counterparts. It is no wonder that in spite of increasing costs, college enrollments are rising steadily.

1. Underline the topic sentence of the paragraph.
2. Does the paragraph focus on causes or effects? How do you know?

____

3. List the main effect the paragraph identifies.

____

4. What is the cause of these effects?

____

◆ PRACTICE 7.22

Following are four topic sentences for cause-and-effect paragraphs. List three causes or effects for each sentence.

1. Indoor air pollution is caused by a number of items we use every day.

____

____

2. Indoor air pollution can have harmful effects on our health.

____

____

3. Cell phones are popular for several reasons.

____

____

4. Cell phones have changed our society.

____

____

◆ PRACTICE 7.23

Choose one of the topics below as the subject of a cause-and-effect paragraph.

Causes of the inability to fall sleep
Effects of lack of communication on a relationship
Effects of computer spell checkers
Effects of Internet chat rooms
Causes of drunk driving
Why you attend the college you do
Causes of a particular television show's popularity
The effects of global warming
Why you belong to a particular school or community organization
The effects of watching too much television
Why certain students succeed
The effects of a positive (or negative) attitude
The causes of cheating
The consequences of cheating

◆ PRACTICE 7.24

On a separate sheet of paper, write a cause-and-effect paragraph on the topic you chose in Practice 7.23. When you have finished, use the Self-Assessment Checklist on page 119 to help you revise your paragraph.

◆ PRACTICE 7.25

On a separate sheet of paper, write a final, edited draft of your cause-and-effect paragraph.

F Comparison and Contrast

When you **compare** two things, you concentrate on their similarities. When you **contrast** them, you concentrate on their differences. (Sometimes, people use the term *comparison* to refer to both similarities and differences.) When you write a **comparison-and-contrast paragraph**, you examine the similarities or differences (or both) between two people, two things, or two ideas.

FOCUS Topics for Comparison and Contrast

To write an effective comparison-and-contrast paragraph, you have to discuss two things that have enough in common so that the comparison makes sense. For example, it would be difficult (and not very useful) to compare dogs and telephones. (They do not share any significant characteristics.) It would, however, be easy to compare dogs and cats. (Both are mammals, both like to play, and both make good pets.)

There are two methods for structuring a comparison-and-contrast paragraph: subject by subject and point by point.

Subject-by-Subject Comparisons

In a **subject-by-subject** comparison, you discuss all the points you are going to make about one subject, and then you discuss the same points for the second subject. This method of organization works well if you are discussing just a few points for each subject. A subject-by-subject comparison has the following structure.

Subject A
    Point 1
    Point 2
    Point 3

Writing Tip

Transitional words and phrases used in comparison and contrast include *however, in contrast, similarly,* and *on the one hand . . . on the other hand.*

Computer Tip

Many word-processing programs have an outline feature that helps you automatically format the different levels of your outline. Some also have a document-map view that gives you an overview of your essay's organization.

Subject B
  Point 1
  Point 2
  Point 3

In the following paragraph, the writer uses a subject-by-subject comparison to compare two methods of transportation—cars and trains.

Last year, when I took the train to Boston to visit my sister, I had a chance to compare this method of transportation with the way I usually travel, by car. Driving to Boston from Philadelphia takes about six-and-a-half hours. I often drive alone with only my car radio and CD player for company. By the third hour, I am bored and tired. Traffic is also a problem. The interstate roads I take are crowded and dangerous. If my attention wanders, I can get into serious trouble. If there is an accident, I may have to wait for more than an hour until the police clear the highway. A train ride, however, is a much better experience. Often, I meet other students and get into interesting conversations. If I am tired, I can take a nap, and if I am hungry, I can get a snack. If I really feel motivated, I can even catch up on my schoolwork. Best of all, I never get stuck in traffic, and when I arrive in Boston, I am rested and ready for a day with my sister.

Forest Williams (student)

In his topic sentence, the writer clearly states what two things he will be comparing, and the rest of his paragraph presents the points that support his comparison. In the first half of the paragraph, the writer discusses the disadvantages of driving. In the second half, he discusses the advantages of taking the train. Notice that he signals the shift from his discussion of cars to his discussion of trains with the transition *however*.

Point-by-Point Comparisons

When you write a **point-by-point** comparison, you make a point about one subject and then discuss the same point in relation to the other subject. You use this alternating pattern throughout the paragraph. This arrangement is best for a paragraph in which you discuss many points because it helps readers to compare specific points as they read. A point-by-point comparison has the following structure.

Point 1
  Subject A
  Subject B
Point 2
  Subject A
  Subject B
Point 3
  Subject A
  Subject B

Writing Tip

Many everyday writing tasks require comparison and contrast. For example, in a letter to your local school board, you might compare two methods of teaching reading before recommending one of them.

Notice how the author of the following paragraph uses a point-by-point comparison to compare students who commute to those who live on campus.

Some people say that there is no difference between students who commute and those who live on campus, but I disagree. Just come to an eight o'clock class any morning, and the differences are obvious. Commuters are fighting to keep awake after their one-hour ride to school. Dorm students are wide awake after a brisk ten-minute walk to class. As a result of being sleep deprived, commuters are frequently grumpy and irritable. Dorm students, however, are generally alert and in good spirits. After all, they have gotten an extra hour of sleep. The differences between dorm students and commuters do not end in class. After class, the dorm students go back to their rooms to nap before their next class. Commuters must find something to occupy their time before the next class. Often, this means walking around campus trying to find a quiet spot to rest. After classes are finished for the day, the dorm students go back to their rooms. The commuters, who by this time are exhausted, trudge wearily to the bus stop and wait for the process to begin again the next morning.

Margaret Caracappa (student)

This point-by-point comparison begins with a topic sentence that clearly states what two subjects will be compared. The writer goes on to discuss a series of points, making a point about commuters and then a related point about dorm students. She signals shifts from one subject to another by repeating the words *dorm students* and *commuters.*

✓ SELF-ASSESSMENT CHECKLIST: Writing a Comparison-and-Contrast Paragraph

- ☐ Does your topic sentence indicate what two things you will compare?
- ☐ Do the two things you are comparing have enough in common so that the comparison makes sense?
- ☐ Have you used a subject-by-subject or a point-by-point comparison? Why?
- ☐ Have you discussed the same or similar points for both subjects?
- ☐ Have you used appropriate transitional words and phrases?

◆ PRACTICE 7.26

Read this comparison-and-contrast paragraph, and answer the questions that follow it.

Having been both a smoker and a nonsmoker, I feel qualified to compare the two ways of life. When I smoked, I often found myself banished from public places such as offices, restaurants, and stores when I felt the urge to smoke. I would huddle with my fellow smokers outside, enduring all kinds of weather just for the pleasure of a cigarette. As more and more people stopped smoking, I found myself banished from private homes, too, if I gave in to my craving. I spent a lot of money on cigarettes, and the prices seemed to rise faster and faster. In my sanest moments, I worried about lung cancer and heart disease. My colds lingered and often turned into bronchitis. Climbing stairs and running left me breathless. Now that I have been smoke-free for over a year, I can go anywhere and socialize with anyone. The money I have saved in the last year on cigarettes is going to pay for a winter vacation in sunny Florida. After not smoking for only a few weeks, I could breathe more easily. I had more energy for running and climbing stairs. I have avoided colds so far, and I'm not as worried about lung and heart disease. In fact, I've been told that my lungs should be as healthy as those of a nonsmoker within another year or so. Quitting smoking has proved to be one of the smartest moves I've ever made.

1. Underline the topic sentence of the paragraph.
2. Does this paragraph deal mainly with similarities or differences?

   ____

   How do you know?

   ____

   ____

3. Is this paragraph a subject-by-subject or a point-by-point comparison? How do you know?

   ____

   ____

   ____

   ____

   ____

4. List some of the contrasts the writer describes. The first contrast has been listed for you.

   When she was a smoker, she often had to smoke outside of public and private places. As a nonsmoker, she can go anywhere.

   ____

   ____

   ____

   ____

   ____

   ____

◆ PRACTICE 7.27

Following are four topic sentences for comparison-and-contrast paragraphs. First, identify the two things being compared. Then list three similarities or differences for the two subjects. For example, if you were comparing two authors, you could show the similarities and/or differences in the subjects they write about, their styles of writing, and what kinds of readers they attract.

1. My life plan has changed considerably since I was a child.

   ____

   ____

   ____

2. The media's portrayal of young people has been very negative in recent years, but the true picture is more positive.

   ____

   ____

   ____

3. These two styles of music are very similar.

   ____

   ____

   ____

4. As soon as I get to my job, I become a different person.

   ____

   ____

   ____

◆ PRACTICE 7.28

Choose one of the following topics (or one of your own choice) as the subject of a comparison-and-contrast paragraph. Then, on a separate sheet of paper, list as many similarities or differences as you can for the topic you have chosen. Use the invention strategies discussed in 5B to help you think of similarities and differences.

Two different parts of the country
The differences between two political candidates
What you thought college would be like before you started and what it actually is like
Two different sports
How you and your best friend or sibling are alike (or different)
Two different recording artists
Writing letters and sending email
The music you listen to and the music your parents listen to

Technology today and 100 years ago
How people see you and how you really are
Dog owners and cat owners
The work of two different writers or musicians
Differences in the lives of the rich and the poor in the United States
Two different jobs you've had
Childhood and young adult years
Living in a city and living in a small town

◆ PRACTICE 7.29

On a separate sheet of paper, write a comparison-and-contrast paragraph on the topic you chose in Practice 7.28. When you have finished, use the Self-Assessment Checklist on page 123 to help you revise your paragraph.

◆ PRACTICE 7.30

On a separate sheet of paper, write a final, edited draft of your comparison-and-contrast paragraph.

G Classification

When you **classify**, you sort items into categories. In a **classification paragraph**, you explain to readers how a variety of items can be sorted into categories. When you classify items, none of them should fit into more than one category. For example, you would not classify novels into mysteries, romance novels, and paperbacks because both mystery novels and romance novels could also be paperbacks.

The following is an example of a classification paragraph.

> **● Writing Tip**
> Transitional words and phrases used in classification include *first, second, third, next, last,* and *another.*

Rocks can be sorted into three categories. The first type of rock, igneous rock, is molten rock that has cooled and solidified. Igneous rocks, such as pumice and granite, are formed when volcanic eruptions bring molten rock to the earth's surface. Other types of igneous rock are formed when molten rock solidifies slowly underground. The second type of rock, sedimentary rock, is formed from the sediment that is deposited at the bottom of the ocean. Sedimentary rocks, such as sandstone and shale, are deposited in layers, with the oldest sediments on the bottom and newest on the top. The final type of rock, metamorphic rock, is created by heat and pressure. These rocks are buried deep below the earth's surface for millions of years. The weight and high temperatures that they are exposed to alters their structure and their mineral composition. The most common metamorphic rocks are marble, slate, gneiss, and quartzite.

Bethany Cooper (student)

The topic sentence of the paragraph above clearly identifies the paragraph's subject—rocks—and the three categories into which they will be sorted. The rest of the paragraph discusses these three categories, one at a time. The shift from one category to another is signaled by transitional phrases (*The first type of rock, The second type of rock, The final type of rock*).

SELF-ASSESSMENT CHECKLIST: Writing a Classification Paragraph

- Have you sorted items into categories?
- Are the categories distinct from one another?
- Does your topic sentence identify your subject as well as the categories into which items are sorted?
- Do transitional words and phrases signal the shift from one category to another?

Writing Tip

Many everyday writing tasks require classification. For example, you could justify your request to your local school board for extended after-school hours by classifying the various needs that students have.

◆ PRACTICE 7.31

Read the following classification paragraph, and answer the questions that follow.

Because high-profile athletes receive high salaries and the love and admiration of sports fans, many of them find ways to give back to the community. One way to give back is through charitable foundations to help young fans. Michael Jordan and the Chicago Bulls, for example, built a Boys' and Girls' Club on Chicago's West Side, and Troy Aikman set up a foundation that builds playgrounds for children's hospitals. Another way athletes contribute to their communities is through mentoring. Many high-profile athletes participate in programs designed to encourage young people to stay in school and avoid drugs. Shaquille O'Neal's Shaq's Paq, for example, provides mentoring for inner-city children. The Philadelphia 76ers visit schools and have donated over five thousand books to local libraries. The final way athletes contribute is by responding to emergencies in a community and trying to help. For example, Ike Reese of the the Philadelphia Eagles recently began collecting clothing and food for a needy family. Vince Carter's Embassy of Hope Foundation distributes food to needy families at Thanksgiving and hosts a Christmas party for disadvantaged families. These are some of the many important and useful ways that high-profile athletes give back to their communities.

1. Underline the paragraph's topic sentence.
2. List the categories that the writer uses to present the ways that high-profile athletes give back to their communities.

____

____

____

3. List the transitional words and phrases that let the reader know when a new category is being introduced.

____

____

____

◆ PRACTICE 7.32

Following are four topic sentences for classification paragraphs. For each sentence, list three categories under which information could be discussed.

1. On every road in the United States, motorists encounter three types of drivers.

____

____

2. Students can be sorted into several distinct categories.

____

____

3. Advertisers try to appeal to women in several ways.

____

____

4. Reality shows, the most popular type on television, consist of a variety of types.

____

____

◆ PRACTICE 7.33

Choose one of the topics below as the subject of a classification paragraph.

Types of exercise
Skin-care products
Electronic toys for young children
Snack foods
English instructors
Sports fans
College courses
Parenting styles
Types of stress
Kinds of nonverbal communication
Ways of arguing
Kinds of college pressures
Types of friends
Popular music

◆ PRACTICE 7.34

On a separate sheet of paper, write a classification paragraph on the topic you chose in Practice 7.33. When you have finished, use the Self-Assessment Checklist on page 127 to help you revise your paragraph.

◆ PRACTICE 7.35

On a separate sheet of paper, write a final, edited draft of your classification paragraph.

H Definition

A **definition** tells what a word means. When you want your readers to know exactly how you are using a specific term, you define it. When most people think of definitions they think of the **formal definitions** they see in a dictionary. These definitions have a three-part structure that includes the term to be defined, the general class to which the term belongs, and the things that make the term different from other terms in its class.

Term	**Class**	**Differentiation**
Ice hockey	is a game	that is played on ice by two teams on skates using curved sticks to try to hit a puck into the opponent's goal.

A single-sentence formal definition is often not enough to define a technical term, a concept (*happiness* or *success,* for example), or a complicated subject. In these cases, you will have to write a longer definition in a **definition paragraph**. In a definition paragraph, the topic sentence identifies the term to be defined (and may include a brief formal definition as well). The rest of the paragraph develops this definition by means of one or more of the patterns of development discussed in this chapter.

The following paragraph defines the term *blog.*

> A *blog,* short for *Web log,* is a frequently updated Web site that contains a series of dated entries. Usually the entries are arranged in reverse chronological order, with the most recent appearing first. Blogs resemble online journals, containing the thoughts of the blogger about his or her life or about what is happening on the Web or in the wider world. Entries can be unrelated, or they can focus on particular themes or topics. Unlike journals, however, blogs often include links between entries or links to other sites, frequently other blogs. Blogs first appeared in the 1990s and since then have become very popular. Because anyone with an Internet connection can publish one, blogs vary quite a bit in content and quality. Although some blogs have just a few readers, others, such as those written by popular radio talk-show hosts, may be read by thousands of readers each day.
>
> Charnette Carrington (student)

The topic sentence of the paragraph gives a short formal definition of the term that the paragraph will discuss. The paragraph then goes on to expand this definition, using description, exemplification, and narration to develop the definition. Throughout the paragraph, the writer uses the transitional words and phrases that are appropriate for the individual patterns she uses to develop her definition.

FOCUS Definition

A definition paragraph may develop a definition by negation, telling what the term is not—for example, "Unlike journals, however, blogs often include links. . . ."

Writing Tip

Many everyday writing tasks require definition. For example, in a letter to your local newspaper, you could support one candidate for political office by defining your ideal public official.

✓ SELF-ASSESSMENT CHECKLIST: Writing a Definition Paragraph

- ☐ Does your topic sentence identify the term to be defined?
- ☐ Have you included a formal definition?
- ☐ Have you developed the rest of the paragraph using one or more of the patterns discussed in this chapter?

◆ PRACTICE 7.36

Read this definition paragraph, and answer the questions that follow.

Like a VCR, a DVR (digital video recorder) unit consists of a box and a remote control, but because a DVR records programs onto a hard drive, it gives viewers complete control over what they watch. A DVR works in three ways. First, it continuously records television shows while viewers are watching them. If viewers want to go to the kitchen for a snack, the DVR keeps recording while they're gone, and when they get back, they can replay what they missed. They can also replay scenes to clarify information. For example, if an umpire calls a pitch a ball, and viewers think that the pitch is a strike, they can replay it. The second way a DVR works is that it records whatever viewers program it to. For example, it will record every episode of a show, whenever that show is on, for a month or for a whole season: it will even skip reruns. If the show moves to a different time slot, the DVR searches for it and records it. Finally, a DVR "learns" what shows viewers like and eventually begins to record those shows—without even being programmed.

1. Underline the topic sentence of the paragraph.
2. Underline the writer's one-sentence definition of the subject.
3. List the three functions that the writer presents to help readers understand how a DVR works.

____

____

____

____

4. What patterns of development does the writer use in the definition?

◆ PRACTICE 7.37

Following are four topic sentences for definition paragraphs. Each sentence contains an underlined word or phrase. List two ways you could develop an extended definition of the underlined word or phrase.

1. Community policing is a method of fighting crime.

2. Napster is an online site used for downloading music.

3. Liquid bandages are a new way to treat cuts and scrapes.

4. An abridged dictionary contains a limited number of words.

◆ PRACTICE 7.38

Choose one of the topics below as the subject of a definition paragraph. After you define the term in a sentence, you may use exemplification, narration, description, process, cause and effect, comparison and contrast, classification, or definition—whichever works best—to develop your definition. Use the invention strategies discussed in 5B to help you generate material.

A symbol of your religion (for example, a star, crucifix, or crescent)
A style of popular music (for example, rhythm and blues)
A technical term
A tool found in most households
A fad
Success
A foreign term
A good day
Sexual harassment
Stress
An ideal mate
Freedom
Happiness

◆ PRACTICE 7.39

On a separate sheet of paper, write a definition paragraph on the topic you chose in Practice 7.38. When you have finished, use the Self-Assessment Checklist on page 130 to help you revise your paragraph.

◆ PRACTICE 7.40

On a separate sheet of paper, write a final, edited draft of your definition paragraph.

I Argument

Word Power

controversy a dispute between sides holding different views

controversial marked by controversy

So far, we have discussed paragraphs that are developed by means of *exemplification, narration, description, process, cause and effect, comparison and contrast, classification*, and *definition*. In these paragraphs, the main idea stated in the topic sentence is straightforward, not controversial or debatable. In an **argument paragraph**, however, the main idea *is* debatable: the topic sentence states a position on an issue, but reasonable people may disagree with this position. The rest of the paragraph supports the topic sentence with facts, examples, and reasons.

To write an effective argument paragraph, follow these guidelines.

- *Write a clear topic sentence that states your position.* Using *should, should not,* or *ought to* in your topic sentence will make your position on the issue clear to readers.

  The city *ought to* lower the wage tax.

  The school *should* change its drop/add policy.

- *Present convincing support.* Include facts, examples, and reasons that support your topic sentence. At first, your support will consist mainly of information from your own experience. Later, when you become a more experienced writer, you will support your points with information you get from research.
- *Address opposing arguments.* Try to anticipate possible opposing arguments and argue against them. By addressing these objections, you strengthen your position.

The following paragraph argues against animal experimentation.

Writing Tip

Transitional words and phrases used in argument include *the first reason, the second reason, therefore, furthermore,* and *in conclusion.*

<u>Scientists should no longer experiment on animals</u>. The work many scientists have already done on animal behavior suggests that animals feel, think, and even communicate with each other. For example, work with dolphins and whales shows how smart these animals are. Not only can they be trained, but they can also think. It seems that the gap between us and the rest of the animal kingdom is getting smaller. This is making it more and more difficult to justify animal experiments. Of course, some people will say that animal experimenta-

tion is necessary to help save human lives. But the fact is that most experiments that are done on animals are not necessary, and even the few that are necessary could be done in ways that would cut down on or even eliminate suffering and death. For this reason, it is hard not to feel uneasy about scientific experiments on animals.

Agaja Reddy (student)

This paragraph begins with a topic sentence that states the writer's position on the issue and then presents facts, examples, and reasons to support the topic sentence. After the writer has presented her points, she addresses the opposing argument that animal experimentation is needed to save human lives. She ends with a sentence that sums up her position. Throughout the paragraph, transitional words and phrases—*for example, of course, the fact is,* and *for this reason*—lead readers through the argument.

✓ SELF-ASSESSMENT CHECKLIST: Writing an Argument Paragraph

- Does your topic sentence clearly state your position? Is your position debatable?
- Do you support your topic sentence with specific facts, examples, and reasons?
- Have you addressed possible opposing arguments?
- Have you used appropriate transitional words and phrases?

Writing Tip

Many everyday writing tasks require argument. For example, in a letter to your local newspaper, you might argue for or against a law banning drivers from using cell phones in moving vehicles.

◆ PRACTICE 7.41

Read this argument paragraph, and answer the questions that follow it.

Many American voters never cast a ballot, and voter turnout is often below 50 percent even in presidential elections. It is tragic that people give up this hard-won right. It is in each person's best interest to vote. The most important reason to vote is that government affects every aspect of our lives. It is foolish not to have one's say about who makes the laws and regulations people have to live with. If a citizen does not vote, he or she loses control over what taxes one must pay, the educational system, health care, the environment, and even what roads will be built and which bridges repaired. Another reason to vote is to support a particular political party. If a person believes in that party's policies, it is important to vote to elect that party's candidates and keep them in power. Many people seem to think a single vote doesn't matter, but even if one's candidate does not win, one's vote isn't wasted. The voter has expressed his or her opinion by voting, and the government in power is affected by public opinion. Remember that to keep our democracy working and to participate in government, all citizens must exercise their right to vote.

1. Underline the topic sentence of the paragraph. Why do you think the writer places the topic sentence where he does?

____

____

____

2. What is the issue that the writer is dealing with?

____

____

____

____

What is the writer's position on the issue?

____

____

3. List some of the reasons the writer uses to support his position. The first reason has been listed for you.

The most important reason to vote is that government affects every aspect of our lives.

____

____

____

____

4. Where does the writer address an opposing argument?

____

____

◆ PRACTICE 7.42

Following are four topic sentences for argument paragraphs. For each statement, list three points that could support the statement. For example, if you were arguing in favor of banning smoking in all public places, you could say that smoking is a nuisance, a health risk, and a fire hazard.

1. Employers should offer flexible time schedules to employees.

____

____

____

2. Women's college sports teams should be supported on an equal level with men's teams.

____

____

____

3. Driving under the influence of alcohol is a widespread problem among young people.

____

____

____

4. The space exploration program benefits everyone.

____

____

____

◆ PRACTICE 7.43

Choose one of the following topics (or one of your own choice) as the subject of an argument paragraph. Then, on a separate sheet of paper, state your position on the issue and list as much support (facts, examples, and reasons) as you can to back up your position. Use the invention strategies discussed in 5B to help you think of supporting points.

- Why you would be a good president
- Why stricter gun control is a good (bad) idea
- Is college necessary for success?
- Is our right to privacy being lost?
- Why capital punishment is a good (bad) idea
- A law that should be changed
- Why a particular improvement is needed in your town or neighborhood
- Courses or requirements that your school should change or add
- Why laws requiring motorcycle riders to wear helmets are a good (bad) idea
- Why workplaces should offer childcare facilities
- An environmental policy or issue
- A health-care issue
- Safety on your campus
- Financial aid policies at your school
- Campus drug or alcohol policies

◆ PRACTICE 7.44

On a separate sheet of paper, write an argument paragraph on the topic you chose in Practice 7.43. When you have finished, use the Self-Assessment Checklist on page 133 to help you revise your paragraph.

◆ PRACTICE 7.45

On a separate sheet of paper, write a final, edited draft of your argument paragraph.

■ REVISING AND EDITING

Look back at your response to the Seeing and Writing exercise on page 104. First, determine which pattern of development your paragraph most closely matches. Then consult the appropriate Self-Assessment Checklist (Exemplification, p. 105; Narration, p. 108; Description, p. 112; Process, p. 115; Cause and Effect, p. 119; Comparison and Contrast, p. 123; Classification, p. 127; Definition, p. 130; or Argument, p. 133). Next, referring to Chapter 6 if necessary, evaluate your paragraph for unity, development, and coherence. Finally, make any necessary revisions.

✓ REVIEW CHECKLIST:
Patterns of Paragraph Development

- ☐ Exemplification paragraphs use specific examples to support the topic sentence. (See 7A.)
- ☐ Narrative paragraphs tell a story by presenting a series of events in time order. (See 7B.)
- ☐ Descriptive paragraphs use specific details to communicate a dominant impression. (See 7C.)
- ☐ Process paragraphs explain how something works or how something is done. (See 7D.)
- ☐ Cause-and-effect paragraphs tell readers why something happened or is happening or how one thing affects something else. (See 7E.)
- ☐ Comparison-and-contrast paragraphs explain how two things are alike or how they are different. (See 7F.)
- ☐ Classification paragraphs explain how a variety of items can be sorted into categories. (See 7G.)
- ☐ Definition paragraphs tell what a word or term means. (See 7H.)
- ☐ Argument paragraphs support a position on a debatable issue. (See 7I.)

CHAPTER 8

Moving from Paragraph to Essay

PREVIEW

In this chapter, you will learn

- to understand essay structure (8A)
- to decide on a topic (8B)
- to use invention strategies (8C)
- to state your thesis (8D)
- to select and arrange ideas (8E)
- to draft your essay (8F)
- to revise and edit your essay (8G)

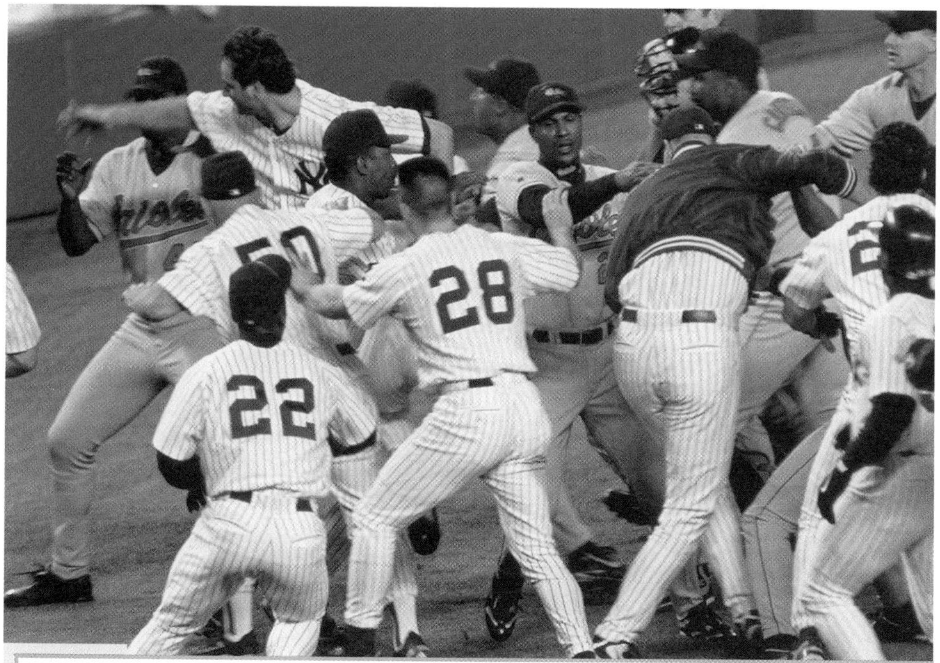

SEEING AND WRITING

Do you think there is too much violence in sports? Why or why not? Look at the picture above as you think about these questions. This chapter will take you through the process of writing an essay about the topic of violence in sports.

Word Power

brawl a noisy fight

altercation a quarrel

A Understanding Essay Structure

In the previous chapters, we have been discussing paragraphs. Now we will focus on essays. An **essay** is a group of paragraphs about one subject. In this chapter, you will see how the strategies you learned for writing paragraphs can also be helpful in writing essays.

For information on how to write a paragraph, see Chapter 5.

In some ways, essays and paragraphs are similar. In a paragraph, the main idea is presented in a topic sentence, and the rest of the paragraph supports this main idea.

Paragraph

The **topic sentence** states the main idea of the paragraph.

Support develops the main idea with details, facts, and examples.

Writing Tip
Many writing situations outside of school require you to write more than one paragraph. The skills you learn in this chapter can also be applied to these writing tasks.

In an essay, the main idea is presented in a **thesis statement**. The first paragraph—the **introduction**—presents the thesis statement. The main part of the essay consists of several **body paragraphs** that support the thesis statement. (Each of these body paragraphs contains a topic sentence that states the paragraph's main idea, one point in support of the essay's thesis.) The essay ends with a **conclusion** that restates the thesis statement (in different words) and brings the essay to a close. This essay structure is called **thesis and support**.

Thesis-and-Support Essay

Opening remarks introduce the subject to be discussed.

The **thesis statement** presents the main idea of the essay in the last sentence of the first paragraph.

Introduction

Topic sentence (first point)

Support (details, facts, examples)

Topic sentence (second point)

Support (details, facts, examples)

Body paragraphs

Topic sentence (third point)

Support (details, facts, examples)

Body paragraphs

The **restatement of the thesis** summarizes the essay's main idea.

Closing remarks present the writer's last thoughts on the subject.

Conclusion

The rest of this chapter will introduce you to the process of writing a **thesis-and-support essay**.

B Deciding on a Topic

Most of the essays you write in college will be in response to assignments that your instructors give you. In your writing class, you may be given general assignments such as the following ones:

- Discuss something your school could do to improve the lives of returning older students.
- Examine a decision you made that changed your life.
- Write about someone you admire.

Before you can respond to these general assignments, you will need to ask yourself some questions. Exactly what could your school do to improve the lives of older students? What decision did you make that changed your life? What person do you admire? By asking yourself questions like these, you can narrow these general assignments to specific **topics** that you can write about.

- Free day care for students
- The effects of giving up smoking
- My grandfather

◆ PRACTICE 8.1

The following assignments are too general for an essay of four or five paragraphs. In the blank that follows each assignment, narrow the topic down so it is suitable for a brief essay.

Example: How has technology made your life easier?

How my computer makes my college work easier

1. A personal problem you have solved

   ____

2. Write an essay that offers some survival skills to students at your school

   ____

3. A problem in your community

   ____

4. Violence in the media

   ____

5. Censorship

   ____

C Using Invention Strategies

For a discussion of these invention strategies, see 5B.

Once you have a topic, you need to find something to say about it. You do this by using invention strategies—*freewriting, brainstorming, clustering,* or *journal writing*—just as you do when you write a paragraph.

◆ PRACTICE 8.2

Reread the Seeing and Writing exercise on page 137, and review section 5B of this text. Then, on a separate sheet of paper, use whatever invention strategies you like to help you generate material for an essay on violence in sports. If your instructor gives you permission, you may discuss your ideas with other students.

D Stating Your Thesis

Once you have used one or more invention strategies to help you find information about your topic, you need to decide what specific points you want to make about this topic. You begin doing this by looking through your invention material to see what main idea it can support. You express this main idea in a single sentence called a **thesis statement**.

Topic	*Thesis Statement*
Free day care for students	Free day care on campus would improve the lives of the many students who are also parents.

Topic	*Thesis Statement*
The effects of giving up smoking	Giving up smoking saved me money and gave me self-respect.
My grandfather	Even though he is over sixty years older than I am, my grandfather is my role model.

To be effective, a thesis statement must do two things:

- *An effective thesis statement must make a point about your topic.* For this reason, it must do more than simply state a fact or announce the subject of your essay.

STATEMENT OF FACT	Free day care is not available on our campus.
ANNOUNCEMENT	In this essay, I will discuss free day care on campus.
EFFECTIVE THESIS STATEMENT	Free day-care on campus would improve the lives of the many students who are also parents.

- *An effective thesis statement must be specific and clearly worded.*

VAGUE THESIS STATEMENT	Giving up smoking helped me a lot.
EFFECTIVE THESIS STATEMENT	Giving up smoking saved me money and gave me self-respect.

FOCUS Stating Your Thesis

The thesis that you state at this stage of the writing process is not definite; it is *tentative.* As you write, you will probably change this tentative thesis—perhaps several times.

◆ PRACTICE 8.3

In the space provided, indicate whether each of the following items is a fact (F), an announcement (A), a vague statement (VS), or an effective thesis (ET). If your instructor gives you permission, you can break into groups and do this exercise collaboratively.

Examples

I spend an hour each day, five days a week, working on college algebra. F

College algebra is my favorite course. ET

1. In this paper, I will discuss challenging and high-paying careers that are open to math majors. ____
2. Following some specific strategies can help students improve their grades. ____
3. Domestic violence is a problem. ____
4. Several local programs that help victims of domestic violence deserve more funding. ____
5. Flexible work hours have many advantages for both employers and employees. ____
6. A community center can help strengthen a neighborhood by providing needed programs and services. ____
7. Neighborhood community centers are a good idea. ____
8. Many students must work while attending college. ____
9. The minimum wage is below $6 an hour in many states. ____
10. An increase in the minimum wage is necessary and long overdue. ____

◆ PRACTICE 8.4

Carefully review the material you have gathered for your essay about violence in sports. Then write a tentative thesis statement for your essay on the following lines.

____

____

E Selecting and Arranging Ideas

After you have decided on a tentative thesis statement, your next step is to decide on the individual points you will use to support it. When you have identified the points you will discuss, list them in the order in which you intend to write about them. For example, you might arrange the points from most general to most specific or from least important to most important. You can use this list of points as a rough outline for your essay.

◆ PRACTICE 8.5

Copy the tentative thesis statement you wrote in Practice 8.4 on the lines below.

____

____

Now, review the material you came up with in Practice 8.2, and decide which points you will use to support your thesis statement. List those points on the lines below.

____

____

____

____

Finally, arrange these points in the order in which you plan to write about them. Cross out any points that do not support your thesis statement.

1. ____

2. ____

3. ____

4. ____

5. ____

F Drafting Your Essay

Once you have decided on a thesis and have arranged your points in the order in which you will present them, you are ready to draft your essay. Each paragraph should include a topic sentence that states a point in support of the thesis. It should also include the details, facts, and examples readers will need to understand the point.

Keep in mind that you are writing a rough draft, one that you will revise and edit later. Your goal at this point is simply to get your ideas down so that you can react to them. Even so, your draft should have a thesis-and-support structure.

Here is the first draft of an essay by David Weaver, a student in an introductory writing class. Before he wrote his essay, David went through the process discussed in this chapter: he decided on a topic, brainstormed and wrote a journal entry, decided on a tentative thesis, and selected and arranged ideas.

Writing Tip

Put brackets around questions you think of as you write [like this]. Later, when you revise your work, you can think of answers to the questions.

Computer Tip

Don't be afraid to skip around in your document while you draft. You can go back to add an idea that occurs to you, or you can write a later section first if you find that easier.

My Grandfather, My Role Model

My grandfather, Richard Weaver, is seventy years old and lives in Leola, a small town outside Lancaster, Pennsylvania. When I was eight, I lived with my grandparents for almost a year. During that time, my grandfather became my role model.

When I lived with my grandparents, there was never a dull moment. My grandfather always had interesting and unusual ideas. He showed me that you don't have to spend money or go places to have a good time. An afternoon in his workshop was more than enough to keep me entertained all day. Working next to my grandfather, I learned the value of having patience and of doing a job right the first time.

If there ever is a problem, you can always count on my grandfather because he is a very caring and understanding person. He not only cares about his family, but he also cares about the whole community. He is known in the community as a caring and sharing person. Whenever anyone needs help, he is always there—whatever the cost or personal inconvenience.

One major thing that my grandfather taught me is always to be honest. He told me that in the long run, honesty will be its own reward. He taught me that if you find something that is not yours, you should make an effort to find the person who it belongs to so that the person will not suffer from the loss. This also shows how caring of other people my grandfather is.

These characteristics—doing a job right, caring, and being honest—describe my grandfather. Now that I have grown up, I have adopted these special and important characteristics of his.

◆ PRACTICE 8.6

Reread David Weaver's first draft. What changes would you suggest he make? What might he add? What might he delete? Write your suggestions on the following lines. If your instructor gives you permission, you can break into groups and do this exercise collaboratively.

____

____

____

____

◆ PRACTICE 8.7

Writing Tip

Triple-space your rough drafts. This will make revision easier.

On a separate sheet of paper, write a draft of your essay about violence in sports. Be sure to include the thesis statement you drafted in Practice 8.4 as well as your list of points from the last part of Practice 8.5.

G Revising and Editing Your Essay

When you **revise** your essay, you reconsider the choices you made when you wrote your first draft. As a result of this reevaluation, you rethink (and frequently rewrite) parts of your essay. Some of your changes will be major—

for example, deleting several sentences or even crossing out or adding whole paragraphs. Other changes will be minor—for example, crossing out a sentence or adding or deleting a word or phrase.

Before you begin to revise, try to put your essay aside for at least an hour or two. Time away from your essay will help you distance yourself from your writing so you can see it critically. When you do start to revise, keep in mind that revision is not a neat process. Don't be afraid to revise directly on your first draft, marking it up with lines, arrows, and crossouts as well as writing between the lines and in the margins.

When you are finished revising, **edit** your essay, concentrating on grammar, punctuation, mechanics, and spelling.

To make your revision and editing more orderly and more efficient, you may want to use the following checklists to guide you.

Computer Tip

Be sure to revise and edit on a printed hard copy of your essay at least once. Many errors are easier to spot on a hard copy than on a computer screen.

Computer Tip

When you cut material from your draft, paste it at the end of the draft or in a separate file. Do not delete material until you are sure you will not need it.

✓ SELF-ASSESSMENT CHECKLIST: Revising Your Essay

- ☐ Does your essay have an introduction, a body, and a conclusion?
- ☐ Does your essay have a clearly worded thesis statement?
- ☐ Does your thesis statement make a point about your topic?
- ☐ Does each body paragraph have a topic sentence?
- ☐ Does each body paragraph focus on one point that supports the thesis statement?
- ☐ Are the body paragraphs unified, well developed, and coherent? (See Chapter 5.)
- ☐ Does your conclusion restate your thesis?

✓ SELF-ASSESSMENT CHECKLIST: Editing Your Essay

Editing for Common Sentence Problems

- ☐ Have you avoided run-ons and comma splices? (See Chapter 14.)
- ☐ Have you avoided sentence fragments? (See Chapter 15.)
- ☐ Do your subjects and verbs agree? (See Chapter 16.)
- ☐ Have you avoided illogical shifts? (See Chapter 17.)
- ☐ Have you avoided dangling and misplaced modifiers? (See Chapter 18.)

(continued on the following page)

(continued from the previous page)

Editing for Grammar

- Are your verb forms and verb tenses correct? (See Chapters 19 and 20.)
- Have you used nouns and pronouns correctly? (See Chapters 21 and 22.)
- Have you used adjectives and adverbs correctly? (See Chapter 23.)

Editing for Punctuation, Mechanics, and Spelling

- Have you used commas correctly? (See Chapter 25.)
- Have you used apostrophes correctly? (See Chapter 26.)
- Have you used capital letters where they are required? (See Chapter 27.)
- Have you used quotation marks correctly where they are needed? (See Chapter 27.)
- Have you spelled every word correctly? (See Chapter 28.)

Computer Tip

Use the Search function to find common spelling errors that the spell checker will not catch—the use of *there* instead of *their,* for example.

Writing Tip

Schedule an appointment with your instructor or with a writing lab tutor if you think you will need help with revising your essay.

When David Weaver revised his essay about his grandfather, he decided to change his tentative thesis statement so that it reflected what he had actually written. In addition, he added topic sentences to help readers see how his body paragraphs related to his thesis statement. To do this, he added transitional words and phrases (*one thing; another thing; the most important thing*). He also added examples to clarify several generalizations that he had made in his body paragraphs. (He took some of these examples from his journal.) Finally, he expanded his introduction and conclusion.

After he finished revising and editing his essay, David proofread it to make sure that he had not missed any errors. Then he made sure his essay conformed to his instructor's guidelines.

FOCUS Guidelines for Submitting Your Papers

Always follow the requirements that your instructor gives you for submitting papers.

- Use good-quality 8½- by 11-inch paper.
- Unless your instructor tells you otherwise, type your name, your instructor's name, the course name and number, and the date (day, month, year) in the upper left-hand corner, one-half inch from the top.

(continued on the following page)

(continued from the previous page)

- Type on one side of each sheet of paper.
- Double-space your work.
- Leave one-inch margins on all sides of the page.
- Type your last name and the page number in the upper right-hand corner of each page (including the first page).

Here is the final draft of David's essay.

```
David Weaver                                      Weaver 1
Professor Yanella
Composition 101
18 Oct. 2003
```

My Grandfather, My Role Model

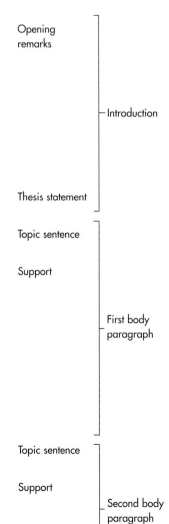

My grandfather, Richard Weaver, is seventy years old and lives in Leola, a small town outside of Lancaster, Pennsylvania. He has lived there his entire life. As a young man, he apprenticed as a stone mason and eventually started his own business. He worked as a stone mason until he got silicosis and had to retire. He now works part time for the local water department. When I was eight, my mother was very sick, and I lived with my grandparents for almost a year. During that time, my grandfather taught me lessons about life and became my role model. [Opening remarks; Thesis statement — Introduction]

One thing my grandfather taught me is that I did not have to spend money or go places to have a good time. An afternoon in his workshop was more than enough to keep me entertained all day. We spent many hours together working on small projects, such as building a wagon, and large projects, such as building a tree house. My grandfather even designed a pulley system that carried me from the roof of his house to the tree house. Working next to my grandfather, I also learned the value of patience and of hard work. He never cut corners or compromised. He taught me that it was easier to do the job right the first time than to do it twice. [Topic sentence; Support — First body paragraph]

Another thing my grandfather taught me is the importance of helping others. Whenever anyone needs help, my grandfather is always there—whatever the cost or personal inconvenience. One afternoon a year ago, a friend called him from work and asked him to help fix a broken water pipe. My grandfather immediately canceled his plans and went to help. When he was a member of the [Topic sentence; Support — Second body paragraph]

Weaver 2

volunteer fire department, my grandfather refused to quit even though my grandmother thought the job was too dangerous. His answer was typical of him: he said that because people depended on him, he could not let them down.

Third body paragraph — Topic sentence; Support

The most important thing my grandfather taught me is that honesty is its own reward. One day, when my grandfather and I were in a mall, I found a wallet. I held it up and proudly showed it to my grandfather. When I opened it up and saw the money inside, I couldn't believe it. I had wanted a mountain bike for the longest time, but every time I had asked my grandfather for one, he had told me to be thankful for what I already had. So when I saw the money, I thought that my prayers had been answered. My grandfather, however, had other ideas. He told me that we would have to call the owner of the wallet and tell him that we had found it. Later that night, we called the owner (his name was on his driver's license inside the wallet), and he came over to pick up his money. As soon as I saw him, I knew that my grandfather was right. The owner looked as if he really needed the money. When he offered me a reward, I told him no. After he left, my grandfather told me how proud of me he was.

Conclusion — Restatement of thesis; Closing remarks

These characteristics—doing a job right, being caring, and being honest—make my grandfather my role model. Now that I have grown up, I have adopted these special and important qualities of his. I only hope that someday I can pass them on to my own children and grandchildren the way my grandfather passed them on to me.

◆ PRACTICE 8.8

What material did David add to his draft? What did he delete? Why do you think he made these changes? Write your answers on the following lines.

____

____

____

____

____

____

____

◆ PRACTICE 8.9

Reread the final draft of David's essay. Do you think this draft is an improvement over the previous one? What other changes could David have made? Write your suggestions on the following lines.

___

___

___

___

___

___

___

■ REVISING AND EDITING

■ Using the Self-Assessment Checklist for revising your essay on page 145 as a guide, evaluate the essay that you wrote in this chapter. Can you support your points more fully? What points can you delete? Can any ideas be stated more clearly? (You may want to get feedback by exchanging essays with another student.) On the following lines, describe any changes you think you should make to your draft.

___

___

___

___

___

___

___

___

■ Revise and edit the draft of your essay, writing any new material between the lines or in the margins. Then, edit this revised draft, using the Self-Assessment Checklist for editing your essay on pages 145–146 to find errors in grammar, punctuation, mechanics, and spelling.

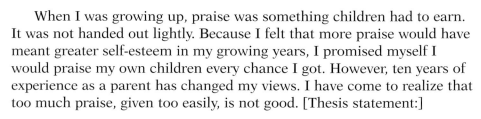

CHAPTER REVIEW

◆ EDITING PRACTICE

After reading the following incomplete essay, write an appropriate thesis statement on the lines provided. (Make sure your thesis statement clearly communicates the essay's main idea.) Next, fill in the topic sentences for the second, third, and fourth paragraphs. Finally, restate the thesis (in different words) in your conclusion.

To Praise or Not to Praise

Father applauding daughter's performance

When I was growing up, praise was something children had to earn. It was not handed out lightly. Because I felt that more praise would have meant greater self-esteem in my growing years, I promised myself I would praise my own children every chance I got. However, ten years of experience as a parent has changed my views. I have come to realize that too much praise, given too easily, is not good. [Thesis statement:]

____

____

____

[Topic sentence for the second paragraph:] ____________________

____

____

When children feel they are valued, they learn more easily and work harder when the going gets tough. Self-doubt makes children too frightened of failure to take risks and overcome obstacles. When my older son, Tim, was a preschooler, I gave him lots of praise to build his self-esteem. My strategy worked. He is now a confident fifth-grader who does well in school and has many friends. I did the same for Zachary, who is six, with the same good results.

[Topic sentence for the third paragraph:] ____________________

____

____

____

When you praise children, they know what is expected of them. They develop a set of inner rules, called a conscience, that with luck will last a lifetime. I believe that praise works better than criticism in molding a child's behavior. For example, when Tim was jealous of his newborn baby brother, my husband and I did not respond with criticism or threats. Instead, we encouraged Tim to help take care of the baby and praised him for doing so. He caught on, and his jealousy disappeared. If we had criticized or threatened him, I am sure his natural jealousy of the baby would have gotten worse.

[Topic sentence for the fourth paragraph:] ______________________

____

____

One of the harmful effects of praising my children too much was that they did not continue working on anything once they were praised for it. If I told them a first draft of a report or a drawing or a kite they were making was good, they put it aside and stopped working on it. Then they would get angry if I tried to get them to improve their work. I finally learned not to praise things that needed more effort. I learned to say things like, "Tell me more about the topic of this report. It's interesting. What else do you know about it?" It took a while before I learned how to say things so that I was not criticizing the children but also was not overpraising them.

[Restatement of thesis in conclusion:] ______________________

____

____

____

My children seem to be less dependent on praise than they used to be, and they work harder at getting things right. I hope to use these new techniques in my future career as a preschool teacher and also teach them to other parents.

◆ COLLABORATIVE ACTIVITIES

1. Working with another student, find an article in a magazine or a newspaper about a controversial issue that interests both of you. Then identify the thesis statement in the article and the main points used to support that thesis. Underline topic sentences that state these points, and make a list of the details, facts, and examples that support each topic sentence. How does the article use the thesis-and-support structure to discuss the issue? How could the article be improved?
2. Working in a small group, develop thesis statements suitable for essays on two of the following topics.

   True friendship

   Professional athletes' salaries

   Censoring the Internet

   The value of volunteer work

   A course I will always remember

Improving the public schools

A favorite electronic gadget

A community problem

3. Choose one of the thesis statements you wrote for activity 2. Working with another student, make a list of at least three points that could be used to support the thesis.

✓ REVIEW CHECKLIST: Moving from Paragraph to Essay

- ☐ Many essays have a thesis-and-support structure: the thesis statement presents the main idea, and the body paragraphs support the thesis. (See 8A.)
- ☐ When you write an essay, begin by deciding on a topic. (See 8B.)
- ☐ Use one or more invention strategies to narrow your focus and find ideas to write about. (See 8C.)
- ☐ State your main idea in a thesis statement. (See 8D.)
- ☐ List the points that best support your thesis, and arrange them in the order in which you plan to discuss them. (See 8E.)
- ☐ As you write your first draft, make sure your essay has a thesis-and-support structure. (See 8F.)
- ☐ Revise your essay. (See 8F, 8G.)
- ☐ Edit the final draft of your essay. (See 8G.)

UNIT THREE

Writing Effective Sentences

CHAPTER

9

Writing Simple Sentences

PREVIEW

In this chapter, you will learn

- to identify a sentence's subject (9A)
- to recognize singular and plural subjects (9B)
- to identify prepositions and prepositional phrases (9C)
- to distinguish a prepositional phrase from a subject (9C)
- to identify action verbs (9D)
- to identify linking verbs (9E)
- to identify main verbs and helping verbs (9F)

SEEING AND WRITING

If you met a person who had never been to McDonald's, what would you tell him or her about this fast-food restaurant? Look at the picture above, and then write a paragraph that answers this question.

A **sentence** is a group of words that expresses a complete thought. A sentence includes a subject and a verb.

McDonald's is an American institution.

Word Power

institution a well-known person, place, or thing; something that has become associated with a particular place

A Identifying Subjects

The **subject** of a sentence tells who or what is being talked about in the sentence.

Marissa did research on the Internet.

Research helped her find a topic for her paper.

It was due in March.

The subject of a sentence can be a noun or a pronoun. A **noun** names a person, place, or thing—*Marissa, research.* A **pronoun** takes the place of a noun—*I, you, he, she, it, we, they.*

For more on avoiding problems with subjects, see 24A and 24B.

FOCUS Simple and Complete Subjects

A sentence's **simple subject** is just a noun or a pronoun.

house witch she it they

A sentence's **complete subject** is the simple subject along with all the words that describe it.

our new house

the haunted house

a wicked witch

A two-word name, such as *Victor Frankenstein,* is a simple subject.

◆ PRACTICE 9.1

ON THE WEB
For more practice identifying subjects, visit Exercise Central at <bedfordstmartins.com/foundationsfirst>.

Underline the simple subject of each of the following sentences twice. Then, underline the complete subject of each sentence (the noun or pronoun that tells who or what the sentence is about and also all the words that describe the subject).

Example: Reality shows are very popular with television viewers.

(1) Reality TV actually began in the 1960s. (2) One early television reality show was called *Candid Camera*. (3) This show was on the air from 1960 to 1966. (4) Hidden cameras recorded people in unusual situations. (5) A man in a coffee shop once dunked his doughnut into strangers' coffee cups. (6) The strangers' reactions were shown on television. (7) They did not know about the cameras. (8) The host revealed the presence of *Candid Camera* after a few minutes. (9) Many viewers learned something about psychology from this show. (10) *Candid Camera*'s creator even won an award from the American Psychological Association.

◆ PRACTICE 9.2

Write in a simple subject that tells *who* or *what* is being talked about in the sentence.

Example: The ___wind___ howled.

1. __________ was terrified.
2. The __________ was very loud.
3. __________ banged on the roof.
4. The __________ barked in the distance.
5. The __________ rapped on the window.
6. __________ screamed and ran to the door.
7. Opening the door, __________ saw a frightening sight.
8. __________ closed the door immediately.
9. Outside, the __________ grew stronger.
10. Finally, __________ and __________ arrived.

◆ PRACTICE 9.3

The following sentences are not complete because they have no subjects. Complete each sentence by adding a subject—a word or words telling *who* or *what* is being talked about in the sentence.

Example: Runs a small business.

My sister runs a small business.

1. Crashed through the picture window.

   ____

2. Are my least favorite foods.

   ____

3. Gave the players a pep talk during halftime.

   ____

4. Fell from the sky.

   ____

5. Placed the glass slipper on Cinderella's foot.

   ____

6. Always makes me cry.

   ____

7. Disappeared into a black hole.

____

8. Really meant a lot to me.

____

9. Ate five pounds of chocolate-covered cherries.

____

10. Lived happily ever after in a cave.

____

B Recognizing Singular and Plural Subjects

Writing Tip

Sometimes an *-ing* word can be a singular subject: *Studying is important.*

The subject of a sentence can be *singular* or *plural.* A **singular subject** is one person, place, or thing (*Marissa, research, she*).

A **plural subject** is more than one person, place, or thing (*students, papers, they*).

Students often do research on the Internet.

For information on subject-verb agreement with compound subjects, see 16C.

A plural subject that joins two subjects with *and* is called a **compound subject**.

Marissa and Jason did research on the Internet.

◆ PRACTICE 9.4

Each item listed here could be the subject of a sentence. Write *S* after each item that could be a singular subject, and write *P* after each item that could be a plural subject.

ON THE WEB
For more practice recognizing singular and plural subjects, visit Exercise Central at <bedfordstmartins.com/foundationsfirst>.

Examples

Joey Ramone S

The Ramones P

Joey and Johnny Ramone P

1. hot-fudge sundaes ____
2. the USS *Enterprise* ____
3. a blue-eyed baby girl ____
4. the McCaughey septuplets ____
5. my Web site ____
6. three blind mice ____
7. Betty and Barney Rubble ____

8. her two children ____

9. Texas ____

10. Ruben Blades ____

◆ PRACTICE 9.5

First, underline the complete subject in each sentence. Then label each singular subject *S*, and label each plural subject *P*. (Remember that a compound subject is plural.)

Example: The Vietnam Veterans Memorial (S) opened to the public on November 11, 1982.

1. The memorial honors men and women killed or missing in the Vietnam War.
2. More than 58,000 names appear on the black granite wall.
3. More than two and a half million people visit the Memorial each year.
4. People leave mementoes at the site.
5. Some visitors, for example, leave letters and photographs.
6. Other people leave items like combat boots, stuffed animals, rosaries, and dog tags.
7. One man leaves a six-pack of beer each year.
8. Visitors also leave cigarettes, flowers, canned food, and clothing.
9. Spouses, children, parents, and friends leave offerings for men and women lost in the war.
10. A Persian Gulf War veteran left his medal for his father.

C Identifying Prepositional Phrases

As you have seen, every sentence needs a subject and a verb. As you try to identify sentence subjects, you may be confused by nouns or pronouns that cannot be subjects because they are part of prepositional phrases. If you learn to identify prepositional phrases, you will not have this problem.

A **prepositional phrase** is made up of a **preposition** (a word like *on, to, in,* or *with*) and its **object** (a noun or pronoun).

Preposition	+	*Object*	=	*Prepositional Phrase*
on		the roof		on the roof
to		Leah's apartment		to Leah's apartment
in		my Spanish class		in my Spanish class
with		her		with her

Writing Tip

A **phrase** is a group of words that is missing a subject or a verb or both. A phrase cannot stand alone as a sentence. (See 15B.)

Writing Tip

Prepositions are often combined with other words to form familiar expressions: *Debbie is addicted to chocolate.* (See 24L.)

Because the object of a preposition is a noun or a pronoun, it may look like the subject of a sentence. However, the object of a preposition can never be a subject. To identify a sentence's subject, cross out every prepositional phrase.

SUBJECT — PREPOSITIONAL PHRASE

The price ~~of a new home~~ ~~in the San Francisco Bay area~~ is very high.

After you cross out the prepositional phrases, you will easily be able to identify the sentence's subject. Remember, every prepositional phrase is introduced by a preposition.

For more on prepositions, see 24K–24M.

Frequently Used Prepositions

about	behind	for	off	toward
above	below	from	on	under
across	beneath	in	onto	underneath
after	beside	including	out	until
against	between	inside	outside	up
along	beyond	into	over	upon
among	by	like	through	with
around	despite	near	throughout	within
at	during	of	to	without
before	except			

◆ PRACTICE 9.6

Each of the sentences in the following paragraph includes at least one prepositional phrase. To identify a sentence's subject, first cross out each prepositional phrase. Then underline the simple subject.

Example: The Internet has changed our world ~~in many ways~~.

ON THE WEB
For more practice identifying prepositional phrases, visit Exercise Central at <bedfordstmartins.com/foundationsfirst>.

(1) The Internet has been the inspiration for many new businesses. (2) One of the most successful is eBay, an online auction site. (3) This site is an electronic version of a garage sale, collectibles show, and flea market. (4) The company began by selling collectibles. (5) Soon, however, the founders hired a team of business managers. (6) The goal of these managers was to expand the auction. (7) Today auction items consist of antiques, cars, jewelry, DVDs, pet supplies, and many other things. (8) Some of the items are new; others are used. (9) Buyers on eBay browse the site and then place a bid. (10) Sellers pay for listing their items and then for selling them.

D Identifying Action Verbs

An **action verb** tells what the subject does, did, or will do.

Tiger Woods plays golf.

Columbus sailed across the ocean.

Andrea will go to Houston next month.

Action verbs can also show mental or emotional action.

Nirav often thinks about his future.

Wendy loves backpacking.

When the subject of a sentence performs more than one action, the sentence includes two or more action verbs joined to form a **compound predicate**.

Lois left work, drove to Somerville, and met Carmen for dinner.

◆ PRACTICE 9.7

Underline all the action verbs in each of the following sentences.

Example: Many nineteenth-century Americans left their homes and journeyed to unfamiliar places.

(1) During the 1840s, thousands of Americans traveled west to places like Oregon, Nevada, and California. (2) Many travelers began their journey in Independence, Missouri. (3) In towns all around Missouri, travelers advertised in newspapers for strong young companions for the journey west. (4) Thousands of wagons eventually departed from Independence on the dangerous four-month trip to California. (5) Whole families packed their bags and joined wagon trains. (6) The wagons carried food, supplies, and weapons. (7) Some travelers wrote letters to friends and relatives back east. (8) Others wrote in journals. (9) From these letters and journals, we understand the travelers' fear and misery. (10) Traveling 2,500 miles west across plains, deserts, and mountains, many people suffered and died.

ON THE WEB
For more practice identifying action verbs, visit Exercise Central at <bedfordstmartins .com/foundationsfirst>.

◆ PRACTICE 9.8

Insert an action verb in each space to show what action the subject is (or was) performing.

Example: I ___drove___ my car to the grocery store.

1. Good athletes sometimes __________ but often __________.
2. After opening the letter, Michele __________.
3. The little boat __________ and __________ on top of the waves.
4. Thousands of people __________ in the rain.
5. The computer __________, __________, and died.
6. The hurricane __________ the residents and __________ the town.
7. Smoke __________ out of the windows.
8. The Doberman __________.
9. A voice __________ from the balcony.
10. Wanda __________ the door.

E Identifying Linking Verbs

A **linking verb** does not show action. Instead, it connects the subject to a word or words that describe or rename the subject.

Calculus is a difficult course.

In this sentence, the linking verb (*is*) links the subject (*calculus*) to the words that describe it (*a difficult course*).

Many linking verbs, such as *is,* are forms of the verb *be.* Other linking verbs refer to the senses (*look, feel, seem,* and so on).

Tremaine looks very handsome today.

Time seemed to pass quickly.

Frequently Used Linking Verbs

act	become	look	sound
appear	feel	remain	taste
be (am, is, are, was, were)	get	seem	turn
	grow	smell	

◆ PRACTICE 9.9

Underline the verb in each of the following sentences. Then, in the blank, indicate whether the verb is an action verb (*AV*) or a linking verb (*LV*).

ON THE WEB
For more practice identifying linking verbs, visit Exercise Central at <bedfordstmartins.com/foundationsfirst>.

Example: Working mothers face difficult decisions. AV

1. Some women leave careers to raise their children. ____
2. My neighbor Jeanne was a graphic designer for twelve years. ____
3. She quit work to stay home with her baby. ____

4. Now her son is six years old and in first grade. _____
5. Jeanne feels ready to return to an office job. _____
6. Twenty years ago, employers usually rejected applicants like Jeanne. ___
7. Even now, employers are sometimes suspicious of gaps in an applicant's employment history. _____
8. However, two companies offered jobs to Jeanne last week. _____
9. They appreciate her skills and experience. _____
10. Today, taking time out to raise a family is not necessarily a career-ending decision. _____

◆ PRACTICE 9.10

Underline the linking verb in each of the following sentences. Then, circle the complete subject and the word or words that describe it.

Example: The juice <u>tasted</u> sour.

1. The night grew cold.
2. The song seems very familiar.
3. In 2000, George W. Bush became the forty-third president of the United States.
4. College students feel pressured by their families, their instructors, and their peers.
5. Many people were outraged at the mayor's announcement.
6. The cheese smelled peculiar.
7. The fans appeared upset by their team's defeat.
8. After the game, the crowd turned ugly.
9. Charlie got sick after eating six corn dogs.
10. A mother's love remains strong and true.

F Identifying Main Verbs and Helping Verbs

Many verbs are made up of more than one word. For example, the verb in the following sentence is made up of two words.

Andrew <u>must make</u> a choice.

In this sentence, *make* is the **main verb**, and *must* is a **helping verb**. A sentence's **complete verb** is made up of the main verb plus all the helping verbs that accompany it.

Helping verbs include forms of *be, have,* and *do* as well as the words *must, will, can, could, may, might, should,* and *would.*

For information on forming negative statements and questions with phrasal verbs, see 24G.

- Some helping verbs, like forms of *be* and *have,* combine with main verbs to give information about when the action occurs.

  Ana has worked at the diner for two years.

- Forms of *do* combine with main verbs to form questions and negative statements.

  Does Ana still work at the diner?

  Ana does not work on Saturdays.

- Other helping verbs indicate ability (*can*), possibility (*may*), necessity (*should*), obligation (*must*), and so on.

  Ana can choose her own hours.

  Ana may work this Saturday.

  Ana should take a vacation this summer.

  Ana must work hard to earn money for college.

Writing Tip

Sometimes other words come between the parts of a complete verb: *Victoria can really succeed in life.*

Writing Tip

Some complete verbs include several helping verbs: *Brian should have called sooner.*

FOCUS Helping Verbs with Participles

Present participles, such as *thinking,* and many irregular **past participles**, such as *gone,* cannot stand alone as main verbs in a sentence. They need a helping verb to make them complete.

INCORRECT Samantha gone to the dentist.

CORRECT Samantha has gone to the dentist.

For information on past participles, see Chapter 20. For information on how to recognize incomplete sentences, see Chapter 15.

◆ PRACTICE 9.11

Each of these sentences includes one or more helping verbs as well as a main verb. Underline the complete verb (the main verb and all the helping verbs) in each sentence. Then, place a check mark above the main verb.

ON THE WEB
For more practice identifying main verbs and helping verbs, visit Exercise Central at <bedfordstmartins.com/foundationsfirst>.

Example: Elizabeth II has been ✔ Queen of England since 1952.

1. Obese adolescents may risk serious health problems as adults.
2. The candidates will name their running mates within two weeks.
3. Henry has been thinking about his decision for a long time.
4. Do you want breakfast now?
5. I could have been a French major.
6. This must be the place.

7. I have often wondered about my family's history.
8. You should have remembered the mustard.
9. Jenelle has always loved animals.
10. Research really does take a long time.

◆ PRACTICE 9.12

Some of the following sentences have only a main verb. Other sentences have a main verb and one or more helping verbs. In each sentence, underline the main verb twice and the complete verb once.

Example: Many teenagers have used email every day for years.

1. Text messaging has become very popular with teenagers.
2. Teens send written messages by cell phone.
3. In fact, many prefer this new method of commucation to email.
4. With text messaging, they can "talk" with friends from school, home, or almost anywhere.
5. They just need fast fingers and a working knowledge of the keypad.
6. Parents and teachers have voiced some objections to text messaging.
7. For one thing, these shortened messages often use incorrect spelling and grammar.
8. For example, a typical message might say, "Txt msgz R kewl."
9. Text messaging can also be expensive.
10. Companies charge users up to 10 cents to send or receive a message.

■ REVISING AND EDITING

Look back at your response to the Seeing and Writing exercise on page 155. Reread it carefully, and then complete the following tasks.

- Put a check mark above the simple subject of every sentence.
- Underline the complete subject (the simple subject plus all the words that describe it) of every sentence once.
- Underline the complete verb (the main verb plus all the helping verbs) of every sentence twice.
- Circle all the helping verbs in each sentence, and put a check mark above the main verb.

CHAPTER REVIEW

◆ EDITING PRACTICE

Read the following essay. Underline the complete subject of each sentence once, and underline the complete verb of each sentence twice. To help you locate the subject, cross out the prepositional phrases. The first sentence has been done for you.

The Triangle Shirtwaist Company Fire

~~On March 25, 1911~~, a terrible event drew attention ~~to unsafe conditions in garment factories across the United States~~. The Triangle Shirtwaist Company occupied the top floors of a ten-story building in New York City. The company employed more than five hundred people, mainly young immigrant women. These women operated sewing machines. The workers could not leave the building during working hours. In fact, the owners locked most of the exit doors during the day.

The Triangle Shirtwaist Company fire

The factory had always been overcrowded and cluttered with scraps of paper and cloth. On that March afternoon, some trash caught fire. The flames spread quickly through the building. Many of the workers were trapped at their sewing machines or behind the locked doors. Fire engine ladders could not reach the upper floors. The fire escapes collapsed under the weight of so many people. In their terror, some people leaped to their deaths from the eighth and ninth floors of the burning building. By late afternoon, one hundred forty-six people had died.

Woman (left) wearing a shirtwaist

No one was ever officially blamed for the tragedy at the Triangle Shirtwaist Company. However, some things did change because of that disaster. For example, American labor unions grew stronger after the fire. Workers now have shorter work weeks and better working conditions. In addition, fire safety is very important at most workplaces. Government agencies investigate on-the-job conditions. With these safeguards, a nightmare like the Triangle Shirtwaist Company fire should never happen again.

◆ COLLABORATIVE ACTIVITIES

1. Working in a group of three or four people, write a subject on one slip of paper. On another slip, write a prepositional phrase; on a third, write a verb. Fold up the slips, keeping subjects, prepositional phrases, and verbs in separate piles. Choose one slip from each pile, and use them to create a sentence, adding whatever other words are necessary.
2. Working in a group of three or four people, have one person write a noun on a blank sheet of paper and pass the paper to the next student, who should add a verb that makes sense with the noun. Then have the second person pass the paper to the third person, who should do one of the following:

   - add words that describe the noun
   - add one or more helping verbs to the main verb
   - begin a new sentence with a new noun

   Keep passing the paper until your group has completed a story several sentences long.
3. *Composing original sentences* Working in a group, create five simple sentences. Make sure each sentence contains a subject and a verb. When you have finished, check the sentences to make sure each sentence begins with a capital letter and ends with a period.

☑ REVIEW CHECKLIST:
Writing Simple Sentences

- The subject tells who or what is being talked about in the sentence. (See 9A.)
- A subject can be singular or plural. (See 9B.)
- The object of a preposition cannot be the subject of a sentence. (See 9C.)
- An action verb tells what the subject does, did, or will do. (See 9D.)
- A linking verb connects the subject to a word or words that describe or rename the subject. (See 9E.)
- Many verbs are made up of more than one word. The complete verb in a sentence includes the main verb plus all the helping verbs. (See 9F.)

CHAPTER

10

Writing Compound Sentences

PREVIEW

In this chapter, you will learn

- to form compound sentences with coordinating conjunctions (10A)
- to form compound sentences with semicolons (10B)
- to form compound sentences with conjunctive adverbs (10C)

■ SEEING AND WRITING

Suppose you wanted to sell this car. Look at the picture above, and then write a paragraph in which you describe the car in a way that would make someone want to buy it.

Word Power

classic something typical or traditional; something that has lasting importance or worth

Writing Tip

A **clause** is a group of words that contains a subject and a verb. An **independent clause** can stand alone as a sentence; a **dependent clause** cannot. For more on dependent clauses, see Chapter 11.

A **compound sentence** is made up of two or more simple sentences joined by a coordinating conjunction, a semicolon, or a conjunctive adverb.

A Forming Compound Sentences with Coordinating Conjunctions

The most basic kind of sentence, a **simple sentence**, consists of a single **independent clause**: one subject and one verb.

Many college students major in psychology.

Many other students major in business.

A **compound sentence** is made up of two or more simple sentences (independent clauses). One way to create a compound sentence is by joining two simple sentences with a **coordinating conjunction**. Always place a comma before the coordinating conjunction.

Many college students major in psychology, but many other students major in business.

Coordinating Conjunctions

and	for	or
but	nor	so
		yet

◆ PRACTICE 10.1

Each of the following compound sentences is made up of two simple sentences joined by a coordinating conjunction. Underline the coordinating conjunction in each compound sentence. Then bracket the two simple sentences. Remember that each simple sentence includes a subject and a verb.

Example: [I do not like unnecessary delays], nor [do I like lame excuses].

1. Speech is silver, but silence is golden.
2. I fought the law, and the law won.
3. The house was dark, so he didn't ring the doorbell.
4. He decided to sign a long-term contract, for he did not want to lose the job.
5. They will not surrender, and they will not agree to a cease-fire.
6. I could order the chicken fajitas, or I could have chili.
7. She has lived in California for years, yet she remembers her childhood in Kansas very clearly.
8. Professor Blakemore was interesting, but Professor Salazar was inspiring.
9. Melody dropped French, and then she added Italian.
10. Give me liberty, or give me death.

ON THE WEB
For more practice forming compound sentences with coordinating conjunctions, visit Exercise Central at <bedfordstmartins.com/foundationsfirst>.

Coordinating conjunctions join ideas that are of equal importance.

Idea (Simple Sentence)	+	**Coordinating Conjunction**	+	**Idea (Simple Sentence)**	=	**Compound Sentence**
Brenda is a vegetarian	+	but	+	Larry eats everything	=	Brenda is a vegetarian, but Larry eats everything.

Coordinating conjunctions describe the relationship between two ideas, showing how and why the ideas are connected. Different coordinating conjunctions have different meanings.

- To indicate addition, use *and.*

  Edgar Allan Poe wrote horror fiction in the nineteenth century, and Stephen King writes horror fiction today.

- To indicate contrast or contradiction, use *but* or *yet.*

  Poe wrote short stories, but King writes both stories and novels.

  Poe died young, yet his stories live on.

- To indicate a cause-and-effect connection, use *so* or *for.*

  I liked *Carrie,* so I decided to read King's other novels.

  Poe's "The Tell-Tale Heart" is a chilling tale, for it is about a horrible murder.

- To present alternatives, use *or.*

  I have to finish *Cujo,* or I won't be able to sleep.

- To eliminate alternatives, use *nor.*

  I have not read *The Green Mile,* nor have I seen the movie.

Writing Tip
Plus and *also* indicate addition, but they are not coordinating conjunctions. They cannot be used to join two simple sentences the way coordinating conjunctions can. (Incorrect: *I have a lot of homework, plus I'm exhausted.* Correct: *I have a lot of homework, and I'm exhausted.*)

Writing Tip
However indicates a contradiction, but it is not a coordinating conjunction. (See 10C.)

Writing Tip
Therefore indicates a cause-and-effect connection, but it is not a coordinating conjunction. (See 10C.)

Writing Tip
When you use *nor* to create a compound sentence, the verb comes before the subject in the second part of the sentence.

FOCUS Using Commas with Coordinating Conjunctions

When you use a coordinating conjunction to join two simple sentences into a compound sentence, always place a comma before the coordinating conjunction.

We can see a movie, or we can go to a club.

However, do not use a comma before a coordinating conjunction that does not join two complete sentences.

INCORRECT We can see a movie, or go to a club.

CORRECT We can see a movie or go to a club.

◆ PRACTICE 10.2

Fill in the coordinating conjunction—*and, but, for, nor, or, so,* or *yet*—that most logically links the two parts of each of the following compound sentences. Remember to insert a comma before each coordinating conjunction.

Example: Many people travel abroad to adopt children, ___for___ adopting internationally is often easier than adopting an American child.

(1) Many people today desperately want children ______ they are unable to conceive a child. (2) For many of these people, adoption is the answer ____ a lot of them will choose international adoption. (3) Children adopted by Americans frequently come from orphanages in poor countries ____ starting a new life in the United States is not always easy for these children. (4) Loving parents and a stable home may be very appealing ______ the child is also leaving a familiar world behind. (5) Years ago, adoption experts told adoptive parents to ignore their children's background ____ most children adopted internationally had no sense of their culture. (6) For example, many Korean children adopted in the 1950s were given American names ____ they often settled in towns with no other Asian children. (7) Now, however, adopted children have a very different experience ____ they adjust more easily. (8) Today, adoptive parents usually try to learn about their children's native country and language ____ teaching adopted children about their native culture is considered essential. (9) Adoptive parents often form support groups for adopted children from a particular country ____ in these groups, their children can meet others with similar backgrounds. (10) Today's adoptive parents no longer ignore their children's cultural backgrounds ____ do they try to make their children conform to an "American" standard.

◆ PRACTICE 10.3

Using the coordinating conjunctions provided, add a complete independent clause to each of the following pairs of sentences to create two different compound sentences. Remember that each coordinating conjunction establishes a different relationship between ideas.

Example

They married at age eighteen, and *they had ten children*________.

They married at age eighteen, so *they grew up together*________.

1. Date rape is a complex and emotional issue, so ____.

   Date rape is a complex and emotional issue, but ____.

2. Drunk drivers should lose their licenses, for ____.

   Drunk drivers should lose their licenses, or ____.

3. A smoke-free environment has many advantages, and ____.

   A smoke-free environment has many advantages, but ____.

4. Female pilots have successfully flown combat missions, yet ____.

   Female pilots have successfully flown combat missions, so ____.

5. The death penalty can be abolished, or ____.

   The death penalty cannot be abolished, nor ____.

◆ PRACTICE 10.4

Add coordinating conjunctions to combine these sentences where necessary to relate one idea to another. Remember to put a comma before each coordinating conjunction you add.

Example: Drive-in movies were a popular form of entertainment in the 1950s. ~~Today,~~ *, but today* only a few drive-ins remain.

(1) Americans love the freedom and independence of driving a car. (2) They also love movies. (3) Not surprisingly, the United States was the home of the very first drive-in movie theater. (4) The first drive-in opened in New Jersey in 1934. (5) The second one, Shankweiler's Drive-In in Orefield, Pennsylvania, opened in the same year. (6) Today, the very first drive-in no longer exists. (7) There is not a single drive-in theater remaining in the entire state of New Jersey. (8) However, Shankweiler's is still open for business. (9) Fans of drive-in theater history have something to celebrate. (10) Shankweiler's Drive-In still has the in-car speakers that moviegoers used to hang in their car windows. (11) They are rarely used. (12) Instead, drive-in visitors simply turn on the car radio to hear the movie sound. (13) Shankweiler's broadcasts movie soundtracks on FM stereo. (14) Anyone with a car, a love of movies, and a sense of history should make a trip to Shankweiler's Drive-In.

◆ PRACTICE 10.5

Write an original compound sentence on each of the following topics. Use the specified coordinating conjunction, and remember to put a comma before the coordinating conjunction in each compound sentence.

Example: *Topic:* course requirements
Coordinating conjunction: but

Composition is a required course for all first-year students, but history is not required.

____

1. *Topic:* the high cost of textbooks
   Coordinating conjunction: so

____

____

____

2. *Topic:* interracial dating
   Coordinating conjunction: but

____

____

____

3. *Topic:* two things you hate to do
   Coordinating conjunction: and

   ____

   ____

4. *Topic:* why you made a certain decision
   Coordinating conjunction: for

   ____

   ____

5. *Topic:* something you regret
   Coordinating conjunction: yet

   ____

   ____

6. *Topic:* two possible career choices
   Coordinating conjunction: or

   ____

   ____

7. *Topic:* two chores you would rather not do
   Coordinating conjunction: nor

   ____

   ____

8. *Topic:* one reason you came to college
   Coordinating conjunction: for

   ____

   ____

9. *Topic:* your favorite musician and musical group
   Coordinating conjunction: and

   ____

   ____

10. *Topic:* a first impression that turned out to be wrong
    Coordinating conjunction: but

    ____

    ____

B Forming Compound Sentences with Semicolons

Another way to create a compound sentence is by joining two simple sentences with a **semicolon**.

The Democrats held their convention in Boston; the Republicans held their convention in New York.

A semicolon connects two ideas. Sometimes you use a semicolon to show a close connection between two ideas.

The Democrats supported gun control; they also supported universal health insurance.

Sometimes you use a semicolon to show a strong contrast between two ideas.

The Democrats supported gun control; the Republicans did not.

FOCUS Avoiding Sentence Fragments

A semicolon can only join two complete sentences. It cannot join a sentence and a fragment.

INCORRECT Because New York City has excellent public transportation [FRAGMENT]; it was a good choice for the convention.

CORRECT New York City has excellent public transportation; it was a good choice for the convention.

For more on avoiding sentence fragments, see Chapter 15.

◆ PRACTICE 10.6

Each of the following items consists of a simple sentence followed by a semicolon. For each item, add another simple sentence to create a compound sentence.

Example: Some people love to watch sports on television; others would rather play a game than watch one.

ON THE WEB
For more practice forming compound sentences with semicolons, visit Exercise Central at <bedfordstmartins .com/foundationsfirst>.

1. Baseball is known as "America's pastime"; ______________________________.

2. The most-played sport in the United States is probably basketball; ______________________________.

3. Soccer has gained popularity in recent years; ______________________________.

4. American football requires size and strength; ______________________________.

5. Professional sports teams usually give their fans something to cheer about; ______________________________.

6. The Olympic Games honor athletes from around the world; ________
____.

7. Individual athletes compete in sports such as track and field; ________
____.

8. Some athletes are models of good sportsmanship; ________
____.

9. A good coach knows how to encourage an athlete; ________
____.

10. Many children admire sports heroes; ________
____.

C Forming Compound Sentences with Conjunctive Adverbs

Another way to create a compound sentence is by joining two simple sentences with a **conjunctive adverb**. When a conjunctive adverb joins two sentences, a semicolon always comes *before* the conjunctive adverb, and a comma always comes *after* it.

> Women's pro basketball games are often sold out; however, not many people watch the games on television.

Frequently Used Conjunctive Adverbs

also	however	still
besides	instead	subsequently
consequently	meanwhile	then
eventually	moreover	therefore
finally	nevertheless	thus
furthermore	otherwise	

Although you can use just a semicolon to link similar or contrasting ideas, adding a conjunctive adverb shows the exact relationship between ideas. Different conjunctive adverbs convey different meanings.

Writing Tip

Do not capitalize the word that follows a semicolon unless it is a proper noun. (See 27A for more on capitalization.)

- Some conjunctive adverbs signal addition: *also, besides, furthermore, moreover.*

  > Golf can be an expensive sport; besides, it can be hard to find a public golf course.

- Some conjunctive adverbs show a cause-and-effect connection: *therefore, consequently, thus.*

Professional baseball players are bigger and stronger than ever before; therefore, home runs have become more common.

- Some conjunctive adverbs indicate contradiction or contrast: *nevertheless, however, still.*

    Some of the world's best athletes are track stars; nevertheless, few of their names are widely known.

- Some conjunctive adverbs present alternatives: *otherwise, instead.*

    Shawn got a football scholarship; otherwise, he could not have gone to college.

    He didn't make the first team; instead, he backed up other players.

- Some conjunctive adverbs indicate time relationships: *finally, meanwhile, subsequently, then.*

    The popularity of women's tennis has been growing; meanwhile, the popularity of men's tennis has been declining.

Writing Tip

When you use a conjunctive adverb or a transitional expression to join two sentences, be sure to use a semicolon, too. If you leave out the semicolon, you create a run-on. (See 14B.)

FOCUS Transitional Expressions

Like conjunctive adverbs, **transitional expressions** can join two simple sentences into one compound sentence.

Soccer has become very popular in the United States; in fact, more American children play soccer than any other sport.

Note that here too a semicolon comes *before* the transitional expression, and a comma comes *after* the transitional expression.

Frequently Used Transitional Expressions

after all	in contrast
as a result	in fact
at the same time	in other words
for example	of course
for instance	on the contrary
in addition	that is
in comparison	

◆ PRACTICE 10.7

Each item below consists of a simple sentence followed by a semicolon and a conjunctive adverb or transitional expression. For each item, add an independent clause to create a complete compound sentence.

Example: Shopping malls have spread throughout the country; in fact, *they have replaced many main streets*.

ON THE WEB

For more practice forming compound sentences with conjunctive adverbs, visit Exercise Central at <bedfordstmartins.com /foundationsfirst>.

1. Nearly every community is near one or more shopping malls; as a result, ____.

2. Some malls include hundreds of stores; moreover, ____.

3. Malls include restaurants as well as stores; therefore, ____.

4. Some malls serve as social centers; in fact, ____.

5. Shopping at malls offers many advantages over traditional shopping; however, ____.

6. Malls offer many employment opportunities; for example, ____.

7. Malls provide a safe, attractive, climate-controlled atmosphere; nevertheless, ____.

8. Many stores seem to have similar merchandise; in addition, ____.

9. The Mall of America, in Minnesota, even includes an amusement park; therefore, ____.

10. Some people think malls are wonderful; still, ________________________

____

____.

◆ PRACTICE 10.8

In each of the following sentences, add a semicolon and a comma to set off the conjunctive adverb or transitional expression that joins the two independent clauses.

Example: Many people are concerned about the environment; however, new technology offers solutions to some of the problems we face.

1. Every day, Americans use about 9.3 billion barrels of gasoline to power their cars and trucks as a result our environment is deteriorating.
2. To save the environment, engineers are looking into other types of fuel at the same time they are redesigning gasoline-powered vehicles to improve their mileage and reduce their emissions.
3. One of the newly designed cars is called a hybrid because it combines gasoline and electric power consequently this car uses less fuel and causes less pollution.
4. Another new type of vehicle will run on hydrogen fuel cells in fact the U.S. government plans to have 3 percent of cars use this technology by 2007.
5. The only emission from cars powered by hydrogen fuel cells is water nevertheless these cars create other problems.
6. Engineers have to find ways to produce and distribute large amounts of hydrogen in addition they have to find a way to keep the carbon dioxide created by hydrogen out of the atmosphere.
7. Some engineers believe that solar power is a good alternative fuel source unfortunately solar-powered cars are complicated to design.
8. The solar car must have a number of solar cells attached to it moreover batteries are needed for storing sunlight to use on cloudy, rainy, or snowy days.

9. Most of these new types of cars have already been designed and tested meanwhile many other problems related to them have yet to be resolved.
10. All of the new cars are cheaper to operate and more friendly to the environment than the gasoline-powered engines in use today still it remains to be seen which design will be most appealing to consumers.

◆ PRACTICE 10.9

Consult the list of conjunctive adverbs on page 176 and the list of transitional expressions on page 177 to choose a word or an expression that logically connects each pair of sentences below into one compound sentence. Be sure to punctuate appropriately.

; however, many

Example: Quilt making is a familiar form of folk art. ~~Many~~ other kinds of folk art are less familiar.

1. Cutting paper into decorative designs is a popular form of folk art. It exists in different cultures around the world.
2. In Germany, artists produce pictures called *scherenschnitte*. French artists produce *silhouettes*, and Chinese artists produce *hua yang*.
3. The Mexican art of paper cutting, called *papel picado,* is very precise. Small, sharp chisels and a hammer are used to cut the paper.
4. The designs are cut into fifty or more layers of colored tissue paper. The cut paper is used as decorations for celebrations.
5. The designs depend on the celebration. Illustrations might celebrate religious figures or christenings.
6. Typically, the *papel picado* are made for the Mexican festival of the Days of the Dead. The images include skeletons performing everyday activities.
7. To make the designs, artisans must first draw a pattern. They lay the pattern on the tissue paper.
8. Next, the artists place the chisel on the outlines of the pattern. They pound the chisel through the layers to a lead sheet located beneath it.

9. With the entire design cut out, it is time to separate the layers. The artists extend the banners and hang them on the walls or ceilings.
10. One Mexican village is well known for its paper-cutting designs. Families in this village compete to see whose work is best.

◆ PRACTICE 10.10

Using the specified topics and conjunctive adverbs or transitional expressions, create five compound sentences. Be sure to punctuate correctly.

Example: *Topic:* popular music
Conjunctive adverb: nevertheless

Most popular singing groups today seem to have been put together by a committee; nevertheless, many of these groups sell millions of records.

1. *Topic:* finding a job
Transitional expression: for example

2. *Topic:* gun control
Conjunctive adverb: otherwise

3. *Topic:* teenage pregnancy
Transitional expression: as a result

4. *Topic:* recycling
Conjunctive adverb: still

5. *Topic*: watching television
Conjunctive adverb: however

■ REVISING AND EDITING

Look back at your response to the Seeing and Writing exercise on page 168. Underline every compound sentence. Have you used the coordinating conjunction, conjunctive adverb, or transitional expression that best communicates your meaning? Have you punctuated these sentences correctly? Make any necessary revisions.

Now, look for a pair of short simple sentences in your writing that you could combine, and use one of the three methods discussed in this chapter to join them into one compound sentence.

CHAPTER REVIEW

◆ EDITING PRACTICE

The following student essay contains many short, choppy simple sentences. To revise it, link pairs of sentences by adding an appropriate coordinating conjunction, by adding a semicolon, or by adding an appropriate conjunctive adverb or transitional expression. (There are many different correct ways to revise the essay.) Remember to put commas before coordinating conjunctions that join two simple sentences and to use semicolons and commas correctly with conjunctive adverbs and transitional expressions. The first two sentences have been combined for you.

The State Fair

Like most Americans, I do not live on a farm; in fact, I live in the suburbs. However, my parents both grew up on farms. My mother's parents had a family farm in Indiana. My father's parents raised wheat and sugar beets in Colorado. My parents decided not to farm. They knew enough about agriculture to understand how difficult and uncertain that life could be. My grandparents have all died. I do not have much contact with rural life. That is why I love to go to the state fair every year.

A state fair

The fair has carnival rides and stands selling all kinds of junk food. My favorite part of the fair is the livestock pavilion. One barn contains beef cattle. There, visitors admire the giant Black Angus bull from a safe distance. They walk past rows of white-faced Herefords. Another barn has dairy cattle of all kinds. Brown Swiss stand beside black-and-white Holsteins. If I arrive at the right time, I might see a milking demonstration. A butter sculpture might be on display in the milking barn. There might be fresh butter and milk shakes for sale.

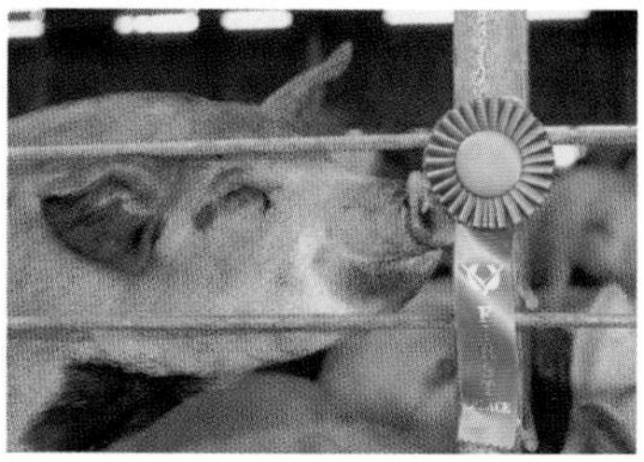

A prize pig

Every animal has commercial possibilities. Otherwise, the farmers would not raise them. The dairy cows, for instance, are not the only milk producers at the fair. The goat barn has a dairy center where people can buy goat cheese. The sheep barn also has a cheese shop. Sheep farmers sell wool and handmade sweaters. They give sheep-shearing and yarn-spinning demonstrations. Some animals will end up as meat. The people who raise them cannot think of them as pets.

Plants are another feature of the fair. The gardening exhibit offers advice on gardening and landscape design. Unfortunately, I do not have a garden. I do not expect to have one in the near future. When I pass this area, I simply admire the work of other people. Another area shows prize-winning fruits and vegetables. Giant, glossy green peppers might take home the grand prize. The winner might be a basket of tart, firm apples.

A prize-winning pie

After the fair, I sometimes wish I had a chance to live on a farm. I am glad that I don't have to live a farmer's life day in and day out. Still, I will keep going to the state fair every year. That way, I can enjoy the experience without having to do the work.

◆ COLLABORATIVE ACTIVITIES

1. Working in a small group, use a coordinating conjunction to join each sentence in the left-hand column with a sentence in the right-hand column to create ten compound sentences. Use as many different coordinating conjunctions as you can to connect ideas. Be sure each coordinating conjunction you choose conveys a logical relationship between ideas, and remember to put a comma before each one. You may use some of the listed sentences more than once. (Many different

combinations—some serious and factually accurate, some humorous—are possible.)

Miniskirts get shorter every year.
Those shoes are an ugly color.
Berries usually ripen in the summer.
Wild mushrooms grow all over the world.
I bought seven pairs of earrings.
His pants are dragging on the ground.
Everyone at work has to wear a uniform.
The yard is full of dandelions.
Ostrich eggs are enormous.
Cherry tomatoes make excellent snacks.

Some come with a belt.
They are torn and dirty.
My mother hates them.
Some kinds are edible.
The silver ones are my favorites.
Only experts should pick them.
Digging them up is my job.
I will not try them on.
I love to throw them in salads.
Each one could make several omelettes.

2. Working in a group of three or four students, invent a new sport. Begin by writing one rule of the game in the form of a simple sentence. Then, pass the paper to the person on your right. That person should expand the rule into a compound sentence.

Example

ORIGINAL RULE The ball must not touch the ground.

CHANGED RULE The ball must not touch the ground; moreover, the players can only move it with their elbows.

Keep going until you have five complete rules. Then work together to write additional sentences describing the playing area, teams, uniforms, or anything else about the game that you like. Use compound sentences whenever possible.

3. *Composing original sentences* Working in a group, create six compound sentences. Make sure that each compound sentence includes two simple sentences, each with a subject and a verb. Two sentences should join clauses with coordinating conjunctions, two with semicolons, and two with conjunctive adverbs or transitional expressions. When you have finished, check the sentences again to make sure you have punctuated them correctly.

✓ REVIEW CHECKLIST: Writing Compound Sentences

- A coordinating conjunction—*and, but, for, nor, or, so,* or *yet*—can join two simple sentences into one compound sentence. A

(continued on the following page)

(continued from the previous page)

comma always comes before the coordinating conjunction. (See 10A.)

- A semicolon can join two simple sentences into one compound sentence. (See 10B.)
- A conjunctive adverb or transitional expression can join two simple sentences into one compound sentence. When it joins two sentences, a conjunctive adverb or transitional expression is always preceded by a semicolon and followed by a comma. (See 10C.)

CHAPTER

11

Writing Complex Sentences

PREVIEW

In this chapter, you will learn

- to form complex sentences with subordinating conjunctions (11A)
- to punctuate dependent clauses introduced by subordinating conjunctions (11B)
- to form complex sentences with relative pronouns (11C)
- to punctuate dependent clauses introduced by relative pronouns (11D)

Word Power

estranged separated from someone else by feelings of hostility or indifference

diverge to separate and go in different directions

dependent relying on another for support

independent free from the influence or control of others

SEEING AND WRITING

Which childhood friends have you lost touch with? Why don't you see them anymore? Look at the picture above, and then write a paragraph that answers these questions.

In this chapter, you will learn to combine dependent and independent clauses to create complex sentences. A **complex sentence** is made up of one independent clause and one or more dependent clauses. A **clause** is a group of words that contains both a subject and a verb.

An **independent clause** can stand alone as a sentence.

INDEPENDENT CLAUSE Tanya was sick yesterday.

A **dependent clause** cannot stand alone as a sentence. It needs other words to complete its meaning.

DEPENDENT CLAUSE Because Tanya was sick yesterday

What happened because Tanya was sick yesterday? To answer this question, you need to add an independent clause that completes the idea in the dependent clause. Combining these two clauses creates a single **complex sentence.**

COMPLEX SENTENCE [DEPENDENT CLAUSE: Because Tanya was sick yesterday,] [INDEPENDENT CLAUSE: I had to work a double shift.]

Writing Tip

Sometimes the independent clause comes first in a complex sentence: *I had to work a double shift because Tanya was sick yesterday.*

A Forming Complex Sentences with Subordinating Conjunctions

One way to create a complex sentence is to join two simple sentences (independent clauses) with a **subordinating conjunction**—a word like *although* or *because.* The subordinating conjunction will signal the relationship between the two simple sentences. For example, look at the following two sentences.

TWO SENTENCES The election was close. The state supreme court did not order a recount.

What is the connection between the close election and the action of the court? By adding a subordinating conjunction, you can make the relationship between these two ideas clear.

COMPLEX SENTENCE Although the election was close, the state supreme court did not order a recount.

Here the subordinating conjunction *although* indicates that one event happened in spite of the other.

Frequently Used Subordinating Conjunctions

after	if only	till
although	in order that	unless
as	now that	until
as if	once	when
as though	provided	whenever
because	rather than	where
before	since	whereas
even if	so that	wherever
even though	than	whether
if	though	while

Different subordinating conjunctions express different relationships between dependent and independent clauses.

Relationship between Clauses	*Subordinating Conjunction*	*Example*
Time	after, before, since, until, when, whenever, while	Before the storm hit land, the people evacuated the town.
Reason or cause	as, because, since	The senator suggested raising the retirement age because the Social Security program was running out of money.
Result or effect	in order that, so that	We need to put computers in all public libraries so that everyone can have access to the Internet.
Condition	even if, if, unless	Global warming will get worse unless we do something now.
Contrast	although, even though, though	Even though he dropped out of college, Bill Gates was able to start Microsoft.
Location	where, wherever	Where there's smoke, there's fire.

Writing Tip
A clause that begins with a subordinating conjunction does not express a complete thought. Used by itself, it is a sentence fragment. (See 15D.)

◆ PRACTICE 11.1

Write an appropriate subordinating conjunction in each blank. Consult the list of subordinating conjunctions on page 187 to make sure you choose a conjunction that establishes the proper relationship between ideas. (The required punctuation has been provided.)

ON THE WEB
For more practice forming complex sentences with subordinating conjunctions, visit Exercise Central at <bedfordstmartins.com/foundationsfirst>.

Example: ___*When*___ people work together in a small space, they all need to mind their manners.

(1) ______________ in the past every person working for a company might have had his or her own office, workers today are likely to share space with other people. (2) In fact, many companies provide small cubicles instead of large offices ______________ office space is expensive. (3) ______________ the company has plenty of space, many managers want employees to work in cubicles or simply to have desks in an open area. (4) These managers think sharing a space makes people work together ______________ they feel like a team. (5) ______________ workers share space, they may feel less isolated than they would in separate offices. (6) However, employees in a shared office space have to be considerate ______________ they are spending so much time close to their coworkers. (7) For example, people should not cut fingernails,

brush hair, or apply makeup at their desks ________________ no one else is nearby. (8) Also, ________________ coworkers overhear personal telephone conversations, they should try to ignore what they hear. (9) ________________ telephone technology is very advanced, people should remember to avoid shouting on the telephone. (10) Indeed, when sharing office space, people should behave ________________ they would like others around them to behave.

◆ PRACTICE 11.2

Complete each of the following complex sentences by finishing the dependent clause on the line provided. Make sure you supply both a subject and a verb.

Example: Some students succeed in school because *they have good study habits*.

1. After ________________________, these students review their lecture notes and reread the assignment.
2. They memorize facts from the notes even though ________________ ________________________.
3. Sometimes these students copy key words from lectures onto note cards so that ________________________________.
4. Teachers sometimes give surprise quizzes since ________________ ________________________.
5. Students might do poorly on these quizzes unless ________________ ________________________.
6. Even if ________________________________, they are prepared for the unexpected.
7. Wherever ________________________________, good students ask questions to be sure they understand the assignment.
8. When ________________________, good students begin their research early.

9. They narrow the topic and develop a tentative thesis before ____________ ____________.

10. Since ____________, good students are always prepared.

B Punctuating with Subordinating Conjunctions

To punctuate a complex sentence that contains a subordinating conjunction, follow these rules.

- Place a comma after the dependent clause when it comes *before* the independent clause.

  Although they had no formal training as engineers, Orville and Wilbur Wright built the first airplane.

- Do not use a comma when the dependent clause comes *after* the independent clause.

  Orville and Wilbur Wright built the first airplane although they had no formal training as engineers.

◆ PRACTICE 11.3

Some of the following complex sentences are punctuated correctly, and some are not. Put a *C* next to every sentence that is punctuated correctly. If the punctuation is not correct, edit the sentence to correct it.

Example: Roller coasters have thrilled riders since they became popular in the 1920s. C

1. Although today's roller coasters are made of steel the early ones were made of wood. ____
2. One of the original coasters, the Cyclone at New York's Coney Island, is still popular because people are nostalgic for earlier times. ____
3. Another great old wooden coaster, the Boulder Dash in Connecticut, is unique because it was built into the side of a mountain. ____
4. These early coasters achieved speeds of up to sixty miles per hour while they dropped down hills as much as eighty-five feet high. ____
5. Today's steel coasters go faster and higher than earlier rides, because technology has improved coaster designs. ____

ON THE WEB
For more practice punctuating with subordinating conjunctions, visit Exercise Central at <bedfordstmartins.com/foundationsfirst>.

6. The Superman Ride of Steel in Agawam, Massachusetts, is considered one of today's best rides, because it gives riders the sensation of flying like a superhero. ____
7. The Dueling Dragons at Universal Studios in Orlando is unusual, because it consists of two coasters—one named Fire, the other named Ice. ____
8. In Pimm, Nevada, the Desperado has a yellow track, so that it is visible from the interstate highway linking Los Angeles with Las Vegas. ____
9. Since it is 310 feet high the Millennium Force in Sandusky, Ohio, uses elevator cables rather than the typical chain lift. ____
10. Whether they are made of wood or steel, roller coasters continue to thrill and entertain their riders. ____

◆ PRACTICE 11.4

Combine each of the following pairs of sentences to form one complex sentence, using the subordinating conjunction that follows the pair. Make sure you include a comma where one is required.

Example: *Although people* ~~People~~ fear dreadful viruses such as Ebola*, not* ~~. Not~~ enough has been done to equip health-care workers in Africa with medical supplies. (although)

1. Many Westerners rarely think about problems in Africa. The lack of money for medical supplies should concern everyone. (although)
2. Contagious diseases in African countries often spread. Hospitals and medical personnel there do not have basic equipment. (because)
3. An outbreak of Ebola virus appeared in northern Uganda in 2000. Doctors and nurses caring for Ebola patients lacked disinfectants and latex gloves. (when)
4. Ebola spreads. Bodily fluids from an infected person come into contact with the skin of a healthy person. (whenever)
5. The Ebola virus makes a patient bleed heavily. Medical workers without gloves face grave danger. (because)

6. Health-care workers must take precautions in an Ebola outbreak. Their skin never touches the skin of their patients. (so that)
7. The virus is named for the Ebola River in Zaire. It first appeared there in human beings. (where)
8. The Ugandan outbreak raged. Doctors and nurses did their best to contain it. (while)
9. A doctor and several nurses died of the Ebola virus. More than half of the patients survived. (even though)
10. Wealthier nations should help poor countries acquire basic medical supplies. Medical workers have a better chance of stopping these infections from spreading. (so that)

◆ PRACTICE 11.5

Use each of the subordinating conjunctions below in an original complex sentence. Make sure you punctuate the sentences correctly.

Example

subordinating conjunction: even though

My little sister finally agreed to go to kindergarten even though she was afraid.

1. *subordinating conjunction:* because

____

____

2. *subordinating conjunction:* after

____

____

3. *subordinating conjunction:* even if

____

____

4. *subordinating conjunction:* until

____

____

5. *subordinating conjunction:* whenever

____

____

C Forming Complex Sentences with Relative Pronouns

Another way to create a complex sentence is to join two simple sentences (independent clauses) with a **relative pronoun** (*who, which, that,* and so on). The relative pronoun creates a dependent clause and shows its relationship to the rest of the sentence. For example, consider the following pair of sentences.

TWO SENTENCES Tiger Woods had won every major golf tournament by the year 2000. He was only twenty-four years old at the time.

Adding a relative pronoun creates a dependent clause that describes a noun or a pronoun in the independent clause.

COMPLEX SENTENCE Tiger Woods, who was only twenty-four years old at the time, had won every major golf tournament by the year 2000.

Relative Pronouns

that	which	whoever	whomever
what	who	whom	whose

◆ PRACTICE 11.6

In each of the following complex sentences, underline the dependent clause once, and underline the relative pronoun twice. Then, draw an arrow from the relative pronoun to the noun or pronoun it describes.

Example: Indian Americans who wish to maintain their heritage celebrate Diwali, the Festival of Lights.

1. This holiday, which lasts five days, involves special foods, candles, prayers, and presents.
2. The roots of this celebration are in Hinduism, which is one of the oldest religions in the world.
3. Among the special sweets baked for this holiday are cakes that contain saffron, almonds, butter, and milk.

ON THE WEB
For more practice forming complex sentences with relative pronouns, visit Exercise Central at <bedfordstmartins.com/foundationsfirst>.

4. Offerings are made to Krishna, who is one of the three main gods of Hinduism.
5. In the evenings, families light candles that represent the banishing of ignorance and darkness.
6. On the first day of the celebration, people who want prosperity during the coming year decorate their houses with rice flour and red footprints.
7. The second day celebrates a legend about Krishna, who is said to have rescued sixteen thousand daughters of gods and saints from a demon king.
8. The third and most important day consists of feasts, gifts, pilgrimages to temples, and visits to friends whom the family wishes to see.
9. The fourth day, which is associated with legends about mountains, is considered a good day to start a new venture.
10. On the last day, families, who meet to exchange gifts, express their love for one another.

D Punctuating with Relative Pronouns

Sometimes a dependent clause introduced by a relative pronoun is set off with commas; sometimes it is not. If the dependent clause is **restrictive**—that is, if it contains essential information—it should *not* be set off with commas.

RESTRICTIVE CLAUSE The bus that takes me to school is always late.

In this sentence, the writer is not talking about just any bus; she is talking about the particular bus that takes her to school. Without the clause *that takes me to school,* the meaning of the sentence would be different. Because the dependent clause is restrictive—that is, it is essential to the meaning of the sentence—it is not set off with commas.

However, if a dependent clause introduced by a relative pronoun is **nonrestrictive**—that is, if it does not contain information that is essential to the meaning of the sentence—it should be set off by commas.

NONRESTRICTIVE CLAUSE The *Titanic,* which sank in 1912, carried more than two thousand passengers.

In this sentence, the dependent clause *which sank in 1912* provides extra information, but the sentence communicates the same main idea without it (the *Titanic* carried more than two thousand passengers). Because the dependent clause is nonrestrictive—that is, it is not essential to the meaning of the sentence—it is set off with commas.

FOCUS Introducing Restrictive and Nonrestrictive Clauses

Which always introduces a nonrestrictive clause. *That* always introduces a restrictive clause. *Who* can introduce either a restrictive or a nonrestrictive clause.

The concert, which took place in a football stadium, was very good. (Here, *which* introduces a nonrestrictive clause.)

The sneakers that I wear when I work out are white and green. (Here, *that* introduces a restrictive clause.)

Ernest Hemingway, who wrote *The Old Man and the Sea*, won the Nobel Prize in Literature in 1954. (Here, *who* introduces a nonrestrictive clause.)

The person who robbed the bank was captured almost immediately. (Here, *who* introduces a restrictive clause.)

Writing Tip

Who always refers to people; *that* and *which* refer to things.

◆ PRACTICE 11.7

Read the following sentences. If the dependent clause in the sentence is restrictive, write *R* in the blank; if the clause is nonrestrictive, write *N*. Then, if necessary, correct the punctuation of the sentence.

Example: The ideal of equality for women in the workplace, which is not yet a reality, is supported by most Americans. N

1. Working women who have more career opportunities today than ever before are successful in many fields. ____
2. However, women may still encounter a "glass ceiling," which is a phenomenon that occurs when companies refuse to hire women for top positions. ____
3. After getting a position of power which almost always involves supervising other employees, women may face additional problems. ____
4. Many workers whose bosses are female feel some resentment. ____

ON THE WEB

For more practice punctuating with relative pronouns, visit Exercise Central at <bedfordstmartins.com/foundationsfirst>.

5. Workers admitted unhappiness with their female bosses on surveys, that questioned both male and female employees. ____
6. Female employees, who might be expected to sympathize with female bosses, resent them as much as the male employees do. ____
7. Employees are likely to consider criticism that comes from a female boss as unfair. ____
8. They accept criticism from male bosses which says a lot about the roles of men and women in our society. ____
9. People, who admire a tough attitude in a man, may not like the same attitude in a woman. ____
10. The news that younger workers do not seem to share these attitudes about female supervisors is encouraging. ____

◆ PRACTICE 11.8

Combine each of the following pairs of sentences into one complex sentence, using the relative pronoun that follows the pair. Be sure to punctuate correctly, using commas to set off only nonrestrictive clauses, not restrictive clauses.

, which inspired the great American novel Moby Dick,

Example: Whaling ^ was once a part of American culture. ~~Whale hunting inspired the great American novel *Moby Dick*.~~ (which)

1. In the nineteenth century, American whalers sailed around the world to hunt whales. Their jobs were very dangerous. (who)
2. Whale oil provided light in many American homes. It burns very brightly. (which)
3. Today, U.S. laws protect several species of whale. They are considered to be in danger of extinction. (that)
4. Most Americans approve of the U.S. ban on whaling. They no longer need whale oil or other whale products. (who)
5. Whale hunting is the focus of a disagreement between the United States and Japan. The two countries have different ideas about whaling. (which)

6. In 2000, Japanese whalers doubled the number of whales they killed. Japanese whalers had been killing some whales every year for research. (who)
7. Some of the whales killed in the Japanese hunt are considered by the U.S. government to be endangered. They include minke whales, Bryde's whales, and sperm whales. (which)
8. Whale meat is a special treat to some Japanese. They consider eating whale to be a part of Japanese culture. (who)
9. The U.S. government argues that the Japanese whale hunt is not for research, but for businesses. The businesses want whale meat to sell to restaurants. (that)
10. Many Japanese do not like the feeling that the United States is trying to tell them what to do. They may not think the Japanese whale hunt is a good idea. (who)

◆ PRACTICE 11.9

Complete the following items by creating complex sentences. Make sure that the clause of the complex sentence contains a subject and a verb, and be sure to punctuate correctly.

Example: A hamburger that *has been barbecued on a grill on a sunny summer day is one of my favorite things*.

1. When my mother ______________________________.
2. My best friend, who ______________________________.
3. If you ever ______________________________.
4. Although most people ______________________________.
5. My dream job, which ______________________________.

■ REVISING AND EDITING

Look back at your response to the Seeing and Writing exercise on page 186. Underline every complex sentence, and circle the subordinating conjunction or relative pronoun. Then, check to make sure your punctuation is correct. Do you have a pair of simple sentences that could be combined with a subordinating conjunction or a relative pronoun? Would combining sentences make the connection between them clearer? If so, revise the sentence pair to create a complex sentence.

CHAPTER REVIEW

◆ EDITING PRACTICE

Read the following essay, and then revise it by using subordinating conjunctions or relative pronouns to combine pairs of short sentences. Be sure to punctuate correctly. The first sentence has been revised for you.

El Día de los Niños

Until the late 1990s, there was no special day in the United States on which to honor children. In 1996, young Latinos held a national summit in Texas, ~~They~~ *where they* established El Día de los Niños, or the Day of the Children.

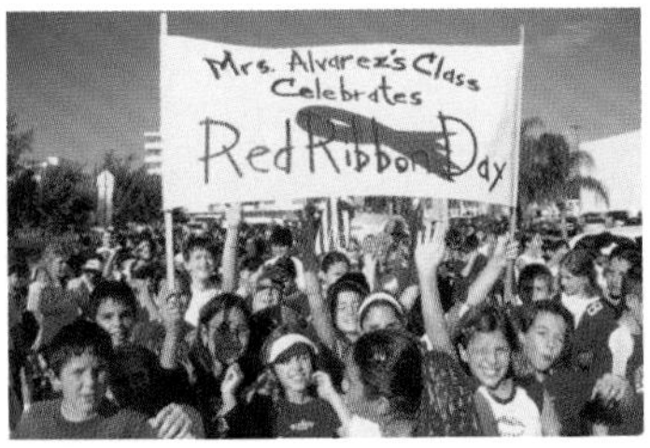

Nine hundred adults and youth from twenty-two states came to the summit. They came to consider challenges facing young Latinos. At the summit, parents agreed to be involved with their children. They agreed to teach them about their culture, heritage, and language. They also agreed to inspire them with goals and dreams. The community wanted the children to succeed. They said that they would set up programs to discuss critical issues facing these young people.

El Día de los Niños is sponsored by the National Latino Children's Institute (NLCI). Communities are supposed to celebrate the day on April 30. They must pass a city resolution recognizing the day. The day is supposed to follow principles in the NLCI handbook. Children must be at the center of the events. The activities should be safe. The events also should be positive and uplifting.

NLCI recognizes many other programs for Latinos. Each year, they select outstanding community-based programs. These programs are called La Promesa. An example of a Promesa program is the Latino Dollars for Scholars of Rhode Island. It raises money and scholarships for students. Another program is Platicamos Salud in Arizona. Promoters provide information on prenatal care and other health-care issues.

America is a melting pot. People from many Hispanic countries around the world have come here. They want to become Americans. They want to keep—and celebrate—the best features of their culture.

◆ COLLABORATIVE ACTIVITIES

1. Working in a group of four students, develop a list of four well-known actors. Now, working in pairs, write a simple sentence about each actor on the list. Following each sentence, write a subordinating conjunction or relative pronoun in parentheses. When both pairs have finished, trade papers. Then, turn each simple sentence into a complex sentence by using the subordinating conjunction or relative pronoun suggested. Finally, get back together with your group, and compare sentences.

   Example
   Samuel L. Jackson was relatively unknown before *Pulp Fiction*. (although)

   Although Samuel L. Jackson was relatively unknown before *Pulp Fiction,* he is now a very popular actor.

2. As a group, create the plot of a film starring all the people on the list of actors your group generated in activity 1. Explain what part each actor plays. Use a subordinating conjunction or relative pronoun in each sentence you write.
3. Using simple sentences, write one paragraph addressed to a Hollywood studio explaining one reason why the studio should make the film your group created in activity 2. Then, exchange paragraphs so that another member of your group can create complex sentences from the simple sentences you wrote. When your group has finished editing all four paragraphs, work together to turn the paragraph(s) with the best reason(s) into a letter arguing for the production of your film.
4. *Composing original sentences* Working in a small group, write five complex sentences. Make sure that each one contains (1) a dependent clause with a subordinating conjunction, a subject, and a verb and

(2) an independent clause with a subject and a verb. When you have finished, check the sentences again to make sure you have punctuated them correctly.

✓ REVIEW CHECKLIST: Writing Complex Sentences

- A complex sentence consists of one independent clause and one or more dependent clauses. (See 11A.)
- Subordinating conjunctions—such as *after, although, because, when,* and *while*—can join two simple sentences into one complex sentence. (See 11A.)
- Always use a comma after a dependent clause when it comes before the independent clause in the sentence. Do not use a comma when the dependent clause follows the independent clause. (See 11B.)
- Relative pronouns can join two simple sentences into one complex sentence. Adding a relative pronoun creates a dependent clause that describes a noun or a pronoun in the independent clause. (See 11C.)
- If a dependent clause introduced by a relative pronoun is restrictive, it should not be set off by commas. If the dependent clause is nonrestrictive, it should be set off by commas. (See 11D.)

CHAPTER

12

Fine-Tuning Your Sentences

PREVIEW

In this chapter, you will learn

- to vary sentence openings (12A)
- to choose exact words (12B)
- to use concise language (12C)
- to avoid clichés (12D)

SEEING AND WRITING

Do you think publicly funded artworks like this one enrich our cities, or do you think the money they cost could be put to better use elsewhere? Look at the picture above, and then write a paragraph in which you explain your position.

Word Power

subsidize to give financial support to a project

priority an important or urgent goal

commission to place an order for something

In Chapters 9 through 11, you learned to write simple, compound, and complex sentences. Now, you are ready to focus on fine-tuning your sentences.

Computer Tip

Use the Search or Find command to locate every *The, This,* and *It* you used at the beginning of a sentence. If necessary, revise your work to vary sentence openings.

A Varying Sentence Openings

When all the sentences in a paragraph begin in the same way, the paragraph may seem dull and repetitive. In the following paragraph, for example, every sentence begins with the subject.

The AIDS quilt contains thousands of panels. Each panel represents a death from AIDS. One panel is for a young college student. Another panel is for an eight-year-old boy. This panel displays his baseball cap. A third panel displays a large picture of a young man. This panel includes a quotation: "Blood saved his life, and it took it away."

The subject matter of this paragraph is interesting, but the style is not. Beginning every sentence with the subject makes the paragraph choppy and monotonous. You can make your paragraphs more interesting by varying your sentence openings.

Beginning with Adverbs

Writing Tip
An adverb modifies a verb, an adjective, or another adverb. See 23A.

Instead of beginning every sentence with the subject, you can begin some sentences with **adverbs**.

The AIDS quilt contains thousands of panels. Sadly, each panel represents a death from AIDS. One panel is for a young college student. Another panel is for an eight-year-old boy. This panel displays his baseball cap. Finally, a third panel displays a large picture of a young man. This panel includes a quotation: "Blood saved his life, and it took it away."

Adding the adverbs *sadly* and *finally* makes the paragraph's sentences flow more smoothly.

Beginning with Prepositional Phrases

For a list of frequently used prepositions, see 9C.

You can also begin some sentences with **prepositional phrases**. A prepositional phrase is a preposition (*of, by, along,* and so on) and all the words that go along with it (*of the people, by the curb, along the road*).

Writing Tip
An adverb or a prepositional phrase that opens a sentence is generally followed by a comma. However, if an introductory prepositional phrase has fewer than three words, the comma is optional. See 25B.

The AIDS quilt contains thousands of panels. Sadly, each panel represents a death from AIDS. One panel is for a young college student. Another panel is for an eight-year-old boy. In the center, this panel displays his baseball cap. Finally, a third panel displays a large picture of a young man. Under the picture, this panel includes a quotation: "Blood saved his life, and it took it away."

◆ PRACTICE 12.1

Computer Tip
Keep a list of possible sentence openings (adverbs and prepositional phrases, for example) in a separate file. Refer to this file to find different ways to begin your sentences.

Several sentences in the following passage contain adverbs and prepositional phrases that could be moved to the beginnings of the sentences. Revise the passage to vary the sentence openings by moving adverbs to the beginnings of three sentences and moving prepositional phrases to the beginnings of three other sentences. Be sure to place a comma after these adverbs and prepositional phrases.

Example: *In recent years, stock* ~~Stock~~ car racing has grown very popular ~~in recent years.~~

(1) Stock car racing has grown from humble beginnings into a multibillion-dollar sport since the 1940s. (2) NASCAR, the National

Association of Stock Car Auto Racing, was formed in 1949. (3) The association originally raced stock cars—unmodified Fords and Chevys. (4) The Daytona 500 was the first stock car race televised in 1960. (5) The deaths of three drivers in 1964 led to safety modifications in the stock cars. (6) Only the stock car body remains the same today. (7) Stock cars are still inspected according to strict rules, however. (8) Stock car racing entered a new era in the 1980s after President Reagan came to watch driver Richard Petty's 200th and final win. (9) The death of racing legend Dale Earnhardt in 2000 brought wide attention to the sport. (10) NASCAR jackets, NASCAR books, and other NASCAR merchandise add to the sport's revenues today.

ON THE WEB
For more practice varying sentence openings, visit Exercise Central at <bedfordstmartins.com/foundationsfirst>.

◆ PRACTICE 12.2

Listed below are three adverbs and three prepositional phrases. To vary sentence openings in the passage that follows, add each of these words or phrases to the beginning of one sentence. Be sure your additions connect the passage's ideas clearly and logically. Remember to add commas where they are needed.

Finally	In the wild
Fortunately	With their cuddly teddy-bear looks
Now	In addition

Example: ~~Breeding~~ *Fortunately, breeding* giant pandas in zoos may help prevent their extinction.

(1) Giant pandas are a favorite animal for people of all ages. (2) The fact that they are endangered concerns animal lovers around the world. (3) Saving the panda has been a priority for wildlife conservation experts for decades, but it is not an easy task. (4) A giant panda needs a huge area without many human beings in it, and each adult panda requires about ten tons of bamboo a year for food. (5) Wilderness areas are increasingly rare in China, the giant panda's home. (6) Poachers hunt giant pandas for their thick black-and-white fur coats.

(7) Some endangered wild animals have been saved by breeding programs in zoos, but panda-breeding programs have struggled. (8) One

panda cub, born at the San Diego Zoo in August 1999, managed to survive the difficult first weeks and thrive in captivity. (9) The cub, known as Hua Mei, was the first giant panda to be born outside of China. (10) Hua Mei's mother, Bai Yun, took very good care of her tiny cub and gave birth to a new cub in 2003. (11) Wildlife conservationists hope that Bai Yun's success story will help them increase the numbers of giant pandas. (12) There may be a bright future for this popular animal after all.

B Choosing Exact Words

When you revise your writing, check to make sure you have used words that clearly express your ideas. Try to replace general words with more specific ones.

Specific words refer to particular people, places, and things. **General** words refer to entire classes of things. Sentences that contain specific words create a clearer, stronger picture for readers than sentences containing only general ones. Consider the following sentences.

GENERAL The old car went down the street.

SPECIFIC The pink 1959 Cadillac convertible glided smoothly down Main Street.

GENERAL I would like to apply for the job you advertised.

SPECIFIC I would like to apply for the assistant manager's job you advertised in the Sunday *Inquirer.*

In each pair of sentences, the sentence that includes specific words is clearer and more interesting than the one that does not.

FOCUS Overused Words

Try to avoid vague, overused words like these.

good	terrific	bad
nice	great	interesting

◆ PRACTICE 12.3

In the following passage, underline the specific words that help you experience the scene the writer describes. The first sentence has been done for you.

(1) The world of *Anna in the Tropics,* a Pulitzer Prize–winning play by Nilo Cruz, is hot and steamy. (2) The play is set in 1929 in a small Cuban cigar factory near Tampa, Florida. (3). This was before the development of cigar-rolling machines, so the workers rolled the cigars by hand. (4) The stage is bathed in harsh white and yellow light, and the workers' benches are as brown as the hanging tobacco leaves. (5) Their clothing is dark and drab. (6) The blue ocean can be glimpsed far away through the high windows. (7) Into this hot, dull scene comes a handsome young man known as the lector, who has been hired to read to the workers to make their work less boring. (8) In contrast to the workers, the lector is dressed in a sharply pressed white suit. (9) The book he chooses to read aloud is *Anna Karenina,* a novel about doomed Russian lovers. (10) The novel's subject heats up several romantic triangles among the factory workers, and violence results.

ON THE WEB
For more practice choosing exact words, visit Exercise Central at <bedfordstmartins.com/foundationsfirst>.

◆ PRACTICE 12.4

Below are five general words. In the blank beside each, write a more specific word related to the general word. Then, use the more specific word in a sentence of your own.

Example

tool claw hammer

Melanie pried the rusty nails out of each weather-beaten board with a claw hammer.

1. game ____________________

____

____

2. house ____________________

____

____

3. job ____________________

____

____

4. exercise ______________________

____

____

5. car ______________________

____

____

◆ PRACTICE 12.5

The following paragraph is a vaguely worded job-application letter. Rewrite the paragraph on a separate page, substituting specific words for the general words of the original and adding details where necessary. Start by making the first sentence, which identifies the applicant and the job, more specific. Then, add specific information about the applicant's background and qualifications, expanding the original paragraph into a three-paragraph letter.

> I am currently attending college and would like to apply for the position advertised. I have a strong interest in that field. My background includes high school and college coursework that relates to this position. I also have personal experience that would make me a good choice. I am qualified for this job, and I would appreciate the opportunity to be considered. Thank you for your consideration.

C Using Concise Language

Wordy constructions get in the way of clear communication. **Concise language**, however, says what it has to say in as few words as possible. When you revise, cross out words that overload your sentences and add nothing to the meaning, and substitute more concise language where necessary.

WORDY In spite of the fact that the British troops outnumbered them, the colonists fought on.

CONCISE Although the British troops outnumbered them, the colonists fought on.

WORDY There are many people who have serious allergies.

CONCISE Many people have serious allergies.

WORDY It is my opinion that everyone should have good health care.

CONCISE Everyone should have good health care.

WORDY During the period of the Great Depression, many people were out of work.

Writing Tip

A short sentence is not necessarily a concise one. A sentence is concise when it contains only the words needed to convey its ideas.

Writing Tip

Try to avoid flowery language and complicated sentences. Remember, good writing is clear and concise.

CONCISE During the Great Depression, many people were out of work.

WORDY In the newspaper article, it said the situation was serious.

CONCISE The newspaper article said the situation was serious.

FOCUS Using Concise Language

The following phrases add nothing to a sentence. You can usually delete them or substitute a more concise phrase with no loss of meaning.

Wordy	*Concise*
It is clear that	(delete)
It is a fact that	(delete)
The reason is that	Because
It is my opinion that	(delete)
Due to the fact that	Because
Despite the fact that	Although
At the present time	Today/Currently
At that time	Then
In most cases	Usually
In order to	To

Unnecessary repetition can also make your writing wordy. When you revise, delete repetition that adds nothing to your sentences.

WORDY Seeing the ocean for the first time was the most exciting and thrilling experience of my life.

CONCISE Seeing the ocean for the first time was the most exciting experience of my life.

WORDY Some people can't make their own decisions by themselves.

CONCISE Some people can't make their own decisions.

◆ PRACTICE 12.6

To make the following sentences more concise, cross out wordy expressions and unnecessary repetition, substituting more concise expressions where necessary.

Example: ~~It is a fact that over~~ Over 150,000 people participated in a demonstration at the World Trade Organization meeting in 2003.

ON THE WEB

For more practice using concise language, visit Exercise Central at <bedfordstmartins.com/foundationsfirst>.

1. Protesters demonstrating at the World Trade Organization's meeting in Seattle in 1999 disrupted the meeting.
2. Before the occurrence of these protests, few Americans felt strongly about the World Trade Organization.
3. There were some violent incidents that happened in Seattle.
4. The protesters came from many different and varied backgrounds.
5. Some of the protesters were interested mainly in protecting the environment, which was their main cause.
6. Other people among the protesters were concerned about poverty in developing nations.
7. The Seattle protest was not an isolated event that happened only once.
8. Every year, the annual meetings of the World Trade Organization and the International Monetary Fund attract protesters.
9. Many young people are getting involved in these protests due to the fact that they believe a global economy should help the poor as much as the wealthy.
10. There are many people who disagree strongly about the practices of international business organizations.

◆ PRACTICE 12.7

The following passage is wordy. Cross out unnecessary words, and make any revisions that may be needed.

> **Example:** Soap and water can clean hands as well as antibacterial ~~germ-fighting~~ products.

(1) A few years ago, antibacterial cleaning products were introduced to the American market all across the country. (2) These products are promoted in commercial advertisements. (3) The ads try to make people afraid and fearful of the germs in their homes. (4) Mothers of children are often the targets of these scary commercials. (5) When the ads first appeared, frightened people immediately began buying antibacterial soap to kill off the invisible germs they could not see.

(6) It is a fact that ordinary soap does not kill every household germ.

(7) However, new research suggests that antibacterial products may kill good germs that are helpful to human beings. (8) These products may also strengthen dangerous bacteria due to the fact that the strongest germs will still survive. (9) Scientists have warned that children who grow up in germ-free homes may get sick from normally harmless bacteria that do not usually hurt people. (10) Therefore, in the final analysis, antibacterial products may do more harm than good.

D Avoiding Clichés

Clichés are phrases—like *raining cats and dogs* and *hard as a rock*—that have been used so often that people no longer pay attention to them. Clichés do nothing to improve writing; in fact, they get in the way of clear communication.

To make your point effectively, replace a cliché with a direct statement or a fresh expression.

CLICHÉ After a year of college, I learned that what goes around comes around.

REVISED After a year of college, I learned that if I don't study, I won't do well.

CLICHÉ With the pressures of working and going to school, I feel as if I am on a treadmill.

REVISED With the pressures of working and going to school, I feel as if I am constantly trying to walk up the down escalator.

Computer Tip

Keep a file of overused expressions you encounter in your reading and writing. Refer to this file as you revise.

◆ PRACTICE 12.8

Cross out any clichés in the following sentences. Then, either substitute a fresher expression, or restate the idea in more direct language.

Example: A cup of coffee is a needed ~~shot in the arm~~ boost for many hard-working Americans.

(1) Many Americans get their get up and go from a morning cup of coffee. (2) Today, many find that designer coffees go down smooth as silk. (3) In fact, there are more designer coffees than you can shake a stick at. (4) Some coffees are made from beans imported from the four corners of the globe, from such places as Hawaii, Sumatra, and Kenya. (5) Others have flavors that melt in your mouth, such as hazelnut, vanilla,

ON THE WEB

For more practice avoiding clichés, visit Exercise Central at <bedfordstmartins.com/foundationsfirst>.

and raspberry. (6) Still other coffee drinks, such as cappuccino, latte, and frappuccino, include lots of milk straight from the cow. (7) Some designer coffees even combine all three elements—exotic beans, strong flavors, and milk—to create a taste that is out of this world. (8) Although a cup of designer coffee doesn't cost an arm and a leg, they are more expensive than a regular cup of Joe. (9) In fact, Seattle, the home of the Starbucks chain, even went out on a limb and tried to tax designer coffees. (10) Although the Starbucks chain is top dog in the designer coffee business today, other chains and individual coffee shops offer just as much bang for the buck.

■ REVISING AND EDITING

Look back at your response to the Seeing and Writing exercise on page 201. Are your sentence openings varied? Revise them if necessary. Next, make sure that your language is as exact and concise as possible. Finally, make sure you have not used any clichés in your writing.

CHAPTER REVIEW

◆ EDITING PRACTICE

Read the following student essay, and then revise it by moving at least three adverbs and at least three prepositional phrases to the beginnings of sentences. Then, revise the essay's sentences so that they use exact words and concise language and do not include clichés. The first sentence has been revised for you.

Suburban Living

A suburb with no sidewalks

Parents want to raise their children in a ~~nice~~ *safe, quiet* place. The suburbs are supposedly "family friendly," so many people move out of urban cities when they have children. Many areas that are in the suburbs are not planned with children in mind. There is nowhere that the kids have to gather and play. Some kids are bored out of their minds in the suburbs and turn to dangerous pastimes. Many parents may find in the long run that their children would have been as happy as clams to grow up in the city.

Parents imagine that children in suburban homes ride bicycles or stroll along pretty streets. However, people take their lives in their hands if they bike down some suburban streets. It is also true that many suburbs have no sidewalks, so pedestrians have to compete with cars. When suburban children visit a friend, their parents usually drive them in a car. The children don't spend enough time doing healthy things as a result.

Overhead view of a suburb with no sidewalks

Children may find the suburbs bad during their teenage years. Meeting the needs of teens is more challenging and difficult than keeping small children amused. Suburbs unfortunately offer few areas where teenagers can gather and get together. Boredom can make teenagers feel down in the dumps. A young person who is smart as a whip may do stupid things out of boredom.

Arieal view of a modern housing development

When all is said and done, suburbs may seem so nice to city people, but they are not small towns. For children, cities with sidewalks, parks, museums, and public transportation may be more interesting than suburbs. Parents who are considering a move for the sake of the children should put on their thinking caps before making a decision.

◆ COLLABORATIVE ACTIVITIES

1. Working in a group of three or four students, make a list of every cliché you can think of. Then, working on your own, write new, fresh expressions to replace the clichés on your list. Finally, discuss the new expressions with the rest of the group, and choose your favorites.
2. Working in the same group, write a paragraph containing two or three of the fresh expressions you listed for activity 1. When you have finished, trade paragraphs with another group. Make any revisions in the paragraph that you think are necessary to vary the paragraph's sentence openings or to eliminate vague language or wordiness. Finally, discuss the changes in your paragraph and the other group's paragraph with the other group.
3. Bring in an article from a newspaper or magazine that you think contains clichés or wordy or vague language. Working in a group, look

through the articles everyone has contributed, and choose the one paragraph that most needs revision. Then, revise the paragraph to eliminate the problems.

4. *Composing original sentences* Working in a group, write five sentences. Be sure to vary your sentence openings, choose exact words, use concise language, and avoid clichés. When you have finished, check the sentences again to make sure you have no errors in grammar, punctuation, or spelling.

☑ REVIEW CHECKLIST: Fine-Tuning Your Sentences

- You can make your sentences more interesting by varying your sentence openings. (See 12A.)
- Try to replace general words with specific ones. (See 12B.)
- Delete wordy expressions, substituting concise language where necessary. (See 12C.)
- Avoid clichés (overused expressions). (See 12D.)

CHAPTER

13

Using Parallelism

PREVIEW

In this chapter, you will learn

- to recognize parallel structure (13A)
- to use parallel structure (13B)

SEEING AND WRITING

In what ways have you changed in the months (or years) since you graduated from high school? In what ways have you stayed the same? Look at the picture above, and then write a paragraph in which you answer these questions.

Word Power

mature full-grown

mellow to gain the wisdom and tolerance that are characteristic of maturity

perspective a view or outlook; the ability to see things as they are

A Recognizing Parallel Structure

In writing, using **parallelism** means repeating the same grammatical structure—for example, all nouns, all verbs, and so on—to express comparable or equivalent ideas.

Paul Robeson was an actor and a singer. (two nouns)

When my brother comes home from college, he eats, sleeps, and watches television. (three verbs)

Elephants are big, strong, and intelligent. (three adjectives)

Jan likes to run, to do aerobics, and to lift weights. (three phrases)

When different grammatical patterns are used to express similar ideas, sentences can seem awkward. For example, see how parallelism makes the following pairs of sentences easier to read.

NOT PARALLEL I like composition, history, and taking math.

PARALLEL I like composition, history, and math. (All three items in the series are nouns.)

NOT PARALLEL The wedding guests danced, ate, and were drinking toasts.

PARALLEL The wedding guests danced, ate, and drank toasts. (All three verbs are in the past tense.)

NOT PARALLEL The Manayunk bike race is long and climbs steeply and is difficult.

PARALLEL The Manayunk bike race is long, steep, and difficult. (All words in the series are adjectives.)

NOT PARALLEL We can go to the movies, or playing miniature golf is an option.

PARALLEL We can go to the movies, or we can play miniature golf. (Both independent clauses have the same structure.)

◆ PRACTICE 13.1

In each of the following sentences, underline the groups of words that are parallel.

Example: The pitcher threw a tantrum in the dugout, threatened his teammates in the locker room, and called a press conference to criticize the coaches.

ON THE WEB
For more practice recognizing parallel structure, visit Exercise Central at <bedfordstmartins.com/foundationsfirst>.

1. The tornado was sudden, unexpected, and destructive.
2. Petra ordered an egg-white omelet, a green salad with no dressing, and two slices of cheesecake.
3. After the test, I wanted to lie down and take a nap.
4. Her friend had tattoos, a pierced nose, and perfect manners.
5. The store's new owners expanded the parking lot and added a deli counter.
6. The vandals broke the windows, painted graffiti on the walls, and threw garbage on the floor.
7. Before she goes to bed, my niece likes a bath, a bottle, and a lullaby.

8. The almanac predicted a long, cold, and snowy winter.
9. A beautiful voice and acting ability are important for an opera singer.
10. Maria bought a bicycle, Terence bought a bus pass, and Sheila bought a pair of hiking boots.

◆ PRACTICE 13.2

In each of the following sentences, decide whether the underlined words are parallel. If so, write *P* in the blank. If not, edit the sentence to make the words parallel.

Examples

The contestants argued, sunbathed, and ~~they~~ watched each other suspiciously. ____

A retired Navy SEAL, a river guide, and a corporate trainer were the last players on the island. _P_

1. Hundreds of people wanted to be on a game show that required them to live on an island, catch their own food, and they could not have contact with the outside world. ____
2. The contestants had to be resourceful and healthy. ____
3. The last person on the island would win a car and a million dollars. ____
4. *Survivor* was modeled on a Swedish game show that had forty-eight contestants and a thirty-thousand-dollar prize. ____
5. The contestants held their breath underwater, rowed a canoe, and rats and caterpillars were eaten by them. ____
6. Many viewers decided that it was much more fun to watch *Survivor* than watching summer reruns. ____
7. Each week, the television audience saw one person win a contest and another person would get voted off the island. ____
8. The corporate trainer was manipulative, argumentative, and he often schemed. ____
9. Some viewers loved him, some viewers hated him, but all of them talked about his victory. ____

10. The show became so popular that the contestants came home to endorsements, acting roles, and becoming famous. ____

B Using Parallel Structure

Parallelism enables you to emphasize related ideas, and it makes your sentences easier to read. Parallel structure is especially important in *paired items, comparisons,* and *items in a series.*

Paired Items

For more on coordinating conjunctions, see 10A.

Use parallel structure for paired items connected by a **coordinating conjunction**—*and, but, for, nor, or, so,* or *yet.*

Jemera takes Alex to day care *and* then goes to work.

You can register to vote now, *or* you can register next week.

You should also use parallel structure for paired items joined by **correlative conjunctions**.

Computer Tip
Use the Search or Find function to look for correlative conjunctions in your writing. Make sure you have used parallel structure.

Correlative Conjunctions

both...and	neither...nor	rather...than
either...or	not only...but also	

Darryl is good *both* in English *and* in math.

The movie was *not only* long *but also* boring.

I would *rather* take classes in the morning *than* take them in the afternoon.

Comparisons

Use parallel structure for comparisons formed with *than* or *as.*

It often costs less to rent a house *than* to buy one.

In basketball, natural talent is *as* important *as* hard work.

Items in a Series

Writing Tip
Use commas to separate three or more items in a series. See 25A.

Use parallel structure for items in a series.

Unemployment is low because of a healthy economy, low inflation, and high consumer demand.

To do well in school, you should attend class regularly, take careful notes, and set aside time to study.

Items in a List

Use parallel structure for items in a numbered or bulleted list.

There are three reasons to go to college:

1. To learn
2. To increase self-esteem
3. To get a better job

> **Writing Tip**
> Elements in an outline should be presented in parallel terms.
> I. Good habits
> A. Exercising
> B. Getting enough sleep
> C. Eating well

◆ PRACTICE 13.3

In each of the following sentences, underline the parts of the sentence that should be parallel. Then, edit each sentence to make it parallel.

Example: Growing orchids can be challenging and ~~brings rewards with it~~ rewarding.

1. When orchids first became popular in the 1880s, the plants were dug up and being collected from the wild.
2. Orchid sellers sent hunters around the world to find and then shipping back thousands of these beautiful plants.
3. If the hunter found a rare species, he took every plant, causing harm to the environment and it also caused damage to the species.
4. Today, orchids can be purchased legally from plant nurseries, orchid clubs, or buyers can go to shows where orchids are traded.
5. As a result, orchids have become both popular and they are inexpensive.
6. In the wild, orchids grow in the rain forest—either in trees as air plants or they grow on the ground as earth plants.
7. Because of their natural habitat, orchids grown at home need bright light, moderate temperatures, and to have good air circulation around them.
8. Orchids are primarily of two types: *monopodial,* which means "single footed," and *sympodial,* the definition of which is "many footed."
9. The single-footed orchid grows up from a single stem, and the many-footed orchid is found growing on several stems.
10. Although amateurs can raise some types of orchids, growing other types of orchids is easier for experts than beginners can grow them.

> **Writing Tip**
> Items listed in a résumé should be in parallel form: *designed ads; drew illustrations; created computer programs.*

ON THE WEB
For more practice using parallel structure, visit Exercise Central at <bedfordstmartins.com/foundationsfirst>.

◆ PRACTICE 13.4

In each of the following sentences, fill in the blanks with parallel words, phrases, or clauses of your own that make sense in context.

Example: When I am at school, my favorite things to do are *hang out with friends*, *go to the cafeteria*, and *play Frisbee in the quad*.

1. My favorite classes are ________ and ________.
2. If I could take any class at school, it would be ________ or ________.
3. To graduate from school, I will need to be able to ________, ________, and ________.
4. The fields I am most interested in are ________, ________, and ________.
5. Fields that do not interest me at all are ________ and ________.
6. When I'm not at school, I enjoy ________, ________, and ________.
7. These activities are [or are not] related to my schoolwork because they ________ and ________.
8. Although these are considered leisure activities, I still learn something from them, such as ________ and ________.
9. Next year, I will either ________ or ________.
10. After I graduate, I hope to ________ or ________.

◆ PRACTICE 13.5

Rewrite the following sentences to create parallel structure.

Example: Every autumn, the leaves of certain trees turn from shades of green to brown, red, yellow, and they also turn orange.

Every autumn, the leaves of certain trees turn from shades of green to shades of brown, red, yellow, and orange.

1. Each leaf is a miniature factory that uses water, carbon dioxide, and it also needs sunlight to make food.

2. Leaves are green in the summer because they contain chlorophyll, a compound found in plants, in algae, and it can also be found in some bacteria.

3. Also present in leaves are other chemicals that give the leaves their orange and also their yellow color.

4. Red leaves get their color from stored sugar that has turned from being a green color to red.

5. Throughout both the spring and also in the summer, these beautiful colors are overshadowed by the green chlorophyll.

6. During the late fall, the chlorophyll fades, and the other colors are emerging.

7. Although too little rain can delay the arrival of fall, dull colors can be caused by too much rain.

8. An early frost can turn leaves brown, but sunny days help to create chemicals that produce the most striking red, gold, and the color purple hues.

9. Warm, wet springs, moderately rainy summers, and a fall that is clear and mild make the best leaf colors.

____

____

10. The leaves we enjoy so much each autumn not only are following nature's plan but they also give us enjoyment.

____

____

REVISING AND EDITING

Look back at your response to the Seeing and Writing exercise on page 213. First, underline every pair or series of words or phrases. Then, revise your work to make sure you have used parallel words where necessary.

CHAPTER REVIEW

◆ EDITING PRACTICE

Read the following essay, which contains examples of faulty parallelism. Then, identify the sentences you think need to be corrected, and make the changes necessary to create parallelism. The first sentence has been edited for you.

A woman playing a theremin during the 1920s

The Strangest Instrument

Many people think that electronic musical instruments are a recent invention and ~~produced by~~ *a product of* modern technology. In some cases, modern computers have changed the recording, playing, and the way music is composed, but the first electronic instrument was created just after World War I. In 1919, a Russian electronics genius named Leon Theremin created an instrument that looked strange and was equally strange sounding. Today, this instrument, which is called a theremin, has a small group of fans but they are devoted.

A theremin

A theremin looks like a metal box with two antennae; one antenna controls volume, and pitch is controlled by the other. A theremin player moves his or her hands over the antennae to change the pitch. The theremin player touches neither the box nor does he or she come in contact with the antennae. Instead, the player's hands become a part of an electrical circuit that creates sound.

Playing the theremin is difficult. Only a handful of professional theremin players are able to make the instrument play the right note and also play it at the right time. Because of its weird, outer-space sound, the theremin has been used to create background music in science fiction movies, horror movies, and films that involve suspense. One of its first uses in Hollywood was in Alfred Hitchcock's 1945 movie *Spellbound,* which starred Gregory Peck and also Ingrid Bergman was featured. The director used the theremin to suggest Peck's amnesia. Soon after, rock bands began experimenting with the theremin to get particular sound effects. One of the most unusual uses and it was memorable was in the Beach Boys' 1966 hit "Good Vibrations." In this song, the theremin's high-pitched and the otherworldly sound can be heard during the refrain, "Good good good good vibrations."

Today, theremin collectors buy expensive early theremins, purchase new theremins, and kits to build theremins. Most collectors would rather have a theremin that they will never learn to play well than not to have one at all. The eerie sound of the theremin, the "magical" way it produces sound, and having an interesting history are rewards enough.

◆ COLLABORATIVE ACTIVITIES

1. Working on your own, write a simple sentence. Then, working in a group of three students, pass the paper to another person in the group, who should add a parallel noun, verb, adjective, phrase, or clause to

the sentence. Next, pass the paper to the third person in the group to check for correct parallelism. Finally, as a group, compare the finished sentences to the originals and discuss the changes.

2. Working on your own, make a list of at least three points to support one of these topics:

   Why I like a particular recording artist

   Why I chose this college

   The most serious problems in my community

   Next, write a sentence that includes all the items on your list. Then, working in a group, read aloud the sentence you wrote. Finally, discuss the parallelism in the finished sentence.
3. Working in a group, decide on a topic for a paragraph. Next, have each student write a sentence containing parallel words, phrases, or clauses. Then, as a group, choose the sentence you like best and write a paragraph that includes that sentence. Be sure that the finished paragraph includes at least three sentences containing parallel items. Be sure to vary the sentences—for example, write one with parallel nouns, one with parallel adjectives, and one with parallel phrases.
4. *Composing original sentences* Working in a group, create five sentences illustrating effective parallelism. When you have finished, check the sentences to make sure you have corrected any errors in grammar, punctuation, or spelling.

✓ REVIEW CHECKLIST: Using Parallelism

- Repeat the same grammatical structure to express comparable or equivalent ideas. (See 13A.)
- Use parallel structure with paired items. (See 13B.)
- Use parallel structure in comparisons formed with *than* or *as.* (See 13B.)
- Use parallel structure for items in a series or in a numbered or bulleted list. (See 13B.)

UNIT FOUR

Solving Common Sentence Problems

CHAPTER 14

Run-Ons and Comma Splices

PREVIEW

In this chapter, you will learn

- to recognize run-ons and comma splices (14A)
- to correct run-ons and comma splices in five different ways (14B)

SEEING AND WRITING

Do you think Barbie is a positive role model for young girls? Why or why not? Look at the picture above, and then write a paragraph in which you answer these questions.

Word Power

role model a person who serves as a model of behavior for someone else to imitate

A Recognizing Run-Ons and Comma Splices

A **run-on** is an error that occurs when two sentences are joined without punctuation.

RUN-ON [The economy has improved] [many people still do not have jobs.]

Writing Tip
A comma can join sentences only when it is followed by a coordinating conjunction. (See 10A.)

Computer Tip
Although grammar checkers can find many errors, they are not good at identifying run-ons and comma splices. Don't depend on the grammar checker to find these types of sentence problems for you.

ON THE WEB
For more practice recognizing run-ons and comma splices, visit Exercise Central at <bedfordstmartins.com/foundationsfirst>.

A **comma splice** is an error that occurs when two sentences are joined with just a comma.

COMMA SPLICE [The economy has improved], [many people still do not have jobs.]

◆ PRACTICE 14.1

Some of the sentences in the following passage are correct, but others are run-ons or comma splices. In the blank after each sentence, write *C* if the sentence is correct, *RO* if it is a run-on, and *CS* if it is a comma splice.

Example: People believe many myths about dieting, it is hard for them to accept the truth. CS

(1) Many people think that cholesterol is bad for them. ____ (2) In fact, cholesterol is necessary, it helps build cells and produce hormones. ____ (3) There is good cholesterol, and there is bad cholesterol. ____ (4) Bad cholesterol accumulates in the arteries good cholesterol travels back to the liver. ____ (5) Many other myths about dieting persist, people accept them as fact. ____ (6) For example, crash diets do not help people lose weight they really cause only temporary weight loss and burn valuable lean muscle. ____ (7) Foods containing fats are not necessarily fattening, the number of calories consumed is what matters. ____ (8) Many dieters rely on low-fat food, yet they can contain as many calories as regular foods. ____ (9) Some people think low-fat milk has less calcium than whole milk actually it has more calcium. ____ (10) These myths may prevent people from losing weight, they can also prevent them from eating healthy foods. ____

B Correcting Run-Ons and Comma Splices

You can correct run-ons and comma splices in five ways.

1. *Create two separate sentences.*

INCORRECT (RUN-ON) Frances Perkins was the first female cabinet member she was President Franklin D. Roosevelt's secretary of labor.

INCORRECT (COMMA SPLICE)	Frances Perkins was the first female cabinet member, she was President Franklin D. Roosevelt's secretary of labor.
CORRECT (TWO SEPARATE SENTENCES)	Frances Perkins was the first female cabinet member. She was President Franklin D. Roosevelt's secretary of labor.

For more on connecting ideas with coordinating conjunctions, see 10A.

2. *Connect ideas with a coordinating conjunction.* If you want to indicate a particular relationship between ideas—for example, a cause-and-effect link or a contrast—use a coordinating conjunction (*and, but, for, nor, or, so,* or *yet*) to connect the ideas. Always place a comma before the coordinating conjunction.

INCORRECT (RUN-ON)	"Strange Fruit" is best known as a song performed by Billie Holiday it was originally a poem.
INCORRECT (COMMA SPLICE)	"Strange Fruit" is best known as a song performed by Billie Holiday, it was originally a poem.
CORRECT	"Strange Fruit" is best known as a song performed by Billie Holiday, but it was originally a poem. (ideas are connected with the coordinating conjunction *but*)

3. *Connect ideas with a semicolon.* If you want to indicate a close connection—or a strong contrast—between two ideas, use a semicolon.

Writing Tip

A semicolon links two complete independent clauses. It cannot connect a clause and a phrase.

INCORRECT (RUN-ON)	Jhumpa Lahiri is the daughter of immigrants from Calcutta she won the Pulitzer Prize for her first book.
INCORRECT (COMMA SPLICE)	Jhumpa Lahiri is the daughter of immigrants from Calcutta, she won the Pulitzer Prize for her first book.
CORRECT	Jhumpa Lahiri is the daughter of immigrants from Calcutta; she won the Pulitzer Prize for her first book. (ideas are connected with a semicolon)

Writing Tip

Conjunctive adverbs include words such as *however* and *therefore;* transitional expressions include *in fact, as a result,* and *for example.* (See 10C.)

4. *Connect ideas with a semicolon and a conjunctive adverb or transitional expression.* To show a specific relationship between two closely related ideas, add a conjunctive adverb or transitional expression after the semicolon.

Word Power

genome a complete set of chromosomes and its associated genes

INCORRECT (RUN-ON)	The human genome project is very important it may be the most important scientific research of the last hundred years.
INCORRECT (COMMA SPLICE)	The human genome project is very important, it may be the most important scientific research of the last hundred years.
CORRECT	The human genome project is very important; in fact, it may be the most important scientific research of the last hundred years. (ideas are connected with a semicolon and the transitional expression *in fact*)

5. *Connect ideas with a subordinating conjunction or relative pronoun.* When one idea is dependent on another, you can turn the dependent idea into a dependent clause by adding a subordinating conjunction

FOCUS Connecting Ideas with Semicolons

A run-on or comma splice often occurs when you use a conjunctive adverb or transitional expression to join two sentences but do not include the required punctuation.

INCORRECT (RUN-ON) It is easy to download information from the Internet however it is not always easy to evaluate the information.

INCORRECT (COMMA SPLICE) It is easy to download information from the Internet, however it is not always easy to evaluate the information.

To correct this kind of run-on or comma splice, put a semicolon before the conjunctive adverb or transitional expression, and put a comma after it.

CORRECT It is easy to download information from the Internet; however, it is not always easy to evaluate the information.

Writing Tip

Remember, a comma is *required* after the conjunctive adverb or transitional expression that links two independent clauses.

For more on connecting ideas with subordinating conjunctions and relative pronouns (and complete lists of these words), see Chapter 11.

(such as *although, because,* or *when*) or a relative pronoun (such as *who, which,* or *that*).

INCORRECT (RUN-ON) J. K. Rowling is now the best-selling author of the Harry Potter books not long ago she was an unemployed single mother.

INCORRECT (COMMA SPLICE) J. K. Rowling is now the best-selling author of the Harry Potter books, not long ago she was an unemployed single mother.

CORRECT Although J. K. Rowling is now the best-selling author of the Harry Potter books, not long ago she was an unemployed single mother. (ideas are connected with the subordinating conjunction *although*)

INCORRECT (RUN-ON) Harry Potter is an orphan he is also a wizard with magical powers.

INCORRECT (COMMA SPLICE) Harry Potter is an orphan, he is also a wizard with magical powers.

CORRECT Harry Potter, who is an orphan, is also a wizard with magical powers. (ideas are connected with the relative pronoun *who*)

Writing Tip

When you use a relative pronoun to correct a run-on or comma splice, the relative pronoun takes the place of a noun or pronoun in the sentence. (For example, in the sentence to the right, *who* takes the place of *he*.)

◆ PRACTICE 14.2

Correct each of the run-ons and comma splices below in one of the following ways: by creating two separate sentences, by connecting ideas with a comma followed by a coordinating conjunction, by connecting ideas with a semicolon, or by connecting ideas with a semicolon and a conjunctive adverb or transitional expression. Be sure the punctuation is correct. Remember to put a semicolon before, and a comma after, each conjunctive adverb or transitional expression.

ON THE WEB
For more practice on correcting run-ons and comma splices, visit Exercise Central at <bedfordstmartins.com/foundationsfirst>.

Example: All over the world, people eat flatbreads, ^and^ different countries have different kinds.

1. Flatbread is bread that is flat usually it does not contain yeast.
2. An example of a flatbread in the United States is the pancake, many Americans eat pancakes with maple syrup.
3. The tortilla is a Mexican flatbread tortillas are made of corn or wheat.
4. A favorite flatbread in the Middle East is the pita, it may have a pocket that can be filled with vegetables or meat.
5. Italians eat focaccia, when they put cheese on a focaccia, it becomes a pizza.
6. Crackers are another kind of flatbread the dough is baked until it is crisp.
7. Indian cooking has several kinds of flatbreads, all of them are delicious.
8. Matzoh resembles a large, square cracker, it is a traditional food for the Jewish holiday of Passover.
9. Fifty years ago, most people ate only the flatbreads from their native lands, today flatbreads are becoming internationally popular.
10. Many American grocery stores sell tortillas, pita bread, and other flatbreads most of their customers love flatbread sandwiches.

◆ PRACTICE 14.3

Correct each of the following run-ons and comma splices by connecting ideas with a subordinating conjunction from the list on page 187 or with a relative pronoun (*who, which,* or *that*).

Examples

Scientists have long experimented with combining different fruits and vegetables~~,~~ ^because^ they want to get the best characteristics of both.

These new products ^, which^ are the result of combining two different species, ~~they~~ are called hybrids.

1. Over the years, several hybrid fruits have come to market these have become popular with consumers.
2. The tangelo is a combination of the tangerine and the grapefruit, it is juicier and easier to peel than either of them.
3. More recently, two more new hybrid fruits have been introduced, these are called pluots and apriums.
4. Pluots have speckled orange and yellow skin, they are nicknamed "dinosaur eggs."
5. They are sweeter and juicier than plums hybrids usually have higher sugar content than their parent fruits.
6. Another plum-apricot combination is called an aprium, it resembles an apricot.
7. Apriums have thin fuzz on their skins they are smaller than pluots.
8. Pluots and apriums may look different, they are tasty additions to the fruit market.
9. Both new fruits are good sources of vitamin A this vitamin is essential for healthy skin.
10. The pluot and aprium are also fat-free, sodium-free, and cholesterol-free, they are good choices for people with dietary restrictions.

◆ PRACTICE 14.4

Review the five strategies for correcting run-ons and comma splices. Then, correct each run-on and comma splice in the following passage in the way that best indicates the relationship between ideas. Be sure to use appropriate punctuation.

Example: Mexican cuisine is very popular among Americans today, *but* ^ this unique blend of dishes is more accurately called Tex-Mex.

(1) Tex-Mex cuisine is a blend of foods and cooking styles it combines the traditions of the Aztec, Toltec, and Maya with European and North American traditions. (2) This cuisine evolved as different cultures merged, this was a result of migration and exploration. (3) Before the arrival of the Spanish explorers, the Mexican diet was based on corn it

could be ground and made into tortillas, tamales, and flour. (4) The corn-based dishes were served with vegetables, and meat, spices, and herbs were added to enhance the flavors. (5) After the Spanish arrived, the cuisine changed, rice, olives, beef, and various fruits were added to the corn dishes. (6) Catholic nuns also contributed to the development of the cuisine they created new pastries and sauces for holy days. (7) Over time, Americans adopted Mexican foods, but they changed them. (8) They added variations and introduced new foods, these included tortillas made of wheat flour rather than corn and enchiladas filled with meat and cheese rather than eaten plain. (9). However, America's Tex-Mex cuisine kept the beans and peppers found in many Mexican dishes, these continue to be a staple of Tex-Mex dishes. (10) Fried ice cream, though, is strictly an American invention it is not found in Mexico.

■ REVISING AND EDITING

Look back at your response to the Seeing and Writing exercise on page 225. Can you spot any run-ons or comma splices? Correct each run-on and comma splice you find. If you do not find any run-ons or comma splices in your own writing, work with a classmate to correct his or her writing, or edit the work you did for another assignment.

CHAPTER REVIEW

◆ EDITING PRACTICE: PARAGRAPH

Read the following paragraph. Then, revise it by carefully correcting each run-on and comma splice. Be sure to use appropriate punctuation. The first error has been corrected for you.

Many city parks are full of pigeons; they are also found on building ledges and monuments. Most people think of pigeons as dirty, disgusting creatures that soil cars, sidewalks, and buildings, others recognize their unique abilities. There are several different types of pigeons one of the most interesting, the passenger pigeon, is now extinct. Passenger pigeons were used during wartime they carried messages in capsules attached to their legs. A pigeon named Cher Ami (French for "dear friend") became famous during World War I for saving two hundred American soldiers lost behind enemy lines, he delivered a message providing their location. A pigeon with similar abilities is the homing pigeon, it will travel hundreds of miles to get back home. No one is sure how these birds find their way some people think they follow the lines in the earth's magnetic field. Others think they use the sun and stars still others think they follow their excellent senses of sight, smell, and hearing. The true explanation is probably a combination of these methods, if one fails, another may take over. There are many other interesting facts about pigeons, to most people they are just an annoyance.

◆ EDITING PRACTICE: ESSAY

Read the following essay. Then, carefully correct each run-on and comma splice. Be sure to use appropriate punctuation. The first error has been corrected for you.

Stripes

Prison inmates in old movies always wear striped uniforms, but most prisons today do not make prisoners wear stripes. Instead, prisoners usually wear brightly colored jumpsuits they even wear street clothes in some prisons. Old-fashioned ideas about prison life are becoming popular again the striped prison uniform is making a comeback.

Most American prisons stopped requiring prisoners to wear stripes at least fifty years ago, at the time, many people felt that wearing stripes was humiliating. However, there is a reason for bringing back striped uniforms these uniforms help people identify escaped prisoners. Most people outside of prisons do not wear jumpsuits with horizontal stripes other popular prison clothing resembles everyday clothing. Denim is a popular uniform material in prisons, denim blends in too well with clothing worn by people on the street. Orange jumpsuits may be noticeable, they also may look too much like the uniforms worn by sanitation workers. Escaped prisoners in striped suits are easy to spot, even at night, the stripes are highly visible.

Prisoners in the 1932 movie I Am a Fugitive from a Chain Gang

Some people still object to striped uniforms they argue that these uniforms are designed to humiliate prisoners. However, in states that have brought back the old uniforms, the stripes are very popular with voters. Many Americans think prison life is too easy they want prisoners to be treated more harshly. Some states make prisoners work on chain gangs striped uniforms are part of this trend toward strict treatment of prisoners.

Movies from the 1930s showed prisoners in black-and-white uniforms, the uniforms instantly identified them as prisoners. Soon, people may begin to think of the striped uniforms as a part of the present instead of the past. Americans may eventually think this a good idea, of course that depends on how they feel about prisoners and prison life in this country.

◆ COLLABORATIVE ACTIVITIES

1. Find two examples of run-ons or comma splices (or one of each). You can look for these errors in papers you have written, in your school newspaper, or online; sometimes, errors like these also appear in national magazines or newspapers. Bring the two examples to class. Then, working with another student, exchange examples, and make corrections to the run-ons or comma splices your classmate found. Finally, discuss your corrections with each other.
2. Copy down four sentences from a television or radio news program, and bring your sentences to class. Then, working in a group of three or four students, pass your sentences to another person in the group. Check to make sure that the sentences you receive contain no run-ons or comma splices.
3. Working in a group, rewrite the sentences transcribed for activity 2, turning them into run-ons or comma splices. Then, exchange the incorrect sentences with another group, and correct their sentences. Finally, compare the original sentences with your corrected sentences and discuss the differences with the other group.
4. *Composing original sentences* Working in a group, collaborate to write five sentences on a topic of the group's choice, being careful to avoid run-ons and comma splices. When you have finished, check the sentences again to make sure you have corrected any errors in grammar, punctuation, or spelling.

✓ REVIEW CHECKLIST: Run-Ons and Comma Splices

- A run-on is an error that occurs when two sentences are joined without punctuation. (See 14A.)
- A comma splice is an error that occurs when two sentences are joined with just a comma. (See 14A.)
- You can correct a run-on or comma splice in one of five ways:
  - by creating two separate sentences;
  - by connecting ideas with a comma followed by a coordinating conjunction;
  - by connecting ideas with a semicolon;
  - by connecting ideas with a semicolon and a conjunctive adverb or transitional expression;
  - by connecting ideas with a subordinating conjunction or relative pronoun. (See 14B.)

CHAPTER

15

Sentence Fragments

SEEING AND WRITING

Why do you think so many young people don't vote? Look at the picture above, and then write a paragraph explaining why you think this situation exists.

PREVIEW

In this chapter, you will learn

- to recognize sentence fragments (15A)
- to correct sentence fragments created when phrases are punctuated as sentences (15B)
- to correct sentence fragments created when verbs are incomplete (15C)
- to correct sentence fragments created when dependent clauses are punctuated as sentences (15D)

Word Power

apathy a lack of interest

apathetic feeling or showing a lack of interest

alienated emotionally withdrawn or unresponsive

A Recognizing Sentence Fragments

A **sentence fragment** is an incomplete sentence. Every sentence must include at least one subject and one verb, and every sentence must express a complete thought. If a group of words does not do *all* these things, it is a fragment and not a sentence—even if it begins with a capital letter and ends with a period.

Writing Tip

Although you often see sentence fragments in advertisements ("A full head of hair in just 30 minutes!"), fragments are not acceptable in college writing.

Computer Tip

Grammar checkers are able to identify many sentence fragments.

ON THE WEB

For more practice recognizing sentence fragments, visit Exercise Central at <bedfordstmartins.com/foundationsfirst>.

SENTENCE A new U.S. president was elected. (includes both a subject and a verb and expresses a complete thought)

FRAGMENT A new U.S. president. (verb is missing)

FRAGMENT Was elected. (subject is missing)

The first fragment—*A new U.S. president*—has no verb: What is being said about the new president? The second fragment—*Was elected*—has no subject: Who was elected? A sentence must have both a subject and a verb and express a complete thought.

◆ PRACTICE 15.1

Each of the following items is a fragment because it lacks a subject, a verb, or both. Add any words needed to turn the fragment into a complete sentence.

Example: The sparkling lake.

The sparkling lake reflected the sunlight.

1. Eats sunflower seeds for breakfast.

2. A terrible scream.

3. Ran and jumped, hoping to win.

4. Answered the question.

5. Wore a purple and pink tutu and waved a magic wand.

6. Harold and Sally, the king and queen of the prom.

7. The mansion on the hill, dark and empty.

____

____

8. The last two pieces of dental floss.

____

____

9. Skidded off the road into a ditch.

____

____

10. The leaves in their fall colors.

____

____

FOCUS Identifying Sentence Fragments

In paragraphs and longer pieces of writing, sentence fragments sometimes appear next to complete sentences. You can often correct a sentence fragment by attaching it to a nearby sentence that includes the missing subject or verb. In the following example, a fragment appears right after a complete sentence:

COMPLETE SENTENCE — FRAGMENT

Okera majored in two subjects. English and philosophy.

To correct the fragment, attach it to the complete sentence that contains the missing subject (*Okera*) and verb (*majored*):

Okera majored in two subjects, English and philosophy.

◆ PRACTICE 15.2

In the following passage, some of the numbered groups of words are missing a subject, a verb, or both. First, identify each fragment by labeling it *F.* Next, decide how each fragment could be attached to a nearby word group to create a complete new sentence. Finally, rewrite the entire passage, using complete sentences, on the lines provided.

Example: Some people use lip balm. ____ To keep their lips from drying out. __F__

Rewrite: *Some people use lip balm to keep their lips from drying out.*

(1) According to some people. _____ (2) Who frequently use lip balm. _____ (3) This product is addictive. _____ (4) The purpose of lip balm. _____ (5) Is to keep the lips. _____ (6) From getting chapped. _____ (7) Can people become dependent on lip balm? _____ (8) Some users say yes. _____ (9) However, the makers of lip balm. _____ (10) Strongly deny that it is addictive. _____

Rewrite:

____

____

____

____

____

____

◆ PRACTICE 15.3

In the following passage, some of the numbered groups of words are missing a subject, a verb, or both. First, underline each fragment. Then, decide how each fragment could be attached to a nearby word group to create a complete new sentence. Finally, rewrite the entire passage, using complete sentences, on the lines provided.

> **Example:** When they feel threatened, bears can be dangerous. And unpredictable.
>
> Rewrite: *When they feel threatened, bears can be dangerous and unpredictable.*

(1) Hikers often wear bells. (2) To make noise on the trail. (3) Especially in areas populated by bears. (4) Bears can hear very well. (5) But cannot see long distances. (6) Sometimes, bears can be frightened by humans. (7) And attack them. (8) However, a bear may hear a person coming. (9) And then is very likely to avoid the person. (10) This is why experienced hikers never go hiking without bells.

Rewrite:

____

____

____

B Correcting Phrase Fragments

A **phrase** is a group of words that is missing a subject or a verb or both. When you punctuate a phrase as if it is a sentence, you create a fragment.

Two kinds of phrases that are often written as sentence fragments are *appositives* and *prepositional phrases.*

Appositive Fragments

An **appositive** is a group of words that identifies, renames, or describes a noun or a pronoun. An appositive cannot stand alone as a sentence. To correct an appositive fragment, add the words needed to make it a complete sentence: the nouns or pronouns that the appositive identifies. (You will often find these words in a nearby sentence.)

For information on using commas with appositives, see 25D.

INCORRECT The *Lethal Weapon* movies have two stars. Mel Gibson and Danny Glover. [APPOSITIVE FRAGMENT: Mel Gibson and Danny Glover.]

CORRECT The *Lethal Weapon* movies have two stars, Mel Gibson and Danny Glover.

Sometimes an expression like *such as* introduces an appositive. Even if an appositive is introduced by *such as,* it still cannot stand alone as a sentence.

INCORRECT Sequels have been made for many popular action movies. Such as *Lethal Weapon, Die Hard, Terminator,* and *The Matrix.* [APPOSITIVE FRAGMENT: Such as *Lethal Weapon, Die Hard, Terminator,* and *The Matrix.*]

CORRECT Sequels have been made for many popular action movies, such as *Lethal Weapon, Die Hard, Terminator,* and *The Matrix.*

Prepositional Phrase Fragments

A **prepositional phrase** consists of a preposition and its object. A prepositional phrase cannot stand alone as a sentence. To correct a prepositional phrase fragment, add the words needed to make it a complete sentence. (You will often find these words in a nearby sentence.)

For more on prepositional phrases, see 9C.

INCORRECT The horse jumped. Over the fence. [PREPOSITIONAL PHRASE FRAGMENT: Over the fence.]

CORRECT The horse jumped over the fence.

ON THE WEB
For more practice correcting phrase fragments, visit Exercise Central at <bedfordstmartins.com /foundationsfirst>.

◆ PRACTICE 15.4

Each of the following phrases is a fragment because it lacks a subject, a verb, or both. Correct each fragment by adding any words needed to turn the fragment into a complete sentence.

Example: With a loud crash.

The bookcase fell to the floor with a loud crash.

1. A high-rise apartment building.

2. On the ledge outside the window.

3. After the race.

4. At the beginning of football season.

5. The excited contestants.

6. During the announcement.

7. Such as a brand-new washing machine.

8. The wealthiest people in town.

9. Before the first flash of lightning.

____

____

10. A gray mist creeping slowly over the grass.

____

____

◆ PRACTICE 15.5

In the following passage, some of the numbered groups of words are appositive fragments or prepositional phrase fragments. First, identify each fragment by labeling it *F.* Then, decide how each fragment could be attached to a nearby word group to create a complete new sentence. Finally, rewrite the entire passage, using complete sentences, on the lines provided.

Example: Mexican artist Frida Kahlo lived and painted. ____ In the first half of the twentieth century. __F__

Rewrite: *Mexican artist Frida Kahlo lived and painted in the first half of the twentieth century.*

(1) She is known to many for her marriage to fellow artist Diego Rivera. ____ (2) A mural painter. ____ (3) She is also famous for her many self-portraits. ____ (4) In these portraits, Kahlo is usually dressed up. ____ (5) In colorful clothes. ____ (6) In her portraits, she is adorned. ____ (7) With jewelry and flowers. ____ (8) The scenes that surround her are often exotic. ____ (9) With a dreamlike atmosphere. ____ (10) Kahlo's paintings express the reality of her own life. ____ (11) A life of great beauty and great pain. ____

Rewrite:

____

____

____

____

____

____

◆ PRACTICE 15.6

In the following passage, some of the numbered groups of words are appositive fragments or prepositional phrase fragments. First, underline each fragment. Then, decide how each fragment could be attached to a nearby word group to create a complete new sentence. Finally, rewrite the entire passage, using complete sentences, on the lines provided.

Example: In 1883, the volcanic island of Krakatoa erupted. ~~Off~~ off the coast of Java.

Rewrite: *In 1883, the volcanic island of Krakatoa erupted off the coast of Java.*

(1) It remains one of the largest eruptions in recorded history and one of the world's largest natural disasters. (2) Nearly forty thousand people died. (3) In the resulting tsunamis. (4) Giant tidal waves reaching one hundred feet high. (5) The force of the eruption caused shifts. (6) In climate. (7) Around the world. (8) Writer Simon Winchester researched this disaster. (9) In 2003, he published a best-selling book. (10) *Krakatoa: The Day the World Exploded.*

Rewrite:

C Correcting Incomplete Verbs

Every sentence must include a **complete verb**. Present participles and past participles are not complete verbs. They need **helping verbs** to complete them.

A **present participle**, such as *rising,* is not a complete verb because it cannot stand alone in a sentence without a helping verb.

Writing Tip

A complete verb consists of the **main verb** and any **helping verbs**. For more on main verbs and helping verbs, see 9F.

FOCUS Using Helping Verbs with Present Participles

To serve as the main verb of a sentence, a present participle must be completed by a form of the verb *be*.

Helping Verb	+	*Present Participle*	=	*Complete Verb*
am		rising		am rising
is		rising		is rising
are		rising		are rising
was		rising		was rising
were		rising		were rising
has been		rising		has been rising
have been		rising		have been rising
had been		rising		had been rising

When you use a present participle without a helping verb, you create a fragment.

FRAGMENT The moon rising over the ocean.

To correct the fragment, add a helping verb.

SENTENCE The moon was rising over the ocean.

An irregular **past participle** is not a complete verb because it cannot stand alone in a sentence without a helping verb.

Writing Tip
Be careful not to create dangling modifiers with participles such as *rising*. (See 18C.)

For a list of irregular past participles, see 20B.

FOCUS Using Helping Verbs with Past Participles

To serve as the main verb of a sentence, a past participle must be completed by a form of the verb *be* or *have*.

Helping Verb(s)	+	*Past Participle*	=	*Complete Verb*
am		hidden		am hidden
is		hidden		is hidden
are		hidden		are hidden
was		hidden		was hidden
were		hidden		were hidden
has		hidden		has hidden
have		hidden		have hidden
had		hidden		had hidden
has been		hidden		has been hidden
have been		hidden		have been hidden
had been		hidden		had been hidden

When you use an irregular past participle without a helping verb, you create a fragment.

FRAGMENT The sun hidden behind a cloud.

To correct the fragment, add a helping verb.

SENTENCE The sun was hidden behind a cloud.

◆ PRACTICE 15.7

ON THE WEB
For more practice correcting incomplete verbs, visit Exercise Central at <bedfordstmartins.com/foundationsfirst>.

Each of the following is a fragment because it does not include a complete verb. Correct each fragment by completing the verb.

Example: She ^is sending an email to her brother in California.

1. My sister forgotten the house where we used to live.
2. Now the nights getting colder.
3. The baby been crying ever since you left.
4. Lately I been too tired to do my homework.
5. Vivian and her daughters gone to the supermarket to pick up some groceries for dinner.
6. They never eaten beef before they moved to this country.
7. Until yesterday, the choir never sung a hymn that featured two soloists.
8. Reverend Martin given beautiful sermons this month.
9. More and more airplanes flying over this neighborhood every day.
10. He swum across this lake at least once a week for twenty years.

D Correcting Dependent Clause Fragments

Every sentence must include a subject and a verb and express a complete thought. A **dependent clause** is a group of words that includes a subject and a verb but does not express a complete thought. A dependent clause cannot stand alone as a sentence.

The following dependent clause is punctuated as if it were a sentence:

FRAGMENT After Jeanette got a full-time job.

This sentence fragment includes a subject (*Jeanette*) and a complete verb (*got*), but it does not express a complete thought. Readers expect the thought to continue, but it stops short. What happened after Jeanette got a full-time job? Was the result positive or negative? To turn this fragment into a sentence, you need to complete the thought.

SENTENCE After Jeanette got a full-time job, she was able to begin paying off her loans.

Dependent Clauses Introduced by Subordinating Conjunctions

Some dependent clauses are introduced by **subordinating conjunctions** (*although, because, if,* and so on).

For more on subordinating conjunctions, see 11A.

The following dependent clause is punctuated as if it were a sentence.

For information on punctuation with subordinating conjunctions, see 11B.

FRAGMENT Although many students study French in high school.

This sentence fragment includes a subject (*many students*) and a complete verb (*study*), but it does not express a complete thought.

One way to correct this fragment is to add an **independent clause** (a complete sentence) to complete the idea and finish the sentence.

Computer Tip

Use the Search or Find function to look for subordinating conjunctions in your writing. (For a list of subordinating conjunctions, see 11A.) Then, check to make sure the sentences in which they appear are complete.

SENTENCE Although many students study French in high school, Spanish is more popular.

Another way to correct the fragment is to leave out the subordinating conjunction *although,* the word that makes the idea incomplete.

SENTENCE Many students study French in high school.

Dependent Clauses Introduced by Relative Pronouns

Other dependent clauses are introduced by **relative pronouns** (*who, which, that,* and so on).

For more on relative pronouns, see 11C.

The following dependent clauses are punctuated as if they were sentences.

FRAGMENT Marc Anthony, who is Puerto Rican.

FRAGMENT Zimbabwe, which was called Rhodesia at one time.

FRAGMENT One habit that has been observed in many overweight children.

Each of these three sentence fragments includes a subject (*Marc Anthony, Zimbabwe, One habit*) and a complete verb (*is, was called, has been observed*). However, they are not sentences because they do not express complete thoughts.

One way to correct each of these fragments is to add the words needed to complete the idea.

For information on punctuation with relative pronouns, see 11D.

SENTENCE Marc Anthony, who is Puerto Rican, records in both English and Spanish.

SENTENCE Zimbabwe, which was called Rhodesia at one time, is a country in Africa.

SENTENCE One habit that has been observed in many overweight children is excessive television viewing.

Another way to correct the fragments is to leave out the relative pronouns that make the ideas incomplete.

SENTENCE Marc Anthony is Puerto Rican.

SENTENCE Zimbabwe was once called Rhodesia.

SENTENCE One habit has been observed in many overweight children.

◆ PRACTICE 15.8

ON THE WEB
For more practice correcting dependent clause fragments, visit Exercise Central at <bedfordstmartins.com/foundationsfirst>.

Correct each of the following dependent clause fragments in two ways. First, turn the fragment into a complete sentence by adding a group of words that completes the idea. Second, turn the fragment into a complete sentence by deleting the subordinating conjunction or relative pronoun that makes the idea incomplete.

Example: Because he wanted to get married.

Revised: *He needed to find a job because he wanted to get married.*

____

Revised: *He wanted to get married.*

____

1. This young man, who has a very promising future.

   Revised: ______________________________

   ____

   Revised: ______________________________

   ____

2. After the music and dancing had stopped.

   Revised: ______________________________

   ____

   Revised: ______________________________

   ____

3. A box turtle that was trying to find water.

   Revised: ______________________________

   ____

   Revised: ______________________________

   ____

4. Even though hang gliding is a dangerous sport.

Revised: ______________________________

____

Revised: ______________________________

____

5. Although most people think of themselves as good drivers.

Revised: ______________________________

____

Revised: ______________________________

____

6. Parents who do not set limits for their children.

Revised: ______________________________

____

Revised: ______________________________

____

7. Frequent-flier miles, which can sometimes be traded for products as well as for airline tickets.

Revised: ______________________________

____

Revised: ______________________________

____

8. Whenever Margaret got up late.

Revised: ______________________________

____

Revised: ______________________________

____

9. While she searched the crowd frantically.

Revised: ______________________________

____

Revised: ______________________________

____

10. A politician, who has to raise huge amounts of money to run for office.

Revised: ______________________________

____

Revised: ______________________________

____

◆ PRACTICE 15.9

All of the following are fragments. Turn each fragment into a complete sentence, and write the revised sentence on the line below the fragment. Whenever possible, try creating two different revisions.

Example: When a huge bat flew out of the closet.

Revised: *I was just climbing into bed when a huge bat flew out of the closet.*

Revised: *When a huge bat flew out of the closet, I decided to check out of the hotel.*

1. Finding a twenty-dollar bill on the sidewalk.

Revised: ______________________________

____

Revised: ______________________________

____

2. To make matters worse.

Revised: ______________________________

____

Revised: ______________________________

____

3. The tiny plastic ballerina spinning inside the music box.

Revised: ______________________________

____

Revised: ____

____

4. Anyone who has ever worked for tips.

Revised: ____

____

Revised: ____

____

5. The basket, which was filled with exotic tropical fruits.

Revised: ____

____

Revised: ____

____

6. Banned from the sport for life.

Revised: ____

____

Revised: ____

____

7. Without a hat or coat.

Revised: ____

____

Revised: ____

____

8. Continuing to play with her toys.

Revised: ____

____

Revised: ____

____

9. Returning to the scene of the crime.

Revised: ____

____

Revised: ____

____

10. Below the surface of the muddy brown river.

Revised: ____

____

Revised: ____

____

■ REVISING AND EDITING

Look back at your response to the Seeing and Writing exercise on page 235. Is every sentence complete? Check every sentence to be sure that it has a subject and a verb, that the verb is complete, and that the sentence expresses a complete thought. If you spot a fragment, revise it by adding the words needed to make it a complete sentence. (Remember, you may be able to correct a fragment simply by attaching it to a nearby sentence or by crossing out a subordinating conjunction or relative pronoun.) If you do not find any fragments in your own writing, work with a classmate to correct his or her writing, or edit work that you did for another assignment.

CHAPTER REVIEW

◆ EDITING PRACTICE: PARAGRAPH

Read the following paragraph, and underline each fragment. Then, correct the fragment by adding the words necessary to complete it, by attaching the fragment to a nearby sentence, or by deleting an unnecessary subordinating conjunction or relative pronoun. The first error has been corrected for you.

Over the past few decades, ~~More~~ more and more people have been recognizing the artwork of nonmainstream artists. Some of these works are called "outsider art." This is valuable and unusual art. That is created by untrained or self-taught artists. Because these artists have not attended art school. They are not familiar with artistic styles and traditions. Their work seems almost childlike. But very original. They make up their own techniques and often choose unusual materials. Such as plywood or plastic bottles. Many outsider artists live on the margins of society. Away from cultural influences. Usually, they are not focused. On showing or selling their art. Outsider art which is becoming more popular among art collectors. Galleries and Web sites are now dedicated to promoting outsider art. In addition, outsider artists showing their work at major museums.

◆ EDITING PRACTICE: ESSAY

Read the following essay, and underline each fragment. Then, correct the fragment by adding the words necessary to complete it, by attaching the fragment to a nearby sentence that completes the idea, or by deleting an unnecessary subordinating conjunction or relative pronoun. The first fragment has been underlined and corrected for you.

The ADA

Many people living in America are familiar with the Americans with Disabilities Act (ADA), which ~~Which~~ protects the rights of disabled people. The ADA was created to guarantee disabled people greater access to all parts of society. Including employment, transportation, and telecommunications. According to the ADA. Employers must provide "reasonable accommodation" for disabled employees, and owners must make their businesses accessible. To patrons with disabilities. In the years since the ADA was passed, however, there has been a lot of debate. Over what "reasonable accommodation" means. And about how the law should be put into action. As a result, the law continues to be reinterpreted and amended.

Student receiving diploma

The act itself took many years. To develop. In 1964, the Civil Rights Act granted protection. To women and to racial and religious minorities. But not to people with disabilities. During the 1970s and 1980s, activism in the disabled community grew. Inspired by the civil rights movement. More people became involved in the fight. For the rights of people with

Sign denoting handicapped parking

disabilities. When it finally passed in 1990, the ADA was a great victory. For the community and for all people with disabilities. The mentally as well as the physically challenged.

Today, the activism continues. Groups like ADA Watch who work to strengthen the power of the ADA and protect it from threats. Unfortunately, other groups want to get rid of the ADA altogether. These groups claim. That accommodating disabled people is too expensive and not good for the economy. They want to make it harder. To enforce the laws. Meanwhile, the disabled community works to keep the laws active and up-to-date.

Fortunately, the disabled community been able to communicate clearly the benefits of the ADA. Although the ADA does not guarantee success for all people with disabilities. It promises them a fair chance. For many, this means an opportunity. To work and to be independent. Ultimately, the ADA benefits everyone. Many accommodations required by the ADA make workspaces and businesses safer for all people. Those with and without disabilities. Americans also strengthen their community and democracy. When they allow everyone to participate.

◆ COLLABORATIVE ACTIVITIES

1. Copy three fragments that you find in magazine or newspaper advertisements, and bring them to class. Then, exchange fragments with another student. Correct the fragments you receive and discuss your corrections with your classmate.
2. Bring a newspaper to class. Working in a group of three or four students, find three headlines that are fragments. Then, working on your own, turn each fragment into a complete sentence. Finally, compare your sentences with those written by other students in your group, and choose the best sentence for each headline.
3. Discuss some of the fragments you worked on in activities 1 and 2. Why were fragments used in the advertisements and the headlines? How are these fragments different from the complete sentences you wrote? Which work more effectively? Why?
4. *Composing original sentences* Working in a group, collaborate to produce five sentences that contain no fragments. Make sure at least one sentence contains a prepositional phrase, at least one contains an appositive, at least one contains a present participle, and at least one con-

tains a past participle. When you have finished, check the sentences to make sure you have corrected any errors in grammar, punctuation, or spelling.

✓ REVIEW CHECKLIST: Sentence Fragments

- ☐ A sentence fragment is an incomplete sentence. Every sentence must include a subject and a verb and must express a complete thought. (See 15A.)
- ☐ Phrases cannot stand alone as sentences. (See 15B.)
- ☐ Every sentence must include a complete verb. (See 15C.)
- ☐ Dependent clauses cannot stand alone as sentences. (See 15D.)

CHAPTER

16

Subject-Verb Agreement

PREVIEW

In this chapter, you will learn

- to understand subject-verb agreement (16A)
- to avoid agreement problems with *be, have,* and *do* (16B)
- to avoid agreement problems with compound subjects (16C)
- to avoid agreement problems when a prepositional phrase comes between the subject and the verb (16D)
- to avoid agreement problems with indefinite pronouns as subjects (16E)
- to avoid agreement problems when the subject comes after the verb (16F)
- to avoid agreement problems with the relative pronouns *who, which,* and *that* (16G)

SEEING AND WRITING

Look at the picture above. Then, using present tense verbs, write a paragraph describing what you see.

Word Power

monument a structure built as a memorial

observer someone who watches attentively

symbol a thing that represents something else

A Understanding Subject-Verb Agreement

A sentence's subject (a noun or a pronoun) and verb must **agree**: singular subjects take singular verbs, and plural subjects take plural verbs.

I walk to work. (The first-person singular pronoun *I* takes the singular verb *walk.*)

You walk to work. (The second-person singular pronoun *you* takes the singular verb *walk.*)

Alex walks to work. (The third-person singular noun *Alex* takes the singular verb *walks.*)

For more on person, see 17B.

Alex and I walk to work. (The compound subject *Alex and I* takes the plural verb *walk*.)

You all walk to work. (The second-person plural pronoun *you* takes the plural verb *walk*.)

They walk to work. (The third-person plural pronoun *they* takes the plural verb *walk*.)

For more on compound subjects, see 16C.

Most subject-verb agreement problems occur in the present tense, where third-person singular subjects require special verb forms. *Regular verbs* in the *present tense* form the third-person singular by adding *-s* or *-es* to the third-person singular form of the verb. In all other tenses, the same form of the verb is used with every subject: *I walked, he walked, they walked; I will walk, she will walk, they will walk.*

Subject-Verb Agreement

	Singular	Plural
1st person	I walk	Alex and I/we walk
2nd person	you walk	you walk
3rd person	he/she/it walks	they walk
	the woman walks	the women walk
	Alex walks	Alex and Sam walk

Writing Tip
Subject-verb agreement presents special problems with the irregular verb *be*. (See 16B.)

◆ PRACTICE 16.1

Underline the correct form of the verb in each of the following sentences. Make sure that the verb agrees with the subject.

Example: Many American musicians (enjoys/enjoy) world music.

(1) Some musicians (travels/travel) to other continents to hear it. (2) The different patterns and rhythms (inspires/inspire) them to compose their own new music. (3) Many people in America (likes/like) the sound of this fusion music. (4) Guitarist Ry Cooder (travels/travel) often to other countries. (5) In Cuba, he (plays/play) with singer Ibrahim Ferrer. (6) In India, he (gets/get) together with Vishwa Mohan Bhatt, a famous sitar player. (7) Singer Paul Simon also (takes/take) trips abroad regularly. (8) The members of Ladysmith Black Mambazo (sings/sing) with him when he visits Africa. (9) He also (records/record) songs with Brazilian musicians. (10) Simon often (brings/bring) these musicians to America to tour with him. (11) Cellist Yo-Yo Ma also (loves/love) to play different kinds of music. (12) He (joins/join) a group of Brazilian

ON THE WEB
For more practice understanding subject-verb agreement, visit Exercise Central at <bedfordstmartins.com/foundationsfirst>.

musicians on his album *Obligado Brazil.* (13) They (succeeds/succeed) in creating beautiful new sounds. (14) These collaborations (keeps/keep) music from getting stale. (15) They also (provides/provide) a way for people from different countries to meet and share their music.

◆ PRACTICE 16.2

Fill in the blank with the correct present tense form of the verb in parentheses.

Example: In this country, the Atkins diet ___attracts___ (attract) many followers.

(1) It is popular because many people ______________ (fear) being fat. (2) Consequently, many people ______________ (look) for reliable ways to stay thin. (3) Like most diet plans, the Atkins diet ______________ (promise) success. (4) Followers of Dr. Atkins ______________ (suggest) eating fewer carbohydrates. (5) Instead of carbohydrates, dieters ______________ (eat) more protein and vegetables. (6) Critics ______________ (argue) that this plan encourages people to eat too much meat. (7) Supporters ______________ (claim) that the diet is healthy. (8) In any case, people ______________ (like) being able to lose weight while eating familiar, fatty foods. (9) The long-term effects ______________ (remain) unknown. (10) Unlike most fads, the Atkins diet, for now, ______________ (seem) to work.

B Avoiding Agreement Problems with *Be, Have,* and *Do*

The verbs *be, have,* and *do* are irregular in the present tense. The best way to avoid problems with these verbs is to memorize their forms.

The past tense forms of be *are shown in 19C.*

Subject-Verb Agreement with Be

	Singular	**Plural**
1st person	I am	we are
2nd person	you are	you are
3rd person	he/she/it is	they are
	Tran is	Tran and Ryan are
	the boy is	the boys are

Subject-Verb Agreement with Have

	Singular	Plural
1st person	I have	we have
2nd person	you have	you have
3rd person	he/she/it has	they have
	Shana has	Shana and Robert have
	the student has	the students have

Writing Tip
For information on forming contractions with the verbs *be, have,* and *do,* see 26A.

Subject-Verb Agreement with Do

	Singular	Plural
1st person	I do	we do
2nd person	you do	you do
3rd person	he/she/it does	they do
	Ken does	Ken and Mia do
	the book does	the books do

For information on forming negative statements and questions with the verb do, *see 24G.*

◆ PRACTICE 16.3

Fill in the blank with the correct present tense form of the verb *be.*

Example: The Tour de France ___is___ a popular bicycle race.

1. Every July, the Tour de France ________ televised all over the world.
2. Lance Armstrong ________ a five-time winner of the Tour de France.
3. Because of him, many people ________ fans of this event.
4. They ________ proud of him for overcoming cancer.
5. They like to watch him because they know he ________ not a quitter.
6. Armstrong also ________ the writer of two best-selling books.
7. Watching him race, I ________ motivated to work harder.
8. The Tour de France ________ a difficult race, lasting three weeks.
9. For an ordinary person, the distances ________ unimaginable.
10. Even if you ________ a skilled cyclist, the Tour de France would be a great challenge.

ON THE WEB
For more practice avoiding agreement problems with be, have, *and* do, *visit Exercise Central at <bedfordstmartins.com/foundationsfirst>.*

◆ PRACTICE 16.4

Fill in the blank with the correct present tense form of the verb *have.*

Example: Every summer, the Forest Service ___has___ to manage forest fires.

1. Managers ______ many decisions to make about what they should and should not allow to burn.
2. Fire management is complicated because many people ______ strong opinions about it.
3. Hikers and campers ______ an interest in keeping the forest green.
4. However, the healthiest forests ______ regular fires.
5. Some environmentalists ______ a problem with allowing a forest fire to burn; they think all fires should be put out immediately.
6. However, when an overprotected forest catches fire, we ______ a bad situation on our hands because of all the dead trees and vegetation.
7. This is a problem because these forests ______ much more fuel to burn.
8. Of course, a fire ______ a greater chance of causing problems if it threatens people or buildings.
9. Most people agree that the government ______ a responsibility to keep people out of danger.
10. When people build a home in the middle of a forest, however, they often ______ no idea what dangers they face.

◆ PRACTICE 16.5

Fill in the blank with the correct present tense form of the verb *do.*

Example: Therapy animals ___do___ many different kinds of community-service work.

1. For example, many dogs ______ important work in schools and hospitals.
2. In some schools, children ______ a "read-to-a-dog" project to promote literacy.

3. Animals ______________ not do their work alone, of course.

4. A person, usually the pet's owner, ______________ therapy along with the animal.

5. The owner ______________ a fair amount of training with the animal to prepare for this kind of work.

6. First, you ______________ an evaluation to make sure the animal is a good candidate.

7. Then the animal ______________ a series of tests to get officially registered.

8. Other animals besides dogs ______________ therapy as well.

9. We ______________ not usually think of hamsters, goats, or birds as being good around people.

10. However, a friendly bird can ______________ an excellent job of putting a person at ease.

◆ PRACTICE 16.6

Fill in the blank with the correct present tense form of *be, have,* or *do.*

Example: All over the world, soccer ______*is*______ (be) a popular sport.

(1) Everywhere except in the United States, soccer ______________ (be) called football. (2) In the United States, however, football ______________ (have) a different meaning. (3) American football ______________ (have) many fans, but most of them ______________ (be) in this country. (4) Soccer ______________ (have) a larger audience worldwide than American football. (5) Soccer ______________ (do) not yet have the popularity in the United States that it ______________ (have) most other places. (6) Nevertheless, the World Cup ______________ (have) more and more U.S. fans every year.

(7) The World Cup ______________ (be) the most important international soccer tournament. (8) Like Olympic events, World Cup

matches ____________ (be) contests between countries, and fans ____________ (have) a patriotic loyalty to their teams. (9) To make its country proud, a devoted team ____________ (do) anything to win. (10) The United States ____________ (have) its own men's and women's soccer teams that play in the World Cup. (11) When our teams ____________ (do) well, we ____________ (be) more interested in the tournament. (12) Fortunately, our teams ____________ (be) internationally competitive. (13) The women ____________ (do) particularly well. (14) The U.S. women's team ____________ (be) almost always one of the top four teams in the world. (15) They ____________ (have) first-place trophies from both the 1991 and 1999 World Cups. (16) As a result, many of these players, like Mia Hamm, ____________ (be) famous and ____________ (have) the admiration and respect of many young soccer players.

(17) American football ____________ (do) a good job of attracting an audience in the United States. (18) Although soccer ____________ (be) not yet the spectator sport that football is, many children in the United States ____________ (be) soccer players. (19) Because of this, soccer ____________ (have) a great future in this country. Perhaps someday, soccer will be the sport Americans think of when they hear the word *football*.

C Avoiding Agreement Problems with Compound Subjects

The subject of a sentence is not always a single word. Sometimes a sentence has a **compound subject**, which consists of two or more words. To avoid agreement problems with compound subjects, follow these rules.

- If the parts of a compound subject are connected by *and*, use a plural verb.

  Every day, Sarah and Tom drive to school.

- If the parts of a compound subject are connected by *or* and both parts are singular, use a singular verb.

  Every day, Sarah or Tom drives to school.

- If the parts of a compound subject are connected by *or* and both parts are plural, use a plural verb.

  Every day, Sarah's parents or Tom's parents drive to school.

- If the parts of a compound subject are connected by *or* and one part is singular and the other part is plural, the verb agrees with the part of the compound subject closest to the verb.

  Every day, Sarah or her friends drive to school.

  Every day, her friends or Sarah drives to school.

◆ PRACTICE 16.7

Underline the correct verb in each of the following sentences.

ON THE WEB
For more practice avoiding agreement problems with compound subjects, visit Exercise Central at <bedfordstmartins .com/foundationsfirst>.

Example: Katie and David (is/are) expecting a baby in June.

1. Toast or pancakes (is/are) my usual breakfast.
2. The teachers and the students (dresses/dress) differently.
3. Her father and mother (works/work) in the suburbs.
4. Diamonds or pearls (costs/cost) more than costume jewelry.
5. The album and the CD (shares/share) the same cover art, but the CD has some additional songs.
6. Thunder and rain or too much heat (spoils/spoil) the fun of hiking in the woods.
7. Winter squash and pumpkins (makes/make) delicious pies.
8. Several tadpoles and a frog (swims/swim) in the pond.
9. Take-out food and restaurants (saves/save) time, but both are more expensive than cooking at home.
10. Dental floss and a toothbrush (protects/protect) your teeth if you use them often.

◆ PRACTICE 16.8

Circle the correct verb in each of the following sentences.

Example: The roof and plumbing (needs/need) immediate repair.

1. Cornmeal or whole wheat flour (is/are) a possible substitute for white flour in that recipe.
2. In wet weather, a raincoat and boots (keeps/keep) me from getting soaked.
3. All U.S. senators and representatives (has/have) Web sites now.

4. A woodchuck or raccoons (eats/eat) all the ripe strawberries in my garden every night.
5. These photograph albums or this envelope (contains/contain) the pictures from our vacation.
6. My futon and easy chair (fills/fill) the whole apartment.
7. I don't remember whether blue or green (is/are) my father's favorite color.
8. Water and iced tea (quenches/quench) thirst better than cola.
9. The bus and the subway (costs/cost) the same.
10. Styrofoam cups and yellowed newspapers (litters/litter) the floor of the waiting room.

D Avoiding Agreement Problems When a Prepositional Phrase Comes between the Subject and the Verb

For more on prepositional phrases and for a list of prepositions, see 9C.

Remember, a verb must always agree with its subject. Do not be confused if a prepositional phrase comes between the sentence's subject and verb. Keep in mind that a noun or pronoun that is part of a prepositional phrase (a phrase that begins with *of, in, between,* and so on) cannot be the subject of the sentence.

A box of chocolates makes a very good gift.
High levels of radon occur in some houses.
Volunteers, including my brother, help clean up the community.

An easy way to identify the subject of a sentence is to cross out the prepositional phrase.

A box ~~of chocolates~~ makes a very good gift.
High levels ~~of radon~~ occur in some houses.
Volunteers, ~~including my brother~~, help clean up the community.

FOCUS Words That Come between the Subject and the Verb

Watch out for phrases that begin with words such as *as well as, in addition to,* or *along with.* Such phrases do not make a singular subject plural.

The mayor, as well as members of the city council, supports the pay increase.

◆ PRACTICE 16.9

In each of the following sentences, cross out the prepositional phrase that separates the subject and the verb. Then, underline the simple subject of the sentence once and the verb that agrees with the subject twice.

Example: Some people ~~in China~~ (travels/travel) by bicycle.

1. A resident of one of China's cities (goes/go) a long distance to work.
2. Westerners in China (expects/expect) to see many bicycles.
3. A black bicycle with a huge, heavy frame (has/have) been a common sight in China for many years.
4. The streets in Beijing and other large cities (has/have) bicycle lanes.
5. Today, the economy of China (is/are) booming.
6. Chinese citizens with high-paying jobs (is/are) not likely to commute by bicycle.
7. A worker with a long commute (does/do) not want to spend hours bicycling to work.
8. A bus in city streets as well as a private car (pollutes/pollute) the air.
9. Many Chinese people under age thirty (does/do) not even know how to ride a bicycle.
10. A Chinese store with a stock of bicycles (rents/rent) the old-fashioned black ones, mainly to tourists.

ON THE WEB

For more practice avoiding agreement problems when a prepositional phrase comes between the subject and the verb, visit Exercise Central at <bedfordstmartins.com/foundationsfirst>.

◆ PRACTICE 16.10

In each of the following sentences, cross out the prepositional phrase that separates the subject and the verb. Then, underline the simple subject of the sentence once and the verb that agrees with the subject twice.

Example: My memory ~~of those ten days~~ (remains/remain) clear.

1. The roots of these plants (goes/go) deep into the soil.
2. Some chess players in the park (meets/meet) every morning.
3. Firefighters on the night shift (takes/take) turns cooking dinner for the crew.
4. The woman across the street (sings/sing) opera while doing her laundry.
5. A wedding with a hundred guests (costs/cost) a small fortune.
6. The lights of Las Vegas (appears/appear) suddenly to travelers in the desert.

7. That book about chimpanzees (was/were) due back at the library last week.
8. Even a movie with expensive special effects (needs/need) an interesting plot.
9. Tickets to this week's performances (is/are) already sold out.
10. The sandy banks along the river (disappears/disappear) during spring floods.

E Avoiding Agreement Problems with Indefinite Pronouns as Subjects

Writing Tip
Many indefinite pronouns end in *-one, -body,* or *-thing.* These pronouns are always singular.

Indefinite pronouns—*anybody, everyone,* and so on—do not refer to specific persons or things. Most indefinite pronouns are singular and take singular verbs.

Everyone likes ice cream.
Each of the boys carries a beeper.
Neither of the boys misses class.
Nobody wants to see the team lose.

Singular Indefinite Pronouns

anybody	either	neither	one
anyone	everybody	nobody	somebody
anything	everyone	no one	someone
each	everything	nothing	something

Some indefinite pronouns are plural—*many, several, few, both, others.* Plural indefinite pronouns take plural verbs.

For more on indefinite pronouns, see 22C.

Many watch the nightly news on television.
Few get their news from the Internet.

ON THE WEB
For more practice avoiding agreement problems, visit Exercise Central at <bedfordstmartins.com/foundationsfirst>.

◆ PRACTICE 16.11

Underline the correct verb in each of the following sentences.

Example: Nobody (likes/like) to get calls from telemarketers.

(1) However, few (manages/manage) to avoid these annoyances. (2) Everyone (seems/seem) to get these calls from time to time. (3) Many

(wants/want) telemarketers to stop. (4) One solution (is/are) the do-not-call list. (5) Everyone (wants/want) to be able to choose whether to get calls from telemarketers. (6) However, everybody in the telemarketing industry (thinks/think) that do-not-call lists will damage their business. (7) They argue that telemarketers (risks/risk) losing their jobs if the do-not-call list is made legal. (8) The two groups disagree; both (argues/argue) that they are defending an essential freedom. (9) Both (thinks/think) the Constitution will protect them. (10) Because this issue is still being decided in the federal courts, neither (is/are) the winner yet.

F Avoiding Agreement Problems When the Subject Comes after the Verb

A verb agrees with its subject even if the subject comes after the verb, as it does in questions.

Where is (V) the ATM (S)?

Where are (V) Zack and Angela (S)?

Why are (V) they (S) running?

If you have trouble identifying the subject, answer the question with a statement.

Where is (V) the ATM (S)? The ATM (S) is (V) inside the bank.

FOCUS *There is* and *There are*

When a sentence begins with *there is* or *there are,* the word *there* is not the subject of the sentence. The subject comes after the form of the verb *be.*

There is (V) still one ticket (S) available for the playoffs.

There are (V) still ten tickets (S) available for the playoffs.

Writing Tip

Try to avoid beginning a sentence with *there is* or *there are.* If possible, write more directly: *One ticket is still available for the playoffs. Ten tickets are still available for the playoffs.*

ON THE WEB
For more practice avoiding agreement problems when the subject comes after the verb, visit Exercise Central at <bedfordstmartins.com/foundationsfirst>.

◆ PRACTICE 16.12

First, underline the simple subject of each sentence. Then, circle the correct form of the verb.

Example: What (is/are) your reasons for applying to this college?

1. There (is/are) an excellent nursing program here.
2. Where (is/are) you planning to live during the semester?
3. There (is/are) an inexpensive dormitory on Third Avenue.
4. What (does/do) the students here usually like best about the school?
5. How difficult (is/are) the placement tests?
6. What (has/have) been the most popular major in the last five years?
7. There (is/are) more people taking business courses today than there were twenty years ago.
8. There (has/have) been few nursing jobs available lately.
9. How many years (does/do) an average student take to graduate?
10. There (is/are) no simple answer to that question.

◆ PRACTICE 16.13

Circle the correct form of the verb *be* in each of the following sentences.

Example: There (is/are) several ways to write a good résumé.

1. There (is/are) a potato in her garden that resembles Richard Nixon.
2. There (is/are) furniture designed by Frank Lloyd Wright in our local museum.
3. There (is/are) three drummers in the high school orchestra.
4. There (is/are) sand in my shoes.
5. There (is/are) stories I've heard that would make your hair stand on end.
6. There (is/are) trains to the shore six or seven times a day.
7. There (is/are) other fish in the sea.
8. There (is/are) a list of names engraved on the side of the monument.

9. There (is/are) nothing on television tonight.

10. There (is/are) many people who deserve this award more than I do.

G Avoiding Agreement Problems with the Relative Pronouns *Who, Which,* and *That*

The relative pronouns *who, which,* and *that* are singular when they refer to a singular word and plural when they refer to a plural word. The verb in the dependent clause introduced by the relative pronoun must agree with the word to which the relative pronoun refers.

For more on who, which, that, *and other relative pronouns, see 11C and 11D.*

Workers who have health insurance are lucky. (The verb *have* is plural because the relative pronoun *who* refers to *workers,* which is plural.)

Anyone who has health insurance is lucky. (The verb *has* is singular because the relative pronoun *who* refers to *anyone,* which is singular.)

The house, which stands at the corner of Fifth and Spring Garden, is open to tourists. (The verb *stands* is singular because the relative pronoun *which* refers to *house,* which is singular.)

Books that have large print are easy to read. (The verb *have* is plural because the relative pronoun *that* refers to *books,* which is plural.)

◆ PRACTICE 16.14

In the blank, write the word that *who, which,* or *that* refers to. Then, circle the correct form of the verb.

ON THE WEB
For more practice avoiding agreement problems with the relative pronouns who, which, *and* that, *visit Exercise Central at <bedfordstmartins.com/foundationsfirst>.*

Example: ___toys___ I found an attic full of toys that (sells/sell) for high prices at antique shows.

_______ 1. Her mother, who (watches/watch) at least two movies a day, is working on a film encyclopedia.

_______ 2. In Hawaii, he saw the whales that (migrates/migrate) through the islands.

_______ 3. Newscasters who constantly (smiles/smile) make me nervous.

__________ 4. She owns the city's first Ethiopian restaurant, which (serves/serve) a young, enthusiastic crowd on weekend nights.

__________ 5. Some countries provide free medical care to all citizens who (needs/need) it.

__________ 6. The two horses that (lives/live) in my neighbor's pasture love to eat sugar cubes.

__________ 7. The baby is going to spill her grape juice, which (leaves/leave) permanent stains.

__________ 8. My brother bought a coffeemaker that (makes/make) very strong coffee.

__________ 9. Their hot water is heated by solar panels, which (charges/charge) a battery for use on cloudy days.

__________ 10. According to the courts, video cameras can film anyone who (appears/appear) in a public place.

◆ PRACTICE 16.15

First, draw an arrow from *who, which,* or *that* to the word it refers to. Then, circle the correct form of the verb.

> **Example:** Tourists who (travels/travel) through central and eastern Pennsylvania are likely to see Amish communities.

(1) The Amish have lived in America for hundreds of years but reject the modern world, which (depends/depend) on electricity and technology. (2) The Amish, who (farms/farm) for a living, choose to live without modern conveniences. (3) People who (lives/live) on Amish farms do all of their work without the help of motorized machinery. (4) Instead, they use horse-drawn equipment that (does/do) not require motors. (5) They value simplicity and self-denial, which (is/are) praised in the Bible. (6) The Amish, who also (dresses/dress) in plain, old-fashioned clothes and who (speaks/speak) Pennsylvania Dutch, seem strange to most modern Americans. (7) However, the Amish are proud of the lifestyle that

(makes/make) them different from the rest of the world. (8) The behavior that (seems/seem) odd to outsiders is the same behavior that (allows/allow) the Amish to be self-sufficient. (9) They have their own code of conduct, which (is/are) known as the *Ordnung,* or order. (10) It is this code that (makes/make) the Amish way of life peaceful and satisfying to those who follow it.

REVISING AND EDITING

Look back at your response to the Seeing and Writing exercise on page 254. Make sure every verb agrees with its subject. (Remember to check for the situations discussed in sections B through G of this chapter.) If you find any incorrect verb forms, cross them out, and write the correct forms above them.

CHAPTER REVIEW

◆ EDITING PRACTICE: PARAGRAPH

Computer Tip

Your computer's grammar checker can spot many subject-verb agreement problems.

Read the following student paragraph. If the underlined verb does not agree with its subject, cross out the verb, and write in the correct form. If it does, write *C* above the verb. The first sentence has been done for you.

Every parent has [C] the right to take time off from work after the birth or adoption of a child. The Family and Medical Leave Act (FMLA) of 1993 promise the same amount of leave to men as it do to women. The law guarantees twelve weeks of unpaid leave to each parent. Although there is several restrictions, anyone who request leave are supposed to receive it. However, many men do not take paternity leave because there are a lot of pressure to keep working. A woman who gives birth are more likely to feel pressure to stay at home with her new baby. Ideally, the law takes pressure off both parents and allow them to spend more time together with their infant.

◆ EDITING PRACTICE: ESSAY

Read the following student essay. If the underlined verb does not agree with its subject, cross out the verb and write in the correct form. If it does, write *C* above the verb. The first sentence has been done for you.

Credit cards

An overdue bill

Credit Card Debt

Alhough it is *C* one of the most expensive ways to be in debt, many people in this country ~~carries~~ *carry* a large credit-card balance. This kind of debt often develops before we realize it are happening. Despite our best intentions, balances creep upward. Even though most of these cards charges extremely high interest rates, most people in this situation never consider taking out a low-interest loan. Few really intends to spend more than they earns. The problem is that credit cards make it easy to spend money that do not exist.

The companies that issues credit cards make them very simple to get. Once people has credit cards, it is easy for them to spend more than they should. Most companies offers benefits for using their card. There is companies that gives clients free airfare or merchandise when they spend a certain amount. Because these offers seem so good, almost everyone have one or more credit cards. Sometimes we forget, however, that the credit-card companies want to keep us in debt. They are happiest when we is unable to pay our bills.

If users are careful, credit cards are not dangerous. However, we live in a culture that encourage us to spend. Too many people falls into this trap, but there is ways to prevent it. First, everyone need to learn how a credit card works and how the credit-card companies makes their money. For example, the minimum payment is often less than the interest owed on the balance. By paying only the minimum, users gets further and further in debt—even though they pay their bills. Companies have many other tricks, which is hard to see at first glance. If we want to use credit cards, we need to take the time to read the rules.

◆ COLLABORATIVE ACTIVITIES

1. Working on your own, write five subjects (people, places, or things) on a sheet of paper. The subjects can be singular or plural. Then, working in a group of three students, pass the paper to another member of the group. On the paper you receive, write a dependent clause beginning with *who, which,* or *that* for each of the five subjects. Then, pass the paper again, and finish the sentences on the paper you receive.

   Example

First Person	*Second Person*	*Third Person*
The pizza	*that has a burned crust*	*tastes funny.*

   Finally, review the paper you started with, and correct any subject-verb agreement errors in the sentences that have been created from your subjects.
2. Each person in the group should write the same five subjects from activity 1 on another sheet of paper. Next, each person should pass his or her paper to another member of the group, who will add a prepositional phrase to follow each subject. Then, the third member of the group will complete the sentences. When you get your paper back, check subject-verb agreement.
3. Working in the same group, choose one sentence from activity 1 and one sentence from activity 2. As a group, write a paragraph that contains both sentences. Make sure that at least one additional sentence contains an indefinite pronoun used as a subject. Check the paragraph to be sure there are no errors in subject-verb agreement. When your group is satisfied with its paragraph, have one member read it to the class.
4. *Composing original sentences* Working in a group of three students, write four sentences in the present tense. Make sure that one sentence has a compound subject, one has a prepositional phrase between the subject and the verb, one has an indefinite pronoun as a subject, and one has a subject that comes after the verb. Make sure none of the sentences contains errors in subject-verb agreement.

☑ REVIEW CHECKLIST: Subject-Verb Agreement

- Singular subjects (nouns and pronouns) take singular verbs, and plural subjects take plural verbs. (See 16A.)
- The irregular verbs *be, have,* and *do* often present problems with subject-verb agreement in the present tense. (See 16B.)
- Compound subjects can cause problems in agreement. (See 16C.)

(continued on the following page)

(continued from the previous page)

- A prepositional phrase that comes between the subject and the verb does not affect subject-verb agreement. (See 16D.)
- Most indefinite pronouns, such as *no one* and *everyone,* are singular and take a singular verb when they serve as the subject of the sentence. (See 16E.)
- A verb agrees with its subject even if the subject comes after the verb. (See 16F.)
- The relative pronouns *who, which,* and *that* are singular when they refer to a singular word and plural when they refer to a plural word. (See 16G.)

CHAPTER

17

Illogical Shifts

PREVIEW

In this chapter, you will learn

- to avoid illogical shifts in tense (17A)
- to avoid illogical shifts in person (17B)
- to avoid illogical shifts in voice (17C)

SEEING AND WRITING

Do you think women should be allowed to serve in combat? Why or why not? Look at the picture above, and then write a paragraph in which you answer these questions.

Word Power

gender sex (male or female)

rigor a hardship or difficulty

parity equality in power or value

A **shift** occurs whenever a writer changes *tense, person,* or *voice* in a sentence or a paragraph. As you write and revise, make sure that any shifts you make are logical—that is, that they occur for a reason.

A Avoiding Illogical Shifts in Tense

Tense is the form a verb takes to show when an action took place or a situation occurred. An **illogical shift in tense** occurs when a writer shifts from one tense to another for no apparent reason.

For more on tense, see Chapters 19 and 20.

ILLOGICAL SHIFT We sat at the table for more than an hour before a server comes and takes our order. (shift from past tense to present tense)

REVISED We sat at the table for more than an hour before a server came and took our order. (consistent use of past tense)

Of course, a shift in tense is often necessary. In the following sentence, for example, a shift from past to present tense shows a change in the writer's attitude between the past and the present.

LOGICAL SHIFT In high school, I just wanted to have fun, but now I want to become a graphic artist.

ON THE WEB
For more practice avoiding illogical shifts in tense, visit Exercise Central at <bedfordstmartins.com /foundationsfirst>.

◆ PRACTICE 17.1

Underline the verbs in the following sentences. Then, correct any illogical shifts by writing the correct verb tense above the line. If a sentence is correct, write *C* in the blank after the sentence.

Examples

Thomas ate meat until he married Meena, but now he is a vegetarian.

C

As I drove through the woods, a deer suddenly ~~runs~~ ran across the road.

____

1. I ordered a CD online, but it takes more than a week to arrive. ____
2. Although the zookeeper warned us about feeding the animals, one couple ignores him. ____
3. Last night, he felt sad; this morning, he is much more cheerful. ____
4. The noon whistle blew, and immediately everyone stop working. ____
5. The baby makes a terrible mess every time he eats. ____
6. The movie was out of focus, so we complain to the manager. ____
7. She offered us free tickets and tells us to use them anytime. ____
8. She sang the blues in Mississippi before she arrives in Detroit. ____
9. Even though the landlord agreed to allow pets, now he wants me to get rid of my dog. ____
10. The deejay played great dance music until the sun comes up. ____

◆ PRACTICE 17.2

Edit the following sentences for illogical shifts in tense. If a sentence is correct, write *C* in the blank.

Example: The New York City Draft Riots occurred in 1863 when President Lincoln ~~announces~~ *announced* a draft for the Civil War. ____

(1) The Civil War began in 1861, and by 1863, both sides needed more soldiers. ____ (2) Abraham Lincoln was president of the United States at that time, and on March 3, 1863, he begins drafting men in the North to fight in the war. ____ (3) Lincoln needs 300,000 more men. ____ (4) Everyone agreed that the draft is not fair. ____ (5) For example, a rich man could pay a "commutation fee" that allows him to hire someone else to fight so that he could stay home. ____ (6) Most people in the North are tired of the war, and not all of them supported the cause of freeing the slaves in the South. ____ (7) On June 12, 1863, the first draftees were chosen, and soon mobs begin to form. ____ (8) There are eventually about fifty thousand people rioting in New York City, and many of the rioters targeted blacks. ____ (9) The mob looted dozens of stores and killed about a hundred people. ____ (10) Federal troops ended the rioting after three days; the troops remained in New York for several weeks. ____

B Avoiding Illogical Shifts in Person

Person is the form a pronoun takes to indicate who is speaking, spoken about, or spoken to.

Person

	Singular	**Plural**
First person	I	we
Second person	you	you
Third person	he, she, it	they

An **illogical shift in person** occurs when a writer shifts from one person to another for no apparent reason.

ILLOGICAL SHIFT Before a person gets a job in the computer industry, you have to take a lot of courses. (shift from third person to second person)

REVISED Before a person gets a job in the computer industry, he or she has to take a lot of courses. (consistent use of third person)

ILLOGICAL SHIFT The students were told that you have to attend a conference each week. (shift from third person to second person)

REVISED The students were told that they had to attend a conference each week. (consistent use of third person plural)

Writing Tip

Be careful not to use the pronoun *he* to refer to a noun, such as *person,* that could be either masculine or feminine. Instead, use *he or she*—or make the noun plural, and use *they.*

For more on subject-verb agreement, see Chapter 16.

◆ PRACTICE 17.3

Correct any illogical shifts in person in the following sentences. If necessary, change any verbs that do not agree with the new subjects. If a sentence is correct, write *C* in the blank.

Example: The guide told us that ~~you~~ we had to learn certain skills to survive in the wilderness. ____

1. The students learned that you needed to use proper lab technique. ____
2. A salesperson can successfully sell products door-to-door; you just have to be persistent. ____
3. I worked on an assembly line where you could not spend more than thirty seconds on each task. ____
4. The manager told me that I should improve my attitude. ____
5. His boss told him that you have to be on time for work every day. ____
6. Maria discovered that you cannot buy friends. ____
7. The officer who stopped us claimed that we had gone through a stop sign. ____
8. You must respect your coworkers if you want to get along in the office. ____

ON THE WEB

For more practice avoiding illogical shifts in person, visit Exercise Central at <bedfordstmartins.com/foundationsfirst>.

9. His brother said that you could find almost anything on the Internet. ____

10. The boss's daughter found out that you could use family connections to get a job but that you needed talent to keep it. ____

◆ PRACTICE 17.4

The following paragraph contains illogical shifts in person. Edit it so that pronouns are used consistently. Be sure to change any verb that does not agree with the new subject.

Example: Most people who use the Internet know that ~~you~~ *they* cannot escape pop-up ads.

(1) Most of us hate these distracting ads because you have to stop whatever you are doing to get rid of them. (2) A person might go online to look for the title of a movie, and they might be interrupted six or eight times by pop-up ads. (3) If a person takes the time to read these ads, you often realize that they are random. (4) Even if someone is just looking for a movie title, they will still be interrupted by ads for cruises or dating services. (5) People are getting fed up because you don't like to waste time with these ads. (6) Fortunately, Internet users now have several ways to avoid pop-ups, and we are using them. (7) For example, they are discovering that you can download free pop-up-blocking software. (8) They are also learning that you can use sites like Google or Ask Jeeves, which ban pop-ups. (9) Over the next few years, companies may realize that you will be at a disadvantage if you use pop-up advertising. (10) Customers will choose pop-up-free sites, and by doing so we will make these irritating ads a thing of the past.

C Avoiding Illogical Shifts in Voice

When a sentence is in the **active voice**, the subject *performs* the action. When a sentence is in the **passive voice**, the subject *receives* the action—that is, if it is acted upon.

ACTIVE VOICE Pablo Neruda won the Nobel Prize in Literature in 1971. (Subject *Pablo Neruda* performs the action.)

PASSIVE VOICE The Nobel Prize in Literature was won by Pablo Neruda in 1971. (Subject *The Nobel Prize in Literature* receives the action.)

An **illogical shift in voice** occurs when a writer shifts from active to passive voice or from passive to active voice for no apparent reason.

ILLOGICAL SHIFT The jazz musician John Coltrane played the saxophone, and the clarinet was also played by him. (active to passive)

REVISED The jazz musician John Coltrane played the saxophone, and he also played the clarinet. (consistent use of active voice)

ILLOGICAL SHIFT *Fences* was written by August Wilson, and he also wrote *The Piano Lesson.* (passive to active)

REVISED August Wilson wrote *Fences,* and he also wrote *The Piano Lesson.* (consistent use of active voice)

FOCUS Changing from Passive to Active Voice

You should use the active voice in most of your college writing because it is stronger and more direct than the passive voice. To change a sentence from passive to active voice, determine who or what performs the action, and make this noun the subject of this new sentence.

PASSIVE VOICE Three world records in track were set by Jesse Owens in a single day. (Jesse Owens performs the action.)

ACTIVE VOICE Jesse Owens set three world records in track in a single day.

Computer Tip
Most grammar checkers can search for use of passive voice and will spot illogical shifts in voice.

◆ PRACTICE 17.5

Correct any illogical shifts in voice in the following sentences, using active voice wherever possible. Change any verb that does not agree with its new subject. If a sentence is correct, write *C* in the blank.

ON THE WEB
For more practice avoiding illogical shifts in voice, visit Exercise Central at <bedfordstmartins.com/foundationsfirst>.

Example: Michael washed his car, but it ~~was not waxed by him~~. (he did not wax)

____

1. A settlement was discussed by the lawyers, but the defendant refused it. ____

2. A good crop was harvested by the farmers, and the farmers' market attracted big crowds. _____
3. Roberto signed up for calculus, so a new calculator was bought by him. _____
4. Lightning struck the chimney, and two bricks fell to the sidewalk below. _____
5. As the waves battered the beach, a surfboard was clutched by a gasping young man. _____
6. A hymn was sung by the choir while the congregation passed the collection plate. _____
7. When Brandon met Jane, she was asked by him for a date. _____
8. The children watched television, and dinner was cooked by their parents. _____
9. Kathy mowed her grandfather's lawn, and his yardwork was also done by her. _____
10. When my father lost his job, my mother worked longer hours. _____

◆ PRACTICE 17.6

The following sentences contain shifts in voice. Revise each sentence by changing the underlined passive-voice verb to the active voice.

Example: Few people talk about apartment insurance, and it <u>is bought</u> by even fewer people.

Few people talk about apartment insurance, and even fewer buy it.

1. Many people think that their personal property <u>is protected</u> by the landlord's insurance, but this insurance covers only the building itself.

____

____

2. A lease does not protect the renter's belongings from fire or water damage, and the renter's property <u>is not protected</u> from theft by a lease.

____

____

3. If the pizza delivery man trips on the carpet and his leg <u>is broken</u>, the tenant is responsible.

____

____

4. Unfortunately, landlords do not require tenants to have insurance, and most accidents <u>are not expected</u> by tenants.

____

____

5. Fortunately, most apartment insurance is inexpensive, and reasonably priced policies <u>are offered</u> by many companies.

____

____

■ REVISING AND EDITING

Look back at your response to the Seeing and Writing exercise on page 273. Revise any illogical shifts in tense, person, or voice.

CHAPTER REVIEW

◆ EDITING PRACTICE: PARAGRAPH

Read the following paragraph, which contains illogical shifts in tense, person, and voice. Then, edit the essay to correct the illogical shifts, making sure subjects and verbs agree. The first sentence has been edited for you.

These days, more people are picking up graphic novels, and ~~we~~ *they* are taking them more seriously than ever before. Graphic novels are book-length comics, and graphic novelists used classic comic techniques. These artists tell their stories through a series of illustrated panels. In addition, thought and speech bubbles are used by them to show what the characters are thinking and saying. Comic books have been read by us for a long time, but we always considered them strictly for children. Now, many people realize that complex stories can be told in comic books. For example, in his famous graphic novels *Maus* and *Maus II,* Art Spiegelman writes about the Holocaust and told us his father's story of survival. The Jewish people are portrayed as mice by Spiegelman, and he represents the Nazis as cats. Some people might think it is strange to deal with such a serious subject in a comic book. However, the comic book format draws readers in and makes you more comfortable. This clever, sad story is especially well suited to the comic book format. In fact, a Pulitzer Prize was won by Spiegelman for *Maus* in 1992.

◆ EDITING PRACTICE: ESSAY

Read the following essay, which contains illogical shifts in tense, person, and voice. Then, edit the essay to correct the illogical shifts, making sure subjects and verbs agree. The first sentence has been edited for you.

A Great Olympic Moment

When swimming fans saw Eric Moussambani, a swimmer from Equatorial Guinea, arrive at the 2000 Olympic Games in Sydney, Australia, they ~~you~~ knew that this athlete had ~~has~~ no chance to win a medal. Fans expected famous athletes and record holders to win the gold medals, and Moussambani's name was not known by them; besides, his qualifying times are much slower than those of other swimmers. The organizers of the games invited Moussambani only because of an Olympic rule allowing athletes to compete without qualifying if you came from a developing country.

Many obstacles were faced by Eric Moussambani, and this explained his poor qualifying time. He had no coach, his country had no swim team, and he trains in the ocean instead of in a pool. In Sydney, Moussambani saw his first Olympic-size pool. As he prepared to swim in his qualifying heat for the 100-meter freestyle race, he hopes just to be able to finish the two laps.

Swimmer Eric Moussambani

Moussambani's qualifying heat begins early in the morning as he stood at the side of the pool with two other "wild-card" swimmers. Before the starting signal was heard by them, the other two swimmers

Swimmer Eric Moussambani

leaped into the pool. Olympic officials disqualified them, and Moussambani had to swim his laps alone.

At first, the crowd pays little attention to the events in the pool because you knew that the qualifying heat would not affect the final outcome of the race. Spectators soon noticed the lone swimmer from Equatorial Guinea, struggling to swim two lengths of the long pool. Moussambani looks exhausted when he reaches the end of his first lap. He was cheered on by the crowd as he splashed slowly toward the finish line because you saw his Olympic spirit. Moussambani was clearly not swimming fast enough to qualify for the finals, but he was trying hard.

Although he did not win, the race was finished by Eric Moussambani. That night, television viewers around the world watched his heroic swim, and their hearts were won by the athlete from Equatorial Guinea. When he tells interviewers that he hoped to find a coach, train hard, and win a medal in the 2004 Olympic Games, television viewers around the world understood, and you hoped that his dream would come true.

◆ COLLABORATIVE ACTIVITIES

1. Working in a group of four students, choose a subject to write sentences about. Each pair of students should write two simple sentences, one using the subject with a present tense verb and the other using the same subject with a past tense verb. Then, work with your partner to combine the two sentences into a single sentence containing an illogical shift. Finally, exchange sentences with the other pair in your group, and correct the shifts in the other pair's sentence.

   Example

SUBJECT	*Three blind mice*
PRESENT TENSE SENTENCE	*Three blind mice hide from the cat.*
PAST TENSE SENTENCE	*Three blind mice ran after the farmer's wife.*
SENTENCE WITH ILLOGICAL SHIFT	*Three blind mice hide from the cat and ran after the farmer's wife.*
CORRECTED SENTENCE	*Three blind mice hid from the cat and ran after the farmer's wife.*

2. Working in a group of three or four students, write a paragraph explaining how to do a simple task. Use *you* as the subject throughout the paragraph. When you have finished, go back and change every other

sentence so that the subject is *a person, someone, people, students,* or some other third-person word or phrase. Then, exchange your paragraph with another group. Correct the illogical shifts in person so that the whole paragraph uses the third person.

3. Bring to class three sentences from newspapers, magazines, or textbooks that use the passive voice. Then, work in a group of three students to revise these sentences. Begin by changing your own sentences to active voice, if possible. Then, give your original sentences to another member of the group and ask him or her to do the same thing. As a group, discuss the answers you came up with. If a sentence is awkward in the active voice, or if you cannot change it to the active voice, discuss the reasons why this is so.
4. *Composing original sentences* Working in a group of three students, write five sentences in the active voice. When you have finished, check the sentences to make sure you have corrected any errors in grammar, punctuation, or spelling.

☑ REVIEW CHECKLIST: Illogical Shifts

- An illogical shift in tense occurs when a writer shifts from one verb tense to another for no apparent reason. (See 17A.)
- An illogical shift in person occurs when a writer shifts from one person to another for no apparent reason. (See 17B.)
- An illogical shift in voice occurs when a writer shifts from active to passive voice or from passive to active voice for no apparent reason. (See 17C.)

CHAPTER

18 Dangling and Misplaced Modifiers

PREVIEW

In this chapter, you will learn

- to identify present participle modifiers (18A)
- to identify past participle modifiers (18B)
- to recognize and correct dangling modifiers (18C)
- to recognize and correct misplaced modifiers (18D)

SEEING AND WRITING

Look at the picture above, and then write a paragraph in which you tell a story from your family's history. If possible, discuss the significance this story has for your family.

Word Power

generation a group of individuals born and living at about the same time

heritage something passed down from previous generations

migrate to move from one region to another

A **modifier** is a word or word group that **modifies** (provides information about) another word in a sentence. Many word groups that act as modifiers are introduced by present participles (*the column supporting the roof*) or past participles (*an afternoon warmed by the sun*). To communicate its meaning, a modifier must clearly refer to the word it modifies.

Writing Tip

A modifier can function as an adjective or as an adverb. An **adjective** modifies a noun or a pronoun. An **adverb** modifies a verb, an adjective, or another adverb. (See Chapter 23.)

A Identifying Present Participle Modifiers

A **present participle modifier** consists of the *-ing* form of the verb along with the words it introduces. The modifier provides information about a noun or a pronoun that appears next to it in a sentence.

PRESENT PARTICIPLE MODIFIER

Remembering what he had come to do, Robert reached in his pocket for the ring.

PRESENT PARTICIPLE MODIFIER

Dancing to the music of Frank Sinatra, Madeline knew she was in love.

FOCUS Placing Present Participle Modifiers

A present participle modifier can come at the beginning, in the middle, or at the end of a sentence.

Returning to the streets they had left, many early rock singers were soon forgotten.

Many early rock singers, returning to the streets they had left, were soon forgotten.

Many early rock singers were soon forgotten, returning to the streets they had left.

◆ PRACTICE 18.1

In each of the following sentences, underline the present participle modifier. Then, draw an arrow from the modifier to the word it modifies.

Example: Singing in the rain, Gene made a splash.

1. The young soldier, fearing for his life, tried to steady his shaky hands.
2. Sailing out into the open ocean, the fishing boat looked very small.
3. The pageant winner clutched her bouquet, smiling professionally.
4. Dropping a book on his desk, the professor cried, "Time's up!"
5. Standing in the barbershop doorway, the two young men asked me for help.
6. Sipping his coffee, Mark prepared to pull the big rig out of the parking lot.
7. The telephone woke me up again, ringing loudly at 2 a.m.
8. Emilia, drawing on her last bit of strength, crossed the finish line first.
9. The foreman irritated me, blowing his whistle loudly in my ear.
10. Roaring toward the waterfall, the river took control of my canoe.

ON THE WEB
For more practice identifying present participle modifiers, visit Exercise Central at <bedfordstmartins.com/foundationsfirst>.

◆ PRACTICE 18.2

In each of the following sentences, underline the present participle modifier. Then, draw an arrow from the modifier to the word it modifies.

Example: Displaying yellow and black markings, yellow jackets are small stinging wasps.

1. Appearing at picnics and other outdoor gatherings, yellow jackets can be a nuisance.
2. These insects can also be dangerous, stinging when disturbed.
3. Yellow jacket stings, causing allergic reactions in many people, kill about fifty Americans every year.
4. Female yellow jackets, reaching the end of their lives, often sting in the fall.
5. Looking for food, the females usually go where people are.
6. Having a taste for sugar, yellow jackets find soft drinks appealing.
7. A garbage can, overflowing with trash, is a feast for yellow jackets.
8. Fruit trees, dropping overripe apples and pears on the ground, provide additional meals for these insects.
9. Eating other harmful insects, yellow jackets have some good qualities.
10. Trying to keep yellow jackets away, people wear light-colored clothing and keep sweet food and drinks covered.

◆ PRACTICE 18.3

Write five sentences that contain present participle modifiers. Then, underline each modifier, and draw an arrow from the modifier to the word it modifies.

Example: *Wearing her new dress, my sister went to Sunday school.*

1. ______________________________

____

2. ______________________________

____

3. ______________________________

____

4. ______________________________

____

5. ______________________________

____

B Identifying Past Participle Modifiers

A **past participle modifier** consists of the past participle form of the verb (usually ending in *-d* or *-ed*) along with the words it introduces. Like a present participle modifier, a past participle modifier provides information about a noun or a pronoun that appears next to it in a sentence.

For more on past participles, see 20A.

> Submitted to the Continental Congress on June 7, 1776, the Declaration of Independence was approved on July 4.

> Invited to the White House, Sojourner Truth met President Abraham Lincoln.

Writing Tip

Not all past participles end in *-d* or *-ed*. Irregular participles—*cut* and *written*, for example—may have different forms.

FOCUS Placing Past Participle Modifiers

A past participle modifier can come at the beginning, in the middle, or at the end of a sentence.

> Shocked by the ruling, the lawyer said she would appeal.

> The lawyer, shocked by the ruling, said she would appeal.

> "I will appeal," said the laywer, shocked by the ruling.

For a list of irregular past participles, see 20B.

◆ PRACTICE 18.4

In each of the following sentences, underline the past participle modifier. Then, draw an arrow from the modifier to the word it modifies.

Example: Planted in rich soil, the sapling soon grew taller than Simon.

1. Plastered with bumper stickers, her old car rattled down the dirt road.
2. Bored to tears with my job, I sent out a new résumé.
3. Sarah scratched her legs, covered with mosquito bites.

ON THE WEB
For more practice identifying past participle modifiers, visit Exercise Central at <bedfordstmartins.com/foundationsfirst>.

4. Waxed and polished, the marble steps gleamed at the entrance to the banquet hall.
5. The roof, buried under two feet of snow, sagged dangerously.
6. Dulled from years of use, the knife could not slice through the lemon peel.
7. Shattered in its fall from the mantle, the vase lay in pieces on the floor.
8. The cyclists, exhausted after the steep hills, agreed to stop at the nearest motel.
9. Her book, rejected by six publishers, eventually became a bestseller.
10. The test, written too quickly, had several confusing questions.

◆ PRACTICE 18.5

In each of the following sentences, underline the past participle modifier. Then, draw an arrow from the modifier to the word it modifies.

Example: Unsolved to this day, the murders of Andrew and Abby Borden occurred in 1892.

(1) The shocking crime, committed in Fall River, Massachusetts, left a wealthy man named Andrew Borden and his wife dead in their home. (2) Attacked with a hatchet, Mr. and Mrs. Borden were both killed on a hot August morning. (3) Horrified at the news of this murder, the people of Fall River were even more astonished when a suspect appeared. (4) The suspect was Mr. Borden's 32-year-old daughter Lizzie, tried for killing her father and stepmother. (5) Lizzie Borden's story, changed repeatedly, made many people suspicious. (6) Asked where she had been at the time of the murders, Lizzie gave several different answers. (7) A possible motive for the killings, discussed in every home in town, was an enormous inheritance. (8) However, no evidence gathered at the house connected Lizzie to the crime. (9) The jury, faced with a circumstantial case, found her not guilty. (10) A children's rhyme, well known more than a century later, judged Lizzie more harshly: "Lizzie Borden took an axe, gave her mother forty whacks."

◆ PRACTICE 18.6

Write five sentences that contain past participle modifiers. Then, underline the modifier, and draw an arrow from the modifier to the word it modifies.

Example: Frightened by the thunder, the cat hid under the couch.

1. ______________________________

2. ______________________________

3. ______________________________

4. ______________________________

5. ______________________________

C Correcting Dangling Modifiers

A **dangling modifier** "dangles" because the word it is supposed to modify is not present in the sentence. Often, a dangling modifier comes at the beginning of a sentence and appears to modify the word that follows it. Consider the following sentence.

DANGLING MODIFIER Working overtime, my salary almost doubled.

In the preceding sentence, the present participle *working overtime* seems to be modifying *salary.* But this makes no sense. How can salary work overtime? The word the present participle modifier should logically modify is missing. To correct this sentence, you need to supply the missing word.

REVISED Working overtime, I almost doubled my salary.

As the example above illustrates, the easiest way to correct a dangling modifier is to supply the word (a noun or pronoun) that the dangling modifier should actually modify.

DANGLING MODIFIER Living in England, his first collection of poems was published. (Did the poetry collection live in England?)

REVISED Living in England, Robert Frost published his first collection of poems.

Computer Tip
Your grammar checker may be able to search for dangling modifiers automatically.

DANGLING MODIFIER Distracted by my cell phone, my car almost drove off the road. (Did the phone distract the car?)

REVISED Distracted by my cell phone, I almost drove my car off the road.

◆ PRACTICE 18.7

ON THE WEB
For more practice correcting dangling modifiers, visit Exercise Central at <bedfordstmartins.com/foundationsfirst>.

Rewrite the following sentences, which contain dangling modifiers, by suppling a word to which each modifier can logically refer.

Example: Dreaming of easy money, the game show was very appealing.

Dreaming of easy money, he thought the game show sounded very appealing.

1. Hanging by one hand from the edge of the roof, the fire escape could not be reached.

2. Sitting at the back of the classroom, the screen was too far away for her to see.

3. Frightened by the alligator, my canoe almost turned over.

4. Getting to the station late, the train was seen leaving.

5. Sitting on the dock in the bay, many fish were caught.

6. Sitting in the back of the auditorium, the announcement could hardly be heard.

7. Given a second chance, her luck ran out.

8. Forced to make a quick decision in the voting booth, the wrong lever was pulled.

9. Feeling sick to her stomach, the bathroom was too far away to reach in time.

____

____

10. Prepared for an afternoon at the baseball game, the rain was unexpected.

____

◆ PRACTICE 18.8

On the lines below, supply a word to which each modifier can logically refer. Then, complete the sentence.

Example: Startled out of a sound sleep, *I jumped out of bed and ran to the window*.

1. Expecting a package, ____.

2. Feared by every student in the class, ____.

3. Wondering why I had decided to go on the trip, ____.

4. Seated in the stadium, ____.

5. Left at the side of the road, ____.

6. Told to remember her manners, ____.

7. Sipping coffee, ____.

8. Trying to hit a home run, ____.

9. Wearing his oldest clothes, ____.

10. Attracted by the smell of food, ____.

D Correcting Misplaced Modifiers

A modifier should be placed as close as possible to the word it modifies. Ideally, it should come right before or right after it. A **misplaced modifier** appears to modify the wrong word because it is placed incorrectly in the sentence. To correct this problem, move the modifier so that it is as close as possible to the word it is supposed to modify.

MISPLACED MODIFIER I ran to the window wearing my bathrobe. (Was the window wearing the bathrobe?)

REVISED Wearing my bathrobe, I ran to the window.

MISPLACED MODIFIER The dog ran down the street frightened by the noise. (Was the street frightened by the noise?)

REVISED Frightened by the noise, the dog ran down the street.

FOCUS Misplaced Modifiers

Not all misplaced modifiers are participles. Prepositional phrases can also be misplaced in a sentence.

MISPLACED MODIFIER My sister served cookies to her friends on tiny plates. (Were the friends sitting on tiny plates?)

REVISED My sister served cookies on tiny plates to her friends.

◆ PRACTICE 18.9

Rewrite the following sentences, which contain misplaced modifiers, so that each modifier clearly refers to the word it logically modifies.

Example: Wallowing in a cool mud bath, Mr. Phelps scratched the back of the prize pig.

Mr. Phelps scratched the back of the prize pig wallowing in a cool mud bath.

1. The angry bull threw every rodeo rider with a ring in its nose.

ON THE WEB
For more practice correcting misplaced modifiers, visit Exercise Central at <bedfordstmartins.com/foundationsfirst>.

2. The trick-or-treaters rang every doorbell carrying enormous bags of candy.

3. Blushing furiously, the bathroom door was quickly closed by Henry.

4. Attracted to the bright light, the candles were surrounded by moths.

5. A car is not likely to be damaged by rust kept in a garage.

6. A group of homeless men camped at the edge of the city under a highway overpass.

7. A bartender served strong drinks with enthusiasm.

8. Decorated with a skull and crossbones, she carefully read the warning label.

9. Blowing kisses, a white limousine waited as the director emerged from the restaurant.

10. Accidentally tying her shoelaces together, nursery school was a struggle for Amy that morning.

Computer Tip

By entering *-ing* or *-ed,* you can use the Search or Find function to find present participles and past participles in your writing. Then, you can check to make sure you have no dangling or misplaced modifiers.

REVISING AND EDITING

Look back at your response to the Seeing and Writing exercise on page 284. First, underline any present or past participle modifiers you find. Then, revise any dangling or misplaced modifiers. Make sure each modifier refers to a word that it can logically describe.

CHAPTER REVIEW

◆ EDITING PRACTICE: PARAGRAPH

Read the following paragraph. Then, rewrite the sentences to correct dangling and misplaced modifiers. In some cases, you may have to supply a word to which the modifier can logically refer. The first sentence has been corrected for you.

many children experience

Learning to read and write, ^ difficulties ^ ~~are experienced by many people.~~ Diagnosed with dyslexia, this disability frightens some people. Frustrated by their attempts to read and write, these activities are avoided by them. They do not want anyone to know they have trouble fearing embarrassment. Feeling stupid, their attention often turns to other activities. Interpreted by teachers as a lack of interest in learning, serious learning problems can be caused by dyslexia. Inherited from learning-disabled family members, intelligence is not related to dyslexia, however. Extremely intelligent people can be dyslexic. Fortunately, more educators are making an effort to identify the problem, knowing how to recognize the signs of dyslexia. Focusing on new and inventive methods, dyslexics can be taught successfully by educators.

◆ EDITING PRACTICE: ESSAY

Read the following essay. Then, rewrite the sentences to correct dangling and misplaced modifiers. In some cases, you may have to supply a word to which the modifier can logically refer. The first sentence has been corrected for you.

The Popcorn Story

~~Usually eaten in a movie theater, most~~ Most Americans do not think much about popcorn, usually eaten in a movie theater. However, popcorn has a long and interesting history. Respected in the past as a food of the gods, Americans need to learn more about popcorn.

Popcorn is truly an American food. Exploring a cave in New Mexico, ears of popping corn more than five thousand years old were found. Arriving from Europe, native peoples offered to sell popcorn to Columbus and his crew. Popcorn was also an important food for the Aztecs in Mexico. Honoring their gods, idols were decorated with strings of popcorn. Writing about a religious ceremony, the fact that popcorn was scattered in front of a god's statue was recorded by a Spanish priest.

Movie popcorn

Brought by the native Americans, the Pilgrims ate popcorn at the first Thanksgiving. Liking this local food, popcorn was eaten as a breakfast food by early American colonists. By the nineteenth century, street vendors sold popcorn from pushcarts. Sold in movie theaters, films were soon associated with popcorn. The popularity of the fluffy white snack continued through the Great Depression.

Arriving in the 1940s, the movie business was hurt by television, and as a result people ate less popcorn. However, things soon changed. Invented in the 1940s, popcorn was the first food cooked in the microwave oven. Preparing their favorite movie food at home, popcorn was made popular again. In the 1950s, people made popcorn in pots on the stove. In the 1960s, people bought popcorn in pre-packaged foil pans that puffed out as the popcorn popped. Later, in the diet-conscious 1980s and 1990s, popcorn was made with electric poppers that used hot air instead of oil.

Popcorn in an electric popper

Popped in a microwave, in an electric popper, or on the stove, American families enjoy popcorn when they watch their favorite television shows or videos. Sold in theaters, a trip to the local multiplex is made a more enjoyable experience. Most Americans are unaware of the long history of their favorite snack.

◆ COLLABORATIVE ACTIVITIES

1. Work in a group of four or five students. On a sheet of paper, one student should write a present or past participle modifier. The next student should then complete the sentence and pass the sheet to a third student, who should write another modifier to continue the thought begun in the first sentence. Keep passing the paper from student to student until the group has written at least six sentences.
2. Look over the sentences your group wrote in activity 1. Then, discuss the ways you decided to complete the sentences. Check to be sure that no modifiers are dangling or misplaced.
3. Working in a group, write five present or past participle modifiers. Then, trade lists with another group. Work together to complete the sentences, making sure that at least two sentences contain dangling or misplaced modifiers (the sillier, the better). Finally, pass the sentences back to the group that wrote the modifiers, and have them correct the sentences.
4. *Composing original sentences* Working together, write five sentences that contain present or past participle modifiers. Make sure that none of the sentences contain a dangling or misplaced modifier. When you have finished, check the sentences again to make sure you have corrected any errors in grammar or punctuation.

✓ REVIEW CHECKLIST: Dangling and Misplaced Modifiers

- ☐ A present participle modifier consists of the present participle (the *-ing* form of the verb) along with the words it introduces. (See 18A.)
- ☐ A past participle modifier consists of the past participle (usually ending in *-d* or *-ed*) along with the words it introduces. (See 18B.)
- ☐ Correct a dangling modifier by supplying a word to which the dangling modifier can logically refer. (See 18C.)
- ☐ Avoid misplaced modifiers by placing modifiers as close as possible to the words they modify. (See 18D.)

UNIT FIVE

Understanding Basic Grammar

CHAPTER

19

Verbs: Past Tense

PREVIEW

In this chapter, you will learn

- to understand regular verbs in the past tense (19A)
- to understand irregular verbs in the past tense (19B)
- to deal with problem verbs in the past tense (19C and 19D)

■ SEEING AND WRITING

Look at the picture above. Then, select a newsworthy event in your life, and write a one-paragraph news story about it. Include a headline, and be sure to use the past tense.

Word Power

memorable worth remembering

newsworthy interesting enough to be worth reporting in the news

unique one of a kind

Verb tense indicates when an action or situation took place. The **past tense** indicates that an action or a situation has already happened.

A Understanding Regular Verbs in the Past Tense

Regular verbs form the past tense by adding *-d* or *-ed* to the **base form** of the verb (the present tense form of the verb that is used with *I*).

FOCUS Regular Verbs in the Past Tense

- Most regular verbs form the past tense by adding *-ed* to the base form of the verb.

  I edited my paper.

  Tia handed in her paper yesterday.

- Regular verbs that end in *-e* form the past tense by adding *-d*.

  He refused to take no for an answer.

  Last summer they biked through northern California.

- Regular verbs that end in *-y* form the past tense by changing the *y* to *i* and adding *-ed*.

  try tried
  vary varied

Writing Tip
All regular verbs use the same form for singular and plural in the past tense: *I cheered, They cheered.*

For more on indicating verb tense, see 24H.

ON THE WEB
For more practice understanding regular verbs in the past tense, visit Exercise Central at <bedfordstmartins.com/foundationsfirst>.

◆ PRACTICE 19.1

Some of the verbs in the following sentences are in the present tense, and some are in the past tense. First, underline the verb in each sentence. Then, on the line after each sentence, write *present* if the verb is present tense and *past* if the verb is past tense.

Examples

James chopped the log into firewood. ___past___

She donates money to the United Fund every year. ___present___

1. Marguerite sings in the choir. __________
2. The audience members hand their tickets to the usher. __________
3. The coach protested the referee's decision. __________
4. One passenger talked loudly on a cell phone. __________
5. The children cried during the scary parts of the movie. __________
6. We sometimes fail to agree. __________
7. The water gurgled down the drain. __________
8. At work, many people switched from coffee to tea. __________
9. The waiters pool their tips. __________
10. My teacher confused everyone with his explanation of grammar. __________

◆ PRACTICE 19.2

Change the present tense verbs in the following passage to past tense. Cross out the present tense form of each underlined verb, and write the past tense form above it.

Example: Julio ~~tries~~ tried every year to get a green card.

(1) A native of Ecuador, he qualifies for the US Green Card Lottery. (2) Hoping to win a permanent residence visa, he reapplies for the lottery every year. (3) He considers himself lucky to be eligible. (4) Lottery applicants need to be from an underrepresented country. (5) Because of the large volume of Mexican immigrants in the United States, the American government rejects applications from Julio's Mexican friends. (6) Moreover, even people who qualify face disappointment. (7) Julio's chances to win remain slim at about 200 to 1. (8) Applicants also face the possibility of fraud. (9) Many companies try to scam applicants by charging them to apply for the lottery. (10) Nevertheless, Julio, along with thousands of others, hopes to win a green card.

B Understanding Irregular Verbs in the Past Tense

Many **irregular verbs** do not form the past tense by adding *-d* or *-ed*. Instead, they use special irregular past tense forms that may look very different from their present tense forms.

The chart that follows lists the base forms and the past tense forms of the most common irregular verbs. If you do not find a verb on this chart, look it up in a dictionary. If the verb is irregular, the dictionary will list its forms after the base form: for example, *get/got/gotten/getting*. (*Get* is the base form, *got* is the past tense form, *gotten* is the past participle, and *getting* is the present participle.)

Computer Tip
Use the Search or Find command to find the irregular verbs that give you the most trouble.

Irregular Verbs in the Past Tense

Base Form	Past Tense	Base Form	Past Tense
awake	awoke	bet	bet
be	was, were	bite	bit
become	became	blow	blew
begin	began	break	broke

(continued on the following page)

(continued from the previous page)

Irregular Verbs in the Past Tense

Base Form	Past Tense	Base Form	Past Tense
bring	brought	make	made
build	built	meet	met
buy	bought	pay	paid
catch	caught	quit	quit
choose	chose	read	read
come	came	ride	rode
cost	cost	ring	rang
cut	cut	rise	rose
dive	dove, dived	run	ran
do	did	say	said
draw	drew	see	saw
drink	drank	sell	sold
drive	drove	send	sent
eat	ate	set	set
fall	fell	shake	shook
feed	fed	shine	shone, shined
feel	felt	sing	sang
fight	fought	sit	sat
find	found	sleep	slept
fly	flew	speak	spoke
forgive	forgave	spend	spent
freeze	froze	spring	sprang
get	got	stand	stood
give	gave	steal	stole
go	went	stick	stuck
grow	grew	sting	stung
have	had	swear	swore
hear	heard	swim	swam
hide	hid	take	took
hold	held	teach	taught
hurt	hurt	tear	tore
keep	kept	tell	told
know	knew	think	thought
lay (to place)	laid	throw	threw
lead	led	understand	understood
leave	left	wake	woke, waked
let	let	wear	wore
lie (to recline)	lay	win	won
light	lit	write	wrote
lose	lost		

◆ PRACTICE 19.3

Use the list of irregular verbs above to help you find the correct past tense form of the irregular verb in parentheses. Then, write the correct form in the space provided.

Example: The defendant ___swore___ (swear) that he had never entered the store.

1. After staying up all night to finish his paper, Nick __________ (sleep) too late to get to class on time.
2. The cat __________ (drink) some spilled champagne on New Year's Eve.
3. The doctor __________ (give) me a flu shot, but I still got sick.
4. Carla __________ (quit) her job when she __________ (win) the lottery.
5. A red balloon __________ (rise) slowly past my office window.
6. Tiger Woods __________ (choose) a club for a short putt.
7. Sharon __________ (tear) down her opponent's campaign posters.
8. Donald Trump __________ (build) a skyscraper that blocked the view from my window.
9. Angel __________ (hurt) Teresa's feelings by criticizing her mother.
10. Jim __________ (feed) his brother's fish too much, so they all died.

ON THE WEB

For more practice understanding irregular verbs in the past tense, visit Exercise Central at <bedfordstmartins.com/foundationsfirst>.

◆ PRACTICE 19.4

In the following passage, fill in the correct past tense form of the irregular verb in parentheses. Refer to the list of irregular verbs on pages 301–302.

Example: After many years in the making, the Women's National Basketball Association (WNBA) finally ___got___ (get) its start in 1996.

(1) Former collegiate star Sheryl Swoopes __________ (become) the first player signed to a WNBA team. (2) Many people immediately __________ (see) the financial possibilities of this new league, and corporations __________ (pay) to sponsor the new teams. (3) Fans, especially young girls, __________ (find) many women to admire. (4) Many people __________ (buy) tickets to the games, and they __________ (come) ready to cheer. (5) Unlike almost every other professional sport, women's professional basketball __________ (draw) more female fans than male fans. (6) Many people appreciated how the WNBA __________ (shake) up the sports establishment in this way. (7) The

players __________ (rise) to the challenges and __________ (fight) hard to keep the WNBA going. (8) As a result, the league __________ (go) from eight teams to sixteen, doubling in size in the first five years of its existence. (9) Some people __________ (say) that the WNBA was doomed to fail. (10) However, the athletes and fans __________ (know) how long women had been waiting for this opportunity.

Writing Tip
Be is the only verb in English with more than one past tense form. For information about subject-verb agreement with *be,* see 16B.

C Problem Verbs in the Past Tense: *Be*

The irregular verb *be* can cause problems for writers because it has two different past tense forms—a singular form and a plural form. The only way to make certain that you use these forms correctly is to memorize them.

Past Tense Forms of the Verb Be

	Singular	**Plural**
1st person	I was tired.	We were tired.
2nd person	You were tired.	You were tired.
3rd person	He was tired.	
	She was tired.	They were tired.
	It was tired.	

◆ PRACTICE 19.5

In each of the following sentences, circle the correct form of the verb *be.*

Example: The toy chicken (was/were) surprisingly loud.

1. Two lighthouses (was/were) visible from the ship.
2. A kitten (was/were) asleep on her lap.
3. After the show, our parents (was/were) ready to go home.
4. With its old, frayed wires, the lamp (was/were) dangerous.
5. From the moment I bought it, the goldfish (was/were) doomed.
6. The children (was/were) hardly able to keep their eyes open after sledding all day.
7. We (was/were) out of the country last summer.

For more on the verb be *in the present progressive tense and the past progressive tense and more on stative verbs, see 24I.*

ON THE WEB
For more practice dealing with problem verbs in the past tense, visit Exercise Central at <bedfordstmartins.com/foundationsfirst>.

8. The barbarians (was/were) just outside the walls of the city.
9. The potato salad (was/were) the best thing about the picnic.
10. A little girl in a witch costume (was/were) the first person to ring my doorbell last Halloween.

◆ PRACTICE 19.6

Edit the following passage for errors in the use of the verb *be*. Cross out any underlined verbs that are incorrect, and write the correct forms above them. If a verb form is correct, label it *C*.

Example: In 1947, the House Un-American Activities Committee (HUAC) began questioning people in the movie industry who ~~was~~ *were* suspected of being Communists.

(1) This investigation was one result of the fear of Communism that defined the Cold War. (2) HUAC were concerned that Communists were using films to spread their ideas. (3) The committee thought that Hollywood were too influential to ignore. (4) Many people in the Hollywood community was called to testify in front of HUAC. (5) The most famous group were the "Hollywood 10." (6) These ten people refused to answer questions about their politics, and each one were sent to prison. (7) Other suspected Communists in the film industry was blacklisted. (8) This meant that they were not allowed to work in the film industry. (9) Some blacklisted screenwriters used false names and was able to continue making movies. (10) Fifty years later, after the end of the Cold War, the Screen Writers' Guild was finally able to add the writers' real names to the credits of the movies they wrote.

D Problem Verbs in the Past Tense: *Can/Could* and *Will/Would*

The helping verbs *can/could* and *will/would* can cause problems for writers because their past tense forms are sometimes confused with their present tense forms.

For more on helping verbs, see 9F.

Can/Could

Can, a present tense verb, means "is able to" or "are able to." *Could,* the past tense of *can,* means "was able to" or "were able to."

Students can use the copy machines in the library.

Columbus told the queen he could find a short route to India.

Could is also used to express a possibility or a wish.

The president wishes he could balance the budget.

Will/Would

Will, a present tense verb, talks about the future from the perspective of the present. *Would,* the past tense of *will,* talks about the future from the perspective of the past.

I will finish writing the report tomorrow.

Last week, I told my boss that I would work an extra shift today.

Would is also used to express a possibility or a wish.

If we moved to the country, we would be able to have a garden.

Felicia would like to buy a new car.

FOCUS ***Can/Could* and *Will/Would***

Can/could and *will/would* never change form, no matter what the subject is.

I can/he can/they can

I could/he could/they could

I will/he will/they will

I would/he would/they would

◆ PRACTICE 19.7

In each of the following sentences, circle the correct form of the helping verb.

Example: When I was a child, I (can/could) play for hours without getting tired.

1. My boss promised that she (will/would) get me tickets for the World Series.
2. Anyone who works hard (can/could) learn to speak a second language.

3. If he liked the book, he (will/would) buy it.
4. Sheila (will/would) have to go to the post office tomorrow.
5. Before she was injured, she (can/could) walk without a cane.
6. I hope the apples (will/would) be ripe before the first frost.
7. The kindergarten teacher is pleased that all the children in the class (can/could) tie their shoes.
8. The guide said that we (will/would) see whales from the boat.
9. The forecast calls for sunny skies, but the parade (can/could) still be rained out.
10. Don bragged that he (can/could) outscore any of us on the basketball court.

◆ PRACTICE 19.8

In the following passage, circle the correct form of the helping verb from the choices in parentheses.

> **Example:** In the 1970s, my father decided that his next car (will/would) get good gas mileage.

(1) Although everyone complains about the high cost of energy, people (can/could) do something about their energy use. (2) As the price of gasoline rises, drivers (will/would) pay more to fill up their vehicles. (3) If car owners switched from gas-guzzling SUVs to hybrid cars, they (will/would) save money and do something good for the environment. (4) Heating oil (can/could) also be a major expense during the winter. (5) Although no one (can/could) do anything about the weather, homeowners (can/could) lower their heating bills if they kept the thermostat turned down and wore sweaters around the house. (6) During the energy crisis of the 1970s, people realized that they (will/would) save energy this way. (7) Keeping a house cooler in winter and warmer in summer helps; if every household took this step, the United States (will/would) dramatically lower its dependence on foreign oil. (8) Even changing a light bulb (can/could) make a difference in energy use. (9) A person who replaces a single light bulb with an energy-efficient compact fluorescent bulb

(will/would) not see a huge difference in the electric bill, but if everyone made this change, the United States (will/would) save a noticeable amount of electricity. (10) People in previous decades were able to make sacrifices to save energy, and Americans today (can/could) lower their energy use, too.

■ REVISING AND EDITING

Look back at your response to the Seeing and Writing exercise on page 299. Underline every past tense verb you have used, and check to make sure you used the correct past tense form in each case. Then, cross out any incorrect forms, and write the correct past tense form of the verb above the line.

CHAPTER REVIEW

◆ EDITING PRACTICE

Read the following essay, which contains errors in past tense verb forms, and decide whether each of the underlined past tense verbs is correct. If the verb is correct, write *C* above it. If it is not, cross out the verb, and write the correct past tense form. The first sentence has been corrected for you. (If necessary, consult the list of irregular verbs on pp. 301–302.)

Crazy Horse

In the second half of the nineteenth century, American Indian tribes fought (C) to keep their land. Crazy Horse, who were chief of the Oglala Sioux, played a key role in these Great Plains Indian wars. Along with other Indian chiefs, such as Sitting Bull and Red Cloud, Crazy Horse resist the invasion of white settlers. A determined leader, he will be one of the last Indian leaders to surrender.

Crazy Horse was someone who want to preserve the Sioux traditions and ways of life. He were also known as an intelligent and brave warrior.

For many years, he successfully defended the Black Hills and keeped them from U.S. military control. The American government want to confine Indians to reservations. However, Crazy Horse learned early that white men can not be trusted, and he fight hard to keep his people on their land.

The battle between General Custer and Crazy Horse

Crazy Horse won many battles. His most famous victory, however, were over General George Custer. In 1876, Crazy Horse meeted Custer at the Battle of Little Bighorn. Custer planned to surprise Sitting Bull at his camp next to the Little Bighorn River. Custer, however, was unprepared for what he encounter, and he losed badly. Crazy Horse and Sitting Bull wiped out Custer's entire unit. Because of this, the battle become known as "Custer's Last Stand."

Crazy Horse on his way to surrender to General Cook

After defeating Custer, Crazy Horse continued to fight the army. However, less than a year after the Battle of Little Bighorn, Crazy Horse surrender to the U.S. Army, and the Sioux finally losed their land. Then, shortly after the Army moved him and his people to a reservation, Crazy Horse were arrested. The Army accuse him of planning a revolt, and once they have him in custody, they killed him.

The Crazy Horse memorial

Many people thinked Crazy Horse were a hero. To many, he was a model of bravery and integrity because he defended his people and sticked to his beliefs. In honor of Crazy Horse, a sculptor named Korczak Ziolkowski begined a huge memorial in 1948. Carved into a mountain in South Dakota, this memorial shows the respect that some people have for Crazy Horse. The Native Americans who requested the statue wanted everyone to know about this important hero.

◆ COLLABORATIVE ACTIVITIES

1. List ten verbs in the present tense. Then, exchange papers with another student, and write the past tense form of each verb beside the present tense form. Exchange papers again, and check the other student's work.
2. Work in a group of three or four students to choose ten verbs from the lists you made for activity 1. Work together to write a sentence for each of the verbs in the present tense. Then, exchange the sentences with

another group, and ask them to rewrite the sentences in the past tense. When you have finished, check each other's work.

3. Working in a group, collaborate on a paragraph about an event that occurred in the past. First, write the paragraph in the present tense, as if the event were happening as you write. Then, exchange paragraphs with another group, and rewrite their paragraph by putting the verbs in the past tense wherever appropriate. When you get your group's paragraph back, check to make sure that all the past tense forms are correct.
4. *Composing original sentences* Working in a group, compose five sentences with past tense verbs. Make sure that the verb forms are correct. When you have finished, check the sentences again to make sure you have corrected any errors in grammar, punctuation, or spelling.

✓ REVIEW CHECKLIST: Verbs: Past Tense

- ☐ The past tense of a verb indicates that an action or situation has already happened. (See 19A.)
- ☐ Regular verbs form the past tense by adding either *-d* or *-ed* to the base form of the verb. (See 19A.)
- ☐ Irregular verbs have irregular forms in the past tense. (See 19B.)
- ☐ *Be* is the only verb in English that has two different forms in the past tense—one for singular and one for plural. (See 19C.)
- ☐ *Could* is the past tense of *can*. *Would* is the past tense of *will*. (See 19D.)

CHAPTER

20

Verbs: Past Participles

PREVIEW

In this chapter, you will learn

- to identify regular past participles (20A)
- to identify irregular past participles (20B)
- to use the present perfect tense (20C)
- to use the past perfect tense (20D)
- to use past participles as adjectives (20E)

SEEING AND WRITING

Look at the picture above, and then write a paragraph about something you really wanted and finally got. Tell how the thing you got has (or has not) lived up to your expectations.

Word Power

crave to have a strong desire for something

envision to imagine

anticipate to look forward to

A Identifying Regular Past Participles

Every verb has a **past participle** form. The past participle form of a regular verb adds *-d* or *-ed* to the base form of the verb (just as the past tense form does). Combined with helping verbs, the past participle is used to form other tenses, such as the **present perfect** (see 20C) and **past perfect** (see 20D), or used as an adjective (see 20E).

Writing Tip

The **base form** is the present tense form of the verb used with *I*.

PRESENT TENSE She repairs her own car whenever it breaks down.

PAST TENSE She repaired her own car before the trip.

PAST PARTICIPLE She has repaired her own car for years.

PAST PARTICIPLE She told him that she had repaired her own car.

In the examples above, note that the helping verb changes its form to agree with its subject but that the past participle always has the same form: *I have repaired/She has repaired.*

ON THE WEB
For more practice identifying regular past participles, visit Exercise Central at <bedfordstmartins.com/foundationsfirst>.

◆ PRACTICE 20.1

Below are the base forms of ten regular verbs. In the spaces after each verb, write the appropriate present tense form, past tense form, and past participle form.

Example
shout

present: She __shouts__ every day.

past: They __shouted__ yesterday.

past participle: I have always __shouted__ too much.

1. agree

   present: He always __________.

   past: We __________ yesterday.

   past participle: They had __________ before the summit meeting.

2. love

   present: She __________ them.

   past: You __________ them last week.

   past participle: He has __________ her for years.

3. drop

   present: He always __________ the ball.

   past: I __________ that course last semester.

   past participle: She has always __________ the children off at day care before work.

4. cry

   present: The baby __________ every night.

   past: He __________ when she left.

   past participle: She had __________ the night before.

5. work

   present: It __________ every time.

past: I __________ the late shift last year.

past participle: You have __________ since you were fourteen years old.

6. dance

   present: Marilyn __________ the tango professionally.

   past: They __________ all night at their wedding.

   past participle: We have __________ together for years.

7. gargle

   present: He __________ every morning.

   past: I __________ before work yesterday.

   past participle: They had always __________ until the mouthwash ran out.

8. hesitate

   present: She __________ before she speaks.

   past: We __________ to buy it last week.

   past participle: I have __________ many times.

9. confuse

   present: My teacher __________ me every day.

   past: He __________ us last night.

   past participle: You have __________ us all repeatedly.

10. organize

    present: The collector __________ his records all the time.

    past: I __________ a luncheon in his honor last March.

    past participle: They have __________ all the meetings so far.

◆ PRACTICE 20.2

Fill in the correct past participle form of each verb in parentheses.

Example: An energetic and engaging performer, Cuban singer Celia Cruz had ___*gained*___ (gain) the devotion of fans all over the world.

1. By the time she died in 2003, Celia Cruz had ______________ (live) in the United States for more than forty years.

2. She had ______________ (start) her career in Cuba, where she was one of her country's biggest stars.
3. She had ______________ (escape) to the United States in 1959, fleeing the Communist regime in Cuba.
4. Cruz had always ______________ (refuse) to return to Cuba as long as Castro was in power.
5. Over the years, her many recordings have ______________ (help) to make her music popular in Europe as well as in the United States.
6. Because of her extraordinary vocals, many people around the world have ______________ (learn) to love salsa music.
7. Her music has also ______________ (inspire) many young Latina singers.
8. By the time of her death at the age of 79, Celia Cruz had ______________ (record) more than seventy albums.
9. She had also ______________ (earn) many awards, including five Grammys, two Latin Grammys, three honorary doctorates, and a National Medal of Arts.
10. For her many contributions to Latin music, she had also ______________ (acquire) the title "The Queen of Salsa."

B Identifying Irregular Past Participles

Unlike regular verbs, irregular verbs often have different past tense and past participle forms.

PRESENT TENSE He chooses.
PAST TENSE He chose.
PAST PARTICIPLE He has chosen./He had chosen.

PRESENT TENSE They sing.
PAST TENSE They sang.
PAST PARTICIPLE They have sung./They had sung.

The following chart lists the base form, the past tense form, and the past participle of the most common irregular verbs. If you do not find a verb on this chart, look it up in a dictionary. If the verb is irregular, the dictionary will list its forms after the base form: for example, *get/got/gotten/getting*. (*Get* is the base form, *got* is the past tense form, *gotten* is the past participle, and *getting* is the present participle.)

Irregular Past Participles

Base Form	**Past Tense**	**Past Participle**
awake	awoke	awoken
be (am, are)	was, were	been
beat	beat	beaten
become	became	become
begin	began	begun
bet	bet	bet
bite	bit	bitten
blow	blew	blown
break	broke	broken
bring	brought	brought
build	built	built
buy	bought	bought
catch	caught	caught
choose	chose	chosen
come	came	come
cost	cost	cost
cut	cut	cut
dive	dove, dived	dived
do	did	done
draw	drew	drawn
drink	drank	drunk
drive	drove	driven
eat	ate	eaten
fall	fell	fallen
feed	fed	fed
feel	felt	felt
fight	fought	fought
find	found	found
fly	flew	flown
forgive	forgave	forgiven
freeze	froze	frozen
get	got	got, gotten
give	gave	given
go	went	gone
grow	grew	grown
have	had	had
hear	heard	heard
hide	hid	hidden
hold	held	held
hurt	hurt	hurt
keep	kept	kept
know	knew	known
lay (to place)	laid	laid
lead	led	led
leave	left	left

(continued on the following page)

(continued from the previous page)

Base Form	Past Tense	Past Participle
let	let	let
lie (to recline)	lay	lain
light	lit	lit
lose	lost	lost
make	made	made
meet	met	met
pay	paid	paid
put	put	put
quit	quit	quit
read	read	read
ride	rode	ridden
ring	rang	rung
rise	rose	risen
run	ran	run
say	said	said
see	saw	seen
sell	sold	sold
send	sent	sent
set	set	set
shake	shook	shaken
shine	shone, shined	shone, shined
sing	sang	sung
sit	sat	sat
sleep	slept	slept
speak	spoke	spoken
spend	spent	spent
spring	sprang	sprung
stand	stood	stood
steal	stole	stolen
stick	stuck	stuck
sting	stung	stung
swear	swore	sworn
swim	swam	swum
take	took	taken
teach	taught	taught
tear	tore	torn
tell	told	told
think	thought	thought
throw	threw	thrown
understand	understood	understood
wake	woke, waked	woken, waked
wear	wore	worn
win	won	won
write	wrote	written

◆ PRACTICE 20.3

Below are the base forms of ten irregular verbs. In the spaces after each verb, write the appropriate present tense form, past tense form, and past participle form. If necessary, refer to the chart on pages 315–316.

ON THE WEB
For more practice identifying irregular past participles, visit Exercise Central at <bedfordstmartins.com /foundationsfirst>.

Example
begin

present: The show ____begins____ at 8 p.m. every night.

past: I ____began____ a new book this morning.

past participle: We have ____begun____ to understand.

1. go

   present: The summer vacation always ______________ too quickly.

   past: He ______________ home an hour ago.

   past participle: They have ______________ to Maine every August for twenty years.

2. think

   present: She ______________ carefully about each question.

   past: We ______________ you wanted a job.

   past participle: I have ______________ a lot about that subject.

3. drink

   present: He ______________ only bottled water.

   past: We ______________ six bottles of water after the race.

   past participle: You have just ______________ the last cold soda.

4. win

   present: Every year, his chili ______________ a blue ribbon at the fair.

   past: They ______________ a bowling trophy last night.

   past participle: We have never ______________ anything.

5. feel

   present: It ______________ very warm in here.

   past: He ______________ sick after lunch.

   past participle: They had ______________ exhausted even before the hike.

6. become

present: He ______________ unpleasant when he is under stress.

past: The argument eventually ______________ difficult to ignore.

past participle: Her shoelaces had ______________ loose before she fell.

7. keep

present: It just ______________ raining.

past: We ______________ the doors locked when we went out.

past participle: Simone has always ______________ secrets very well.

8. lie

present: She ______________ on the couch every night after work.

past: The dog ______________ on the rug while we ate.

past participle: You have ______________ there for more than an hour.

9. understand

present: He ______________ more English than he speaks.

past: We ______________ what the teacher wanted.

past participle: My father has never ______________ rap music.

10. write

present: She ______________ long emails.

past: I ______________ to Jack when he was in the Navy.

past participle: My little brother has never ______________ a paper without using his computer.

◆ PRACTICE 20.4

Fill in the correct past participle form of each verb in parentheses. Refer to the chart on pages 315–316 as needed.

Example: Bowhead whales have always ______swum______ (swim) past the Aleutian Islands as they migrate.

(1) Biologists have recently ______________ (make) a surprising discovery in the Arctic Ocean. (2) Bowhead whales, which have ______________ (spend) their winters in the Bering Sea near Alaska for

centuries, may be the world's longest-lived mammals. (3) Members of Alaska's Inupiat tribe have _____________ (keep) up their ancestors' tradition of hunting the bowheads. (4) They have _____________ (catch) several whales each year for generations. (5) Since 1981, Inupiats have _____________ (find) six stone or ivory spear points in the captured whales. (6) No one in today's Inupiat tribe had _____________ (see) a stone or ivory harpoon before these discoveries. (7) These harpoons had not _____________ (be) used by the Inupiats for at least a century. (8) The Inupiats had _____________ (know) for years that whales could live for sixty or more years, but no one had suspected they could live for over a century. (9) Biologists who had _____________ (hear) about the unusual situation analyzed the whales' flesh. (10) They have not yet _____________ (come) to a conclusion, but early results suggest that some bowhead whales may live more than two hundred years.

◆ PRACTICE 20.5

The following passage contains errors in irregular past participles. Cross out any underlined past participles that are incorrect, and write the correct form above them. If the verb form is correct, label it *C*.

become

Example: Recently, the story of the racehorse Seabiscuit has ~~became~~ popular again.

(1) By the 1930s and 1940s, when the horse was racing, Seabiscuit had already became a household name. (2) Now, the publication of a best-selling book and the release of a popular movie have put Seabiscuit's story in the spotlight again. (3) It has catched people's attention because it is the story of a homely underdog who beats a beautiful champion. (4) Seabiscuit started as an average racehorse who had winned few races. (5) A funny-looking horse with stubby legs, he had showed very little interest in running fast. (6) He had not began winning races until he met jockey Red Pollard in 1936. (7) However, because Pollard had lost more races than he had won, people did not think that these two would

be a winning team. (8) In 1939, after they had fight to win people's respect, both horse and jockey suffered multiple injuries. (9) By that point, most people had gived up on them. (10) However, they came back to win in 1940 and have since become American legends.

C Using the Present Perfect Tense

For more on helping verbs, see 9F.

The **present perfect tense** consists of the present tense of the helping verb *have* plus the past participle.

The Present Perfect Tense
(have or has + past participle)

Singular	**Plural**
I have gained.	We have gained.
You have gained.	You have gained.
He has gained.	They have gained.
She has gained.	
It has gained.	

Computer Tip
Most grammar checkers automatically find problems with past participles and even suggest the correct form.

For more on the past tense, see 20A.

The present perfect tense has two uses. Use the present perfect tense to indicate that an action or activity began in the past and continues into the present.

PRESENT PERFECT TENSE The Gallup poll has predicted elections since the 1930s. (The predicting began in the past and continues into the present.)

Use the present perfect tense to indicate that an action has just occurred.

PRESENT PERFECT TENSE I have just voted. (The voting has just occurred.)

Writing Tip
Use the words *just, now, already,* and *recently* to show that an action has just occurred.

ON THE WEB
For more practice using the present perfect tense, visit Exercise Central at <bedfordstmartins.com/foundationsfirst>.

◆ PRACTICE 20.6

In each of the following sentences, form the present perfect tense by filling in the correct form of *have* and the correct past participle form of the verb in parentheses.

Example: The invention of the cochlear implant ___has___ ___given___ (give) many deaf people the chance to get back some of their hearing.

(1) The cochlear implant, an electronic device that is surgically implanted in the inner ear, __________ __________ (be)

available since the 1980s. (2) Although an implant cannot fully bring back a person's hearing, it ______________ ______________ (make) it easier for some people to function in the hearing world. (3) People who ______________ ______________ (choose) to get cochlear implants can usually hear well enough to use a telephone. (4) Children who get the implants early enough ______________ ______________ (be) able to learn to speak. (5) However, this device ______________ ______________ (cause) a heated debate within the deaf community. (6) Many deaf people ______________ ______________ (speak) out against cochlear implants. (7) They are proud of their deafness and feel that they ______________ ______________ (lead) full and satisfying lives, using American Sign Language (ASL) as their main means of communication. (8) They do not think that their lives are inferior because they are deaf; to the contrary, they think that cochlear implants ______________ ______________ (hurt) deaf culture. (9) As a result, although some people ______________ ______________ (welcome) cochlear implants, others wish that the implants were not available. (10) The invention of this device ______________ ______________ (cause) more controversy than anyone ever thought possible.

◆ PRACTICE 20.7

Circle the appropriate verb tense (past tense or present perfect) from the choices in parentheses.

Example: Don Larsen (threw/has thrown) the ceremonial first pitch in the first game of the 2000 World Series.

(1) Baseball fans (enjoyed/have enjoyed) talking about their favorite games for more than a century. (2) One of the most famous games ever played (was/has been) the fifth game of the 1956 World Series. (3) The New York Yankees (played/have played) the Brooklyn Dodgers in the World Series that year. (4) In game five, the Yankees' Don Larsen (pitched/has pitched) a perfect game, allowing no hits and no runs. (5) People

who (saw/has seen) that game agree that they (never saw/have never seen) anything like it since. (6) Perfect games (were always/have always been) extremely rare. (7) Only a few pitchers (ever had/have ever had) a perfect game, and so far, no one other than Larsen (ever threw/has ever thrown) a perfect game in the World Series. (8) The Yankees (won/have won) the 1956 World Series in seven games. (9) In 1957, the Brooklyn Dodgers (moved/have moved) to Los Angeles. (10) The 1956 World Series (was/has been) the last all–New York series until 2000, when the Mets (played/have played) the Yankees.

◆ PRACTICE 20.8

Fill in the appropriate tense (past tense or present perfect) of the verb in parentheses.

Example: For centuries, Muslims ___have fasted___ (fast) for Ramadan, the ninth month in the Muslim calendar.

(1) Muslims believe that it ______________ (be) during this month in about 610 A.D. that the prophet Muhammad ______________ (receive) the Koran. (2) To show their appreciation for this holy event, Muslims ______________ (decide) to fast every year during the month of Ramadan. (3) Ever since, Muslims ______________ (continue) to celebrate this month by fasting during daylight hours. (4) Since the seventh century, this month of fasting ______________ (be) a time for spiritual growth and renewal. (5) It also ______________ (become) a time for Muslims to focus on family as well as on charity and self-sacrifice. (6) Every night, after they ______________ (break) their fast, people gather with family and friends to eat and pray. (7) When they ______________ (get) through the entire month, they celebrate with a three-day festival. (8) The festival ______________ (be) added more recently, however, and is more a matter of tradition than religion. (9) Because Muslims follow a lunar calendar, they ______________ (celebrate) Ramadan in every season. (10) Last year, Ramadan ______________ (fall) in the early winter, just before Christmas.

D Using the Past Perfect Tense

The **past perfect tense** consists of the past tense of the helping verb *have* plus the past participle.

The Past Perfect Tense
(had + past participle)

Singular	**Plural**
I had returned.	We had returned.
You had returned.	You had returned.
He had returned.	They had returned.
She had returned.	
It had returned.	

Use the past perfect tense to indicate that one past action occurred before another past action.

PAST PERFECT TENSE — The job applicant told (PAST) the receptionist that he had arrived (PAST PERFECT).

This sentence discusses two actions that happened in the past. The verb in the first part of the sentence (*told*) is in the past tense. The verb in the second part of the sentence (*had arrived*) is in the past perfect tense. The use of the past perfect tense indicates that the job applicant arrived at the interview *before* he talked to the receptionist.

◆ PRACTICE 20.9

Circle the appropriate verb tense (present perfect or past perfect) from the choices in parentheses.

Example: Many businesses today (have invested/had invested) in "detective" software to monitor their staff.

1. Before this software became available, many employers (have become/had become) convinced that their employees were not always working when they were online.
2. "Detective" software (has allowed/had allowed) companies to track the Web sites that their workers visit.
3. Originally, manufacturers of this software (have marketed/had marketed) their product mostly to businesses.
4. Now, it is widely available, and many people (have bought/had bought) this kind of software for their own personal use.

ON THE WEB
For more practice using the past perfect tense, visit Exercise Central at <bedfordstmartins.com/foundationsfirst>.

5. Previously, parents (have been/had been) unable to monitor what their children were doing online.
6. Now, using this "detective" technology, parents (have been/had been) tracking their young children's searches and even blocking certain inappropriate sites.
7. In addition, husbands and wives (have used/had used) this software to find out what their spouses were doing online.
8. Although this "detective" software (has taken/had taken) away some privacy, it also (has given/had given) us more control.
9. Nowadays, most people (have developed/had developed) a healthy suspicion of computers and are aware that others may be watching.
10. Those who (have hoped/had hoped) for complete privacy now realize that for better or for worse, they are never alone.

◆ PRACTICE 20.10

Fill in the appropriate tense (past tense or past perfect) of the verb in parentheses.

Example: In 1914, Sir Ernest Shackleton ____*set*____ (set) out with twenty-seven men to cross the Antarctic continent.

(1) No one ______________ (do) this before, and Shackleton ______________ (hope) to be the first. (2) However, he ______________ (fail) to reach his goal. (3) Early in the journey, the ship, called the *Endurance,* ______________ (run) into ice in the Weddell Sea. (4) The ice ______________ (destroy) the ship and ______________ (halt) the expedition. (5) Although Shackleton ______________ (plan) to end the journey on the other side of Antarctica, the team never even ______________ (make) it to the Antarctic continent. (6) After they ______________ (lose) the *Endurance,* the crew ______________ (have) only three small lifeboats. (7) They ______________ (spend) the next year trying to get back to their starting point. (8) Their difficult journey home through the dark, frozen, uninhabited sea ______________ (become) one of the greatest survival stories of

all time. (9) Miraculously, by 1916, the entire crew ______________ (arrive) home safely. (10) None of them ______________ (die). (11) On previous expeditions, Shackleton ______________ (show) himself to be an excellent leader; this time, he ______________ (prove) that he could lead a group safely through the most hostile territory on earth.

E Using Past Participles as Adjectives

In addition to functioning as a verb, the past participle can function as an **adjective**, modifing a noun that follows it.

My aunt sells painted furniture.

I like fried chicken.

The past participle is also used as an adjective after a **linking verb**—*be, become, seem,* and so on.

Mallory was surprised.

My roommate became depressed.

The applicant seemed qualified for the job.

Writing Tip

A linking verb—such as *seemed* or *looked*—connects a subject to the word that describes it. (See 9E.)

See 23A for more on the use of adjectives as modifiers.

◆ PRACTICE 20.11

The following passage contains errors in past participle forms used as adjectives. Cross out any underlined participle that is incorrect, and write the correct form above it. If the participle form is correct, label it *C.*

ON THE WEB

For more practice using the past participles as adjectives, visit Exercise Central at <bedfordstmartins.com/foundationsfirst>.

Example: A pet should wear identification in case it becomes lost. (C)

(1) Every year, thousands of pets are abandon in the United States. (2) When a cute puppy or kitten grows up, its owners sometimes decide that they are tire of it. (3) In other cases, the unconcern owners, unable to take their pet to a new home, decide that it will be better off in the wild. (4) Then the poor creature may be thrown out of a car along a highway far from home or leave in a deserted area. (5) These animals are often injure; many do not survive. (6) Animal rescue groups, usually run by local governments, try to make sure that as many abandoned animals as possible can be save. (7) The animals that are rescue do not

necessarily experience a happy ending, however. (8) Overcrowded animal shelters often have to kill many of these unwanted pets. (9) "No-kill" shelters do exist, but they are often swamp with unwanted animals and in desperate need of funding. (10) Everyone who considers getting a pet must be certain that he or she is committed to caring for the animal.

◆ PRACTICE 20.12

After each of the following verbs in items 1–10 below, write the correct past participle form. Then, use each of the past participles in one of the phrases listed in items 11–20.

Example

break *past participle:* broken

a broken window

1. make *past participle:* ______________
2. fry *past participle:* ______________
3. register *past participle:* ______________
4. defeat *past participle:* ______________
5. wear *past participle:* ______________
6. hide *past participle:* ______________
7. swear *past participle:* ______________
8. frost *past participle:* ______________
9. cut *past participle:* ______________
10. pave *past participle:* ______________
11. a ______________ road
12. a bouquet of ______________ flowers
13. ______________ enemies
14. ______________ green tomatoes
15. a ______________ nurse
16. a bed neatly ______________
17. ______________ camera
18. a ______________ birthday cake
19. the ______________ team
20. a ______________ patch on the rug

◆ PRACTICE 20.13

In each of the following pairs of sentences, find and underline the past participle that is used as an adjective after a linking verb. Then, combine the two sentences into one longer sentence, with the past participle modifying a noun that follows it.

Example

The lobster was boiled. It was our main course.

The boiled lobster was our main course.

1. The quarterback played for the rest of the quarter. He was injured.

2. The sales clerk was annoyed. She did not want to assist any customers.

3. The figs were dried. Rafika put them in a dish.

4. Anders did not realize he had broken the rules. They were unwritten.

5. His beard was pointed. The baby stared at it for several minutes.

6. My boss was outraged. She wanted to fire us all.

7. His fingers were burned. He put them in his mouth.

8. Mr. Duven keeps his passport in a box. The box is locked.

9. The answers were expected. The students did not give them.

____

____

10. The mysterious stranger produced several documents. They were forged.

____

____

■ REVISING AND EDITING

Look back at your response to the Seeing and Writing exercise on page 311. Did you use the present perfect or past perfect tense? If so, underline the helping verbs and past participles. Then, check to make sure that you used these tenses correctly. Cross out any incorrect verb forms, and write your corrections above them.

CHAPTER REVIEW

◆ EDITING PRACTICE

Read the following essay, which contains errors in the use of past participles and the past, present perfect, and past perfect tenses. Decide whether each of the underlined verbs is correct. If it is correct, write *C* above it. If it is not, cross it out and write in the correct verb form. The first sentence has been done for you.

Aaron McGruder and *The Boondocks*

In 1997, Aaron McGruder created (C) the comic strip *The Boondocks*. Although since then, *The Boondocks* has attracted national attention, at that time McGruder have not yet graduated from college. The first *Boondocks* cartoon was published in his college newspaper. He has began drawing it because he was disappoint with the comics he was seeing. He wanted to make a comic strip that examined serious issues, particularly issues of race. Those who saw *The Boondocks* know that he

CHAPTER

Nouns 21

PREVIEW

In this chapter, you will learn

- to identify nouns (21A)
- to recognize singular and plural nouns (21B)
- to form plural nouns (21C)

■ SEEING AND WRITING

What objects do you treasure? Why? Look at the picture above, and then write a paragraph in which you answer these questions.

Word Power

memento a reminder of the past; a keepsake (the plural form is *mementos*)

memorabilia objects valued because of their link to historical events or culture

A Identifying Nouns

A **noun** is a word that names a person (*actor, Denzel Washington*), an animal (*elephant, Babar*), a place (*city, Houston*), an object (*game, Monopoly*), or an idea (*theory, Darwinism*).

FOCUS Common and Proper Nouns

Most nouns, called **common nouns**, name general classes of people, places, or things. Common nouns begin with lowercase (not capital) letters.

prince   holiday

Some nouns, called **proper nouns**, name particular people, places, or things. A proper noun always begins with a capital letter.

Prince Charming   Memorial Day

ON THE WEB
For more practice identifying nouns, visit Exercise Central at <bedfordstmartins.com /foundationsfirst>.

◆ PRACTICE 21.1

In each of the following sentences, underline every noun. Label common nouns *C* and proper nouns *P*.

Example: Day of the Dead (P) is a holiday (C) celebrated in Mexico (P) and in other countries (C) in Latin America (C).

1. This holiday is celebrated every year to honor the spirits of the dead.
2. The celebration occurs in early November, just after people in the United States celebrate Halloween.
3. This holiday originated with the Aztecs, who held a similar ritual.
4. However, the holiday now has Christian as well as Indian features.
5. Today, people observe the Day of the Dead differently in different regions.
6. Usually, families visit the graves of their ancestors and bring them offerings of food.
7. In Mexico City, residents usually have a festival and decorate the town with skeletons and skulls made of papier-mâché.
8. For some people, this day is a religious occasion.
9. In many places, tourists come to watch the celebration.
10. Many Americans travel to Mexico to see the elaborate decorations and eat the traditional food.

B Recognizing Singular and Plural Nouns

A **singular noun** names one thing: *book, family.* A **plural noun** names more than one thing: *books, families.*

For more on identifying plural nouns, see 24C.

FOCUS Singular and Plural Nouns

Recognizing whether a noun is singular or plural is particularly important when a noun is the subject of a sentence. This is because subjects and verbs must always be in **agreement**: a singular subject requires a singular verb; a plural subject requires a plural verb.

SINGULAR The book sits on the shelf.

PLURAL The books sit on the shelf.

For more on subject-verb agreement, see Chapter 16.

Because many plural nouns end in *-s*, you can often tell whether a noun is singular or plural by looking at its ending. However, many other nouns that end in *-s* are singular (*gas, series, focus*), and some plural nouns have special forms and do not end in *-s* (*men, women, children*).

Sometimes, a noun is introduced by a **determiner**, a word that specifically identifies the noun or limits its meaning (*this house,* not *that house*). In these cases, the determiner tells you whether the noun is singular (*this house*) or plural (*these houses*).

For more on plural forms of nouns, see 21C.

Using Determiners with Nouns

Determiners That Introduce Singular Nouns	Determiners That Introduce Plural Nouns
a	all
an	both
another	few
each	many
every	most
one	several
that	these
this	those
	two, three, etc.

Writing Tip

Sometimes, a determiner is followed not by a noun but by *of* or *of the:* for example, *each of us, many of the reasons.* The same rules for subject-verb agreement apply in these cases.

ON THE WEB
For more practice recognizing singular and plural nouns, visit Exercise Central at <bedfordstmartins.com/foundationsfirst>.

◆ PRACTICE 21.2

In the following passage, fill in the blanks with appropriate singular or plural nouns.

Example: This classroom is too cold.

(1) Every ______________ seems to last too long. (2) Most ______________ do not expect these ______________ to be as long as they are. (3) One ______________ can last two or three ______________. (4) Most ______________ simply do not have enough free time. (5) Several ______________ have complained about this ______________. (6) I have heard few ______________, however. (7) Is there a ______________? (8) Each ______________ should speak up. (9) One ______________ can make a ______________. (10) Several ______________ can make a ______________.

◆ PRACTICE 21.3

In the following paragraph, singular and plural nouns that follow determiners are underlined. Decide whether the correct singular or plural form is used for each underlined noun. If the form is correct, write *C* above the noun. If it is incorrect, cross it out; then, write in the correct singular or plural noun form.

Example: One ~~women~~ woman at the United Nations has worked hard for women's rights around the world.

(1) Over thirty years ago, Nafis Sadik was an obstetricians from Pakistan. (2) In 1971, she took a positions with the United Nations Population Fund. (3) At that time, the Population Fund offered few option to women who wanted fewer children. (4) One choices was sterilization, but many woman were unwilling to take such a permanent step. (5) After several year at the Population Fund, Dr. Sadik became the executive director of this program. (6) Population growth is still a problem around the world, but under Dr. Sadik, the U.N. Population Fund found another focus. (7) The Population Fund now supports the right of every women around the world to have access to education and health care. (8) The fund believes that those women who have access to information and

medical care will plan their families wisely. (9) This concept may sound basic, but unfortunately, women in many country have very little freedom. (10) Allowing women to make their own choices about family planning still makes many person uncomfortable.

C Forming Plural Nouns

Some nouns form plurals in predictable ways; others do not.

Regular Noun Plurals

Most nouns add *-s* to form plurals. Other nouns, whose singular forms end in *-s, -ss, -sh, -ch, -x,* or *-z,* add *-es* to form plurals. Some nouns that end in *-s* or *-z* double the *s* or *z* before adding *-es*.

Singular	*Plural*
chair	chairs
zoo	zoos
campus	campuses
kiss	kisses
wish	wishes
bunch	bunches
box	boxes
quiz	quizzes

Irregular Noun Plurals

Some nouns form plurals in unusual ways.

- Some nouns have plural forms that are the same as their singular forms.

Singular	*Plural*
one fish	two fish
this species	these species
a series	several series

- Nouns ending in *-f* or *-fe* form plurals by changing the *f* to *v* and adding *-es* or *-s*.

Singular	*Plural*
each half	both halves
one life	nine lives
a thief	many thieves
that loaf	those loaves
the first shelf	several shelves

Exceptions to this rule include the words *roof* (plural *roofs*), *proof* (plural *proofs*), and *belief* (plural *beliefs*).

Writing Tip

When a noun has an irregular plural, the dictionary lists its plural form: *man, men.*

- Most nouns ending in *-y* form plurals by changing the *y* to *ie* and adding *-s*.

Singular	*Plural*
a new baby	more babies
one berry	many berries

Note, however, that when a vowel (*a, e, i, o,* or *u*) comes before the *y*, the noun has a regular plural form: *turkey* (plural *turkeys*), *day* (plural *days*).

- A **compound noun**—two or more nouns that function as a unit—generally forms the plural just as other nouns do: by adding *-s* at the end (*baby doll, baby dolls*). However, most hyphenated compound nouns form plurals by adding *-s* to the *first word* of the compound.

Singular	*Plural*
Ben's brother-in-law	Ben's two favorite brothers-in-law
a husband-to-be	all the husbands-to-be
one runner-up	many runners-up

- Other irregular plurals must be memorized.

Singular	*Plural*
that child	those children
a good man	a few good men
one woman	several women
my left foot	both feet
a wisdom tooth	my two front teeth

◆ PRACTICE 21.4

ON THE WEB
For more practice forming plural nouns, visit Exercise Central at <bedfordstmartins.com/foundationsfirst>.

Next to each of the following singular nouns, write the plural form of the noun. Then, circle the irregular plurals. (If you are not sure of a word's plural form, check the dictionary. Irregular plurals will be listed there.)

Example: hamburger *hamburgers* goose *(geese)*

1. lady-in-waiting ______
2. wolf ______
3. potato ______
4. band ______
5. bench ______
6. knife ______
7. calendar ______
8. boss ______
9. highway ______
10. sheep ______
11. cheese ______
12. bandit ______
13. enemy ______
14. cactus ______
15. calf ______
16. mouse ______
17. tax ______
18. projector ______
19. stomach ______
20. fly ______

◆ PRACTICE 21.5

Proofread the underlined nouns in the following paragraph, checking for correct singular or plural form. If a correction needs to be made, cross out the noun, and write the correct form above it. If the noun is correct, write *C* above it.

Example: Choreographer Yuen Wo Ping has been working in movies (*C*) for more than forty ~~yeares~~ *years*.

(1) He became famous in many countrys for directing the martial arts scenes in *The Matrix* and *Crouching Tiger, Hidden Dragon.* (2) Since then, he has done the choreography for both *Matrix* sequelles and for Quentin Tarantino's *Kill Bill.* (3) He has also done action scenes for several other movies. (4) Yuen started out as one of many fighter-in-trainings under the instruction of his father, a kung fu authority. (5) In the 1960s, he started his career, working alongside many other novice actors and stuntman in movies and television. (6) In the 1970s, he became a director and did a series of action filmes starring a then-relatively unknown Jackie Chan. (7) As a director, Yuen proved he had a talent for developing exciting storys that were full of comedy as well as action. (8) Yuen has some distinctive techniques, and fans recognize his unique waies of doing things. (9) For instance, Yuen will often have performers use ordinary objects, such as brushs or robe sleeves, to represent knifes and other weapons. (10) In fact, he would not hesitate to make an actor wear fake buck tooths if he thought he could get a laugh out of it.

■ REVISING AND EDITING

Look back at your response to the Seeing and Writing exercise on page 331. First, underline every noun. Then, check to be sure you have capitalized every proper noun and formed plurals correctly.

CHAPTER REVIEW

◆ EDITING PRACTICE

Read the following essay, which contains noun errors. Make any editing changes you think are necessary. The first sentence has been edited for you.

Who Is Home Schooled and Why?

Close to a million or more ~~childs~~ children are home schooled in the United ~~states~~ States. This number has been growing steadily over the past ten year. These days, parents have many different reason for choosing home schooling. It used to be that most home-schooling parentes were either liberal hippies who wanted to give their kids more freedom or conservative Christians who wanted to protect their childrens from sinful influences. Now, many parents say that they are simply in search of a higher quality of education for their children.

A parent home schooling children

Recent changes in education have given schools less flexibility, and most school now rely on standardized testing more than they did in past yeares. Some parents disagree with this focus on test scores and have decided they prefer a different approach. By doing the teaching themselves, they can choose to emphasize their child's intellectual inquiry instead of these test score. For some minoritys, the lack of minority role modeles in traditional classrooms is enough of a reason to leave the public school system. In many area of the country, an African American could go through twelve year of public schooling without ever having an African American Teacher. By home schooling, parents can choose the adults who will affect their children's lifes.

Another common motive for choosing home schooling is the failure of the public schools to meet many children's specific needs. For example, gifted children may not be getting all the different challenge they need, and students with learning disabilitys are often not getting the help they need either. At home, children can get more individual attention and can pursue the activitys that interest them. A child who loves history can spend the day at an art museum, and a child who struggles in math can have the time and space to try several alternative learning strategys.

Recently, there has been a rise in the number of home-schooled children in other populations, such as military familys. Because the military moves peoples frequently, the children of military personnels change school systems every couple of year. By home schooling, parents can offer their kids some much-needed stability. Other parents choose to go this route simply because they want to spend more time with their children. Few parent-to-bes imagine giving up their careers to teach their children. However, some parents (usually woman) do, and they often find unexpected rewards in home schooling their children.

All in all, there seem to be as many reason to home school as there are people doing it. Of course, it is not an option for every families; there are minus as well as pluses to home schooling. For example, there is less socializing and less competition in a home environment. Many critic worry that home-schooled children will not be prepared to enter college or to face the real world. However, there are many success story. For example, nineteen-year-old Christopher Paolini, who was home schooled, recently watched his book *Eragon* reach the top of the *New York Times* best-seller list.

◆ COLLABORATIVE ACTIVITIES

1. Working in a group, complete the following chart by listing nouns related to each category, writing one noun on each line. If the noun is a proper noun, be sure to capitalize it. When you have completed the chart, work together to add to the chart the plural form of each singular noun and the singular form of each plural noun. (Use a different

color pen, and write these forms beside the nouns.) If the noun has only one form, circle it.

Sports	*Politics*	*Television*	*College*	*Holidays*

2. Continuing to work in the same group, write a sentence on a sheet of paper using one of the nouns from activity 1. Pass the paper to the person next to you; on the sheet you receive, write a related sentence, but use a different noun. Keep passing the sheets and adding sentences until you have a paragraph of at least six sentences on each page.
3. From the paragraphs composed in activity 2, choose the one that your group likes best, and work together to expand it. Then, exchange paragraphs with another group in class. Rewrite the other group's paragraph, substituting a noun from your chart for one of the nouns in each sentence the other group has written. Finally, read the paragraphs to the class, and choose the funniest revision.
4. *Composing original sentences* Working in a group, write five sentences. Make sure that you have used at least one proper noun, at least one determiner that introduces a singular noun, at least one determiner that introduces a plural noun, and at least two plural nouns with irregular plurals. Then, check the nouns carefully to be sure that the forms are correct. When you have finished, check the sentences again to make sure you have corrected any errors in grammar, punctuation, or spelling.

✓ REVIEW CHECKLIST: Nouns

- A noun is a word that names a person, an animal, a place, an object, or an idea. (See 21A.)
- A singular noun names one thing; a plural noun names more than one thing. (See 21B.)
- Most nouns add *-s* to form plurals. Some nouns have irregular plural forms. (See 21C.)

CHAPTER

22

Pronouns

PREVIEW

In this chapter, you will learn

- to identify pronouns (22A)
- to understand pronoun-antecedent agreement (22B)
- to solve special problems with pronoun-antecedent agreement (22C)
- to eliminate vague and unnecessary pronouns (22D)
- to understand pronoun case (22E)
- to solve special problems with pronoun case (22F)
- to identify reflexive and intensive pronouns (22G)

SEEING AND WRITING

If you had a vanity license plate, what would you want it to say? Why? Look at the picture above, and then write a paragraph in which you answer these questions.

Word Power

vanity an excessive pride in one's appearance or achievements

vanity plate a license plate that can be customized for an extra charge

A Identifying Pronouns

A **pronoun** is a word that refers to and takes the place of a noun or another pronoun.

Evan wanted to change his life, so <u>he</u> decided to enlist in the Air Force. (*He* takes the place of *Evan*.)

Without pronouns, you would have to repeat the same nouns over and over again.

Evan wanted to change his life, so Evan decided to enlist in the Air Force.

Pronouns, like nouns, can be singular or plural. Singular pronouns always take the place of singular nouns.

Julia forgot to pick up Max, so she went back to get him. (*She* takes the place of *Julia; him* takes the place of *Max.*)

Plural pronouns always take the place of plural nouns.

Kyle and Mike took their little brother fishing. (*Their* takes the place of *Kyle and Mike.*)

Keep in mind that the pronoun *you* can be either singular or plural.

When the fans met the rock star, they said, "We're crazy about you." The rock star replied, "I couldn't do it without you." (The first *you* is singular; it takes the place of *rock star.* The second *you* is plural; it takes the place of *fans.*)

Writing Tip

Too many pronouns can make a paragraph monotonous, especially when pronouns begin several sentences in a row. See 12A for tips on how to vary your sentence openings.

For lists of pronouns, see 22C (three lists), 22E, and 22G.

◆ PRACTICE 22.1

In each of the following sentences, underline the pronoun. Then, in the blank after each sentence, write *S* if the pronoun is singular or *P* if the pronoun is plural.

Example: He ate twelve pancakes for breakfast. S

1. She sold flowers on the street corner. _____
2. It was a very dull book. _____
3. We spent hours trying to get tickets to the game. _____
4. When the alarm rang, I turned it off. _____
5. The neighborhood is so quiet that it seems deserted. _____
6. Derek, you should try out for the cross-country team. _____
7. The boy looked hungry, but he did not ask for any food. _____
8. The room is clean, children, but you forgot to make the beds. _____
9. Strangers turned away when we asked for help. _____
10. If Cathy had married Heathcliff, they might have been happy. _____

ON THE WEB

For more practice identifying pronouns, visit Exercise Central at <bedfordstmartins.com/foundationsfirst>.

B Understanding Pronoun-Antecedent Agreement

As you learned in 22A, a pronoun takes the place of either a noun or another pronoun. The word to which the pronoun refers is called its **antecedent**. In the following sentence, the noun *runner* is the antecedent of the pronoun *he.*

The runner slowed down, but he did not stop.

A pronoun must always agree with its antecedent. If an antecedent is singular, the pronoun must also be singular. In the sentence above, the antecedent *runner* is singular, so the pronoun that refers to it (*he*) is also singular.

If the antecedent is plural, the pronoun must also be plural.

The runners slowed down, but they did not stop.

Here, the antecedent *runners* is plural, so the pronoun that refers to it (*they*) is also plural.

◆ PRACTICE 22.2

In each of the following sentences, a pronoun is underlined. In the blank after each sentence, write the noun that is the antecedent of the underlined pronoun. Then, draw an arrow from the pronoun to its antecedent.

ON THE WEB
For more practice understanding pronoun-antecedent agreement, visit Exercise Central at <bedfordstmartins.com/foundationsfirst>.

Example: When the kittens were awake, they were constantly eating.

kittens

1. The woman spoke out angrily before she left. ______
2. A frog's skin is so thin that it absorbs pesticides. ______
3. The hitchhiker put out a thumb, but his face showed no hope. ______
4. Felicia won her first karaoke contest and took Friday off. ______
5. When the two lawyers started dating, they decided to stop working together. ______
6. Tino, you cannot graduate without a foreign-language credit. ______
7. Esteban saw a film that he hated. ______
8. Mr. and Mrs. McCoy almost missed their bus to Florida. ______
9. Fries taste good, but they are not very nutritious. ______
10. As Bob crossed the street, a truck narrowly missed him. ______

◆ PRACTICE 22.3

In the following passage, fill in each blank with the appropriate pronoun (*it* or *they*).

Example: For generations, people on earth have asked questions about Mars because ___it___ is the closest planet to us.

(1) When the *Viking 1* spacecraft orbited Mars in July 1976, __________ sent photographs back to the National Aeornautics and Space Administration (NASA). (2) Some people who saw one of these photographs were surprised when __________ thought it showed a face. (3) The face seemed to be about a mile long, and __________ appeared to have eyes, a nose, and a mouth. (4) Science fiction fans suggested the face was a kind of monument and wondered if __________ had been built by a former Martian civilization. (5) However, when more detailed photos were taken in 1998, __________ showed only rocky cliffs where the face had been seen. (6) People have not lost their interest in the red planet, and __________ continue to pay attention to new discoveries. (7) In 2003, Mars came closer to Earth than __________ had been in sixty thousand years. (8) In the month of August, Mars looked like an unusually bright orange star, and __________ outshone every other star and planet in the sky. (9) Taking their telescopes, many people went outside so that __________ could observe the planet for themselves. (10) From the Hubble Space Telescope, NASA took the most detailed photos to date of Mars as __________ reached its closest distance from Earth.

◆ PRACTICE 22.4

In the following passage, circle the antecedent of each underlined pronoun. Then, draw an arrow from the pronoun to its antecedent.

Example: Americans are more disappointed with the public education system than they used to be.

(1) Some reformers think that if schools have to compete for students, they will be forced to improve. (2) A school voucher system is one way to introduce competition, and it is growing in popularity. (3) School vouchers allow parents to select a school—public or private—of their choice. (4) Some people support a voucher program because they think it

will give children in poor and failing school districts the opportunity to get a high-quality education. (5) According to them, the program would also force bad schools to close their doors. (6) Others, however, tend to oppose the idea because it takes money away from public schools. (7) Mayor Anthony Williams supports school vouchers in his city, Washington, D.C. (8) Washington has some of the richest and some of the poorest people in the nation; as a result, it has a very uneven school system. (9) Citywide voucher programs already exist in Cleveland and Milwaukee, but they are local programs. (10) Many people think that the Washington, D.C., pilot program may have a greater impact nationwide because it is the first federally funded voucher program.

C Solving Special Problems with Pronoun-Antecedent Agreement

To make sure pronouns and antecedents agree, you must know whether an antecedent is singular or plural. Certain kinds of antecedents can cause problems for writers because they are not easy to identify as singular or plural. These troublesome groups of antecedents include *compound antecedents, indefinite pronoun antecedents,* and *collective noun antecedents.*

Compound Antecedents

A **compound antecedent** consists of two or more words connected by *and* or *or: England and the United States; Japan or China.*

Compound antecedents connected by *and* are always plural. They are always used with plural pronouns.

England and the United States drafted soldiers into their armies.

Compound antecedents connected by *or* may be treated as singular or plural. When both words in a compound antecedent connected by *or* are singular, use a singular pronoun to refer to the compound antecedent.

For more on compound subjects, see 16C.

Did Japan or China send its army to war?

When both words are plural, use a plural pronoun.

Volunteer armies or military drafts both have their supporters.

◆ PRACTICE 22.5

In each of the following sentences, underline the compound antecedent, and circle the connecting word (*and* or *or*). Then, circle the appropriate pronoun in parentheses.

ON THE WEB

For more practice solving special problems with pronoun-antecedent agreement, visit Exercise Central at <bedfordstmartins.com/foundationsfirst>.

Example: Music fans and moviegoers are finding many reasons to put (its/their) faith in Queen Latifah.

(1) Her power and intelligence have made (its/their) mark on both films and rap music. (2) Her music speaks about the abuse or the lack of respect women receive and (its/their) effects on women's confidence. (3) Queen Latifah is unafraid of her own power and position and uses (it/them) to express her ideas. (4) Feminist issues and politics are never far from her mind, and (its/their) influence on her is clear. (5) In recent years, Queen Latifah has been less focused on music and more focused on movies and television and (its/their) opportunities. (6) A popular movie or television show often makes (its/their) stars famous. (7) In 2003, the films *Chicago* and *Bringing Down the House* brought Queen Latifah to a new level of fame because of (its/their) high ticket sales and awards. (8) For *Chicago,* Queen Latifah was nominated for a Golden Globe and an Oscar, and her many fans thought she deserved to win (it/them). (9) It is hard to know what Queen Latifah will do next with her skills and talents because (it/they) can be so diverse. (10) Her beauty and independence are inspiring, and (it/they) will clearly take her far.

◆ PRACTICE 22.6

The following passage contains errors in pronoun reference with compound antecedents. Decide whether each underlined pronoun is correct. If it is not, cross out the pronoun, and write the correct pronoun above it. If it is correct, label it *C.*

Example: Because the Spanish conquerors never discovered Machu Picchu, most of the buildings and terraces have kept ~~its~~ *their* original shape.

(1) Many tourists and historians travel to Peru every year to get their fill of Incan culture at this ancient site. (2) The Intihuatana stone and the Torreon provide its visitors with rare examples of Incan shrines. (3) Amateurs or experts can appreciate the beauty of Machu Picchu as well as what it tells them about Incan society and culture. (4) High in the Andes mountains, this religious sanctuary or palace—no one is entirely sure

which—is in a world of their own. (5) The peaks and valleys are dramatic, and they help to define the shape of the terraced city. (6) Similarly, the houses or temples inside the walled site took its shape from the contours of the stone bricks used to build them. (7) The design and the stonework were extremely precise, and because of it, the Incan builders were able to use every inch of space. (8) Amazingly, the architects and the workers had no blueprints to guide them. (9) They also had no large animals or wheeled equipment to help them get a brick or a heavy tool to their place. (10) Today, the buildings and terraces of Macchu Picchu are known as the eighth wonder of the world, and people travel from all over the world to see it.

Indefinite Pronoun Antecedents

Most pronouns refer to a specific person or thing. **Indefinite pronouns**, however, do not refer to any particular person or thing.

Most indefinite pronouns are singular. When the indefinite pronoun antecedent is singular, use a singular pronoun to refer to it.

> Something was out of its usual place. (*Something* is singular, so it is used with the singular pronoun *its*.)

For information on subject-verb agreement with indefinite pronouns as subjects, see 16E.

Singular Indefinite Pronouns

another	everybody	no one
anybody	everyone	nothing
anyone	everything	one
anything	much	somebody
each	neither	someone
either	nobody	something

Writing Tip

Some indefinite pronouns (such as *all, any, more, most, none,* and *some*) can be either singular or plural (*All is lost; All were qualified.*).

FOCUS Singular Indefinite Pronouns with *Of*

The singular indefinite pronouns *each, either, neither,* and *one* are often used in phrases with *of*—*each of, either of, neither of, one of*—followed by a plural noun (*each of the boys*). In such phrases, these indefinite pronoun antecedents are always singular and take singular pronouns.

> Each of the games has its [not *their*] own rules.

Some indefinite pronouns are plural. When the indefinite pronoun antecedent is plural, use a plural pronoun to refer to it.

The whole group wanted to go swimming, but few had brought their bathing suits. (*Few* is plural, so it is used with the plural pronoun *their*.)

Plural Indefinite Pronouns

both	others
few	several
many	

FOCUS Using *His* or *Her* with Indefinite Pronouns

Singular indefinite pronouns that refer to people—such as *anybody, anyone, everybody, everyone, somebody,* and *someone*—require a singular pronoun, such as *his*.

However, using the singular pronoun *his* in such cases suggests that the indefinite pronoun refers to a male. Using *his or her* is an improvement because it acknowledges that the indefinite pronoun may refer to either a male or a female.

Everyone must revise his or her work.

When used over and over again, however, *he or she, him or her,* and *his or her* can create wordy, repetitive sentences. Often, the best solution is to use a plural noun instead of the indefinite pronoun.

All students must revise their work.

◆ PRACTICE 22.7

In each of the following sentences, circle the indefinite pronoun. Then, circle the pronoun in parentheses that refers to the indefinite pronoun antecedent.

Example: Neither my sister Alyssa nor her best friend can do homework without listening to (her/their) radio.

1. Everyone in the business world has to be able to do several tasks at once at (his or her/their) job.

2. People once said that everything should be done in (its/their) own time, but that idea has been replaced at many offices.
3. Instead, anyone searching the classified ads for (his or her/their) ideal job is likely to see the word *multitasking,* a computer term for doing several things at the same time.
4. Nobody who is unable to divide (his or her/their) attention should apply for a job that requires multitasking.
5. Many of today's adults learned to focus on one task at a time, and few have developed (his or her/their) ability to multitask.
6. Teenagers, however, seem able to do many things simultaneously, and many can juggle (his or her/their) tasks with apparent ease.
7. Each of my two teenage sisters spends (her/their) evening talking on the telephone, listening to CDs, and reading email at the same time.
8. When our parents objected, both of my sisters insisted that (she/they) could pay attention to all three tasks.
9. Either of them might do (her/their) math homework in front of the television.
10. Everyone has (his or her/their) opinion about teenagers' multitasking.
11. Although some researchers have studied teenagers' and adults' brains, no one has devoted (his or her/their) research to the effects of multi-tasking on the brain.
12. Some psychologists are concerned about the way teenagers juggle tasks, and several have published books explaining (his or her/their) worries.
13. Multitasking may affect the ability to concentrate, and anybody who habitually does many tasks at once may not work to (his or her/their) full potential.
14. Still, I expect at least one of my sisters to find (herself/themselves) in demand in the job market someday.
15. Businesses love people who can multitask, so someone will do (his or her/their) company a favor someday by hiring my sisters.

◆ PRACTICE 22.8

In the following passage, fill in each blank with an appropriate pronoun. Then, draw an arrow from the pronoun in the blank to its indefinite pronoun antecedent.

Example: Nobody should forfeit his or her chance to participate in the democratic process.

(1) Everyone who can vote should be sure to cast __________ ballot in an election. (2) My father always said, "Anyone who doesn't vote loses __________ right to complain about the way things are in this country." (3) Unfortunately, few of the people who are eligible to vote make __________ opinions known on election day. (4) One of my neighbors devotes __________ time to getting out the vote, and this year I joined him. (5) I telephoned local residents and reminded each of them that __________ should vote on Tuesday. (6) Several who were elderly asked how __________ would get to the polling place. (7) One man, Mr. Jones, told me that either his daughter or his granddaughter would have to come from __________ home thirty miles away to drive him to the polls. (8) I called both and told __________ that I would take Mr. Jones to cast his vote. (9) Many in the United States who are younger take __________ voting responsibilities much less seriously than Mr. Jones does. (10) We should all remember that everything we do has __________ consequences; our government works best when we all participate.

◆ PRACTICE 22.9

Edit the following sentences for errors in pronoun-antecedent agreement. In some sentences, substitute *his or her* for *their* when the antecedent is singular and could refer to a person of either gender. In other sentences, replace the antecedent with a plural word or phrase.

Example: Everyone in the restaurant complained to ~~their~~ his or her waiter.

1. Someone left their key in the lock.
2. Each of the trees grows at their own rate.

3. Everyone on the platform missed their train.
4. Neither of the boys remembers their former home in Oregon.
5. Every telemarketer hated making their calls at dinnertime.
6. Either Sandra or Emily should sign their name here.
7. Anyone would love to give this toy to their children.
8. Neither of these chairs will look as good as they did before the fire.
9. Everyone must email their essays to the professor.
10. Each of us has our own cell phone.
11. Has anybody in this neighborhood lost their dog?
12. Everyone in the office bought their own lottery tickets.
13. Someone hung up without leaving their name or number on the answering machine.
14. Anyone with a drunk-driving conviction ought to have their license revoked.
15. Everyone thought the candidate was charming, but they did not want to vote for him.

Collective Noun Antecedents

Collective nouns are singular words (like *band* and *team*) that name a group of people or things. Because they are singular, collective noun antecedents are used with singular pronouns.

The band was very loud, but it was not very good.

In the sentence above, the collective noun *band* names a group of individual musicians, but it refers to them as a unit. Because *band* is singular, it is used with the singular pronoun *it*.

Frequently Used Collective Nouns

army	committee	government	pack
association	company	group	posse
band	crowd	jury	team
class	family	league	union
club	gang	mob	

Writing Tip
When you refer to a collective noun that is plural—for example, *bands, teams, unions*—you need to use a plural pronoun: *Both teams fired their coaches.*

◆ PRACTICE 22.10

In each of the following sentences, underline the antecedent. If the antecedent is a collective noun, write *coll* above it. Then, circle the correct pronoun in parentheses.

Example: The mob (coll) chased (its/their) victim.

1. A wolf pack sometimes tracks (its/their) prey for a long time.
2. Last night, our football team celebrated (its/their) first victory in two years.
3. The officers carried (its/their) guns all the time.
4. The committee holds (its/their) meeting on the first Friday of every month.
5. The gang displayed (its/their) colors proudly.
6. The crowd roared (its/their) encouragement to the runners.
7. The class applauded (its/their) teacher, Mr. Henry, when he was voted Teacher of the Year.
8. The posse made (its/their) way across the plains.
9. The jury gave (its/their) decision to the court clerk.
10. Some people move (its/their) hands rapidly while speaking.

◆ PRACTICE 22.11

Edit the following passage for correct pronoun-antecedent agreement. First, identify the antecedent of each underlined pronoun. (Some antecedents will be compounds, some will be indefinite pronouns, and some will be collective nouns.) Next, cross out any pronoun that does not agree with its antecedent, and write the correct form above it. If the pronoun is correct, label it *C*.

Example: Grant Fuhr and Tiger Woods won acclaim for ~~his~~ their athletic abilities.

(1) Golf and hockey are very different sports, but they have one thing in common: its players tend to be white. (2) In golf, this situation is changing; no one has broken the records of their sport more frequently than the golfer Tiger Woods. (3) Because of Woods, everyone has altered their view of what a professional golfer looks like. (4) Hockey, however, is

still waiting for its own Tiger Woods even though black hockey players are becoming more common. (5) Willie O'Ree and Grant Fuhr, for example, have been impressive in his contributions to hockey. (6) The National Hockey League broke their color barrier in 1958 when O'Ree joined the Boston Bruins. (7) O'Ree noticed that American fans and Canadian fans differed in their reactions to him: the Americans were more likely to shout racist remarks. (8) Although O'Ree stopped playing in 1961, the National Hockey League recently hired him to head their Diversity Task Force. (9) The Edmonton Oilers and the Calgary Flames have been fortunate to have Fuhr, who is expected to end up in the Hockey Hall of Fame, as its goalie. (10) Either Fuhr or O'Ree can be a role model for their fans even though neither player is as well known as Tiger Woods.

D Eliminating Vague and Unnecessary Pronouns

Vague and unnecessary pronouns clutter up your writing. Eliminating them will make your writing clearer and easier for readers to follow.

Vague Pronouns

A pronoun should always refer to a specific antecedent. When a pronoun has no antecedent, it confuses readers. The pronouns *it* and *they* can be particularly troublesome.

VAGUE PRONOUN In the news report, they said city workers would strike. (Who said city workers would strike?)

VAGUE PRONOUN It says in today's paper that overcrowded prisons are a serious problem. (Who says overcrowded prisons are a problem?)

When you use *it* or *they* as the subject of a sentence, check carefully to be sure the pronoun refers to a specific antecedent in the sentence. If it does not, delete it, or replace it with a noun that communicates your meaning to readers.

REVISED The news report said city workers would strike.

REVISED An editorial in today's paper says that overcrowded prisons are a serious problem.

Writing Tip

Only an intensive pronoun can come right after its antecedent: *I myself prefer to wait.* (See 22G.)

Unnecessary Pronouns

When a pronoun directly follows its antecedent, it is usually unnecessary.

UNNECESSARY PRONOUN — The librarian, he recommended Toni Morrison's *Beloved.*

In the above sentence, the pronoun *he* serves no purpose. Readers do not need to be directed back to the pronoun's antecedent (the noun *librarian*) because it appears right before the pronoun. The pronoun should therefore be eliminated.

REVISED — The librarian recommended Toni Morrison's *Beloved.*

◆ PRACTICE 22.12

ON THE WEB
For more practice eliminating vague and unnecessary pronouns, visit Exercise Central at <bedfordstmartins.com/foundationsfirst>.

The following sentences contain vague and unnecessary pronouns. Rewrite each sentence correctly on the lines below it.

Example: On the Web site, it claimed that a spaceship was following the comet.

The Web site claimed that a spaceship was following the comet.

1. In Canada, they have many sparsely populated areas.

2. My dog, he likes to play in water.

3. The video game that I bought, it broke almost immediately.

4. In the pamphlet, it explained how AIDS is transmitted.

5. Her granddaughter, she lives in another state.

6. On that game show, they know the answers to very difficult questions.

7. These apples, they were damaged in the hailstorm.

____

____

8. On the sidewalk, they were all watching the television in the store window.

____

____

9. The acrobat, he almost fell off the tightrope.

____

____

10. In her class, they do not review grammar.

____

____

E Understanding Pronoun Case

A **personal pronoun**—a pronoun that refers to a particular person or thing—changes form according to the way it functions in a sentence. Personal pronouns can be *subjective, objective,* or *possessive.*

Personal Pronouns

Subjective Case	**Objective Case**	**Possessive Case**
I	me	my, mine
he	him	his
she	her	her, hers
it	it	its
we	us	our, ours
you	you	your, yours
they	them	their, theirs
who	whom	whose
whoever	whomever	

When a pronoun functions as a subject, it is in the **subjective case**.

> She walked along the beach looking for seashells. (The pronoun *She* is the sentence's subject.)

When a pronoun functions as an object, it is in the **objective case**.

> Walking along the beach, Lucia saw them. (The pronoun *them* is the direct object of the verb *saw.*)

Lucia brought him a seashell. (The pronoun *him* is the indirect object of the verb *brought.*)

Lucia gave some seashells to them. (The pronoun *them* is the object of the preposition *to.*)

FOCUS Objects

A **direct object** is a noun or pronoun that receives the action of the verb.

DIR OBJ
Lucia saw seashells. (What did Lucia see?)

DIR OBJ
Lucia saw them. (What did Lucia see?)

An **indirect object** is the noun or pronoun that tells to whom or for whom the verb's action was done.

IND OBJ
Lucia brought Greg a seashell. (For whom did Lucia bring a seashell?)

IND OBJ
Lucia brought him a seashell. (For whom did Lucia bring a seashell?)

A word or word group introduced by a preposition is called the **object of the preposition**. (See 9C.)

OBJ OF PREP
Lucia gave some seashells to Chris and Kelly. (To whom did Lucia give some seashells?)

OBJ OF PREP
Lucia gave some seashells to them. (To whom did Lucia give some seashells?)

When a pronoun shows ownership, it is in the **possessive case**.

Tuan rode his bike to work. (The bike belongs to Tuan.)

Kate and Alex took their bikes, too. (The bikes belong to Kate and Alex.)

◆ PRACTICE 22.13

ON THE WEB
For more practice understanding pronoun case, visit Exercise Central at <bedfordstmartins.com/foundationsfirst>.

Above each of the underlined pronouns, indicate whether it is subjective (S), objective (O), or possessive (P).

S O P
Example: She gave me my first kiss.

1. He played basketball in his first two years of high school.
2. We asked her if she would share her umbrella with us.

3. For a moment, I couldn't remember my name.
4. It gave them great satisfaction to help others.
5. Is this drink mine or yours?
6. You must help me.
7. This is a gift from me to her.
8. The card says, "Happy birthday to you from all of us."
9. Their anniversary is next week, so we are having a party for them at our house.
10. Your car is better than ours or theirs.

◆ PRACTICE 22.14

Above each of the underlined objective case pronouns, indicate whether it is a direct object (DO), an indirect object (IO), or the object of a preposition (OP).

Example: My friends played a clever trick on me. (OP)

1. The president gave him a special citation.
2. The package was sent to them by mistake.
3. The transit officer helped us when we got lost.
4. The band dedicated the last song to her.
5. The owner of the wallet rewarded him very generously.
6. All the attention embarrassed us.
7. I mailed you that check weeks ago.
8. The family always looks to her for the final answer.
9. The clerk handed me my change.
10. Stop tickling me.

F Solving Special Problems with Pronoun Case

When you are trying to decide which pronoun case to use, three kinds of pronouns can be confusing: pronouns in *compounds,* pronouns in *comparisons,* and the pronouns *who* and *whom.*

Pronouns in Compounds

Sometimes, a pronoun is linked to a noun or to another pronoun with *and* or *or* to form a **compound**.

The tutor and I met in the writing lab.

He and I worked to revise my paper.

To decide whether to use the subjective or objective case for a pronoun in a compound, follow the same rules you would apply for a pronoun that is not part of a compound.

- If the compound in which the pronoun appears is the subject of the sentence, use the subjective case.

  Kia and I [not *me*] like rap music.

  She and I [not *me*] went to a concert.

- If the compound in which the pronoun appears is the object of the verb or the object of a preposition, use the objective case.

  The personnel office sent my friend and me [not *I*] the application forms. (object of the verb)

  There is a lot of competition between her and me [not *she and I*] for this job. (object of the preposition)

FOCUS Choosing Pronouns in Compounds

To determine which pronoun case to use in a compound that links a noun and a pronoun, drop the noun and rewrite the sentence with just the pronoun.

Kia and [*I* or *me?*] like rap music.

I like rap music. (not *Me like rap music.*)

Kia and I like rap music.

◆ PRACTICE 22.15

ON THE WEB
For more practice solving special problems with pronoun case, visit Exercise Central at <bedfordstmartins.com/foundationsfirst>.

In each blank, write the correct form (subjective or objective) of the pronouns in parentheses.

Example: We want ___her___ (she/her) to admit her mistake.

1. I asked Marisa and ________ (he/him) to the party.
2. My brother and ________ (I/me) are often mistaken for each other.
3. Many people cannot tell ________ (he/him) and ________ (I/me) apart.
4. The boss divided responsibility for the job between ________ (they/them) and ________ (we/us).

5. __________ (She/Her) and her mother have not spoken in years.

6. Nothing could bring my old girlfriend and __________ (I/me) back together again.

7. __________ (They/Them) and __________ (I/me) have nothing in common.

8. The story about the cockroach always amused Liz and __________ (she/her).

9. I think that __________ (they/them) and their grandchildren should get together more often.

10. This is the last chance for __________ (he/him) and __________ (I/me).

Pronouns in Comparisons

Sometimes, a pronoun appears after the words *than* or *as* in a **comparison**.

> Neil is hungrier than I.
>
> Marriage changed Sonia as much as him.

To decide whether to use the subjective or objective case, write in the words needed to complete the comparison. If the pronoun is a subject, use the subjective case.

> Neil is hungrier than I [am].

If the pronoun is an object, use the objective case.

> Marriage changed Sonia as much as [it changed] him.

FOCUS Choosing Pronouns in Comparisons

Sometimes the pronoun you choose can change the meaning of your sentence. For example, if you say, "She likes potato chips more than I," you mean that she likes potato chips more than you like potato chips.

> She likes potato chips more than I [do].

If, however, you say, "She likes potato chips more than me," you mean that she likes potato chips more than she likes you.

> She likes potato chips more than [she likes] me.

◆ PRACTICE 22.16

In each blank, write the correct form (subjective or objective) of the pronouns in parentheses. In brackets, add the word or words needed to complete the comparison.

Example: My sister is very unemotional; the movie affected me much more than ___[it affected] her___ (she/her).

1. No one could be less qualified than ______ (he/him).
2. Marisol worked as hard as ______ (he/him), but he took all the credit.
3. You eat much more than ______ (I/me), so how do you stay so thin?
4. David exercises as regularly as ______ (she/her).
5. So many people in my family have died young that a visit to the doctor could not frighten you more than ______ (I/me).
6. I play the piano better than ______ (they/them).
7. The trip to Florida cost you as much as ______ (we/us).
8. Francis has a much larger house than ______ (they/them) even though his family is smaller.
9. Clarence pays you a higher hourly rate than ______ (she/her).
10. In these photos, you look as tired as ______ (we/us).

Who and *Whom*

Who is a pronoun that functions as a subject; *whom* is a pronoun that functions as an object. To determine whether to use *who* or *whom,* you need to know how the pronoun functions within the clause in which it appears.

- When the pronoun is the subject of the clause, use *who.*

  I wonder who teaches that course. (*Who* is the subject of the clause *who teaches that course.*)

- When the pronoun is the object, use *whom.*

  I wonder to whom the course will appeal. (*Whom* is the object of the preposition *to* in the clause *to whom the course will appeal.*)

Mr. Brennan is the instructor whom we all like. (*Whom* is the direct object of the verb *like* in the clause *whom we all like.*)

Writing Tip

In conversation, people often use *who* for both the subjective case (*I wonder who teaches that course*) and the objective case (*I wonder who this course will appeal to*). In writing, always use *whom* for the objective case: *I wonder to whom this course will appeal.*

◆ PRACTICE 22.17

In each of the following sentences, circle the correct form of *who* or *whom* in parentheses.

Example: Students (who/whom) need a break from studying should try out for the play.

1. Anyone (who/whom) auditioned for the high school musical had to know how to sing and dance.
2. The choreographer with (who/whom) the drama teacher worked had little experience with high school students.
3. Many students (who/whom) enjoyed helping with the production did not want to appear onstage.
4. The girl (who/whom) the music teacher wanted to be the star did not get the part.
5. Ms. Morgan, (who/whom) taught drama, did not want her to star in the musical.
6. Ms. Morgan, (who/whom) complained that the girl had never learned her lines, argued for Janelle, a shy sophomore.
7. Few other teachers knew (who/whom) Janelle was.
8. Fortunately, she turned out to be someone for (who/whom) acting was easy.
9. The boy (who/whom) played her love interest was a football star.
10. He was the actor (who/whom) got the most applause.

G Identifying Reflexive and Intensive Pronouns

Like other pronouns, *reflexive pronouns* and *intensive pronouns* always agree with their antecedents. Although these two kinds of pronouns have different functions, their forms are exactly the same.

Reflexive Pronouns

Reflexive pronouns always end in *-self* (singular) or *-selves* (plural). These pronouns indicate that people or things did something to themselves or for themselves.

Christina bought herself a new watch.

You need to pace yourself when you exercise.

Eliza and Jill made themselves a plate of nachos.

Intensive Pronouns

Intensive pronouns also end in *-self* or *-selves*. Unlike reflexive pronouns, however, they always appear directly after their antecedents. Intensive pronouns are used for emphasis.

I myself have a friend with an eating disorder.

The actor himself did all the dangerous stunts.

They themselves questioned their motives.

Reflexive and Intensive Pronouns

Singular Forms

Antecedent	*Reflexive or Intensive Pronoun*
I	myself
you	yourself
he	himself
she	herself
it	itself

Plural Forms

Antecedent	*Reflexive or Intensive Pronoun*
we	ourselves
you	yourselves
they	themselves

ON THE WEB
For more practice identifying reflexive and intensive pronouns, visit Exercise Central at <bedfordstmartins.com/foundationsfirst>.

◆ PRACTICE 22.18

In each of the following sentences, fill in the correct reflexive or intensive pronoun.

Example: You should take ___yourselves___ out for dinner to celebrate your anniversary.

1. She ________________ had always walked to school, and she told her children they should do the same thing.
2. The legislators gave ________________ a raise.

3. The cat curled ____________________ up on the bedspread and dozed off.
4. Einstein ____________________ could not have solved that algebra problem.
5. I caught a frightening glimpse of ____________________ in the mirror after my haircut.
6. My sister hates to weigh ____________________ at the doctor's office.
7. If you fall, pick ____________________ up and start over again.
8. You ____________________ told me that this material would not be on the final exam.
9. The toddlers covered ____________________ with mud before their mother could stop them.
10. They bought the property for thousands of dollars, but they tore down the house ____________________ almost immediately afterward.

■ REVISING AND EDITING

Look back at your response to the Seeing and Writing exercise on page 341. Underline every pronoun you have used, and check your work carefully to be sure that all your pronouns and antecedents agree. (Remember, singular pronouns must refer to singular antecedents, and plural pronouns must refer to plural antecedents.) Eliminate any vague or unnecessary pronouns. Finally, check to make sure you have used correct pronoun case.

CHAPTER REVIEW

◆ EDITING PRACTICE

Read the following essay, which contains pronoun errors. Check for errors in pronoun case and pronoun-antecedent agreement as well as for any vague or unnecessary pronouns. Then, make any editing changes you think are necessary. The first sentence has been edited for you.

School Schedules: Time for a New Tradition

All parents worry
~~Every~~ working ~~parent worries~~ at least a little about allowing their school-age children to be at home alone in the afternoon. On the news every night, they talk about criminals, peer pressure, and drugs that could endanger unsupervised young people. Many parents, they feel guilty about having to be at work while their children are at home after school. Many employers and politicians whom have tried to improve day care have not yet done much to solve the problem of school days that are shorter than work days.

In an article I read, it suggested a solution to this problem: a longer school day and school year. A middle school or high school today still has their school calendar set by the needs of nineteenth-century farm families. The school day ends at three o'clock because anyone living on a farm needs the time before dark to do their chores. Summer, it is a time for harvesting, so no school is held during that time. However, they no longer need to schedule school around farming in most parts of the United States today. Very few children whom attend school now live on working farms. Why shouldn't a child be in school during their parents' business day?

Children doing farm chores

This suggestion may horrify every student in the United States, but it could eventually help them. Students in Europe and Asia, they have between ten and sixty more days of school each year than we American students do. Japanese students are in school 240 days each year, while American students are only required to be in school 180 days. In Norway, the government has recently made the switch to longer school days for their children. Norwegian teachers discovered that them and the children got to spend more time together planning activities and interacting. Everyone found the new extended schedule more rewarding—even the students. Acknowledging that the traditional school calendar is outdated, several other countries, including Germany, are also in the process of changing its school days to match parents' work days more closely.

A student doing his homework

A longer school day could keep young Americans safer, put his or her parents at ease, and perhaps even help American schools become more competitive. Many of the countries that choose a longer school calendar are the same ones that consistently outperform us academically. Japanese, Korean, and Taiwanese students all spend many more hours in school than us. They spend almost twice as much time on core academic subjects and study twice as much. Typically, a student in one of these countries takes shorter vacations and forgets less of what they learn. An American student spends more time watching television and getting themselves in trouble. However, some schools in the United States are already following the trend toward a longer school year and longer school days. Several states are offering pilot programs or incentives to its schools. Many charter school students are already spending more time at school and discovering that they have more time to spend on art and music, subjects that are often overlooked in traditional public schools. Maybe someday the 180-day school-year calendar will seem to we Americans a foolish thing of the past.

◆ COLLABORATIVE ACTIVITIES

1. Working in a small group, write a sentence with a compound subject on a sheet of paper, and then pass the sheet to the person on your left. On the sheet you get from the person on your right, write a new sentence that includes a pronoun that refers to the compound subject that student wrote, and then pass your sheet to the person on your left. On the next sheet you get, write a new sentence using *who* or *whom* to refer to the subject on that sheet. Repeat this process until each of you has a paragraph six to eight sentences long.
2. Choose the paragraph from activity 1 that your group likes best. Then, exchange paragraphs with another group. Check each other's work, making sure that pronoun case and pronoun-antecedent agreement are correct.
3. Turn your group's paragraph from activity 2 into a test for another group in your class. After you receive the corrected version of your paragraph from another group, go through the paragraph and add errors in pronoun-antecedent agreement and pronoun case. Then, exchange paragraphs with a different group. Try to correct every error introduced in the other group's test paragraph.
4. *Composing original sentences* Working as a group, write five original sentences. Be sure to use at least one indefinite pronoun, at least one compound subject, and at least one comparison with a pronoun. Then,

check pronoun case and pronoun-antecedent agreement carefully. When you have finished, check the sentences again to make sure you have corrected any errors in grammar, punctuation, or spelling.

✓ REVIEW CHECKLIST: Pronouns

- A pronoun is a word that refers to and takes the place of a noun or another pronoun. (See 22A.)
- The word to which a pronoun refers is called the pronoun's antecedent. (See 22B.)
- Compound antecedents connected by *and* are plural and are used with plural pronouns. Compound antecedents connected by *or* may take singular or plural pronouns. (See 22C.)
- Most indefinite pronoun antecedents are singular. Therefore, they are used with singular pronouns. (See 22C.)
- Collective noun antecedents are singular and must be used with singular pronouns. (See 22C.)
- A pronoun should always refer to a specific antecedent. (See 22D.)
- When a pronoun directly follows its antecedent, it is usually unnecessary. (See 22D.)
- Personal pronouns can be in the subjective, objective, or possessive case. (See 22E.)
- Pronouns present special problems when they are used in compounds and comparisons. The pronouns *who* and *whom* also cause problems. (See 22F.)
- Reflexive pronouns and intensive pronouns must agree with their antecedents in person and number. (See 22G.)

CHAPTER

23

Adjectives and Adverbs

PREVIEW

In this chapter, you will learn

- to identify adjectives and adverbs (23A)
- to understand comparatives and superlatives (23B)
- to identify demonstrative adjectives (23C)

■ SEEING AND WRITING

Look at the picture above, and then write a paragraph in which you describe the costume you would wear to this party. Why would you choose this costume?

Word Power

masquerade (verb) to wear a mask or disguise; (noun) a costume party at which guests wear masks

A Identifying Adjectives and Adverbs

Adjectives and adverbs are words that modify—that is, describe or identify—other words. By using these modifying words, you can make your sentences more precise and more interesting.

Identifying Adjectives

An **adjective** answers the question *What kind? Which one?* or *How many?* Adjectives modify nouns or pronouns.

> The Spanish city of Madrid has exciting nightlife. (The adjective *Spanish* modifies the noun *city;* the adjective *exciting* modifies the noun *nightlife.*)
>
> It is lively because of its many clubs and tapas bars. (The adjective *lively* modifies the pronoun *it.*)

Writing Tip

Some adjectives, such as *Spanish,* are capitalized because they are formed from proper nouns. (Proper nouns name particular people, animals, places, or things.) For more on proper nouns, see 21A.

◆ PRACTICE 23.1

For information on placing adjectives in order, see 24J.

In each of the blanks in the following paragraph, write an adjective from the list below. Cross each adjective off the list as you use it. Be sure to choose an adjective that makes sense in each sentence.

ON THE WEB

For more practice identifying adjectives and adverbs, visit Exercise Central at <bedfordstmartins.com/foundationsfirst>.

> **Example:** It is ___unusual___ for a group of famous writers to form a rock group.

talented	big	willing	diverse
famous	rare	devoted	~~unusual~~
wild	tiny	modest	successful

(1) The group called Rock Bottom Remainders is made up entirely of ______________ authors. (2) Its ______________ members include Amy Tan, Dave Barry, and Stephen King. (3) They play to raise money for charity, and they sometimes make ______________ fools of themselves in the process. (4) Amy Tan, for instance, will often wear a ______________ leather outfit that shows lots of skin when she is performing with the group. (5) Usually, she wears more ______________ clothes. (6) She does not get the chance to show her ______________ side too often. (7) The Rock Bottom Remainders' ______________ concerts take place only once or twice a year. (8) The band is ______________ at raising money because people want to see their favorite authors on stage. (9) Of course, nobody thinks that the authors are ______________ musicians. (10) Their ______________ fans come to see them because they love their writing.

Identifying Adverbs

An **adverb** answers the question *How? Why? When? Where?* or *To what extent?* Adverbs modify verbs, adjectives, or other adverbs.

> The huge Doberman barked angrily. (The adverb *angrily* modifies the verb *barked.*)

Still, we felt quite safe. (The adverb *quite* modifies the adjective *safe.*)

Very slowly, we held out a big juicy steak. (The adverb *very* modifies the adverb *slowly.*)

◆ PRACTICE 23.2

In each of the blanks in the following paragraph, write an adverb from the list below. Cross each adverb off the list as you use it. Be sure to choose an adverb that makes sense in each sentence.

Example: I waited ___wearily___ for the train.

quickly	heavily	easily	unusually	uncomfortably
noisily	rudely	bravely	really	~~wearily~~

(1) The subway train screeched __________ into the station. (2) The doors __________ slid open, and departing passengers __________ elbowed their way out. (3) Entering passengers struggled __________ to get through the narrow doors. (4) It was __________ hot for April, and people were sweating __________ in the steamy underground tunnel. (5) I stood jammed __________ in the middle of the car, praying I'd be able to wriggle out __________ when I reached my stop. (6) What a __________ great way to start the work day!

Telling Adjectives and Adverbs Apart

Many adverbs are formed when the ending *-ly* is added to an adjective.

Adjective	*Adverb*
bad	badly
nice	nicely
quick	quickly
quiet	quietly
real	really
slow	slowly

Writing Tip

Some adjectives—*lovely, friendly,* and *lively,* for example—end in *-ly.* Be careful not to use these words as adverbs.

Because the adjective and adverb forms of these words are similar, you may sometimes be confused about which form to use in a sentence. Remember, adjectives modify nouns or pronouns; adverbs modify verbs, adjectives, or other adverbs.

ADJECTIVE Kim likes the slow dances. (*Slow* modifies the noun *dances.*)

ADVERB Kim likes to dance slowly. (*Slowly* modifies the verb *dance.*)

Writing Tip

The word *fast* has the same form whether it is used as an adjective or as an adverb: *Tracy has a fast car. It goes as fast as a sportscar.*

ADJECTIVE Mark Twain's real name was Samuel L. Clemens. (*Real* modifies the noun *name.*)

ADVERB It was really generous of him to donate his time. (*Really* modifies the adjective *generous.*)

◆ PRACTICE 23.3

In the following passage, circle the correct form (adjective or adverb) from the choices in parentheses.

Example: India has a (real/really) productive film industry.

(1) Bollywood, as the Indian film industry is called, has been making movies for (near/nearly) seventy-five years. (2) It puts out more than a thousand movies every year, releasing films even more (frequent/frequently) than Hollywood. (3) However, Bollywood movies are made very (different/differently) from Hollywood ones. (4) They are often made (quick/quickly) and with a relatively small budget. (5) They also use musical numbers more (free/freely). (6) At least a half a dozen times per film, characters will (spontaneous/spontaneously) break into song and dance. (7) The songs themselves often become (wide/widely) known. (8) The plots of Bollywood movies are usually melodramatic; the stories often focus on romance or revenge, and the films always end (happy/happily). (9) Most of the films are made entirely in and around Bombay, and Bollywood films are (real/really) popular in India. (10) More recently Bollywood has also found a receptive audience abroad, with the South Asian immigrant community in the United States showing a (particular/particularly) strong interest in these films. (11) In many large cities, Bollywood films are (regular/regularly) shown in movie theaters, and a musical about Bollywood, *Bombay Dreams,* opened on Broadway in 2004.

FOCUS *Good* and *Well*

Be careful not to confuse *good* and *well.* Unlike regular adjectives, whose adverb forms add the ending *-ly,* the adjective *good* is irregular. Its adverb form is *well.*

(continued on the following page)

(continued from the previous page)

Remember, *good* is an adjective; *well* is an adverb. Use *good* to modify a noun or pronoun; use *well* to modify a verb, an adjective, or another adverb.

ADJECTIVE John Steinbeck was a good writer. (*Good* modifies the noun *writer.*)

ADVERB He wrote particularly well in the novel *The Grapes of Wrath.* (*Well* modifies the verb *wrote.*)

However, always use *well* when you are describing someone's health.

He wasn't at all *well* [not *good*] after he won the pie-eating contest.

◆ PRACTICE 23.4

In the following passage, circle the correct form (*good* or *well*) in parentheses.

Example: Have Americans treated U.S. veterans (good/well) enough?

(1) Some U.S. veterans of twentieth-century wars were treated (good/well); others, unfortunately, were not. (2) In the 1940s, most American veterans of World War II came home to a (good/well) life. (3) No one doubted that these men and women had done a (good/well) thing by going to war. (4) The G.I. Bill ensured that many of them were able to get a (good/well) education. (5) In the prosperous postwar economy, (good/well) jobs were not difficult to find. (6) Unfortunately, things were not nearly as (good/well) for the veterans who returned from the Vietnam War. (7) Many Americans felt that the U.S. involvement in that war was not a (good/well) idea. (8) Some blamed the soldiers who had gone to Vietnam even though most of them had done their jobs as (good/well) as they could. (9) Rather than being (good/well) respected, the returning veterans were sometimes treated with contempt. (10) In addition, injured soldiers often ended up in veterans' hospitals that were not (good/well) staffed. (11) By comparison, veterans of the two Gulf Wars have been (good/well) received when they returned home. (12) Even people who did not support the war did not take out their anger on the soldiers who

fought so (good/well). (13) Still, veterans of today's wars must deal with underfunded veterans' hospitals, and improvements in veteran care are much needed and (good/well) deserved. (14) No matter what the public may think of a war, it is important to treat veterans (good/well) when they return home.

B Understanding Comparatives and Superlatives

Adjectives and adverbs are sometimes used to compare two or more people or things. The **comparative form** of an adjective or adverb compares *two* people or things. The **superlative form** of an adjective or adverb compares *more than two* people or things. Special forms of the adjectives and adverbs are used to indicate these comparisons.

ADJECTIVE These shoes are ugly.

COMPARATIVE The brown shoes are uglier than the black ones.

SUPERLATIVE The purple ones are the ugliest of all.

ADVERB Will you be able to get home soon?

COMPARATIVE I may not be home until midnight, but I will try to get there sooner.

SUPERLATIVE Unfortunately, the soonest I can leave work is 7:30.

For advice on using articles with superlative forms, see 24F.

FOCUS Adverbs with No Comparative or Superlative Forms

Some adverbs—such as *almost, very, somewhat, quite, extremely, rather,* and *moderately*—do not have comparative or superlative forms.

Forming Comparatives and Superlatives

Adjectives and adverbs form the comparative with *-er* or *more* and the superlative with *-est* or *most.*

ADJECTIVES

To form the comparative of a one-syllable adjective, add *-er.* To form the superlative of a one-syllable adjective, add *-est.*

young younger youngest

To form the comparative of an adjective that has two or more syllables, use *more*. To form the superlative of an adjective that has two or more syllables, use *most*.

beautiful   more beautiful   most beautiful

ADVERBS

Most adverbs end in *-ly*. To form the comparative of an adverb that ends in *-ly*, use *more*. To form the superlative of an adverb that ends in *-ly*, use *most*.

slowly   more slowly   most slowly

Some other adverbs form the comparative with *-er* and the superlative with *-est*.

soon   sooner   soonest

Writing Tip
Two-syllable adjectives ending in *-y* do not form the comparative and superlative with *more* and *most*. Instead, they change the *y* to an *i* and then add *-er* or *-est:* for example, *funny, funnier, funniest*.

Solving Special Problems with Comparatives and Superlatives

The following four rules will help you avoid errors with comparatives and superlatives.

1. Never use both *-er* and *more* to form the comparative.

   The comic could have been a lot funnier. (not *more funnier*)

2. Never use both *-est* and *most* to form the superlative.

   Scream was the scariest (not *most scariest*) movie I ever saw.

3. Never use the superlative when you are comparing only two things.

   Beth is the younger (not *youngest*) of the two sisters.

4. Never use the comparative when you are comparing more than two things.

   This is the worst (not *worse*) of my four part-time jobs.

◆ PRACTICE 23.5

In the blank at the right, fill in the comparative form of each adjective or adverb.

Examples

rich *richer*

embarrassed *more embarrassed*

1. strong ________________   3. quickly ________________
2. playful ________________   4. traditional ________________

ON THE WEB
For more practice understanding comparatives and superlatives, visit Exercise Central at <bedfordstmartins.com/foundationsfirst>.

5. neat ______	13. easy ______
6. neatly ______	14. easily ______
7. fair ______	15. useful ______
8. mature ______	16. poor ______
9. young ______	17. hard ______
10. intense ______	18. gently ______
11. blue ______	19. deep ______
12. new ______	20. lazy ______

◆ PRACTICE 23.6

In the blank at the right, fill in the superlative form of each adjective or adverb.

Examples

rich ___richest___

embarrassed ___most embarrassed___

1. strong ______	11. blue ______
2. playful ______	12. new ______
3. quickly ______	13. easy ______
4. traditional ______	14. easily ______
5. neat ______	15. useful ______
6. neatly ______	16. poor ______
7. fair ______	17. hard ______
8. mature ______	18. gently ______
9. young ______	19. deep ______
10. intense ______	20. lazy ______

◆ PRACTICE 23.7

Fill in the correct comparative form of the word in parentheses.

Example: In 1961, the East German government erected the Berlin Wall to make it ___harder___ (hard) for residents of Communist East Berlin to travel to West Berlin.

1. Originally, the wall was made of barbed wire, but it was later replaced by ______ (strong) concrete.

2. The wall stayed up for twenty-eight years and might have stayed up _______________ (long) if the Communist government of East Germany had not been so weak.
3. When the wall came down in 1989, people around the world saw _______________ (clear) that Communist rule in East Germany would soon end.
4. In 1990, East Germany was reabsorbed into the Federal Republic of Germany, and most people were _______________ (happy).
5. All Berliners could travel around their city _______________ (free).
6. However, the eastern side of Berlin remained _______________ (depressed) economically than the western side.
7. The population of East Germany was _______________ (poor), and many of its residents did not have the money to travel to the western part of the country.
8. Differences between east and west still remain today despite _______________ (free) movement between the two sides.
9. In recent years, some East Germans have even begun looking back _______________ (favorable) at their Communist past.
10. Now that fifteen years have passed, East Germans are free to have _______________ (warm) feelings toward their past.

◆ PRACTICE 23.8

Fill in the correct superlative form of the word in parentheses.

Example: Sports fans must be the *most obsessive* (obsessive) people in the world.

(1) Today's extreme sports often seem to be designed to show which athlete is the _______________ (crazy). (2) The human obsession with extremes is not new, however; records showing who could run the _______________ (fast) or swim the _______________ (far) go back more than a century. (3) Only the _______________ (tiny) minority of people will ever compete well enough in any sport to approach a world record. (4) Anyone else who wants to be a record

holder must scan the *Guinness Book of World Records* to find the record he or she can ________________ (easy) break. (5) Athletic ability is not the ________________ (necessary) skill for many events listed in the *Guinness Book of World Records.* (6) One young man simply stayed awake for the ________________ (long) period on record. (7) Another grew to the ________________ (great) height seen in modern times. (8) Of course, his record would be one of the ________________ (difficult) to break. (9) Growing hair and fingernails and peeling an apple will never be Olympic sports, but people have set some of the ________________ (surprising) records in those events. (10) After looking through the *Guinness Book of World Records,* many people conclude that extreme sports are not, after all, the ________________ (bizarre) obsession a person can have.

FOCUS *Good/Well* and *Bad/Badly*

The adjectives *good* and *bad* and their adverb forms, *well* and *badly,* are irregular. They do not form the comparative and superlative in the same way other adjectives and adverbs do. Because their forms are so irregular, you must memorize them.

Adjective	*Comparative Form*	*Superlative Form*
good	better	best
bad	worse	worst
Adverb	*Comparative Form*	*Superlative Form*
well	better	best
badly	worse	worst

◆ PRACTICE 23.9

Fill in the correct comparative or superlative form of *good, well, bad,* or *badly.*

Example: There is nothing ___worse___ (bad) than getting one telemarketing call after another.

1. One of the ____________ (good) options for people who are tired of getting telemarketing calls is our state's do-not-call list.

2. The __________ (bad) telemarketing experience of my life was the night I got sixteen calls between 6 and 8 p.m.
3. I had never wanted anything __________ (badly) than I wanted to stop the harassment.
4. I considered changing my telephone number, but a local consumer advocate gave me a __________ (good) idea.
5. That evening, I was the __________ (well) prepared I had ever been for telemarketing calls.
6. The first telemarketer mangled my name even __________ (badly) than usual.
7. When he asked how I was, I told him that I felt __________ (well) than I had in a long time.
8. Mispronouncing my name in several different ways, he garbled it the __________ (badly) just before I interrupted him to tell him my name was on the state do-not-call list.
9. He reacted __________ (well) than I had expected: he thanked me politely for my time and hung up.
10. The __________ (bad) part of the do-not-call list was waiting thirty days for it to take effect, but since then, my evenings have been peaceful.

C Identifying Demonstrative Adjectives

Demonstrative adjectives do not describe other words. These adjectives—*this, that, these,* and *those*—simply identify particular nouns.

This and *that* identify singular nouns.

This book is much more interesting than that one.

These and *those* identify plural nouns.

These books are novels, but those books are biographies.

◆ PRACTICE 23.10

In the following passage, circle the correct form of the demonstrative adjective in parentheses.

Example: (That/Those) African-American musicians who came out of Detroit in the 1960s had a unique sound.

ON THE WEB
For more practice identifying demonstrative adjectives, visit Exercise Central at <bedfordstmartins.com/foundationsfirst>.

(1) (That/Those) sound came to be known as Motown, after Motown Records, which in turn was named for Detroit, the "Motor City." (2) The sound was characterized by a powerful lead singer accompanied by (that/those) distinctive harmonizing backup vocals. (3) Some of the musicians who played in (this/these) style are Diana Ross and the Supremes, Gladys Knight and the Pips, and Smokey Robinson and the Miracles. (4) The names of (this/these) Motown groups often had two parts—the lead singer and the backup group. (5) (This/These) kind of group became famous under the direction of Motown Records owner Barry Gordy. (6) Many of (this/these) singers are still famous today. (7) Recently, some of (that/those) musicians who were not well known have gotten more attention. (8) In particular, the record company's in-house band, the Funk Brothers, has gotten credit for creating (that/those) recognizable Motown sound. (9) The 2002 movie *Standing in the Shadows of Motown* highlights the work of (this/these) band. (10) The band is also featured at the Motown Museum in Detroit, which is dedicated to memorializing (this/these) group of extraordinary musicians.

■ REVISING AND EDITING

Look back at your response to the Seeing and Writing exercise on page 367. First, underline every adjective and adverb. Have you used any comparatives or superlatives? Any demonstrative adjectives? If so, check to be sure you have used the correct forms. Then, add or substitute descriptive words you need to make your writing more precise and more interesting.

CHAPTER REVIEW

◆ EDITING PRACTICE

Read the following essay, which contains errors in the use of adjectives and adverbs. Make any changes necessary to correct adjectives that are incorrectly used instead of adverbs, adverbs that are incorrectly used instead of adjectives, errors in the use of comparatives and superlatives, and errors in the use of demonstrative adjectives. You may also add adjectives or adverbs that you feel would make the writer's ideas clearer or more specific. The first sentence has been edited for you.

Satanic Corporations?

These days, most people know that those ~~real~~ really bizarre stories about kidney thieves and microwaved pets are simply urban legends. This myths are everywhere—in newspapers, on the radio, and especially on the Internet. Some of the unbelievablest urban legends make people suspicious right away. However, incredible large numbers of people are still willing to believe rumors about big corporations. The more outrageouser the claims about a corporation, the more likely it is that people will put out the word to boycott the company's products.

The famousest urban legend about a corporation claims that the president of Procter & Gamble appeared on television in the 1980s to say that he was a Satanist. These executive also reportedly said that he gave 10 percent of the company's profits to the Church of Satan. These comments were supposedly made to a talk show host—sometimes reported to be Merv Griffin but most oftenest said to be Phil Donahue. Of course, no Procter & Gamble executive had appeared on any talk show, and no sane businessperson would say such things on television, but the story spread quick. These rumors damaged the company name really bad.

As a result, Procter & Gamble issued publicly statements denying the comments. The company changed its century-old logo because some people believed that the moon and stars on the company's packages were a symbol of the Church of Satan. These tactics did not work very good, so finally, Procter & Gamble began to sue people who were spreading these story. One Kansas City couple eventual paid Procter & Gamble $75,000 for their part in spreading the rumor. Since then, the company has been doing more better.

The old Procter & Gamble logo

More recent, McDonald's and other companies have been targeted with similar stories about Satanism. Who starts these maliciously rumors? Some people suspect business rivals who could make financial gains from this urban legends, but no one really knows. Why do people believe such stories? Perhaps they believe subconsciously that big corporations are bad for consumers. Perhaps they do not trust business executives. Whatever the reason, many people do believe the rumors, and Procter & Gamble and other companies have found them more hard to disprove than any competitor's claims.

◆ COLLABORATIVE ACTIVITIES

1. Working on your own, write five simple sentences on a sheet of paper. Then, working in a group of three, pass your page to another student in your group. Add one adjective and one adverb to one of the sentences on the paper you receive. Keep passing the pages among the three of you until modifying words have been added to every sentence on each sheet. Then, working together, check to make sure all the adjectives and adverbs are used correctly.
2. Working in the same group, choose one sentence from each of the three pages that you agree is the most interesting. Work together to write a one- or two-paragraph story using all three of these sentences. When you have finished, try to add several more adjectives and adverbs to the story.
3. Exchange stories from activity 2 with another group. Then, rewrite the other group's story by changing every adjective and adverb you can find. Make the story as different from the original as you can. When you have finished, exchange the stories again and make any necessary corrections.
4. *Composing original sentences* Working in a group of three, write five original sentences. Make sure each sentence contains at least one adverb and at least one adjective. In addition, include at least one comparative form of an adjective or adverb, at least one superlative form of an adjective or adverb, and at least one demonstrative adjective. Then, check the adjectives and adverbs carefully to be sure you have used them correctly. When you have finished, check the sentences again to make sure you have corrected any errors in grammar, punctuation, or spelling.

☑ REVIEW CHECKLIST: Adjectives and Adverbs

- Adjectives modify nouns or pronouns. (See 23A.)

(continued on the following page)

(continued from the previous page)

- Adverbs modify verbs, adjectives, or other adverbs. (See 23A.)
- To compare two people or things, use the comparative form of an adjective or adverb. To compare more than two people or things, use the superlative form of an adjective or adverb. (See 23B.)
- Adjectives and adverbs form the comparative with *-er* or *more* and the superlative with *-est* or *most.* (See 23B.)
- The adjectives *good* and *bad* and their adverb forms, *well* and *badly,* have irregular comparative and superlative forms. (See 23B.)
- Demonstrative adjectives—*this, that, these,* and *those*—identify particular nouns. (See 23C.)

CHAPTER

24

Grammar and Usage Issues for ESL Writers

PREVIEW

In this chapter, you will learn

- to include subjects in sentences (24A)
- to avoid special problems with subjects (24B)
- to identify plural nouns (24C)
- to understand count and noncount nouns (24D)
- to use determiners with count and noncount nouns (24E)
- to understand articles (24F)
- to form negative statements and questions (24G)
- to indicate verb tense (24H)
- to recognize stative verbs (24I)
- to place adjectives in order (24J)
- to choose correct prepositions (24K)
- to use prepositions in familiar expressions (24L)
- to use prepositions in phrasal verbs (24M)

SEEING AND WRITING

Do you think U.S. ballots should be available in languages other than English? If not, why not? If so, what languages should be represented? Why? Look at the picture above, and then write a paragraph that answers these questions.

Word Power

ballot a written or printed paper on which voters indicate their choices in an election

Learning English as a second language involves more than just learning grammar. In fact, if you have been studying English as a second language, you may know as much English grammar as many native speakers do. Still, you will need to learn conventions and rules that are second nature to most (although by no means all) native speakers. This chapter covers the grammar and usage issues that give nonnative speakers the most trouble.

A Including Subjects in Sentences

In almost all cases, English requires that every sentence state its subject. In fact, every dependent clause must also have a subject.

INCORRECT My parents do not make much money although work hard. (Who works hard?)

CORRECT My parents do not make much money although they work hard.

English even requires a false or "dummy" subject to fill the subject position in sentences like this one.

It is hot here.

It is not correct to write just *Hot here* or *Is hot here.*

◆ PRACTICE 24.1

Each of the following sentences is missing the subject of a dependent or an independent clause. On the lines after each sentence, rewrite it, adding an appropriate subject.

ON THE WEB
For more practice including subjects in sentences, visit Exercise Central at <bedfordstmartins.com/foundationsfirst>.

Example: The essay was interesting even though had some errors.

The essay was interesting even though it had some errors.

1. Will rain all day tomorrow.

2. She was excited after answered a question in class.

3. Javier studied so that could become an American citizen.

4. Was not my fault.

5. Sofia watched television programs for children when was learning English.

6. Is a very difficult problem.

7. She waited until was sure they were gone.

8. He missed the bus because overslept that morning.

9. After Jean scored the winning goal, went out to celebrate with his friends.

10. Is quieter than usual in the library today.

B Avoiding Special Problems with Subjects

Writing Tip

Special dictionaries help nonnative speakers answer usage questions. Your college librarian or English instructor can help you find a dictionary that meets your needs.

Some languages commonly begin a sentence with a word or phrase that has no grammatical link to the sentence but that states clearly what the sentence is about. If you speak such a language, you might write a sentence like this one.

INCORRECT Career plan I am studying to be a computer scientist.

A sentence like this cannot occur in English. The phrase *career plan* cannot be a subject because the sentence already includes one: the pronoun *I*, which agrees with the verb *am studying*. In addition, *career plan* is not connected to the rest of the sentence in any other way. One way to revise this sentence is to rewrite it so that *career plan* is the subject.

For more on subjects, see 9A.

CORRECT My career plan is to become a computer scientist.

Another way to revise the sentence is simply to delete *career plan*.

CORRECT I am studying to become a computer scientist.

Standard English also does not permit a two-part subject in which the second part is a pronoun referring to the same person or thing as the first part.

INCORRECT My sister she is a cardiologist.

CORRECT My sister is a cardiologist.

When the real subject follows the verb, and the normal subject position before the verb is empty, it must be filled by a "dummy" subject, such as *there.*

INCORRECT Are tall mountains in my country.

CORRECT There are tall mountains in my country.

◆ PRACTICE 24.2

The following sentences contain problems with subjects. Rewrite each sentence correctly on the lines provided. (Some of the sentences can be corrected in more than one way.)

ON THE WEB
For more practice avoiding special problems with subjects, visit Exercise Central at <bedfordstmartins.com /foundationsfirst>.

Example: Are no roads in the middle of the jungle.

There are no roads in the middle of the jungle.

1. The old woman she sells candles in the shop downstairs.

2. Are six kinds of rice in the cupboard.

3. Dmitri he rides his bicycle ten miles every day.

4. The doctor says is hope for my father.

5. My neighbor she watches my daughter in the evenings.

6. My former home I grew up in a village near the Indian Ocean.

7. My job it starts at six o'clock in the morning.

____

____

8. Plan for the future Mr. Esposito hopes to buy his own taxi someday.

____

____

9. The best thing in my life I feel lucky that my family is together again.

____

____

10. My brother's big problem at school he is afraid of his teacher.

____

____

C Identifying Plural Nouns

In English, most nouns add *-s* to form plurals. Every time you use a noun, ask yourself whether you are talking about one item or more than one, and choose a singular or plural form accordingly. Consider this sentence.

For more on singular and plural nouns, see Chapter 21.

The books in both branches of the library are deteriorating.

The three nouns in this sentence are underlined: one is singular (*library*), and the other two are plural (*books, branches*). You might think that the word *both* is enough to indicate that *branch* is plural, and that it is obvious that there would have to be more than one book in any branch of a library. But even if the sentence includes information that tells you that a noun is plural, you must always use a form of the noun that shows explicitly that it is plural.

◆ PRACTICE 24.3

In each of the following sentences, underline the plural nouns.

Example: Her daughters love to tease their friends.

ON THE WEB
For more practice identifying plural nouns, visit Exercise Central at <bedfordstmartins.com/foundationsfirst>.

1. Elena has twin toddlers and two older children.
2. She works two jobs, and her feet hurt every evening.
3. Bella and Mikhail are teenagers with typical teen interests and hobbies.

4. Bella loves animals and has a cat, a gerbil, and three white mice.
5. Mikhail is interested in sports and music.
6. The twin girls are three years old.
7. They are identical twins who already love to play tricks on people.
8. They always tell babysitters the wrong names.
9. Elena never dresses them in matching outfits, but sometimes the girls want to wear the same clothes.
10. Elena plans to give them different haircuts.

D Understanding Count and Noncount Nouns

A **count noun** names one particular thing or a group of particular things: *a teacher, a panther, a bed, an ocean, a cloud; two teachers, five panthers, three beds, two oceans, fifteen clouds.* A **noncount noun**, however, names things that cannot be counted: *gold, cream, sand, blood, smoke.*

Count nouns usually have a singular form and a plural form: *cloud, clouds.* Noncount nouns usually have only a singular form: *smoke.* Note how the nouns *cloud* and *smoke* differ in the way they are used in sentences.

CORRECT The sky is full of clouds.
CORRECT The sky is full of smoke.
INCORRECT The sky is full of smokes.

CORRECT I see ten clouds in the distance.
INCORRECT I see ten smokes in the distance.

Writing Tip

Sometimes a noncount noun such as *smoke* appears to have a plural form (*smokes*). Although such forms end in *-s,* they are verbs and not plural nouns: *He smokes two cigars a day.*

You can often use either a count noun or a noncount noun to communicate the same idea.

Count	*Noncount*
people (plural of *person*)	humanity (not *humanities*)
tables, chairs, beds	furniture (not *furnitures*)
letters	mail (not *mails*)
tools	equipment (not *equipments*)
facts	information (not *informations*)

Some words can be either count or noncount, depending on the meaning intended.

COUNT Students in this course are expected to submit two papers.
NONCOUNT These artificial flowers are made of paper.

FOCUS Count and Noncount Nouns

Here are some general guidelines for using count and noncount nouns.

- Use a count noun to refer to a living animal, but use a noncount noun to refer to the food that comes from that animal.

  COUNT There are several live lobsters in the tank.

  NONCOUNT This restaurant specializes in lobster.

- If you use a noncount noun for a substance or class of things that can come in different varieties, you can often make that noun plural if you want to talk about those varieties.

  NONCOUNT Cheese is a rich source of calcium.

  COUNT Many different cheeses come from Italy.

- If you want to shift from a general concept to specific examples of it, you can often use a noncount noun as a count noun.

  NONCOUNT You have a great deal of talent.

  COUNT My talents do not include singing.

ON THE WEB
For more practice understanding count and noncount nouns, visit Exercise Central at <bedfordstmartins.com/foundationsfirst>.

◆ PRACTICE 24.4

In each of the following sentences, identify the underlined word as a count or noncount noun. If it is a noncount noun, circle the *N* following the sentence, but do not write in the blank. If it is a count noun, circle the *C*, and then write the plural form of the noun in the blank.

Examples

She was filled with admiration for the turtle. (N) C ________

A seagull watched from a safe distance. N (C) *seagulls*

1. Rosa walked across the sand. N C ________
2. The moon shone brightly. N C ________
3. The moon was reflected in the water. N C ________
4. A sea turtle came out of the waves. N C ________

5. She crawled slowly up the <u>beach</u> and dug a hole for her eggs. N C ___________

6. A turtle egg feels like <u>leather</u>. N C ___________

7. Rosa felt <u>sympathy</u> for the turtle. N C ___________

8. An <u>enemy</u> could be nearby, waiting to attack the turtle or eat her eggs. N C ___________

9. The enemy could even be a human being who likes to eat <u>turtle</u>. N C ___________

10. Rosa sighed with <u>relief</u> when the turtle finished laying her eggs and swam away. N C ___________

E Using Determiners with Count and Noncount Nouns

Determiners are adjectives that *identify* rather than describe the nouns they modify. Determiners may also *quantify* nouns (that is, indicate an amount or a number).

When a determiner is accompanied by one or more other adjectives, the determiner always comes first. For example, in the phrase *my expensive new digital watch, my* is a determiner; you cannot put *expensive, new, digital,* or any other adjective before *my.*

Determiners include the following words.

- Articles: *a, an, the*
- Demonstrative pronouns: *this, these, that, those*
- Possessive pronouns: *my, our, your, his, her, its, their*
- Possessive nouns: *Sheila's, my friend's,* and so on
- *Whose, which, what*
- *All, both, each, every, some, any, either, no, neither, many, most, much, a few, a little, few, little, several, enough*
- All numerals: *one, two,* and so on

A singular count noun must be accompanied by a determiner—for example, <u>*my*</u> *watch* or <u>*the*</u> *new digital watch,* not just *watch* or *new digital watch.* Noncount nouns and plural count nouns, however, sometimes have determiners but sometimes do not. *This honey is sweet* and *Honey is sweet* are both acceptable, as are *These berries are juicy* and *Berries are juicy.* (In each case, the meaning is different.) However, you cannot say *Berry is juicy*; say instead, <u>*This*</u> *berry is juicy,* <u>*Every*</u> *berry is juicy,* or <u>*A*</u> *berry is juicy.*

FOCUS Determiners

Some determiners can be used only with certain types of nouns.

- *This* and *that* can be used only with singular nouns (count or noncount): *this berry, that honey.*
- *These, those, a few, few, many, both,* and *several* can only be used with plural count nouns: *these berries, those apples, a few ideas, few people, many students, both sides, several directions.*
- *Much* and *a little* can be used only with noncount nouns: *much affection, a little honey.*
- *Some* and *enough* can be used only with noncount or plural count nouns: *some honey, some berries, enough trouble, enough problems.*
- *A, an, every,* and *each* can be used only with singular count nouns: *a berry, an elephant, every possibility, each citizen.*

ON THE WEB

For more practice using determiners with count and noncount nouns, visit Exercise Central at <bedfordstmartins.com/foundationsfirst>.

◆ PRACTICE 24.5

In each of the following sentences, underline the more appropriate choice from each pair of words or phrases in parentheses.

Example: (Many/Much) people communicate via email.

1. (Each/All) email user must check messages carefully.
2. (This/These) messages may contain attachments that have viruses.
3. Computer viruses cause (many/much) distress to email users.
4. (Widespread several/Several widespread) attacks occur once or twice a year.
5. (A few/A little) viruses can destroy a computer's hard drive.
6. When viruses are new, (few/little) information is available about them.
7. It is important to do (a few/a little) investigating before opening an attachment.
8. Knowing the source of (every/enough) attachment can help prevent infection.
9. (Few/Little) computer users open attachments from people they do not know.
10. It is nice to know that (most/much) email messages do not contain viruses.

F Understanding Articles

The definite article *the* and the indefinite articles *a* and *an* are determiners that tell readers whether the noun that follows is one they can identify (*the book*) or one they cannot yet identify (*a book*).

Definite Articles

When the definite article *the* is used with a noun, the writer is saying to readers, "You can identify which particular thing or things I have in mind. The information you need to make that identification is available to you. Either you have it already, or I am about to supply it to you."

Readers can find the necessary information in the following ways.

- By looking at other information in the sentence

  Meet me at the corner of Main Street and Lafayette Road.

  In this example, *the* is used with the noun *corner* because other words in the sentence tell readers which particular corner the writer has in mind: the one located at Main and Lafayette.
- By looking at information in other sentences

  Aisha ordered a slice of pie and a cup of coffee. The pie was delicious. She asked for a second slice.

  Here, *the* is used before the word *pie* in the second sentence to indicate that it is the same pie identified in the first sentence. Notice, however, that the noun *slice* in the third sentence is preceded by an indefinite article (*a*) because it is not the same slice referred to in the first sentence. There is no information that identifies it specifically.
- By drawing on general knowledge

  The earth revolves around the sun.

  Here, *the* is used with the nouns *earth* and *sun* because readers are expected to know which particular things the writer is referring to.

In the following three cases, *the* is always used rather than *a* or *an*.

1. Before the word *same: the same day*
2. Before the superlative form of an adjective: *the youngest son*
3. Before a number indicating order or sequence: *the third time*

For information on the superlative forms of adjectives and adverbs, see 23B.

Indefinite Articles

When an indefinite article is used with a noun, the writer is saying to readers, "I don't expect you to have enough information right now to identify a particular thing that I have in mind. I do expect you to recognize that I'm referring to only one item."

Consider the following sentences.

We need a table for our computer.

I have a folding table; maybe you can use that.

In the first sentence, the writer has no actual table in mind. Because the table is indefinite to the writer, it is clearly indefinite to the reader, so *a* is used, not *the*. The second sentence refers to an actual table, but because the writer does not expect the reader to be able to identify the table specifically, it is also used with *a* rather than *the*.

FOCUS Indefinite Articles

Unlike the definite article, the indefinite articles *a* and *an* occur only with singular count nouns. *A* is used when the next sound is a consonant, and *an* is used when the next sound is a vowel. In choosing *a* or *an,* pay attention to sounds rather than to spelling: *a house, a year, a union,* but *an hour, an uncle.*

No Article

Only noncount and plural count nouns can stand without articles: *butter, chocolate, cookies, strawberries* (but *a cookie* or *the strawberry*).

For more on count and non-count nouns, see 24D.

Nouns without articles can be used to make generalizations.

Infants need affection as well as food.

The absence of articles before the nouns *infants, affection,* and *food* indicates that this statement is not about particular infants, affection, or food but about infants, affection, and food in general. Remember not to use *the* in such sentences. In English, a sentence like *The infants need affection as well as food* can refer only to particular, identifiable infants and not to infants in general.

Articles with Proper Nouns

For more on proper nouns, see 27A.

Proper nouns may be divided into two classes: names that take *the* and names that take no article.

- Names of people do not take articles: *Napoleon, Mahatma Gandhi.* However, if a name is used in the plural to refer to members of a family, it takes *the: the Osbournes, the Kennedys.*
- Names of places that are plural in form usually take *the: the Andes, the United States.*
- Names of most places on land (cities, states, provinces, and countries) take no article: *Salt Lake City, Mississippi, Alberta, Japan.* Names of most bodies of water (rivers, seas, and oceans) take *the: the Mississippi, the Mediterranean, the Pacific.* However, names of lakes and bays do not take articles: *Lake Erie* and *San Francisco Bay.*

- Names of streets take no article: *Main Street.* Names of highways take *the: the Belt Parkway.*

◆ PRACTICE 24.6

In the following passage, decide whether each blank space needs a definite article (*the*), an indefinite article (*a* or *an*), or no article. If a definite or an indefinite article is needed, write it in the space provided. If no article is needed, leave the space blank.

ON THE WEB
For more practice understanding articles, visit Exercise Central at <bedfordstmartins .com/foundationsfirst>.

Example: Salma Hayek was born in __a__ little town in Veracruz, Mexico.

(1) ____ father of Salma is of Lebanese descent, and her mother is of Spanish origin. (2) At ____ age of twelve, Salma's parents sent her away to ____ small boarding school in ____ state of Louisiana in ____ United States. (3) Salma was asked to leave that school after ____ brief stay because she was ____ rebellious girl. (4) After high school, Salma decided to move to ____ Mexico City to attend ____ large university. (5) ____ frustrated college student soon decided she wanted ____ career in acting. (6) Salma's parents didn't like ____ idea of her becoming ____ actress. (7) Salma began performing in ____ variety of plays and ____ television commercials. (8) She finally became ____ star of ____ very popular soap opera in ____ Mexico. (9) In 1991, Salma moved to ____ apartment in ____ California. (10) She had eighteen months of ____ English lessons before obtaining ____ big movie role. (11) Salma played ____ role of Mexican artist Frida Kahlo in ____ movie *Frida.* (12) Salma earned ____ nomination for ____ Academy Award for best actress in 2003.

G Forming Negative Statements and Questions

Negative Statements

To form a negative statement, add the word *not* directly after the first helping verb of the complete verb.

For more on helping verbs, see 9F.

Global warming has been getting worse.

Global warming has <u>not</u> been getting worse.

When there is no helping verb, a form of the verb *do* must be inserted before *not*.

Automobile traffic contributes to pollution.

Automobile traffic does not contribute to pollution.

For information on subject-verb agreement with the verb do, *see 16B.*

Remember that when *do* is used as a helping verb, the form of *do* used must match the tense and number of the original main verb. Note that in the negative statement above, the main verb loses its tense and appears in the base form (*contribute,* not *contributes*).

NOTE: If the main verb is *am, is, are, was,* or *were,* do not insert a form of *do* before *not: Harry was late; Harry was not late.*

Questions

To form a question, move the helping verb that follows the subject to the position directly before the subject.

The governor has tried to compromise.

Has the governor tried to compromise?

The governor has worked on the budget.

Has the governor worked on the budget?

A helping verb never comes before the subject if the subject is a question word (such as *who* or *which*) or contains a question word.

Who is talking to the governor?

Which bills have been vetoed by the governor?

As with negatives, when the verb does not include a helping verb, you must supply a form of *do*. To form a question, put *do* directly before the subject.

The governor works hard.

Does the governor work hard?

NOTE: If the main verb is a form of *be* (*am, is, are, was,* or *were*), do not insert a form of *do* before the verb. Instead, move the verb so it precedes the subject: *Harry was late; Was Harry late?*

◆ PRACTICE 24.7

Rewrite each of the following sentences in two ways: first, turn the sentence into a question; then, rewrite the original sentence as a negative statement.

Example: Moths are living in my closet.

Question: Are moths living in my closet?

Negative statement: Moths are not living in my closet.

1. The sparrows are searching for winter food.

Question: ______________________________

Negative statement: ______________________________

2. Wild raspberries grow all along these dirt roads.

Question: ______________________________

Negative statement: ______________________________

____

3. I answered her email immediately.

Question: ______________________________

Negative statement: ______________________________

4. Shiho felt sick after eating the pizza.

Question: ______________________________

Negative statement: ______________________________

5. The porcupine attacked my dog.

Question: ______________________________

Negative statement: ______________________________

6. Final exams will be given during the last week of school.

Question: ______________________________

Negative statement: ______________________________

____

7. Gunnar saw the robbery at the convenience store.

Question: ______________________________

Negative statement: ______________________________

____

8. The telephone has been ringing all morning.

Question: ______________________________

Negative statement: ______________________________

9. He is working on the problem right now.

Question: ______________________________

Negative statement: ______________________________

ON THE WEB

For more practice forming negative statements and questions, visit Exercise Central at <bedfordstmartins.com/foundationsfirst>.

10. She dropped the box of dishes on the concrete floor.

Question: ______________________________

Negative statement: ______________________________

____

H Indicating Verb Tense

For more on verb tense, see Chapters 19 and 20.

In English, a verb's form indicates its **tense**—when the action referred to by the verb took place (for instance, in the past or in the present). Be sure to use the appropriate tense of the verb even if the time is obvious or if the sentence includes other indications of time (such as *two years ago* or *yesterday*).

INCORRECT Yesterday, I get a letter from my sister Yunpi.

CORRECT Yesterday, I got a letter from my sister Yunpi.

I Recognizing Stative Verbs

Stative verbs usually tell us that someone or something is in a state that will not change, at least for a while.

Hiro knows American history very well.

The **present progressive** tense consists of the present tense of *be* plus the present participle (*I am going*). The **past progressive** tense consists of the past tense of *be* plus the present participle (*I was going*). Most English verbs show action, and these action verbs can be used in the progressive tenses. Stative verbs, however, are rarely used in the progressive tenses.

INCORRECT Hiro is knowing American history very well.

FOCUS Stative Verbs

Verbs that are stative often refer to mental states—for example, *know, understand, think, believe, want, like, love,* and *hate.* Other stative verbs include *be, have, need, own, belong, weigh, cost,* and *mean.* Certain verbs of sense perception, like *see* and *hear,* are also stative even though they can refer to momentary events rather than unchanging states.

Many verbs have more than one meaning, and some of these verbs are active with one meaning but stative with another. An example is the verb *weigh.*

ACTIVE The butcher is weighing the meat.

STATIVE The meat weighs three pounds.

In the first sentence above, the verb *weigh* means "to put on a scale"; it is active, not stative, as the use of the present progressive tense shows. In the second sentence, however, the same verb means "to have weight," so it is stative, not active. It would be incorrect to say, "The meat is weighing three pounds."

◆ PRACTICE 24.8

In each of the following sentences, circle the verb. Then, correct any problems with stative verbs by crossing out the incorrect verb tense and writing the correct verb tense above the line. If a sentence is correct, write *C* in the blank after the sentence.

ON THE WEB
For more practice recognizing stative verbs, visit Exercise Central at <bedfordstmartins.com/foundationsfirst>.

Example: Ahmed ~~is wanting~~ (wants) to take advanced calculus next semester.
____

1. Ahmed is studying mathematics in college. ____
2. He is also knowing a lot about astronomy. ____
3. He is understanding the movements of planets and stars. ____
4. He was being president of the school's Astronomy Club last year. ____
5. Ahmed is working his way through school. ____
6. He is having a job at a gas station. ____
7. He is hating the boring work there. ____
8. Ahmed is needing the money for his tuition. ____
9. Little by little, he is earning enough to help his family. ____
10. Ahmed is knowing he has to keep his boring job for now. ____

J Placing Modifiers in Order

Adjectives and other modifiers that come before a noun usually follow a set order.

Required Order

- Determiners always come first in a series of adjectives: *these fragile glasses.* The determiners *all* or *both* always precede any other determiners: *all these glasses.*

For more on determiners, see 24E.

- If one of the modifiers is a noun, it must come directly before the noun it modifies: *these wine glasses.*
- All other adjectives are placed between the determiners and the noun modifiers: *these fragile wine glasses.* If there are two or more of these adjectives, the following order is preferred.

Preferred Order

- Adjectives that show the writer's attitude generally precede adjectives that merely describe: *these lovely fragile wine glasses.*
- Adjectives that indicate size generally come early: *these lovely large fragile wine glasses.*

◆ PRACTICE 24.9

ON THE WEB
For more practice placing adjectives in order, visit Exercise Central at <bedfordstmartins.com/foundationsfirst>.

Arrange each group of modifiers in the correct order, and rewrite the complete phrase in the blank.

Example: (rubber, a, red, pretty) ball

a pretty red rubber ball

1. (family, old, a, pleasant) tradition

____

2. (some, disgusting, work) boots

____

3. (four, pampered, Anita's) poodles

____

4. (three, the, circus, funny) clowns

____

5. (my, annoying, both) sisters

____

6. (son's, his, favorite, television) show

____

7. (a, wedding, delightful, outdoor) celebration

____

8. (cat, furry, ugly, this) toy

____

9. (birthday, a, wonderful, chocolate) cake

____

10. (traveling, all, these, banjo) players

____

K Choosing Correct Prepositions

A **preposition** links a noun or pronoun (or a word or word group that functions as a noun) to other words in the sentence. The word the preposition introduces is called the object of the preposition. A preposition and its object combine to form a **prepositional phrase**: *on the table, near the table, under the table.* Thus, prepositions show the precise relationships between words—for example, whether a book is *on, near,* or *under* a table.

I thought I left the book on the table or somewhere near the table, but I found it under the table.

The prepositions *at, in,* and *on* sometimes cause problems for nonnative speakers of English. For example, to identify the location of a place or an event, you can use *at, in,* or *on.*

- The preposition *at* specifies an exact point in space or time.

  Please leave the package with the janitor at 150 South Street. I will pick it up at 7:30 tonight.

- Expanses of space or time are treated as containers and therefore require *in.*

  Jean-Pierre went to school in the 1970s.

- *On* must be used in two cases: with names of streets (but not with exact addresses) and with days of the week or month.

  We will move into our new office on 18th Street either on Monday or on March 12.

L Using Prepositions in Familiar Expressions

Many **idioms** (familiar expressions) end with prepositions. Learning to write clearly and **idiomatically**—in keeping with the conventions of written English—means learning which preposition is used in each expression. If you find this difficult, you are not alone. Even native speakers of English sometimes have trouble choosing the correct preposition.

The sentences that follow illustrate idiomatic use of prepositions in various expressions. Note that sometimes different prepositions are used with the same word. For example, both *on* and *for* can be used with *wait* to form two different expressions with two different meanings: *He waited on their table; She waited for the bus.* Which preposition you choose depends on your meaning. (In the list that follows, pairs of similar expressions that end with different prepositions are bracketed.)

Expression with Preposition	*Sample Sentence*
acquainted with	It took the family several weeks to become acquainted with the new neighbors.
addicted to	I think Abby is becoming addicted to pretzels.
agree on (a plan or objective)	It is vital that all members of the school board agree on goals for the coming year.
agree to (a proposal)	Striking workers finally agreed to the terms of management's offer.
angry about or at (a situation)	Taxpayers are understandably angry about (or at) the deterioration of city recreation facilities.
angry with or at (a person)	When the mayor refused to hire more police officers, his constituents became angry with (or at) him.
approve of	Amy's adviser approved of her decision to study in Guatemala.
bored with	Just when Michael was getting bored with his life, he met Sharon.
capable of	Dogs may be able to fetch and roll over, but they certainly are not capable of complex reasoning.
consist of	The deluxe fruit basket consisted of five pathetic pears, two tiny apples, a few limp bunches of grapes, and one lonely kiwi.
contrast with	Coach Headley's relaxed style contrasts sharply with the previous coach's more formal approach.
convenient for	The proposed location of the new day-care center is convenient for many families.
deal with	Many parents and educators believe it is possible to deal with the special needs of autistic children in a regular classroom.
depend on	Children depend on their parents for emotional as well as financial support.
differ from (something else)	The music of Norah Jones differs from the music of Alicia Keys.
differ with (someone else)	I strongly differ with your interpretation of my dream about *The Wizard of Oz*.
emigrate from	My grandfather and his brother emigrated from the part of Russia that is now Ukraine.
grateful for (a favor)	If you can arrange an interview next week, I will be very grateful for your time and trouble.
grateful to (someone)	Jerry Garcia was always grateful to his loyal fans.
immigrate to	Many Cubans want to leave their country and immigrate to the United States.
impatient with	Keshia often gets impatient with her four younger brothers.

interested in	Diana, who was not very interested in the discussion of the Treaty of Versailles, stared out the window.
interfere with	Sometimes it is hard to resist the temptation to interfere with a friend's life.
meet with	I hope I can meet with you soon to discuss my research paper.
object to	The defense attorney objected to the prosecutor's treatment of the witness.
pleased with	Marta was very pleased with Eric's favorable critique of her speech.
protect against	Nobel Prize winner Linus Pauling believed that large doses of vitamin C could protect people against the common cold.
reason with	When a two-year-old is having a tantrum, it is nearly impossible to reason with her.
reply to	If no one replies to our ad within two weeks, we will advertise again.
responsible for	Parents are not responsible for the debts of their adult children.
similar to	The blood sample found at the crime scene was remarkably similar to one found in the suspect's residence.
specialize in	Dr. Casullo is a dentist who specializes in periodontal surgery.
succeed in	Lisa hoped her M.B.A. would help her succeed in a business career.
take advantage of	Some consumer laws are designed to prevent door-to-door salespeople from taking advantage of buyers.
wait for (something to happen)	Snow White slept while she waited for her prince to arrive.
wait on (in a restaurant)	We sat at the table for twenty minutes before someone waited on us.
worry about	Why worry about things you cannot change?

◆ PRACTICE 24.10

In the following passage, fill in each blank with the correct preposition.

ON THE WEB
For more practice using prepositions in familiar expressions, visit Exercise Central at <bedfordstmartins.com/foundationsfirst>.

Example: Naomi's family lives ___in___ a small house ___on___ Parsons Street.

(1) Naomi emigrated __________ Ghana when she was a teenager. (2) Her family settled __________ New Jersey, __________ the East Coast of the United States. (3) Naomi had studied English __________

Ghana, but she was not prepared for the kind of English spoken __________ the United States. (4) The other students __________ her class sometimes laughed __________ her pronunciation. (5) Still, she studied hard, and her high school teachers were pleased __________ her progress. (6) Naomi was interested __________ attending college and getting a nursing degree. (7) She knew that she was capable __________ doing well __________ college classes if she could continue to improve her English. (8) Before sending an application __________ a local college, Naomi met __________ an admissions officer to discuss her application. (9) Everyone __________ the admissions office was encouraging, and Naomi decided to take advantage __________ their offers to help her. (10) __________ April 12, Naomi's mother called her __________ her after-school job to tell her that the college had accepted her.

M Using Prepositions in Phrasal Verbs

Some verbs, called **phrasal verbs**, consist of two words, a verb and a preposition. If the preposition introduces a prepositional phrase, the preposition comes immediately after the verb. In the following sentence, *at* introduces the prepositional phrase *at the video monitor;* therefore, *at* must come immediately after the verb.

CORRECT Please look at the video monitor.
INCORRECT Please look the video monitor at.

In other phrasal verbs, words that look like prepositions do not always function as prepositions. For example, in the sentence below, the second word of the verb (*up*) does not introduce a prepositional phrase; instead, it combines with the first word of the verb to form a two-word verb with its own meaning. Verbs like these are also not usually separated.

CORRECT The student spoke up without hesitation.
INCORRECT The student spoke without hesitation up.

Some Common Inseparable Phrasal Verbs

come across	grow up
get along	run into
give in	speak up
go over	stay away

In some cases, however, a phrasal verb may be split. For example, some phrasal verbs, called **transitive verbs**, express an action toward an object. When the object of a transitive verb is a noun, the second word of the verb can come either before or after the object. In the sentence below, *turn off* is a transitive verb. Because the object of the verb *turn off* is a noun (*printer*), the second word of the verb can come either before or after the verb's object.

CORRECT Please turn off the printer.

CORRECT Please turn the printer off.

When the object of a transitive verb is a pronoun, however, these two-word verbs *must* be split, and the pronoun must come between the two parts.

CORRECT Please turn it off.

INCORRECT Please turn off it.

Some Common Separable Phrasal Verbs

ask out	hang up	put back	throw away
bring up	let in	put on	try out
call up	let out	shut off	turn down
drop off	look over	take down	turn off
fill out	make up	take off	wake up
give away	put away	think over	

Remember, when the object of the verb is a pronoun, these two-word verbs must be split, and the pronoun must come between the two parts: *take (it) down, put (it) on, let (it) out, make (it) up,* and so on.

◆ PRACTICE 24.11

In each of the following sentences, look closely at the phrasal verb. In each case, determine whether the preposition introduces a prepositional phrase or is part of the verb. Then, decide whether the preposition is correctly placed in the sentence. If it is, write *C* in the blank after the sentence. If the preposition needs to be moved, edit the sentence.

Example: Suspecting that her job search would be difficult, Juanita put ~~off it~~ *it off* as long as possible. _____

1. Juanita knew it was important to show off her strongest skills on her résumé. _____
2. She prepared a draft and printed up it. _____

ON THE WEB
For more practice using prepositions in phrasal verbs, visit Exercise Central at <bedfordstmartins.com/foundationsfirst>.

3. Juanita was worried about having mistakes on her résumé. ____
4. She had a friend look it at for errors. ____
5. When the friend gave back it to her, Juanita was relieved to find that it had very few mistakes. ____
6. Next, she bought a newspaper with classified ads and checked out them for jobs. ____
7. She also came across job postings at job Web sites like <hotjobs.com> and <monster.com>. ____
8. Juanita found several interesting jobs, and she wrote up a personalized cover letter for each one. ____
9. She mailed off them to her prospective employers. ____
10. She desperately wanted some interviews, and she waited patiently for some calls so she could set up them. ____

REVISING AND EDITING

Look back at your response to the Seeing and Writing exercise on page 382. Review this chapter; then, make any necessary grammar and usage corrections to your writing. When you have finished, add any additional transitional words and phrases you need to make your ideas clear to your readers.

CHAPTER REVIEW

◆ EDITING PRACTICE

Read the following essay, which contains errors in the use of subjects, articles and determiners, stative verbs, and idiomatic expressions containing prepositions. Look carefully at each underlined word or phrase. If it is not used correctly, cross it out and write the correct word or phrase above the line. If the underlined word or phrase is correct, write *C* above it. The first error has been corrected for you.

The Electoral College

Presidential elections in the United States follow rules that are sometimes confusing. Many Americans ~~are believing~~ believe that the winning candidate is the person who has gotten the most votes. However, a total number of votes for a candidate may not matter. The Electoral College, an organization consisting with electors from every state, actually selects the president. In forty-eight of the fifty states, the candidate who wins in the state gets all of its electoral votes. When the election is being very close, the person who gets the majority of the popular vote may not win the presidency.

The Continental Congress created the Electoral College on 1787, before George Washington was elected president. Since those time, the United States has depended for the Electoral College to name the president. If the no candidate earns a majority of the Electoral College votes, the House of Representatives decides the election. In 1824, John Quincy Adams was elected by the House of Representatives even though he had received only the third of the popular vote.

Were two more elections in the nineteenth century in which the apparent winner lost in the Electoral College. At 1876, the Electoral College chose Rutherford B. Hayes, who had lost for Samuel Tilden in the popular vote. In 1888, Benjamin Harrison won fewer votes than Grover Cleveland, but Harrison won more electoral votes and became president for one term.

Americans become very interested of the Electoral College when an election is close, as in 2000 when George W. Bush narrowly defeated Al Gore. Most Americans think that every vote should be equally important in the democracy. Some people feel that the Electoral College system makes some votes more important than others. Members of Congress have not yet had enough complaints about the Electoral College system to give up it. Perhaps some twenty-first-century Congress will finally object on the system enough to change it.

George Washington

John Quincy Adams

Rutherford B. Hayes

Benjamin Harrison

◆ COLLABORATIVE ACTIVITIES

1. Working in a group of three or four students, write down as many determiners as you can think of. Next, make a list of ten adjectives. Then, list ten nouns. Finally, combine the determiners and adjectives (in the correct order) in front of the nouns. Be as creative, original, and funny as you can. Choose your group's best phrase and write it on the board.
2. Working in the same group, write ten sentences using the phrases you wrote in activity 1. Make sure that each sentence contains at least one prepositional phrase. Then, exchange sentences with another group. Look over the other group's sentences, and correct any errors you find.
3. Working in the same group, choose one sentence that your group wrote in activity 2. Then, write a short paragraph that begins with this sentence. Use as many specific, interesting nouns and prepositional phrases as you can, and include at least one two-word verb. Finally, have one member of the group read the paragraph aloud to the class.
4. *Composing original sentences* Working in the same group, write five additional original sentences. Make sure that you use at least two plural nouns, at least one noncount noun, at least one negative statement or question, at least one stative verb, and at least one idiomatic expression with a preposition. Check the articles and prepositions carefully. When you have finished, check the sentences again to make sure you have corrected any errors in grammar, punctuation, or spelling.

☑ REVIEW CHECKLIST: Grammar and Usage Issues for ESL Writers

- In almost all cases, English sentences must state their subjects. (See 24A and 24B.)
- In English, most nouns add *-s* to form plurals. Always use a form of the noun that indicates that it is plural. (See 24C.)
- English nouns may be count nouns or noncount nouns. A count noun names one particular thing or a group of particular things (*a teacher, oceans*). A noncount noun names something that cannot be counted (*gold, sand*). (See 24D.)
- Determiners are adjectives that identify rather than describe the nouns they modify. Determiners may also indicate amount or number. (See 24E.)
- The definite article *the* and the indefinite articles *a* and *an* are determiners that indicate whether the noun that follows is one readers can identify (*the book*) or one they cannot yet identify (*a book*). (See 24F.)
- To form a negative statement, add the word *not* directly after the first helping verb of the complete verb. To form a question, move the helping verb that follows the subject to the position directly before the subject. (See 24G.)

(continued on the following page)

(continued from the prevous page)

- A verb's form must indicate when the action referred to by the verb took place. (See 24H.)
- Stative verbs indicate that someone or something is in a state that will not change, at least for a while. Stative verbs are rarely used in the progressive tenses. (See 24I.)
- Adjectives and other modifiers that come before a noun usually follow a set order. (See 24J.)
- The prepositions *at, in,* and *on* sometimes cause problems for nonnative speakers of English. (See 24K.)
- Many familiar expressions end with prepositions. (See 24L.)
- When the preposition in a phrasal verb introduces a prepositional phrase, the preposition comes right after the verb. In other phrasal verbs, the second word can come before or after the object. (See 24M.)

UNIT SIX

Understanding Punctuation, Mechanics, and Spelling

CHAPTER

25

Using Commas

PREVIEW

In this chapter, you will learn

- to use commas in a series (25A)
- to use commas to set off introductory phrases (25B)
- to use commas to set off parenthetical words and phrases (25C)
- to use commas with appositives (25D)
- to use commas to set off nonrestrictive clauses (25E)
- to use commas in compound and complex sentences (25F)
- to use commas in dates and addresses (25G)

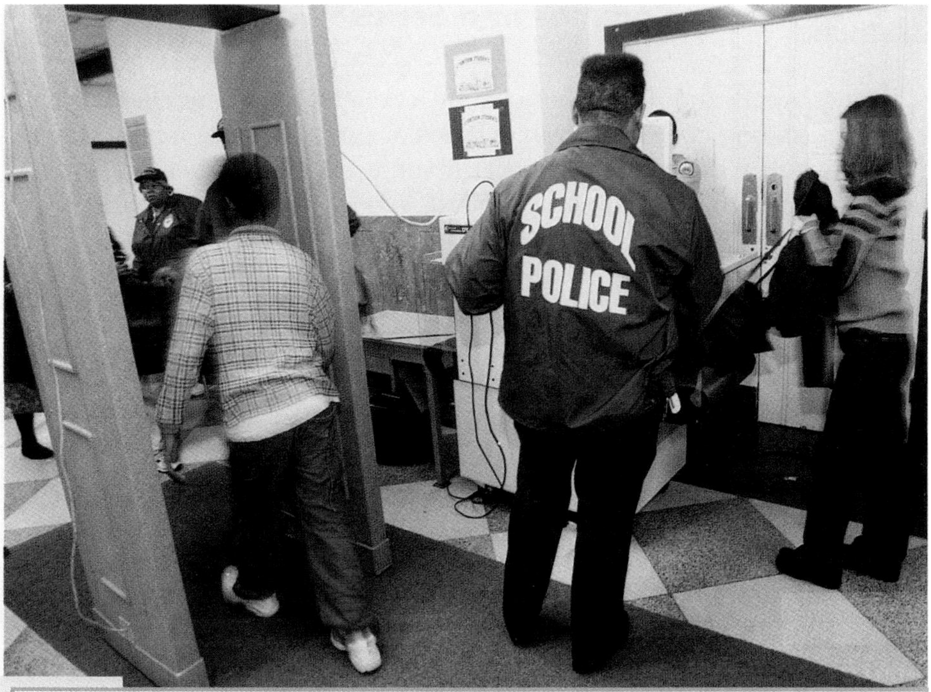

■ SEEING AND WRITING

What kind of security do you think is needed in America's high schools? Why? Look at the picture above, and then write a paragraph in which you answer these questions.

Word Power

surveillance the close observation of a person or a group of people, especially a person or group under suspicion

A **comma** is a punctuation mark that separates words or groups of words within sentences. In this way, commas help readers by keeping ideas distinct from one another. As you will learn in this chapter, commas also have several other uses.

A Using Commas in a Series

Use commas to separate items in a **series** of three or more words or word groups (phrases or clauses).

Writing Tip

Do not use a comma before the first item in a series or after the last item in a series.

Hamlet, Macbeth, and *Othello* are tragedies by William Shakespeare. (series of three nouns linked by *and*)

Hamlet, Macbeth, or *Othello* will be assigned this semester. (series of three nouns linked by *or*)

Brian read *Hamlet,* started *Macbeth,* and skimmed *Othello.* (series of three phrases linked by *and*)

Hamlet is a tragedy, *Much Ado about Nothing* is a comedy, and *Richard III* is a history play. (series of three clauses linked by *and*)

FOCUS Using Commas in a Series

Newspapers and magazines usually leave out the comma before the coordinating conjunction in a series of three or more items. However, your writing will be clearer if you use a comma before the coordinating conjunction (*and, or, but,* and so on) in this situation.

UNCLEAR The party had 200 guests, great food and rock music blaring from giant speakers. (Did food as well as music come from the speakers?)

CLEAR The party had 200 guests, great food, and rock music blaring from giant speakers.

However, do not use *any* commas if all the items in a series are separated by coordinating conjunctions.

The party had 200 guests and great food and rock music blaring from giant speakers.

ON THE WEB

For more practice using commas in a series, visit Exercise Central at <bedfordstmartins.com/foundationsfirst>.

◆ PRACTICE 25.1

Edit the following sentences for the correct use of commas in a series. If the sentence is correct, write *C* in the blank.

Example: We stowed our luggage, took our seats, and fastened our seat belts. ____

1. The intersection was crowded with buses cars and trucks. ____
2. The boys are either in the house, in the yard or at the park. ____
3. *Star Wars, Alien,* and *Blade Runner* are classic science fiction movies. ____
4. Jo Ellen took a walk Roger cleaned the house and Phil went to the movies. ____
5. A good marriage requires patience, honesty and hard work. ____

6. Volunteers collected signatures accepted donations and answered phones. _____
7. We did not know whether to laugh, cry, or cheer. _____
8. Owls are outstanding hunters because they are strong, quick and silent. _____
9. The kitchen is to the left the guest room is upstairs and the pool is out back. _____
10. This computer is fast, has plenty of memory, and comes with an extra-large monitor. _____

B Using Commas to Set Off Introductory Phrases

Use a comma to set off an **introductory phrase** (a group of words that opens a sentence) from the rest of the sentence.

> For best results, take this medicine with a full glass of water.
>
> In case of fire, keep calm.
>
> After the concert, we walked home through the park.

Computer Tip

Your grammar checker can find many places where a comma is missing, especially when the comma should set off an introductory phrase.

◆ PRACTICE 25.2

Edit the following sentences for the correct use of commas with introductory phrases. If the sentence is correct, write *C* in the blank.

Example: From its first performance, the band was a huge success. _____

Writing Tip

When an introductory prepositional phrase has fewer than three words, you do not need to use a comma: *In 1986 the* Challenger *exploded on takeoff.* However, your sentences will be clearer if you include commas after *all* introductory phrases.

1. At the end of the game the bus took the team home. _____
2. Most of the time weather travels from west to east. _____
3. After the holiday season many stores take inventory. _____
4. During chemistry class, Margaret asked a number of interesting questions. _____
5. Racing against the clock Silvio finished the corporate earnings report. _____
6. Due to a reduction in funding some elementary schools have suspended their music programs. _____
7. Often feared bats are actually helpful creatures. _____

ON THE WEB
For more practice using commas to set off introductory phrases, visit Exercise Central at <bedfordstmartins.com/foundationsfirst>.

8. According to some experts eating too much protein can have negative effects. ____
9. Without access to telephones more than half the world's population depends on face-to-face communication. ____
10. At the current rate of global warming oceans could rise a foot or more within the next 100 years. ____

C Using Commas to Set Off Parenthetical Words and Phrases

Often a word or phrase is just an aside or afterthought that the sentence can do without. Because such words and phrases could be enclosed in parentheses, they are known as **parenthetical words and phrases**. Always use commas to set off parenthetical words and phrases.

For lists of some frequently used conjunctive adverbs and transitional expressions, see 10C.

Many parenthetical words and phrases are **conjunctive adverbs** (such as *however* and *therefore*) or **transitional expressions** (such as *in fact* and *for example*).

In fact, Scott Gomez grew up in Alaska.
He is, however, a center for the New Jersey Devils.
He plays for the NHL, of course.

Note that parenthetical words and phrases can come at the beginning, in the middle, or at the end of a sentence.

Of course, he plays for the NHL.
He plays, of course, for the NHL.
He plays for the NHL, of course.

Remember, wherever they appear, parenthetical words and phrases must be set off from the rest of the sentence by commas.

FOCUS Using Commas in Direct Address

Always use commas to set off the name of a person (or an animal) whom you are addressing (speaking to directly). Use commas whether the name of the person addressed appears at the beginning, in the middle, or at the end of a sentence.

Spike, roll over and play dead.
Roll over, Spike, and play dead.
Roll over and play dead, Spike.

◆ PRACTICE 25.3

Edit the following sentences for the correct use of commas with parenthetical words and phrases. If the sentence is correct, write *C* in the blank.

Example: The Dallas Cowboys, surely, are one of football's most famous teams. __C__

1. Bill how did you do on the test? ____
2. The plane therefore never got off the ground. ____
3. In addition, an exercise class is relatively inexpensive. ____
4. We wanted to make a good impression of course. ____
5. When you give your speech Jeanne be sure to speak clearly. ____
6. In fact even experienced professionals make mistakes. ____
7. The party consequently was a disaster. ____
8. How old are you, anyway? ____
9. Don't forget the key to the cabin Amber. ____
10. However no one knew what the outcome would be. ____
11. Furthermore the team had lost its best defensive player. ____
12. The mayor unfortunately had weathered a number of scandals. ____
13. What do you suggest we do for Zach Dr. Chen? ____
14. No one can say, moreover, how the economy will change in the future. ____
15. Besides genetics is the next medical frontier. ____

ON THE WEB
For more practice using commas to set off parenthetical words and phrases, visit Exercise Central at <bedfordstmartins.com/foundationsfirst>.

◆ PRACTICE 25.4

Edit the sentences in the following paragraph for the correct use of commas with parenthetical words and phrases. If the sentence is correct, write *C* in the blank.

Example: Tiger Woods, unlike other golfers, seems to have unlimited talent. ____

(1) For example Tiger Woods is an exceptional golf player. ____ (2) Moreover experts say his skills are nearly perfect. ____ (3) His golf game, consequently is difficult to beat. ____ (4) He dominates most of

the tournaments he enters in other words. ____ (5) In fact, Woods is one of the best golf players in history. ____ (6) After all he has broken many long-standing records. ____ (7) His success moreover has come at a young age. ____ (8) Also he finishes ahead of more experienced players. ____ (9) There may finally be no one to challenge him on the golf course. ____ (10) Furthermore, he has increased the popularity of golf among young people. ____

◆ PRACTICE 25.5

Choose five items from the list of words and phrases provided, and then write three sentences for each parenthetical word or phrase—one with the parenthetical expression at the beginning of the sentence, one with the parenthetical expression in the middle, and one with the parenthetical expression at the end.

Examples

In fact, some dinosaurs were highly intelligent creatures.

Some dinosaurs, in fact, were highly intelligent creatures.

Some dinosaurs were highly intelligent creatures, in fact.

after all	in contrast
as a result	in fact
at the same time	in other words
consequently	nevertheless
for example	subsequently
however	therefore
in addition	

1a. ____

____

b. ____

____

c. ____

____

2a. ____

____

b. ______________________________

____

c. ______________________________

____

3a. ______________________________

____

b. ______________________________

____

c. ______________________________

____

4a. ______________________________

____

b. ______________________________

____

c. ______________________________

____

5a. ______________________________

____

b. ______________________________

____

c. ______________________________

____

D Using Commas with Appositives

Use commas to set off an **appositive**, a word or word group that identifies, renames, or describes a noun or a pronoun.

> Luis Valdez, an award-winning playwright, wrote *Los Vendidos* and *Zoot Suit*. (*An award-winning playwright* is an appositive that describes the noun *Luis Valdez*.)
>
> The Cisco Kid rode in on his horse, a white stallion. (*A white stallion* is an appositive that describes the noun *horse*.)
>
> She, the star of the show, applauded the audience. (*The star of the show* is an appositive that identifies the pronoun *she*.)

FOCUS **Using Commas with Appositives**

An appositive can appear at the beginning, in the middle, or at the end of a sentence. Wherever it appears, it is always set off from the rest of the sentence by commas.

> A Native American writer, Sherman Alexie wrote the novel *Reservation Blues.*
>
> One of Alexie's poems, "Defending Walt Whitman," is about a basketball game.
>
> One of Alexie's books was made into a film, *Smoke Signals*.

ON THE WEB
For more practice using commas with appositives, visit Exercise Central at <bedfordstmartins.com /foundationsfirst>.

◆ PRACTICE 25.6

Edit the following sentences for the correct use of commas to set off appositives. If the sentence is correct, write *C* in the blank.

Example: Hawaii's capital, Honolulu, is on the island of Oahu. ____

1. My mother Sandra Thomas used to work for the city. ____
2. Coca Cola, a popular drink has been around for decades. ____
3. The convention is in Chicago my hometown. ____
4. A rookie he approached the suspect nervously. ____
5. The world's tallest mountain Mount Everest is in Nepal. ____
6. Life on earth could not exist without our nearest star the sun. ____
7. Aloe a common houseplant, has medicinal value. ____
8. An excellent dancer, she won the competition easily. ____
9. Elvis Presley a white singer, was influenced by African-American music. ____
10. Adam Smith was a leading figure in economics the study of wealth and society. ____

◆ PRACTICE 25.7

In each of the following sentences, add an appositive that identifies or describes the noun or pronoun it refers to.

Example: The movie, ___a western___, is one of George's favorites.

1. Grace, ______________________, came to visit yesterday.
2. That item, ______________________, is very expensive.
3. ______________________, he passed the test easily.
4. *Alice's Adventures in Wonderland,* ______________________, is a classic.
5. Ted enjoyed his meal, ______________________.
6. That building, ______________________________, used to be a factory.
7. ______________________, coffee is often served in the morning.
8. We like to talk to Suzanne, ______________________.
9. Biology, ______________________, is fascinating.
10. My great-grandmother had carefully folded the garment, ______________________.

E Using Commas to Set Off Nonrestrictive Clauses

Use commas to set off **nonrestrictive clauses**, groups of words that are not essential to a sentence's meaning. Do not use commas to set off **restrictive clauses**.

A **restrictive clause** contains essential information and is therefore *not* set off from the rest of the sentence by commas.

> The artist who was formerly known as Prince is now known as Prince again.

In the above sentence, the clause *who was formerly known as Prince* supplies specific information that is essential to the idea the sentence is communicating. The clause tells readers which particular artist is now known as Prince again. Without the clause *who was formerly known as Prince,* the sentence does not communicate the same idea because it does not specify which particular artist is now once again known as Prince.

> The artist is now known as Prince again. (Which artist is known as Prince?)

A **nonrestrictive clause** does not contain essential information; therefore, a nonrestrictive clause *is* set off from the rest of the sentence by commas.

> Violent crime in our cities, which increased steadily for many years, is now decreasing.

Here, the underlined clause provides extra information to help readers understand the sentence, but the sentence communicates the same point without this information.

> Violent crime in our cities is now decreasing.

FOCUS *Who, Which,* and *That*

- *Who* can introduce either a restrictive or a nonrestrictive clause.

RESTRICTIVE Many people who watch *Oprah* have bought the books her book club recommends. (no commas)

NONRESTRICTIVE Wally Lamb, who wrote a novel recommended by Oprah's Book Club, saw his book become a best-seller. (clause set off by commas)

- *Which* always introduces a nonrestrictive clause.

NONRESTRICTIVE Natural disasters, which can be terrifying, really appeal to movie audiences. (clause set off by commas)

- *That* always introduces a restrictive clause.

RESTRICTIVE They wanted to see the movie that had the best special effects. (no commas)

ON THE WEB
For more practice using commas to set off nonrestrictive clauses, visit Exercise Central at <bedfordstmartins.com/foundationsfirst>.

◆ PRACTICE 25.8

In each of the following sentences, decide whether the underlined clause is restrictive or nonrestrictive, and then add commas where necessary. If the sentence is correct, write *C* in the blank.

Examples

My boss, who loves fishing, has a picture of his boat in his office. ____

The train that derailed yesterday was empty. __C__

1. Clocks that tick loudly can be irritating. ____
2. The reader who graded my essay gave me an A. ____
3. The camera which is automatic often breaks. ____
4. Fish that live in polluted water are unsafe to eat. ____
5. The artist who painted this picture is famous for her landscapes. ____
6. Boxing which requires quick reflexes can be exciting to watch. ____
7. Rafael who finishes work at 5:30 met Carla for dinner at 7:00. ____

8. The Thai restaurant that opened last month is supposed to be excellent. _____

9. Gray wolves which many ranchers dislike are making a comeback in the West. _____

10. The Broadway star who has also appeared in films has many devoted fans. _____

◆ PRACTICE 25.9

Edit the sentences in the following paragraph so that commas set off all nonrestrictive clauses. (Remember, commas are *not* used to set off restrictive clauses.) If the sentence is correct, write *C* in the blank.

Example: The Weavers Society, which is based in Guyana, runs an Internet business. _____

(1) Many people who live in developing countries have difficulty making a living. _____ (2) Modern technology which includes the Internet is changing that. _____ (3) In fact, businesses that use the Internet can reach customers around the world. _____ (4) For example, a group of women who live in Guyana recently started an Internet business. _____ (5) The women who call themselves the Weavers Society needed customers for their work. _____ (6) Their products which they make themselves are handwoven hammocks. _____ (7) A company, that sells satellite telephones, donated some phones to the weavers. _____ (8) The same company which also deals in computers helped the women connect to the World Wide Web. _____ (9) The weavers who could find no customers in their own village soon sold many of their hammocks to customers in other regions. _____ (10) These women have changed the economy of a village that had long been in poverty. _____

◆ PRACTICE 25.10

Edit the sentences in the following paragraph so that commas set off all nonrestrictive clauses. If the sentence is correct, write *C* in the blank.

Example: The Tenth Mountain Division, which has been one of the U.S. Army's most talked about units, was formed in the early 1940s. _____

(1) This unit was trained in backcountry skiing and survival in preparation for fighting German forces that were stationed in the high mountains of Italy. ____ (2) Some of the men, who joined this division during World War II, were top European skiers and climbers. ____ (3) Having escaped from Europe which was occupied by the Nazis these athletes put their skills to use. ____ (4) They joined with American skiers from Ivy League colleges, who were also eager to use their skills, to form this unique military force. ____ (5) They trained in the Colorado mountains for three years which gave them plenty of time to prepare. ____ (6) In 1945, the skiers who trained with the Tenth Mountain Division got to go to Italy and fight. ____ (7) The battle, that eventually earned them fame and respect, was the result of their successful sneak attack on the German forces on Italy's Mt. Belvedere. ____ (8) Many of the troops who fought in the Tenth Mountain Division became famous after the war for other reasons as well. ____ (9) Aspen and Vail which are now two of the most popular ski resorts in the country were founded by veterans of this division. ____ (10) Though the troops who fought in World War II are perhaps the most famous of the ski troops, the Tenth Mountain Division still exists today and has been deployed in recent years to fight in Afghanistan. ____

◆ PRACTICE 25.11

In each of the following sentences, fill in the blank with words that complete the restrictive or nonrestrictive clause.

Example: Movies and video games that *are very violent* have been in the news lately.

1. Action and horror movies, which ________________, often include violent scenes.
2. People who ________________ seem never to get tired of such films.
3. The violence that ________________ is often graphic.
4. Most fans say movie violence, which ________________, is not realistic.

5. They believe movies that ________________ do not pose a danger in real life.
6. However, psychologists who ________________ say viewing on-screen battles can affect people's behavior.
7. They worry that young people who ________________ will use force to settle conflicts in their own lives.
8. Video games that ________________ are the subject of a similar controversy.
9. Many people who ________________ say the games are a safe outlet for strong emotions.
10. The debate over media violence, which ________________, will probably continue for some time.

F Using Commas in Compound and Complex Sentences

In Chapters 10 and 11, you learned how to use commas between the clauses in compound and complex sentences. Here is a brief review.

Compound Sentences

A **compound sentence** is made up of two or more independent clauses (simple sentences) joined by a coordinating conjunction (*and, or, nor, but, for, so, yet*), by a semicolon, or by a conjunctive adverb. When a coordinating conjunction joins the independent clauses, always use a comma before the coordinating conjunction.

Morocco is in North Africa, but Senegal is in West Africa.

> **FOCUS Unnecessary Commas with *And* and *But***
>
> Not every *and* and *but* has a comma before it. Do not use a comma in the following situations.
>
> - Before the coordinating conjunction that separates the two parts of a compound subject
>
>   INCORRECT *The Little Mermaid,* and *Finding Nemo* are two animated films.
>
> *(continued on the following page)*

(continued from the preceding page)

CORRECT *The Little Mermaid* and *Finding Nemo* are two animated films.

- Before the coordinating conjunction that separates the two verbs that make up a **compound predicate**

INCORRECT Snoopy ate a dog biscuit, and took a nap.

CORRECT Snoopy ate a dog biscuit and took a nap.

Complex Sentences

A **complex sentence** is made up of an independent clause and one or more dependent clauses. The clauses are joined by a subordinating conjunction or a relative pronoun. Use a comma after the dependent clause when it comes *before* the independent clause.

Although the African-American men called the Buffalo Soldiers fought bravely in World War II, most were never honored for their heroism.

FOCUS Unnecessary Commas in Complex Sentences

Do not use a comma in a complex sentence when the dependent clause comes after the independent clause.

INCORRECT Many people come to the United States, because they are seeking religious or political freedom.

CORRECT Many people come to the United States because they are seeking religious or political freedom.

ON THE WEB
For more practice using commas in compound and complex sentences, visit Exercise Central at <bedfordstmartins.com/foundationsfirst>.

◆ PRACTICE 25.12

Edit the sentences in the following paragraph for the correct use of commas in compound and complex sentences. If the sentence is correct, write *C* in the blank.

Example: Alaska is a challenging place to live, so its residents must adapt. ____

(1) Alaska is a rugged state and its population is small. ____ (2) Travel there is difficult so people rely on airplanes for transportation. ____ (3) Although many people live in Alaska's cities many others live in small villages. ____ (4) Such villages are scattered across the state and roads do not always reach them. ____ (5) Also, travel by road is not al-

ways possible because the state's Arctic weather can be severe. ____ (6) Even though air travel is expensive it is the best option available in some places. ____ (7) Alaska's bush pilots use small planes because these planes can take off and land in tight spots. ____ (8) When a traditional landing strip is not available a pilot may land on snow or open water. ____ (9) Most of Alaska's air passengers are locals, but visiting hunters and sightseers also fly with bush pilots. ____ (10) Until residents find a better means of transportation bush pilots will enjoy a brisk business in Alaska. ____

G Using Commas in Dates and Addresses

Dates

Use commas in dates to separate the name of the day from the month and to separate the number of the day from the year.

> The first Christmas that Elena's son celebrated was Saturday, December 25, 1999.

When a date that includes commas falls in the middle of a sentence, place a comma after the date.

> Saturday, December 25, 1999, was the first Christmas that Elena's son celebrated.

Writing Tip

Do not use commas between a month and the number of the day (*December 25*) or between a month and the year (*December 2004*).

Addresses

Use commas in addresses to separate the street address from the city and to separate the city from the state or country.

> The British prime minister lives at 10 Downing Street, London, England.

When an address that includes commas falls in the middle of a sentence, place a comma after the address.

> The residence at 10 Downing Street, London, England, has been home for Winston Churchill and for Margaret Thatcher.

Writing Tip

In addresses, do not use a comma between the building number and the street name (*310 Main Street*).

◆ PRACTICE 25.13

Edit the following sentences for the correct use of commas in dates and addresses. Add any missing commas, and cross out any unnecessary commas. If the sentence is correct, write *C* in the blank.

ON THE WEB
For more practice using commas in dates and addresses, visit Exercise Central at <bedfordstmartins.com/foundationsfirst>.

Examples

Atif was born on August 15, 1965. ____

Islamabad, Pakistan, is near his hometown. ____

1. Atif is from Lahore Pakistan. ____
2. On March 12, 1995 his family moved to the United States. ____
3. Their first home was at 2122 Kent Avenue Brooklyn New York. ____
4. Atif and his wife became citizens of the United States in December, 1999. ____
5. They wanted to move to Boston Massachusetts where Atif's cousins lived. ____
6. On Tuesday June 6 2000 the family moved to the Boston area. ____
7. Their new address was 14 Arden Street Allston Massachusetts. ____
8. Atif's daughters started school there on September 5. ____
9. The school is located at 212 Hope Street, Allston. ____
10. Atif's older daughter graduated from the sixth grade on Friday June 28 2002. ____

Computer Tip
Use the Find or Search command to highlight the commas in your writing. Check to see if you have used the commas correctly.

REVISING AND EDITING

Look back at your response to the Seeing and Writing exercise on page 411. First, circle every comma in your writing. Then, review this chapter, and decide whether every comma you have used is necessary. If you find any unnecessary commas, cross them out. When you have finished, reread your work again to make sure you have not left out any necessary commas.

CHAPTER REVIEW

◆ EDITING PRACTICE

Read the following essay, which contains some errors in the use of commas. Add commas where necessary between items in a series and with introductory phrases, conjunctive adverbs or transitional expressions, appositives, and nonrestrictive clauses. Cross out any unnecessary commas. The first sentence has been edited for you.

The Battles of Elizabeth Cady Stanton

In the 1800s, two human rights campaigns divided public opinion. One was abolition the movement to end slavery. The other was women's suffrage the movement to allow women to vote. Elizabeth Cady Stanton was an important figure in both struggles and she helped to bring about their ultimate success.

Cady Stanton was a wife, a mother, and a fierce campaigner. As a girl, she showed an interest in the law. Her father was a lawyer and Cady Stanton argued with him about laws that favored men. Her father however felt girls were inferior to boys. Although he respected his daughter's energy, and intelligence he always wished she had been a boy.

Elizabeth Cady Stanton speaking to women

Cady Stanton attended a women's seminary in Troy New York. Soon after her graduation she began working to end slavery. Her husband, Henry Stanton opposed slavery. He was in fact a delegate to the World Anti-Slavery Convention in London, England. Cady Stanton admired his speaking talent, liberal values and good looks. The two were married on May 1 1840.

Her work toward abolition which included lobbying Congress went on for more than twenty years. At the same time, she longed to improve the lives of women. Women, who had almost no legal rights were treated as the property of men. Cady Stanton believed women would never be equal to men, until they had the right to vote.

A suffragist

Suffrage was an uphill fight, but she devoted herself to it for more than fifty years. She wrote to Congress spoke about women's rights, and published a newspaper called *The Revolution.* Cady Stanton's work which she did while caring for seven children changed women's lives. Her place in history, therefore should be a prominent one.

◆ COLLABORATIVE ACTIVITIES

1. Working in a group of three or four students, list some of the specific dangers that high school students might be exposed to while in school. Next, list security measures that high schools might take to protect

students from these dangers. Once you have completed your lists, work together to write a paragraph that includes at least three dangers to high school students and three possible security measures. Finally, exchange paragraphs with another group. Check one another's paragraphs to be sure commas are used correctly.

2. Bring to class a textbook for one of your courses. Working with a partner, turn to a page in the textbook, and use a pencil to circle every comma on the page. Take turns explaining why each comma is necessary.
3. Working with a partner, take turns interviewing each other, and use the information you get as material for a brief biography of your partner. Find out when and where your partner was born, where he or she has lived, the schools he or she has attended, and so on. Then, write a paragraph that includes all the information you have gathered, being sure to include transitions where necessary. When you have finished, exchange papers with your partner. Check one another's papers to be sure commas are used correctly.
4. *Composing original sentences* Imagine that you are writing a handbook for middle school students on the use of commas. Compose seven sample sentences to show the correct use of commas in each of the following situations:
   - in a series
   - to set off an introductory phrase
   - to set off a parenthetical word or phrase
   - to set off an appositive
   - to set off a nonrestrictive clause
   - in a compound sentence before a coordinating conjunction (*and, but, or,* and so on)
   - in a complex sentence that begins with a dependent clause

   When you have finished, check the sentences again to make sure you have corrected any errors in grammar, punctuation, or spelling.

✓ REVIEW CHECKLIST: Using Commas

- Use commas to separate elements in a series of three or more words or word groups. (See 25A.)
- Use commas to set off introductory phrases. (See 25B.)
- Use commas to set off parenthetical words and phrases. (See 25C.)
- Use commas to set off an appositive from the rest of the sentence. (See 25D.)
- Use commas to set off nonrestrictive clauses. (See 25E.)
- Use commas in compound and complex sentences. (See 25F.)
- Use commas to separate parts of dates and addresses. (See 25G.)

CHAPTER

26

Using Apostrophes

PREVIEW

In this chapter, you will learn

- to use apostrophes to form contractions (26A)
- to use apostrophes to form possessives (26B)
- to revise the incorrect use of apostrophes (26C)

SEEING AND WRITING

Do you believe that men and women are equally qualified for all jobs, or do you think that some jobs should be "men's jobs" or "women's jobs"? Look at the picture above, and then write a paragraph in which you explain your position.

Word Power

tradition a behavior or custom handed down from generation to generation

traditional relating to tradition

An **apostrophe** is a punctuation mark that is used in two situations: to form a contraction and to form the possessive of a noun or an indefinite pronoun.

Writing Tip

Even though contractions are used in speech and informal writing, they are not acceptable in most college or business writing situations.

A Using Apostrophes to Form Contractions

A **contraction** is a word that uses an apostrophe to combine two words. The apostrophe takes the place of the letters that are left out.

I didn't [did not] understand the question.

It's [it is] sometimes hard to see the difference between right and wrong.

Frequently Used Contractions

I	+ am	= I'm		could	+ not	= couldn't
we	+ are	= we're		do	+ not	= don't
you	+ are	= you're		does	+ not	= doesn't
it	+ is	= it's		will	+ not	= won't
I	+ have	= I've		should	+ not	= shouldn't
I	+ will	= I'll		would	+ not	= wouldn't
there	+ is	= there's		let	+ us	= let's
is	+ not	= isn't		that	+ is	= that's
are	+ not	= aren't		who	+ is	= who's
can	+ not	= can't				

Writing Tip

Note that *won't* is different from the other contractions because its spelling is irregular.

◆ PRACTICE 26.1

Edit the following paragraph so that apostrophes are used correctly in contractions.

ON THE WEB

For more practice using apostrophes to form contractions, visit Exercise Central at <bedfordstmartins.com /foundationsfirst>.

Example: Berea College in Kentucky ~~doesnt~~ doesn't require its students to pay tuition.

(1) This means that students from low-income families who cant pay for school can still get a college education. (2) In fact, Berea wont accept anyone who has the ability to pay. (3) The college wants only students who wouldnt otherwise be able to afford to attend a four-year college. (4) There arent many other colleges or universities that offer this kind of support. (5) Berea has made itself unique in other ways as well, in ways that other schools havent. (6) For example, the college has a community-service program thats both respected and appreciated. (7) Its not unusual for Berea students to spend many hours every week volunteering in their Appalachian community. (8) Theyre also all required to have on-campus jobs. (9) This school offers a rare opportunity in an age where income tends to determine whos eligible for college and who isnt. (10) Its unfortunate that more schools havent decided to follow Berea's lead and offer low-cost education.

◆ PRACTICE 26.2

In each of the following sentences, add apostrophes to contractions if needed, and edit to make sure all apostrophes are placed correctly. If a sentence is correct, write *C* in the blank.

Example: Television ~~didnt~~ didn't become popular until the 1950s, but ~~its~~ it's very popular now. _____

1. In many homes, television is'nt a luxury; its a necessity. _____
2. Most people cant imagine life without television, and they dont want to try. _____
3. Theyll argue that theres plenty of high-quality programming on television. _____
4. However, television shows are'nt always the best source of information. _____
5. Theyre designed to appeal to as many people as possible. _____
6. Wouldn't most people prefer to be entertained rather than informed? _____
7. The average American doesnt read nearly as much as he or she watches television. _____
8. It wouldnt hurt us to read more. _____
9. Fifty years ago, people could'nt have imagined how attached wed become to our television sets. _____
10. A generation from now, wholl be able to imagine a world where theres no television? _____

B Using Apostrophes to Form Possessives

Possessive forms show ownership. Nouns (names of people, animals, places, objects, or ideas) and indefinite pronouns (words like *everyone* and *anything*) do not have special possessive forms. Instead, they use apostrophes to show ownership.

> **Writing Tip**
> Possessive pronouns have special forms, such as *its* and *his*. These forms never include apostrophes. For more on possessives, see 22E.

Singular Nouns and Indefinite Pronouns

To form the possessive of singular nouns (including names), add an apostrophe plus an *s*.

The game's score [the score of the game] was very close.

Coach Nelson's goal [the goal of Coach Nelson] was to win.

Some singular nouns end in *-s*. Even if a singular noun already ends in *-s,* add an apostrophe plus an *s* to form the possessive.

The class's new computers were unpacked on Tuesday.

Carlos's computer crashed on Wednesday.

FOCUS Indefinite Pronouns

For more on indefinite pronouns, see 22C.

Indefinite pronouns—words like *everyone* and *anything*—form possessives in the same way singular nouns do: they add an apostrophe and an *s*.

Rodney was everyone's choice [the choice of everyone] for quarterback.

Plural Nouns

Most nouns form the plural by adding *s*. To form the possessive of plural nouns (including names) that end in *-s,* add just an apostrophe. Do *not* add an apostrophe plus an *s*.

The two televisions' features [the features of the two televisions] were very different.

The Thompsons' house [the house of the Thompsons] is on the corner.

Some irregular plural nouns do not end in *-s*. If a plural noun does not end in *-s,* add an apostrophe plus an *s* to form the possessive.

For a list of some irregular plural nouns, see 21C.

The children's room is upstairs.

◆ PRACTICE 26.3

ON THE WEB
For more practice using apostrophes to form possessives, visit Exercise Central at <bedfordstmartins.com/foundationsfirst>.

Rewrite the following groups of words, changing the singular noun or indefinite pronoun that follows *of* to the possessive form.

Example: the plot of the book *the book's plot*

1. the owner of the shop ____________
2. the pilot of the plane ____________
3. the cat of the neighbor ____________
4. the desk of the manager ____________
5. the cell phone of Indira ____________

6. the engine of the truck ______________________
7. the sister of Chris ______________________
8. the guess of anyone ______________________
9. the opinion of the class ______________________
10. the waiting room of the doctor ______________________

◆ PRACTICE 26.4

Rewrite the following groups of words, changing the plural noun that follows *of* to the possessive form.

Example: the rhythm of the dancers the dancers' rhythm

1. the bags of the travelers ______________________
2. the quills of the porcupines ______________________
3. the faces of the women ______________________
4. the room of the children ______________________
5. the car of the ministers ______________________
6. the bills of the customers ______________________
7. the apartment of the Huangs ______________________
8. the voice of the people ______________________
9. the first meeting of the lawyers ______________________
10. the telephone number of the Smiths ______________________

◆ PRACTICE 26.5

In each of the following sentences, fill in the blank with a possessive noun that completes the sentence.

Example: We listened to the orchestra's fine performance.

1. The ______________ finances are in good order.
2. Tamika bought the ______________ outfits on sale.
3. ______________ answer made no sense at all.
4. We watched the ______________ speech on television last night.
5. The noise made by ______________ dog is unbearable.
6. Her ______________ letter came in the mail on Friday.
7. ______________ most recent movie was quite successful.
8. Someone found a ______________ hat on the sidewalk.

9. ______________ interests include water polo and hang gliding.

10. Halfway through the ______________ hike, it started to rain.

◆ PRACTICE 26.6

In each of the following sentences, edit the underlined possessive nouns and indefinite pronouns so that apostrophes are used correctly. If a correction needs to be made, cross out the noun or pronoun, and write the correct form above it. If the possessive form is correct, write *C* above it.

Example: A ~~business'~~ (business's) success depends on the founder's (C) hard work and good luck.

1. In 1888, Lee Kee Lo opened a business in New Yorks Chinatown.
2. He became one of the neighborhoods' best-known grocers.
3. Lee's son, Harold, expanded his fathers' business.
4. He met many customer's financial needs, such as currency exchange.
5. Harold Lees' bank also filled business owners' requests for loans.
6. Then, Harolds' son Arthur changed the business' mission again.
7. He was the familys'—and Chinatowns'—first insurance agent.
8. If someones' property needed to be insured, Arthur Lee's agency took the job.
9. The insurance agencys' office is now run by Arthurs' children.
10. The Lee's business continues to flourish in Lee Kee Lo's original storefront.

C Revising the Incorrect Use of Apostrophes

Watch out for the following problems with apostrophes.

- Be careful not to confuse a plural noun (*girls*) with the singular possessive form of the noun (*girl's*). Do not use apostrophes to form noun plurals.

In the following sentences, the nouns are plural, not possessive. Therefore, no apostrophes are used.

Cats [not *cat's*] can be wonderful pets [not *pet's*].

The Fords [not *Ford's*] went to Disney World.

Writing Tip

Never use an apostrophe with a plural noun unless the noun is possessive.

- Never use apostrophes with **possessive pronouns** that end in *-s*.

Possessive Pronouns	*Incorrect Spelling*
hers	her's
its	it's
ours	our's
yours	your's
theirs	their's

- Do not confuse possessive pronouns with sound-alike contractions. Remember, possessive pronouns never include apostrophes.

Possessive Pronoun	*Contraction*
The dog licked its paw.	It's [it is] not fair.
This apartment is theirs.	There's [there is] the bus.
Whose turn is it?	Who's [who is] there?
Is this your hat?	You're [you are] absolutely right.

Writing Tip

Remember that *it's* is not a possessive pronoun. It is a contraction that means *it is*.

Computer Tip

Your computer's grammar checker is good at finding the places where you have incorrectly used a contraction instead of a possessive form—*it's* for *its*, for example. Always double-check what the grammar checker suggests, consulting a dictionary if you are not sure.

◆ PRACTICE 26.7

In each of the following sentences, circle the correct form (contraction or possessive pronoun) in parentheses.

Example: This is (you're/your) last chance.

1. The elephant sprayed water from (it's/its) trunk.
2. (There's/Theirs) something wrong with this engine.
3. According to the newspaper, (it's/its) supposed to rain tomorrow.
4. The Johnsons say the yellow rake is (there's/theirs).
5. The building was restored to (it's/its) former beauty.
6. (Who's/Whose) in charge of refreshments?
7. Erica says (you're/your) an excellent softball player.
8. Does anyone know (who's/whose) sweater this is?
9. I never use that vase because (it's/its) an antique.
10. (You're/Your) suggestion was the best one presented at the meeting.

ON THE WEB

For more practice revising the incorrect use of apostrophes, visit Exercise Central at <bedfordstmartins.com/foundationsfirst>.

◆ PRACTICE 26.8

In each of the following sentences, check the underlined words to be sure apostrophes are used correctly. If a correction needs to be made, cross out the word, and write the correct version above it. If the noun or pronoun is correct, write *C* above it.

Example: Tulips grew along the garden's (C) edge, even in ~~it's~~ (its) shadiest spots.

1. Songs about lover's trials and triumphs are always popular.
2. The worlds' population won't stop growing for some time.
3. Don't you think its a lovely evening?
4. Children are quick to say which toys are there's.
5. The committee reported it's findings in today's newsletter.
6. All the government agency's were closed.
7. Whose coming to your party?
8. If your such an expert, why can't you fix Lois' dishwasher?
9. You'll need five hundred resident's signatures on you're petition.
10. Both of Henrys sister's made the dresses they're wearing.

◆ PRACTICE 26.9

Write an original sentence for each of these possessive pronouns: *its, your, theirs*. Then, write a sentence for each of these contractions: *it's, you're, there's*. Be sure to use apostrophes only in contractions, not in possessive pronouns.

1. its

____

____

2. your

____

____

3. theirs

____

____

4. it's

____

____

5. you're

____

____

6. there's

____

____

◆ PRACTICE 26.10

Write a short paragraph that includes all these words: *it's, its, birds, bird's nest.*

____

____

____

____

____

■ REVISING AND EDITING

Look back at your response to the Seeing and Writing exercise on page 429. First, circle every apostrophe in your writing. Then, review this chapter to make sure that all the apostrophes in your response are used correctly and that you have not forgotten any necessary apostrophes.

CHAPTER REVIEW

◆ EDITING PRACTICE

Read the following essay, which contains some errors in the use of apostrophes. Edit it to eliminate errors by crossing out incorrect words and writing corrections above them. (Note that this is an informal essay, so contractions are acceptable.) The first sentence has been edited for you.

Dolphins: People with Fins?

dolphins

Tame ~~dolphin's~~ are a common sight at aquariums and water shows. People are fascinated by the dolphins friendly behavior. Many wild dolphins, too, seem comfortable around people. In some ways, the social pattern's of dolphins are'nt so different from those of humans. Maybe dolphins are attracted to humans because their social behavior is similar to our's.

Like people, dolphins socialize in different groups at different times.

Their not limited to a small set of companions. Humans shift from one group of friends or family members to another, and so do dolphins. Also like humans, dolphins tend to have several mates during their lives. The dolphins mating pattern isnt just biological. It's social as well. In fact, its sort of like the human practice of dating.

Dolphin family's also show some human traits. For example, young dolphins stay close to their mother's for several years. The mothers sometimes work together in groups to guard their calves safety. One mother might even babysit for another while shes busy elsewhere. And the family bond does'nt end when the offspring grow up. A mature dolphin may return to it's mothers side when the mother is giving birth to a new calf.

Finally, dolphins seem to pick their friends the same way people do. Dolphins tend to spend time with other's who are the same sex and age. In fact, many dolphins have one or two companions, similar to best friends, who's company they prefer. Male dolphins, especially, tend to have a couple of buddies their often found with. With so many things in common, its no wonder dolphins and humans seem to get along well.

◆ COLLABORATIVE ACTIVITIES

1. Working in a group of four and building on each of your responses to the Seeing and Writing exercise at the beginning of this chapter, think about how the definitions of "men's jobs" and "women's jobs" have changed in recent decades. Then, make two lists:

   - jobs that were once held only by men but are now also performed by women (such as firefighter)
   - jobs that were once held only by women but are now also performed by men (such as nurse)

2. Consulting the lists your group developed in activity 1, work in pairs. One pair of students in each group should list reasons why there should be "men's jobs" and "women's jobs," and one pair should list reasons why both men and women should be able to do any sort of work they choose. Use possessive forms whenever possible—for example, *women's earnings* rather than *the earnings of women.*
3. Bring to class a book, magazine, or newspaper whose style is informal—for example, a popular novel, an entertainment magazine, or the sports section of a newspaper. Working in a group, circle every contraction you can find on one page of each publication. Then, replace

each contraction with the words that combine to form it. Are your substitutions an improvement? (You may want to read a few paragraphs aloud before you reach a conclusion.)

4. *Composing original sentences* Work together with your group to write a total of seven original sentences. Three sentences should include contractions of a pronoun and a verb using an apostrophe (for example: *it's* = *it is*). Four sentences should use singular and plural nouns in the possessive form. Use at least one noun that ends in *-s* and at least one indefinite pronoun. When you have finished, check the sentences again to make sure you have no errors in grammar, punctuation, or spelling.

✓ REVIEW CHECKLIST: Using Apostrophes

- Use apostrophes to form contractions. (See 26A.)
- Use an apostrophe plus an *s* to form the possessive of singular nouns and indefinite pronouns. Even when a noun ends in *-s*, use an apostrophe plus an *s* to form the possessive. (See 26B.)
- Use an apostrophe alone to form the possessive of most plural nouns, including names. (See 26B.)
- Do not use apostrophes with plural nouns unless they are possessive. Do not use apostrophes with possessive pronouns. (See 26C.)

CHAPTER

27 Understanding Mechanics

PREVIEW

In this chapter, you will learn

- to capitalize proper nouns (27A)
- to punctuate direct quotations (27B)
- to set off titles of books, stories, and other works (27C)

■ SEEING AND WRITING

Look at the picture above. Then, write a paragraph in which you describe your favorite contemporary or classic cartoon. Be sure to name the most important characters and to quote some dialogue that you remember.

Word Power

contemporary current; modern

classic something typical or traditional; something that has lasting importance or worth

A Capitalizing Proper Nouns

A **proper noun** names a particular person, animal, place, object, or idea. Proper nouns are always capitalized. The list that follows explains and illustrates the rules for capitalizing proper nouns. It also includes some important exceptions to these rules.

- Always capitalize names of races, ethnic groups, tribes, nationalities, languages, and religions.

  The census data revealed a diverse community of Caucasians, African Americans, and Asian Americans, with a few Latino and Navajo residents. Native languages include English, Korean, and Spanish. Most people identified themselves as Catholic, Protestant, or Muslim.

Writing Tip

The words *black* and *white* are generally not capitalized when they refer to racial groups. However, *African American* and *Caucasian* are always capitalized.

- Capitalize names of specific people and any titles that go along with those names. In general, do not capitalize titles that are used without a name.

  In 2000, President Vicente Fox was elected to lead Mexico.

  The student body president met with the dean.

- Capitalize names of specific family members and their titles. Do not capitalize words that identify family relationships, including those introduced by possessive pronouns.

  Cousin Matt and Cousin Susie are the children of Mom's brother, Uncle Bill.

  My cousins Matt and Susie are the children of my mother's brother Bill, who is my uncle.

For advice on using articles with proper nouns, see 24F.

- Capitalize names of specific countries, cities, towns, bodies of water (lakes, rivers, oceans), streets, and so on. Do not capitalize words that identify unnamed places.

  The Liffey runs through Dublin.

  The river runs through the city.

- Capitalize names of specific geographical regions. Do not capitalize such words when they refer to a direction.

  Louis L'Amour's novels are set in the American West.

  We got lost after we turned west off the freeway.

- Capitalize names of specific buildings and monuments. Do not capitalize general references to buildings and monuments.

  He drove past the Space Needle and toward Pike's Market.

  He drove past the monument and toward the market.

- Capitalize names of specific groups, clubs, teams, and associations. Do not capitalize general references to groups of individuals.

  Members of the Teamsters' Union worked at the Democratic Party convention, the Backstreet Boys concert, and the Sixers-Pacers game.

  Members of the union worked at the party's convention, the rock group's concert, and the basketball teams' game.

For information on capitalizing titles of books, essays, and so on, see 27C.

- Capitalize names of specific historical periods, events, and documents. Do not capitalize general references to periods, events, or documents.

The Emancipation Proclamation was signed during the Civil War, not during Reconstruction.

The document was signed during the war, not during the postwar period.

- Capitalize names of businesses, government agencies, schools, and other institutions. Do not capitalize nonspecific references to such institutions.

Our local Burger King and McDonald's want to hire students from Lincoln High School and Brooklyn College.

Our local fast-food restaurants want to hire high school and college students.

- Capitalize brand names. Do not capitalize general references to kinds of products.

Jan put on her Rollerblades and skated off to Xerox her paper.

Jan put on her in-line skates and skated off to photocopy her paper.

Writing Tip

Trade names that have been part of the language for many years—*nylon,* for example—are no longer capitalized.

- Capitalize titles of specific academic courses. Do not capitalize names of general academic subject areas, except for proper nouns—for example, the name of a language or a country.

Calvin registered for English 101 and Psychology 302.

Calvin registered for English and psychology.

- Capitalize days of the week, months of the year, and holidays. Do not capitalize the names of the seasons (*summer, fall, winter, spring*).

Christmas, Chanukah, and Kwanzaa all fall in December.

Christmas, Chanukah, and Kwanzaa all fall in the winter.

◆ PRACTICE 27.1

Edit the following sentences, capitalizing letters and changing capitals to lowercase letters where necessary.

ON THE WEB

For more practice capitalizing proper nouns, visit Exercise Central at <bedfordstmartins.com/foundationsfirst>.

Example: Archaeologists study the Ojibwa at mackinac State Historic Park in michigan, a State where many members of the group live. [handwritten corrections: M, M, s]

1. The Ojibwa are the largest native american group in north america.
2. Today, they live near the Great lakes in the united states and canada.
3. The ojibwa made maple syrup that was something like the syrup sold in shoprite or safeway.
4. The Ojibwa migrated to the midwest from their original homes near the atlantic ocean.

5. A century before the revolutionary war, Europeans traveled West and met the native peoples who lived there.
6. Many modern Ojibwa live in the cities of Detroit and duluth and on rural Reservations.
7. The american indian movement is an Organization that calls attention to unfair treaties, such as the treaty of 1854.
8. Activist Winona LaDuke, who served as the Principal of an Ojibwa school, is also active in national politics.
9. In November 2000, LaDuke ran for Vice President on the green party ticket.
10. My cousin, aunt Sara's son, learned about the Ojibwa in American history 240.

◆ PRACTICE 27.2

Write a sentence that includes each of the following pairs of words. Capitalize where necessary. Each sentence should be at least six or seven words long.

Example: valentine's day/holiday

Stella's least favorite holiday is Valentine's Day.

1. aunt mary/aunt

____

2. johnson's department store/store

____

3. dr. casey/doctor

____

4. reverend jackson/minister

____

5. american history 210/history

____

6. donald duck/duck

____

B Punctuating Direct Quotations

A **direct quotation** reproduces the *exact* words of a speaker or writer. Direct quotations are always placed within quotation marks.

Brian said, "I've decided to go to business school."

Tolstoy wrote, "Happy families are all alike; every unhappy family is unhappy in its own way."

When a quotation is a complete sentence, as it is in the two examples above, it begins with a capital letter and ends with appropriate end punctuation (a period, a question mark, or an exclamation point). When a quotation falls at the end of a sentence, as it does in the examples above, the period is placed *inside* the quotation marks. If the quotation is a question or an exclamation, the question mark or exclamation point is also placed *inside* the quotation marks.

Regis asked, "Is that your final answer?"

When the vampire attacked, Ted cried, "Help me!"

FOCUS Identifying Tags

A direct quotation is usually accompanied by an **identifying tag**, a phrase—such as *Mike said* or *asked Jeanine*—that identifies the person whose words are being quoted. Identifying tags can appear in a variety of places in a sentence.

Identifying Tag at the Beginning

When the identifying tag comes before the quotation, it is followed by a comma.

Jamie announced, "I really need to cut up all my credit cards."

Identifying Tag at the End

When the identifying tag comes at the end of a sentence, it is followed by a period. A comma (or, sometimes, a question mark or exclamation point) inside the closing quotation marks separates the quotation from the identifying tag.

"I really need to cut up all my credit cards," Jamie announced.

"Do I really need to cut up all my credit cards?" asked Jamie.

Identifying Tag in the Middle

When the identifying tag comes in the middle of a quoted sentence, it is followed by a comma. The first part of the quotation is

(continued on the following page)

(continued from the previous page)

also followed by a comma, which is placed *inside* the quotation marks. Because the part of the quotation that follows the tag is not a new sentence, it does not begin with a capital letter.

> "I'll cut up all my credit cards," Jamie promised, "and then I'll start over."

Identifying Tag between Two Sentences

When the identifying tag comes between two quoted sentences, it is followed by a period, and the second quoted sentence begins with a capital letter.

> "Doing without credit cards will be good for me," Jamie decided. "Paying cash for everything will help me stick to my budget."

FOCUS Indirect Quotations

Be careful not to confuse direct and indirect quotations. A direct quotation reproduces someone's *exact* words, but an **indirect quotation** simply summarizes what was said or written.

Indirect quotations are not placed within quotation marks.

DIRECT QUOTATION — Martin Luther King Jr. said, "I have a dream."

INDIRECT QUOTATION — Martin Luther King Jr. said that he had a dream.

Writing Tip

Note that an indirect quotation is usually introduced by the word *that*.

◆ PRACTICE 27.3

Rewrite each of the following sentences twice. In the first version, place the identifying tag at the end of the sentence. In the second version, place the identifying tag in the middle of the sentence. Be sure to check punctuation and capitalization carefully.

Example: Joe said, "The grapes don't taste as good as they look."

"The grapes don't taste as good as they look," Joe said.

"The grapes," Joe said, "don't taste as good as they look."

1. Sue said, "These clothes are too small for me."

____

____

ON THE WEB

For more practice punctuating direct quotations, visit Exercise Central at <bedfordstmartins.com/foundationsfirst>.

2. Pasqual claimed, "I won the team's soccer match all by myself."

____

____

3. The instructor said, "The exam should not be too difficult."

____

____

4. Councilman Gonzalez announced, "I will do my best to defeat the new tax law."

____

____

____

____

5. The poet Emily Dickinson wrote, "Tell all the truth but tell it slant."

____

____

◆ PRACTICE 27.4

In the following sentences containing direct quotations, first underline the identifying tag. Then, punctuate the quotation correctly, adding capital letters where necessary.

Example: "Injustice anywhere," said Dr. Martin Luther King Jr., "is a threat to justice everywhere."

1. Dorothy Parker said the cure for boredom is curiosity.
2. The guide announced whatever you do, don't leave the group.
3. Why does it always rain on my birthday Patrice asked.
4. Move along, everyone the officer shouted.
5. If you lose this tape Rebecca insisted I'll never lend you anything again.
6. The game isn't over till it's over said baseball legend Yogi Berra.
7. When I walked in, the instructor was saying please be sure to arrive on time.
8. If we get separated Paul asked where should I meet you?

9. High school Kurt Vonnegut observed is closer to the core of the American experience than anything I can think of.
10. I not only use all the brains that I have said Woodrow Wilson but all that I can borrow.

◆ PRACTICE 27.5

The following quotations are followed in parentheses by the names of the people who wrote or said them. On the blank lines, write a sentence that includes the quotation and places the identifying tag in the position that the directions specify. Be sure to punctuate and capitalize correctly.

Example: Let's ask for directions before we get lost. (said by Michelle)

Identifying tag in the middle: "Let's ask for directions," Michelle said, "before we get lost."

1. Fiction is the truth inside the lie. (said by Stephen King)

   Identifying tag at the beginning: ______________________

   ____

2. What's up? (asked by Hector)

   Identifying tag at the end: ______________________

   ____

3. Express yourself. (said by Madonna)

   Identifying tag at the end: ______________________

   ____

4. Brevity is the soul of wit. (written by William Shakespeare)

   Identifying tag at the beginning: ______________________

   ____

5. I am the greatest! (proclaimed by heavyweight champion Muhammad Ali)

   Identifying tag at the end: ______________________

   ____

6. Why is this bag of rice in the refrigerator? (asked by Juan's sister)

   Identifying tag at the beginning: ______________________

   ____

7. No one can make you feel inferior without your consent. (written by Eleanor Roosevelt)

   Identifying tag at the end: ______________________________

   ____

8. Taku is not home. He went to the movies. (said by Hannah)

   Identifying tag in the middle: ______________________________

   ____

9. The best way to have a good idea is to have lots of ideas. (said by scientist Linus Pauling)

   Identifying tag in the middle: ______________________________

   ____

10. Get plenty of rest. You should feel better in a week or so. (said by Dr. Jagu)

    Identifying tag in the middle: ______________________________

    ____

C Setting Off Titles of Books, Stories, and Other Works

Some titles are *italicized* (or underlined to indicate italics). Others are enclosed in quotation marks. In general, underline titles of books and other long works, and enclose titles of shorter works (stories, essays, poems, and so on) in quotation marks.

The following chart indicates which titles should be italicized and which should be enclosed in quotation marks.

Italicized Titles

Books: *The Joy Luck Club*
Newspapers: the *Los Angeles Times*
Magazines: *People, Latina*
Record albums: *Motown Legends*
Long poems: *Paradise Lost*
Plays: *Our Town, Death of a Salesman*
Films: *Lord of the Rings*
Television and radio series: *Eyes on the Prize*

Titles in Quotation Marks

Book chapters: "Writing a Paragraph"
Short stories: "The Lottery"
Essays and articles: "Shooting an Elephant"
Short poems: "The Road Not Taken"
Songs: "The Star-Spangled Banner"
Individual episodes of television or radio series: "The Montgomery Bus Boycott" (episode of *Eyes on the Prize*)

Writing Tip

When you type one of your own papers, do not underline your title or enclose it in quotation marks. Only titles of *published works* are set off in this way.

FOCUS Capitalizing in Titles

Capitalize the first letters of all important words in titles. Do not capitalize an **article** (*a, an,* or *the*), a **preposition** (*to, of, around,* and so on), or a **coordinating conjunction**—unless it is the first or last word of the title (*On the Road, No Way Out*).

◆ PRACTICE 27.6

In each of the following sentences, underline or insert quotation marks around titles. (Remember that titles of books and other long works are underlined and that titles of stories, essays, and other shorter works are enclosed in quotation marks.)

Example: A Good Man Is Hard to Find, a book of stories by Flannery O'Connor, includes "The Life You Save May Be Your Own" and "Good Country People."

ON THE WEB
For more practice setting off titles of books, stories, and other works, visit Exercise Central at <bedfordstmartins.com/foundationsfirst>.

1. The show A Prairie Home Companion has been on public radio for many years.
2. Norah Jones's first album, Come Away with Me, contained the award-winning song Come Away with Me.
3. Did you see the article Chocolate: A Sweet Life after Bitter Start in Wednesday's New York Times?
4. The Partly Cloudy Patriot, a collection of essays by Sarah Vowell, includes The Nerd Voice and Tom Cruise Makes Me Nervous.
5. The song And All That Jazz was written for the musical Chicago.
6. Sylvia Plath's poem The Moon and the Yew Tree was published in Ariel, her best-known book.
7. The textbook Foundations First includes the chapter Understanding Mechanics.
8. When the movie Troy came out, Newsweek featured a review of the film.
9. After studying Shakespeare's play Hamlet, we will read John Milton's book-length poem Paradise Lost.

10. On the Beach was the last episode in the popular television series ER in which Anthony Edwards appeared.

◆ PRACTICE 27.7

Edit the following sentences, capitalizing letters where necessary in titles.

Example: The movie *charley* was based on the short story "flowers for algernon."

1. Lucy's favorite novel is *for whom the bell tolls.*
2. Jack London's short story "to build a fire" is a classic.
3. Recent television cartoons created for adults include *the simpsons* and *king of the hill.*
4. The soundtrack for the movie *the matrix* features songs such as "ultra-sonic sound" and "wake up."
5. The articles "stream of consciousness" and "school's out" in *wired* magazine focus on new technology.

■ REVISING AND EDITING

Look back at your response to the Seeing and Writing exercise on page 440. Check your work carefully. Have you capitalized all proper nouns? Have you used quotation marks correctly to set off direct quotations? Have you punctuated direct quotations correctly? Have you underlined the title of the cartoon you chose to write about and used capital letters throughout? Edit where necessary.

CHAPTER REVIEW

◆ EDITING PRACTICE

Read the following essay, which contains errors in capitalization and in the use of direct quotations and titles. Then, edit the passage to correct the errors. The first sentence has been edited for you.

Until recently, minority actors had trouble finding work in hollywood, where most films starred actors who had european backgrounds. This was true even when the characters they played were Asian, native american, or Hispanic. One example is the movie "West side Story." Natalie Wood, whose parents were Russian immigrants, played the character Maria, who was Puerto Rican. Wood assumed a Puerto Rican accent when she sang songs such as *I Feel Pretty* and *Tonight.*

Anna May Wong

Anna May Wong was an exception to the rule. For years, she was the most famous Chinese-American actress in hollywood. She grew up in Los Angeles, california, and began appearing in movies when she was thirteen years old. In 1924, Wong played her first major role in *The Thief of Bagdad.* Her real name was Wong Liu Tsong. An Executive at a movie studio changed her name to make it sound more American.

Since then, the opportunities for minorities in the movies have grown. In 2002, when Halle Berry and denzel Washington both received academy awards, some people said it was the beginning of a new era for minorities in hollywood. Berry, who won for her performance in Monster's Ball, was the first African-american woman to win the Award. She said in her acceptance speech, This is for every faceless woman who now has a chance because the door tonight has been opened.

Halle Berry

Other people noted, however, that despite the well-deserved recognition of these two prominent minority actors, hollywood still has a long way to go. "Only time will tell," one observer said, "if actors of color will have more opportunities to star in Oscar-potential roles." In the meantime, executives are discovering that having a diverse cast can be an advantage at the Box Office. Actors like Lucy Liu, Will Smith, and Salma Hayek have proven that faces of all colors can sell tickets.

◆ COLLABORATIVE ACTIVITIES

1. Working in a small group, make a list of at least fifteen famous people, places, and historical or news events you have heard of or read about recently. Be sure to capitalize all proper nouns. Next, choose three of

the items on your list, and work together to write a sentence about each person, place, or event, explaining why it is important. Then, exchange papers with another group. Check one another's papers to be sure capital letters are used correctly.

2. Imagine that you and the other members of your group are in charge of creating the American Entertainment Hall of Fame. Make lists of your favorite songs, movies, and television shows. When you have finished, choose one item from each person's list. Then, write a sentence explaining why that song, movie, or television show belongs in the American Entertainment Hall of Fame. When you have finished, exchange papers with another group. Check one another's papers to be sure capital letters, quotation marks, and underlining are used correctly.
3. Working in a group of four, choose two people in the group to take different positions on a topic such as the drinking age, gun control, or required college courses. Next, have these two people present their views to the group. While the discussion is going on, each of the two remaining group members should record a few key statements by each participant. After the discussion has ended, work together to write a paragraph that includes the viewpoints of both participants. Place all direct quotations within quotation marks, and include identifying tags that clearly indicate which person is speaking. When you have finished, exchange paragraphs with another group, and check each other's papers to be sure capital letters and quotation marks are used correctly and all quotations are punctuated correctly.
4. *Composing original sentences* Working in a group of four, write a five- or six-sentence paragraph about your city or neighborhood, capitalizing proper nouns to identify important places, public officials, schools, and natural landmarks. Include at least one direct quotation and one title of a local newspaper and an article in that paper. (The quotation and the article title can be made up.) Then, exchange paragraphs with another group. Check each other's work to be sure capitals and quotation marks are used correctly, and make sure all quotations are punctuated correctly. When you have finished, check your own group's paragraph again to make sure you have corrected any errors in grammar, punctuation, or spelling.

✓ REVIEW CHECKLIST: Understanding Mechanics

- ☐ Capitalize proper nouns. (See 27A.)
- ☐ Always place direct quotations within quotation marks. (See 27B.)
- ☐ In titles, capitalize all important words, as well as the first and the last words. Use quotation marks or underline to set off titles. (See 27C.)

CHAPTER

28

Understanding Spelling

PREVIEW

In this chapter, you will learn

- to become a better speller (28A)
- to know when to use *ie* and *ei* (28B)
- to understand prefixes (28C)
- to understand suffixes (28D)

SEEING AND WRITING

Do you think local, state, and federal governments are right to pass laws that prohibit smoking in public places? Look at the picture above, and then write a paragraph in which you answer this question.

Word Power

ban to forbid somebody from doing something

obligation a course of action demanded of a person by law or conscience

ostracize to exclude from a group

prohibit to forbid

A Becoming a Better Speller

Teachers and employers will expect you to be able to recognize and correct misspelled words. The following suggestions can help you become a better speller.

- *Use a spell checker.* Always use a spell checker if you are writing on a computer. It will identify and correct many typos and misspelled words.

However, keep in mind that spell checkers have limitations. For one thing, they will not identify some misspelled words—for example, some foreign words and proper nouns. In addition, they do not identify typographical errors that create words (*form* instead of *from*) or words that you have used incorrectly (*there* for *their*). Because of these limitations, you still have to know how to spell—even if you do use a spell checker.

- *Use a dictionary.* As you proofread, circle words whose spellings you are not sure of. Look up these words in a dictionary to make sure they are spelled correctly.
- *Proofread carefully.* If spelling is your biggest problem, proofread first for misspellings. Then, go back and check for all other errors. (You might try checking your spelling by starting with the last sentence of your paper and reading backwards to the beginning. This strategy enables you to concentrate on one word at a time without being distracted by the logic and sequence of your ideas.)
- *Keep a personal spelling list.* Write down all the words you misspell. If you keep a writing journal, set aside a few pages in the back for a spelling list. Keep a record of the words your spell checker highlights, and write down any misspelled words that your instructor identifies. (These will usually be circled or marked *sp.*)
- *Look for patterns in your misspellings.* Do you have trouble forming plurals? Do you misspell words with *ei* combinations? Once you have identified these problems, you can focus on eliminating them.
- *Learn the basic spelling rules.* Memorize the spelling rules outlined in this chapter. Each rule you learn can help you spell many words correctly.
- *Review commonly confused words.* Study the commonly confused words in Chapter 29. If any of these words give you trouble, add them to your personal spelling list.
- *Make flash cards.* Copy down words that constantly give you trouble on 3- by 5-inch cards. Review these words when you have time.
- *Use memory cues.* Think of a memory cue that will help you remember how to spell each particularly troublesome word. For example, remembering that *definite* contains the word *finite* will help you remember that *definite* is spelled with an *i,* not an *a.*
- *Learn how to spell the most frequently misspelled words.* Study the words on the following list. If a word gives you trouble, add it to your personal spelling list.

Writing Tip

The best place to check spelling is a good college dictionary, which will also tell you how to pronounce a word and which syllables to stress. For more on using a dictionary, see the appendix of this book, "Building Word Power."

Some Frequently Misspelled Words

across	benefit	definitely	everything
address	calendar	dependent	exercise
all right	cannot	describe	experience
a lot	careful	develop	finally
argument	careless	disappoint	forty
beautiful	cemetery	early	fulfill
becoming	certain	embarrass	generally
beginning	crowded	entrance	government
believe	definite	environment	grammar

(continued on the following page)

(continued from the previous page)

harass	occasion	probably	tomato
height	occur	professor	tomatoes
holiday	occurred	receive	truly
integration	occurrences	recognize	until
intelligence	occurring	reference	usually
interest	occurs	restaurant	Wednesday
interfere	personnel	roommate	weird
judgment	possible	secretary	window
loneliness	potato	sentence	withhold
medicine	potatoes	separate	woman
minute	prejudice	speech	women
necessary	prescription	studying	writing
noticeable	privilege	surprise	written

FOCUS Vowels and Consonants

Knowing which letters are vowels and which are consonants will help you understand the spelling rules presented in this chapter.

VOWELS *a, e, i, o, u*

CONSONANTS *b, c, d, f, g, h, j, k, l, m, n, p, q, r, s, t, v, w, x, z*

The letter *y* may be considered either a vowel or a consonant, depending on how it is pronounced. In *young, y* acts as a consonant because it has the sound of *y;* in *truly,* it acts as a vowel because it has the sound of *ee.*

B Deciding between *ie* and *ei*

Memorize this rule: *i* before *e,* except after *c,* or when *ei* sounds like *ay* as in *neighbor* and *weigh.*

i before e	*except after c*	*or when ei is pronounced ay*
achieve	ceiling	eight
believe	conceive	freight
friend	deceive	neighbor
		weigh

FOCUS Exceptions to the "*i* before *e*" Rule

There are some exceptions to the "*i* before *e*" rule. The exceptions follow no pattern, so you must memorize them.

ancient	foreign	neither	society
caffeine	height	science	species
conscience	leisure	seize	weird
either			

ON THE WEB
For more practice deciding between ie *and* ei, *visit Exercise Central at <bedfordstmartins .com/foundationsfirst>.*

◆ PRACTICE 28.1

In each of the following sentences, proofread the underlined words for correct spelling. If a correction needs to be made, cross out the incorrect words, and write the correct spelling above it. If the word is spelled correctly, write *C* above it.

Example: The winner of the college science (C) competition will ~~recieve~~ receive a full scholarship.

1. If you believe in yourself, you will find it easier to acheive your goals.
2. Sometimes an emergency can turn nieghbors into friends.
3. Niether one of these dresses fits, and the colors aren't flattering either.
4. The frieght charge depends on the wieght of the package.
5. In the future, people will have more leisure than we can conceive of.
6. The children could not control thier grief over the death of the dog.
7. The prosperous soceity of ancient Rome depended on the labor of slaves.
8. The hieght of the cieling was impressive.
9. A criminal may confess to releive a guilty conscience.
10. That unusual species of butterfly must have migrated here from a foriegn country.

C Understanding Prefixes

A **prefix** is a group of letters that is added to the beginning of a word and that changes the word's meaning. Adding a prefix to a word never changes the spelling of the original word.

dis + service = disservice
un + able = unable
co + operate = cooperate

pre + heat = preheat
un + natural = unnatural
over + rate = overrate

◆ PRACTICE 28.2

Write in the blank the new word that results when the given prefix is added to each of the following words.

Example: pre + view = *preview*

1. un + easy = ______
2. dis + satisfied = ______
3. over + cook = ______
4. co + exist = ______
5. un + wind = ______
6. dis + respect = ______
7. under + pay = ______
8. non + sense = ______
9. pre + war = ______
10. tele + communications = ______

ON THE WEB
For more practice understanding prefixes, visit Exercise Central at <bedfordstmartins .com/foundationsfirst>.

D Understanding Suffixes

A **suffix** is a group of letters that is added to the end of a word and that changes the word's meaning or its part of speech. Adding a suffix to a word can cause changes in the spelling of the original word.

Words Ending in Silent *e*

A **silent *e*** is an *e* that is not pronounced. If a word ends with a silent *e*, drop the *e* if the suffix you are adding begins with a vowel.

DROP THE *E*

hope + ing = hoping
continue + ous = continuous

dance + er = dancer
insure + able = insurable

EXCEPTIONS

change + able = changeable
notice + able = noticeable

courage + ous = courageous
replace + able = replaceable

Keep the *e* if the suffix begins with a consonant.

KEEP THE *E*

hope + ful = hopeful
excite + ment = excitement
bore + dom = boredom
same + ness = sameness

EXCEPTIONS

argue + ment = argument
judge + ment = judgment
true + ly = truly
nine + th = ninth

◆ PRACTICE 28.3

ON THE WEB
For more practice understanding suffixes, visit Exercise Central at <bedfordstmartins.com/foundationsfirst>.

Write in the blank the new word that results when the given suffix is added to each of the following words.

Examples

decide + ing = *deciding*

lone + ly = *lonely*

1. adore + able = ______
2. definite + ly = ______
3. judge + ment = ______
4. care + ful = ______
5. whistle + ed = ______
6. invite + ation = ______
7. true + ly = ______
8. dine + ing = ______
9. insure + ance = ______
10. dedicate + ion = ______
11. sense + less = ______
12. disgrace + ful = ______
13. notice + able = ______
14. become + ing = ______
15. amuse + ment = ______
16. write + er = ______
17. imagine + ation = ______
18. place + ment = ______
19. microscope + ic = ______
20. simple + ly = ______

Words Ending in *-y*

When you add a suffix to a word that ends in *-y*, change the *y* to an *i* if the letter before the *y* is a consonant.

CHANGE *Y* TO *I*

beauty + ful = beautiful
try + ed = tried
busy + ly = busily
friendly + er = friendlier

EXCEPTIONS

Keep the *y* if the suffix starts with an *i*.

cry + ing = crying
baby + ish = babyish

Keep the *y* when you add a suffix to some one-syllable words.

shy + er = shyer   dry + ness = dryness

Keep the *y* if the letter before the *y* is a vowel.

KEEP THE *Y*

annoy + ance = annoyance   enjoy + ment = enjoyment
play + ful = playful   display + ed = displayed

EXCEPTIONS

day + ly = daily   say + ed = said
gay + ly = gaily   pay + ed = paid

◆ PRACTICE 28.4

Write in the blank the new word that results when the given suffix is added to each of the following words.

Examples

cry + ed = *cried*

fry + ing = *frying*

employ + ment = *employment*

1. try + ing = ______
2. pay + ed = ______
3. noisy + ly = ______
4. buy + er = ______
5. destroy + ed = ______
6. annoy + ance = ______
7. dry + ness = ______
8. play + ful = ______
9. tiny + er = ______
10. happy + ness = ______
11. busy + ly = ______
12. marry + es = ______
13. reply + ed = ______
14. fifty + eth = ______
15. thirty + ish = ______
16. lonely + ness = ______
17. joy + ful = ______
18. spy + ed = ______
19. day + ly = ______
20. lively + hood = ______

Doubling the Final Consonant

When you add a suffix that begins with a vowel—for example, *-ed, -er,* or *-ing*—double the final consonant in the original word if both these criteria apply: (1) if the last three letters of the word have a consonant-vowel-consonant pattern (cvc) and (2) if the word has one syllable or the last syllable is stressed.

FINAL CONSONANT DOUBLED

cut	+	ing	=	cutting (cvc—one syllable)
bat	+	er	=	batter (cvc—one syllable)
pet	+	ed	=	petted (cvc—one syllable)
commit	+	ed	=	committed (cvc—stress is on last syllable)
occur	+	ing	=	occurring (cvc—stress is on last syllable)

FINAL CONSONANT NOT DOUBLED

answer	+	ed	=	answered (cvc—stress is not on last syllable)
happen	+	ing	=	happening (cvc—stress is not on last syllable)
act	+	ing	=	acting (no cvc)

◆ PRACTICE 28.5

Write in the blank the new word that results when the given suffix is added to each of the following words.

Examples

hit + ing = *hitting*

slow + er = *slower*

1. shop + er = ______
2. squeak + ing = ______
3. prefer + ed = ______
4. thin + est = ______
5. climb + ed = ______
6. wrap + ing = ______
7. fair + est = ______
8. regret + ed = ______
9. begin + ing = ______
10. star + ed = ______
11. write + en = ______
12. swim + er = ______
13. appeal + ing = ______
14. excel + ed = ______
15. exist + ing = ______
16. occur + ed = ______
17. run + er = ______
18. commit + ed = ______
19. trap + er = ______
20. occur + ence = ______

■ REVISING AND EDITING

Type your response to the Seeing and Writing exercise on page 453 if you have not already done so. Then, run a spell check. Did the computer pick up all the errors? Which did it identify? Which did it miss? Correct all the spelling errors in your Seeing and Writing exercise.

CHAPTER REVIEW

◆ EDITING PRACTICE

Read the following essay, which contains spelling errors. As you read, identify the words you think are misspelled. Then, check the list on pages 454–455. If you do not find them there, check a dictionary. Finally, cross out each incorrectly spelled word, and write the correct spelling above the line. The first sentence has been corrected for you.

Body Language

When I was invited to a job ~~interveiw~~ interview last month, I decided to prepare by learning from the ~~expereinces~~ experiences of others. I asked my freinds what to wear, what to say, and how to show that I was qualifyed. An aquaintance who works in a personell department gave me an article titled "Body Language Tips: Get Your Dream Job!" Naturaly, I read the article, and I got a few more helpful hints. Because I got the job, I asume my strategies worked, so let me pass them along.

Body language, or body and facial movments, can certanly reveal alot about a person. In fact, some sceintists claim that body language comunicates more than speech does. Gestures, smiles, posture, eye contact, and even the position of one's head, arms, and legs all can revele whether a person is honest or lying, interested or bored, defensive or coperative.

Using hand gestures to show enthusiasm during a job interview

The article explained how to use body language to do well in an interview. The advice was to maintain eye contact but not to stare at the interviewer. The point is to look intrested without harrassing the interviewer. The experts also said to use hand gestures to show enthusiasm. Again, the trick is not to overdo this because it can make you seem agressive or just plain wierd. A suprising warning was not to cross your arms, which can make you look stubborn. Finaly, at the end of the interview, give the interviewer a firm handshake to show that you are honest and trustworthy.

Maintaining eye contact during a job interview

These tips on body language came in handy at my job interview. And, as they say, sucess speaks for itself.

◆ COLLABORATIVE ACTIVITIES

1. Working with a partner, test each other on the list of frequently misspelled words on pages 454–455. Then, make a list of the words you misspelled, and study these words, using flash cards and memory cues if necessary. Retake the test until you have learned all the misspelled words.
2. Create a personal spelling list, checking a dictionary for the correct spelling of each word. Then, try to identify patterns in your misspelling habits, and memorize the rules and exceptions that apply to your misspellings. Working with a partner, test each other on these words.
3. Work in a small group to create a spelling test for another group. The test can be a list of words, or it can be a paragraph in which you have intentionally misspelled some words. Correct the other group's test.
4. *Composing original sentences* Choose ten of the most troublesome words from your personal spelling list. Then, write a sentence using each word. When you have finished, exchange sentences with another student, and correct any errors in grammar, punctuation, or spelling.

✓ REVIEW CHECKLIST: Understanding Spelling

- Follow the steps to becoming a better speller. (See 28A.)
- *I* comes before *e*, except after *c* or in any *ay* sound, as in *neighbor* and *weigh*. (See 28B.)
- Adding a prefix to a word never affects the word's spelling. (See 28C.)
- Adding a suffix to a word may change the word's spelling. (See 28D.)
- When a word ends with a silent *e*, drop the *e* if the suffix begins with a vowel. Keep the *e* if the suffix begins with a consonant. (See 28D.)
- When you add a suffix to a word that ends with a *-y*, change the *y* to an *i* if the letter before the *y* is a consonant. Keep the *y* if the letter before the *y* is a vowel. (See 28D.)
- When you add a suffix that begins with a vowel, double the final consonant in the original word if (1) the last three letters of the word have a consonant-vowel-consonant pattern (cvc), and (2) the word has one syllable, or the last syllable is stressed. (See 28D.)

CHAPTER

29

Learning Commonly Confused Words

PREVIEW

- In this chapter, you will learn to distinguish word pairs that are often confused.

SEEING AND WRITING

What does America mean to you? Look at the picture above, which depicts a naturalization ceremony, and then write a paragraph in which you answer this question.

Word Power

immigrant a person who leaves one country to permanently settle in another

multicultural of or relating to many cultures

mobility the movement of people from one social group, class, or level to another

naturalization the process of gaining citizenship

Some English words cause spelling problems because they look or sound like other words. The following word pairs are often confused. Learning to distinguish them can help you become a better speller.

Accept/Except *Accept* means "to receive something." *Except* means "with the exception of."

"I accept your challenge," said Alexander Hamilton to Aaron Burr.

Everyone except Darryl visited the museum.

Computer Tip

Your computer's grammar checker can identify many commonly confused words. The word processor's Help files can show you a list of words that it can find.

Affect/Effect *Affect* is a verb meaning "to influence." *Effect* is a noun meaning "result" and sometimes a verb meaning "to bring about."

Jodi's job could affect her grades.

Overexposure to sun can have a long-term effect on skin.

Commissioner Williams tried to effect changes in police procedure.

All ready/Already *All ready* means "completely prepared." *Already* means "previously, before."

Serge was all ready to take the history test.

Gina had already been to Italy.

Brake/Break *Brake* means "a device to slow or stop a vehicle." *Break* means "to smash" or "to detach."

Peter got into an accident because his foot slipped off the brake.

Babe Ruth bragged that no one would ever break his home-run record.

Buy/By *Buy* means "to purchase." *By* is a preposition meaning "close to" or "next to" or "by means of."

Tina wanted to buy a laptop.

He drove by but didn't stop.

He stayed by her side all the way to the hospital.

Malcolm X wanted "freedom by any means necessary."

◆ PRACTICE 29.1

ON THE WEB
For more practice identifying word pairs that are often confused, visit Exercise Central at <bedfordstmartins.com/foundationsfirst>.

Proofread the underlined words in the following sentences for correct spelling. If a correction needs to be made, cross out the incorrect word, and write the correct spelling above it. If the word is spelled correctly, write *C* above it.

Example: The ~~breaks~~ brakes on this car work well, except (C) on icy roads.

1. The sign in the shop read, "If you break any glass item, you have to buy it."
2. Brad was already for the beach except for having forgotten his sunglasses.
3. Some medications effect a person's concentration by causing drowsiness.
4. If we hope to affect change in our government, we have to except our obligation to vote.
5. The college basketball player had already accepted an offer from a professional team by the end of his junior year.
6. Gervase plans to buy a car with antilock breaks.

7. Buy the way, I've all ready taken that course.
8. Mild stress, such as the excitement before a test, can effect a person in a positive way, whereas long-term stress usually has a negative affect.
9. The excited contestant was all ready to accept the prize money she had won.
10. Participating in sports can affect young people strongly and affect a change for the better in their ability to get along with others.

Conscience/Conscious *Conscience* refers to the part of the mind that urges a person to choose right over wrong. *Conscious* means "aware" or "deliberate."

After he cheated at cards, his conscience started to bother him.

As she walked through the woods, she became conscious of the hum of insects.

Elliott made a conscious decision to stop smoking.

Everyday/Every day *Everyday* is a single word that means "ordinary" or "common." *Every day* is two words that mean "occurring daily."

I Love Lucy was a successful comedy show because it appealed to everyday people.

Every day, Lucy and Ethel would find a new way to get into trouble.

Fine/Find *Fine* means "superior quality" or "a sum of money paid as a penalty." *Find* means "to locate."

He sang a fine solo at church last Sunday.

Demi had to pay a fine for speeding.

Some people still use a willow rod to find water.

Hear/Here *Hear* means "to perceive sound by ear." *Here* means "at or in this place."

I moved to the front so I could hear the speaker.

My great-grandfather came here in 1883.

Its/It's *Its* is the possessive form of *it*. *It's* is the contraction of *it is* or *it has*.

The airline canceled its flights because of the snow.

It's twelve o'clock, and we're late.

Ever since it's been in the accident, the car has rattled.

◆ PRACTICE 29.2

Proofread the underlined words in the following sentences for correct spelling. If a correction needs to be made, cross out the incorrect word, and write the correct spelling above it. If the word is spelled correctly, write *C* above it.

Example: Every day, we ~~fine~~ new challenges to face. (C above "Every day"; *find* above "fine")

1. Sarita became conscience of someone staring at her and turned to discover that it was Tony.
2. "Its been a long time since I've seen you here," Tony remarked to Sarita.
3. Sarita smiled as she said, "Its a great place to here jazz."
4. Paul hated paying the fine for parking in a disabled spot, but his conscious bothered him more than losing the money.
5. Everyday, the dog eats it's dinner at precisely 12:00 noon.
6. As soon as a child becomes conscious of right and wrong, his or her conscience begins to develop.
7. This week, everyday has been fine weather.
8. You will fine an outstanding collection of American art right hear in the college museum.
9. The restaurant made a conscience effort to enforce it's "no smoking" policy.
10. The wind had stopped its roaring, but in my mind, I could still hear it.

Know/Knew/New/No *Know* means "to have an understanding of" or "to have fixed in the mind." *Knew* is the past tense form of the verb *know. New* means "recent or never used." *No* expresses a negative response.

I know there will be a lunar eclipse tonight.
He knew how to install a new light switch.
There are no bananas in the fruit bowl.

Lie/Lay *Lie* means "to rest or recline." The past tense of *lie* is *lay. Lay* means "to put or place something down." The past tense of *lay* is *laid.*

Every Sunday, I lie in bed until noon.
They lay on the grass until it began to rain, and then they went home.
Tammy told Carl to lay his cards on the table.
Brooke and Cassia finally laid down their hockey sticks.

Loose/Lose *Loose* means "not fastened" or "not attached securely." *Lose* means "to mislay" or "to misplace."

In the 1940s, many women wore loose-fitting pants.
Sometimes I lose my keys.

Mine/Mind *Mine* is a possessive pronoun that indicates ownership. *Mind* can be a noun meaning "human consciousness" or "intelligence" or a verb meaning "to obey" or "to attend to."

That red mountain bike is mine.

A mind is a terrible thing to waste.

"Mind your manners when you visit your grandmother," Dad said.

Passed/Past *Passed* is the past tense of the verb *pass*. It means "moved by" or "succeeded in." *Past* is a noun meaning "earlier than the present time."

The car that passed me must have been doing more than eighty miles an hour.

David finally passed his driving test.

The novel was set in the past.

Peace/Piece *Peace* means "the absence of war" or "calm." *Piece* means "a part of something."

The prime minister thought he had achieved peace with honor.

My peace of mind was destroyed when the flying saucer landed.

"Have a piece of cake," said Marie.

◆ PRACTICE 29.3

Proofread the underlined words in the following sentences for correct spelling. If a correction needs to be made, cross out the incorrect word, and write the correct spelling above it. If the word is spelled correctly, write *C* above it.

Example: Heads of state ~~no~~ know that peace (C) is hard to achieve.

1. Everyone was amazed when the troops lay down their weapons and went home in peace.
2. The child new he should not eat another peace of candy, but he did it anyway.
3. In the passed, it was more important to mine one's manners than it is today.
4. Jamal past his chemistry final with a high grade, as we knew he would.
5. I loose my way every time I drive to the mall.
6. The car passed us as if there were know speed limit.
7. Janet decided to lay on a lounge chair and enjoy the peace of the garden.

8. The violinist was able to finish playing the piece even though one string had come loose.
9. The new dog had to be trained not to lay on the couch.
10. The children were warned to mine the babysitter, or they would loose their television-watching privileges.

Plain/Plane *Plain* means "simple, not elaborate." *Plane* is the shortened form of *airplane*.

Sometimes the Amish are referred to as the plain people.

Chuck Yeager was the first person to fly a plane faster than sound.

Principal/Principle *Principal* means "first" or "highest" or "the head of a school." *Principle* means "a law or basic assumption."

She had the principal role in the movie.

I'll never forget the day the principal called me into his office.

It was against his principles to tell a lie.

Quiet/Quit/Quite *Quiet* means "free of noise" or "still." *Quit* means "to leave a job" or "to give up." *Quite* means "actually" or "very."

Jane looked forward to the quiet evenings at the lake.

Sammy quit his job and followed the girls into the parking lot.

"You haven't quite got the hang of it yet," she said.

After practicing all summer, Tamika got quite good at softball.

Raise/Rise *Raise* means "to elevate" or "to increase in size, quantity, or worth." The past tense of *raise* is *raised. Rise* means "to stand up" or "to move from a lower position to a higher position." The past tense of *rise* is *rose.*

Carlos raises his hand when the teacher asks for volunteers.

They raised the money for the down payment.

The fans rise every time their team scores a touchdown.

Sarah rose before dawn so she could see the sunrise.

Right/Write *Right* means "correct" or "the opposite of left." *Write* means "to form letters with a writing instrument."

If you turn right at the corner, you will be going in the right direction.

All students are required to write three short papers.

Sit/Set *Sit* means "to assume a sitting position." The past tense of *sit* is *sat. Set* means "to put down or place" or "to adjust something to a desired position." The past tense of *set* is *set.*

I usually sit in the front row at the movies.

They sat at the clinic waiting for their names to be called.

Every semester I set goals for myself.

Elizabeth set the mail on the kitchen table and left for work.

Suppose/Supposed *Suppose* means "to consider" or "to assume." *Supposed* is both the past tense and the past participle of *suppose. Supposed* also means "expected" or "required." (Note that when *supposed* has this meaning, it is followed by *to.*)

Suppose researchers found a cure for AIDS tomorrow.

We supposed the movie would be over by ten o'clock.

You were supposed to finish a draft of the report by today.

◆ PRACTICE 29.4

Proofread the underlined words in the following sentences for correct spelling. If a correction needs to be made, cross out the incorrect word, and write the correct spelling above it. If the word is spelled correctly, write *C* above it.

Example: Everyone in the creative writing class was ~~suppose~~ *supposed* to write (*C*) a short autobiography.

1. According to Miss Manners, you are supposed to raise from your seat when an older person enters the room.
2. The school board hasn't quite selected a new principle for the high school yet.
3. The dress Lindsay is making started out rather plane but is now quite fancy.
4. We watched as the plane raised slowly and disappeared in the clouds.
5. All she wanted was a quite place to set and think for a while.
6. I suppose I should sit this glass on a coaster so as not to damage the wood table.
7. Set the dial to the right level for the kind of fabric you are ironing.
8. Although Yuki was usually quiet, she spoke out in defense of her principals.
9. Do you suppose Raoul will be chosen for the principle role in the play?
10. If the candidate cannot rise enough money, she will have to quite the race for mayor.

Their/There/They're *Their* is the possessive form of *they. There* means "at or in that place." *There* is also used in the phrases *there is* and *there are. They're* is a contraction meaning "they are."

Jane Addams helped poor people improve their living conditions.

I put the book over there.

There are three reasons why I will not eat meat.

They're the best volunteer firefighters I've ever seen.

Then/Than *Then* means "at that time" or "next in time." *Than* is used to introduce the second element in a comparison.

He was young and naive then.

I went to the job interview and then stopped off for a double chocolate shake.

My dog is smarter than your dog.

Writing Tip
Do not use the informal spelling *thru* for *through*.

Threw/Through *Threw* is the past tense of *throw. Through* means "in one side and out the opposite side" or "finished."

Satchel Paige threw a baseball faster than ninety-five miles an hour.

It takes almost thirty minutes to go through the tunnel.

"I'm through," said Clark Kent, storming out of Perry White's office.

To/Too/Two *To* means "in the direction of." *Too* means "also" or "more than enough." *Two* denotes the numeral 2.

During spring break, I am going to Disney World.

My roommates are coming too.

The microwave popcorn is too hot to eat.

"If we get rid of the tin man and the lion, the two of us can go to Oz," said the scarecrow to Dorothy.

Use/Used *Use* means "to put into service" or "to consume." *Used* is both the past tense and the past participle of *use. Used* also means "accustomed." (Note that when *used* has this meaning, it is followed by *to.*)

I use a soft cloth to clean my glasses.

"Hey! Who used all the hot water?" he yelled from the shower.

Mary had used all the firewood during the storm.

After living in Alaska for a year, they got used to the short winter days.

◆ PRACTICE 29.5

Proofread the underlined words in the following sentences for correct spelling. If a correction needs to be made, cross out the incorrect word, and write the correct spelling above it. If the word is spelled correctly, write *C* above it.

Example: ~~Their~~ There are at least two C good reasons not to rent that apartment.

1. It was hard to get use to the cold when they first came to New York from there home in Puerto Rico.
2. The shortstop threw the ball to second base, but it flew on through the air and landed in the bleachers.
3. I'm threw with the two of them and all they're nonsense!
4. Her blind date was more fun then she expected although it was too early to tell if she really liked him.
5. "They're used to staying up until nine," Mrs. Tsang told the babysitter.
6. Four-year-old Zachary got spaghetti sauce all over his face and than use his T-shirt to clean it off.
7. If they had known then what problems there car would have, they never would have bought it.
8. As a new teacher, Spencer use to feel tired at the end of the day.
9. Is there any reason to risk driving after drinking to much at a party?
10. I don't like the food at that restaurant, and it's two expensive too.

Weather/Whether *Weather* refers to the state of the atmosphere with respect to temperature, humidity, precipitation, and so on. *Whether* means "if it is so that; if the cause is that."

The *Farmer's Almanac* says that the weather this winter will be severe.

Whether or not this prediction will be correct is anyone's guess.

Where/Were/We're *Where* means "at or in what place." *Were* is the past tense of *are*. *We're* is a contraction meaning "we are."

Where are you going, and where have you been?

Charlie Chaplin and Mary Pickford were popular stars of silent movies.

We're doing our back-to-school shopping early this year.

Whose/Who's *Whose* is the possessive form of *who*. *Who's* is a contraction meaning "who is" or "who has."

My roommate asked, "Whose book is this?"

"Who's there?" squealed the second little pig as he leaned against the door.

"Who's been sleeping in my bed?" asked Goldilocks.

Your/You're *Your* is the possessive form of *you*. *You're* is a contraction meaning "you are."

> "You should have worn your running shoes," said the hare as he passed the tortoise.
>
> "You're too kind," said the tortoise sarcastically.

◆ PRACTICE 29.6

Proofread the underlined words in the following sentences for correct spelling. If a correction needs to be made, cross out the incorrect word, and write the correct spelling above it. If the word is spelled correctly, write *C* above it.

Example: We're [C] not sure ~~weather~~ [whether] or not this is the right road to take.

1. "Whose going to the party," Tracey asked, "and whose car are we taking?"
2. Orlando, were we went on vacation, has good weather, fine beaches, and many tourist attractions.
3. "Your late for you're appointment," the receptionist said.
4. Someone who's experienced at buying cameras can tell you whether or not to buy that one.
5. Where you surprised at the sudden change in the weather?
6. Do you know whose left this laptop were anyone might take it?
7. By the time your finished with school and work, your energy is all gone.
8. Whether you like it or not, no one is going to make you're decisions for you.
9. Who's car is parked in the spot were my car usually is?
10. Were you excited when you're letter to the editor was printed in the newspaper?

■ REVISING AND EDITING

Look back at your response to the Seeing and Writing exercise on page 463. Make sure you have not misused any of the words listed in this chapter. If you are writing on a computer, use the Search or Find function to locate any words you think you may have misused.

CHAPTER REVIEW

◆ EDITING PRACTICE

Read the following student essay, which contains spelling errors. Identify the words you think are misspelled, and then look them up in a dictionary. Finally, cross out each incorrectly spelled word, and write the correct spelling above the line. The first sentence has been edited for you.

The Minimum Wage

As a student who has worked at her share of minimum-wage jobs, I strongly believe in the ~~principal~~ principle of a "living wage." How, in good conscious, can employers not pay workers enough to support themselves? To this question, many employers reply that rising the minimum wage would have a negative affect on they're businesses. If the minimum wage is set too high, they might have to close. Some small business owners feel that the minimum wage is all ready to high and that they cannot make a fair profit because of labor costs.

Most labor leaders and working people, including myself, do not except this argument. We believe that a minimum wage is suppose to reflect the basic needs of an individual for food, clothing, shelter, and transportation to and from work. The present minimum wage, in my opinion, doesn't provide for these basic necessities. However, I realize that what constitutes a fair amount depends on whose making the estimate. If your an employer, your estimate might differ greatly from mine. Their is also the question of whether the minimum hourly wage should be enough to support just an individual or a family.

In the United States, about forty states have minimum-wage laws or boards that set minimum wages. The first state to pass such a law was Massachusetts in 1912. The federal government first past a minimum wage law in 1938. About 80 percent of all private industries are all ready covered by the federal law. But self-employed workers and employees of small businesses are often not covered by this law.

This is a complex problem that will not be easily layed to rest. As lawmakers struggle to fine a solution, they should investigate just how someone making minimum wage and working a full forty-hour week can survive on that amount of money.

◆ COLLABORATIVE ACTIVITIES

1. After completing the practice exercises in this chapter, make a list of the words that you found confusing, and study their meanings and the sample sentences. Then, have a partner quiz you on these words.
2. Working in a small group, choose one section of this chapter, and write a test on the material it discusses. (Use the practices in this chapter as a model for your test.) Each of your sentences should contain one of the commonly confused words. When you have finished, exchange tests with another group, and take its test. Finally, correct the other group's work on your test.
3. Divide into two teams, and stage a spelling bee. Each team should prepare a list of twenty words and quiz the other, with students on the two teams alternating to try to spell each word. The team that spells the most words correctly is the winner.
4. *Composing original sentences* Working with a partner, choose the five commonly confused word pairs that give you the most trouble. Write sample sentences for the two words in each pair to illustrate the correct use of the commonly confused words.

   Examples
   1. Don't drop that vase or it will break.
   2. I hit the brake suddenly to avoid hitting the deer.

   When you have finished, check the sentences to make sure you have corrected any errors in grammar, punctuation, or spelling.

✓ REVIEW CHECKLIST: Learning Commonly Confused Words

- Memorize the differences between the most commonly confused words.

UNIT SEVEN

Learning College Reading Skills

CHAPTER

30

Readings for Writers

The following eighteen essays by student and professional writers are designed to give you interesting material to read, react to, think critically about, discuss, and write about. Each essay is accompanied by a short introduction that tells you something about the reading and its author. Definitions of some of the words used in the essay appear in **Word Power** boxes in the margins.

Following each essay are four **Thinking about the Reading** discussion questions, some of which can be done collaboratively. (These are marked in the text with a star.) With your instructor's permission, you can discuss your responses to these questions with other students and then share them with the class. Three **Writing Practice** activities also follow each essay.

As you read each of these essays, highlight and annotate it to help you understand what you are reading. (Highlighting and annotating are discussed in Chapter 2.) Then, reread them more carefully in preparation for class discussion and for writing.

TRIGGER-HAPPY BIRTHDAY

Kiku Adatto

Kiku Adatto is writing a book about how childhood is changing in modern America. In this essay, she describes her own experience with paintball birthday parties for children and questions whether they are appropriate for twelve-year-olds like her son.

Some months ago, my twelve-year-old son received a brightly colored invitation to a friend's birthday party, which was being held someplace called Boston Paintball. A few days later, I received a more somber missive: "This is a Release of Liability—read before signing." 1

> **Word Power**
>
> **missive** a letter or message
>
> **liability** a financial and legal responsibility; a debt that must be paid

A couple of clauses stood out. No. 1: "The risk of injury from the activity and weaponry involved in paintball is significant, including the potential for permanent disability and death." No. 4: "I, for myself and on behalf of my heirs, assigns, personal representatives and next of kin, *hereby release... the American Paintball League (A.P.L.), Boston Paintball... with respect to any and all injury, disability, death....*" 2

Welcome to today's birthday party. And by the way, if your kid is killed at the party, it's not our fault. Call me an old-fashioned mother, but I just couldn't sign. Apparently all the other parents did, however; my son's friends told him that everyone had a great time. 3

I decided to visit Boston Paintball to check it out. Located in an old converted warehouse, the place was teeming with white suburban boys. Over at one end, I found another birthday party, for a kid named Max and 10 or so friends. 4

With their parents' help, the kids were putting on safety gear—chest protectors, neck guards and "Star Wars"–style masks. "It's fun," said Max's mom encouragingly, "like a video game." Then a referee held up a paintball gun (which looked like a real semiautomatic) and shot off a few rounds. The boys quickly lined up to get their weapons. 5

Next came the safety orientation. "First rule: don't lift off the masks on the field. We shoot balls at 100 miles an hour. Lift a mask, you'll lose an eye. Second rule: on the field, no shooting point-blank. No taking hostages. No using dead guys as shields. No hitting with fists or with gun butts." Max's dad snapped a few photos and handed out the ammunition. 6

> **Word Power**
>
> **orientation** a meeting in which participants are introduced to a new situation, such as a new school, job, or other activity
>
> **sporadic** infrequent; happening from time to time
>
> **adrenaline** a hormone in the body that produces a rush of energy and excitement in the face of danger

The referee gave the signal, and the game began. 7

But nothing happened. The boys huddled behind the bunkers. Eventually some of them poked their heads out; sporadic shots were fired. A few brave souls ventured into the open. 8

I was watching with the other parents from behind a window in the viewing area. Suddenly a paintball bullet hit the window with a dull thud. I started back. My adrenaline was pumping, but my mind said, "Trust the plexiglass." More bullets splattered the window. It sounded like real gunfire. "Hey, it looks like one of the kids is shooting at us," joked one of the mothers. We all laughed. And moved back from the window. 9

There was a release of tension after the first game. Max appeared in the lobby flushed and jubilant. "It was awesome," he said. "I hit someone." Max's parents laid out pizza. Spirits were high. "I killed a person," a boy said as he downed a Coke. 10

While they ate, I visited the gift shop. Along the back wall were racks of paintball guns—all looking like assault weapons—from the Sniper II at \$249.99 to the Express Pro Autococker at \$749.99. Even without these sou- 11 venirs, paintball is pricey: $29 for kids ($39 for adults), with numerous extra fees. A birthday party for ten boys with pizza can run $450.

Back at Max's party, one boy was pressing a cold Coke can against a welt. I asked Max's mom about the cost. "Max has contributed a hundred bucks of his birthday money to help pay for the party," she said fondly. Suddenly she spotted a welt on another boy's chin. "Oh, my God. How did that happen?" She turned back to me. "He's a little warrior," she said. 12

When paintball was invented nineteen years ago in New Hampshire, it was played by adults who focused less on simulated violence than on self-reliant survival. Today, it is reportedly a billion-dollar business in North America alone, with outdoor theme parks featuring mock Vietcong villages and bases named the Rambo Hotel. It's a business that proudly markets itself as an all-purpose sport: the Boston Paintball Web site said it was great for "stress relief, confidence, company outings, morale boosting" and, of course, "birthdays." 13

Some of the mothers in attendance that day said that paintball is no different from the war games their brothers played a generation ago. I disagree. True, when I was a kid, my friends and I spun violent fantasies, some (like cowboys and Indians) as troubling as the new high-tech games. But there were differences. We didn't pay for admission. The guns weren't lethal. We used our imaginations. And our parents didn't open the paper several times a year to read about kids firing guns in school. 14

Word Power

lethal capable of killing

As I was pulling out of the paintball parking lot, the attendant, a guy in his forties, asked if I had played. I said no. "I don't think it's good, kids and paintball," he said. "They don't realize that they can hurt somebody with those guns." 15

Well I'm with the parking-lot attendant. And as for the contract, I still couldn't sign. 16

Thinking about the Reading

1. In the Release of Liability, what does Boston Paintball say it will *not* be responsible for?
2. Why does Boston Paintball want parents to sign this Release of Liability? Why does Adatto refuse to sign?
3. Compare Adatto's reaction to the paintball game she watches with the reaction of Max's parents. How are their reactions different?

*4. According to Adatto, how is paintball different from the war games children played in the past? Do you agree with her?

Writing Practice

1. Imagine that you are the parent of a twelve-year-old boy who has just been invited to a paintball party. Would you sign the Release of Liability and allow him to participate? Explain your decision.
2. The author seems to make a connection between the violent game of paintball, which is played with weapons that look like real semiautomatics, and the problem of "kids firing guns in school" (paragraph 14). Do you agree or disagree that paintball might encourage violent behavior in real life? Give reasons for your answer.
3. Why do you think paintball is popular among both children and adults? Do you agree that violent games fulfill a useful function in society, such as preventing real-life violence or relieving stress and building confidence, as the Boston Paintball people claim? Explain your position.

FRIENDS

Justin Brines

Have you ever experienced an unlikely friendship that brought unexpected rewards? Student writer Justin Brines describes his friendship with an unforgettable character, Lula May Johnston, who shared with him her unique approach to life.

"Magic dust and persimmon tips—those are the things that keep you fit." That was her favorite saying, and she would mumble it every time she passed by me in the retail store where I worked. Mrs. Lula May Johnston was the only homeless person I've ever known on a personal level. 1

Perhaps the most memorable quality that May (that was what she preferred to be called) possessed was her smell. It was not a loud smell, and it was not an offensive smell either. It was more of a sweet, almost honey-like aroma that followed her everywhere she went. This was surprising to me because my narrow mind assumed that all homeless people smelled bad. Another trademark was her long brown hair; however, usually it was not visible because it was covered with a burgundy hat in both winter and summer. May said that her brain needed padding. You see, she was a little eccentric, and I think that was what made me like her so much. 2

Word Power

eccentric having odd or whimsical ways; behaving in ways that are not usual or customary

commotion a noisy disturbance

Whenever May came into the store, she was always pushing an old steel shopping cart that was covered in rust. Inside the cart were three items. In the child's seat was May's dog, Charlie. According to her, Charlie was a "hundred-percent full-blooded basset hound." The store manager never minded her bringing Charlie into the store because Charlie never barked or caused any kind of commotion. Charlie was only a stuffed animal, but you would never have known it from the way May treated him. She talked to him, petted him, and even fed him "magic dust and persimmon tips." 3

This brings me to the next item in May's cart: a little blue bag with two glass bottles in it. To me, the bottles looked empty. To May, however, they contained her lifeblood. She told me that without her magic dust and persimmon tips she could not live. Every so often, she would turn each bottle up and take a big gulp of the imaginary concoction, acting as though it tasted terrible. (I never tried them.) I once asked her where she got these two substances that were so important in her life. "It's all in your heart, son," she answered. I never asked again. 4

Word Power

concoction a mixture of several ingredients

The third, and probably most important, item in May's cart was her Bible. It was old and worn, and the cover was almost torn off the front. She once told me that all a person needed to survive was God Almighty, a friend, and a heart. May possessed all three of these things; in fact, they were on public display in her cart. 5

May came into the store once a week, always on Tuesday, and walked around. However, she never bought anything. I think the purpose of her ritual walk was to remind me to eat my lunch on the loading dock that day. There, every Tuesday, the store I worked for would trash its damaged items in a large Dumpster. May knew this, and I could always find her rummaging through the refuse. 6

This was when May talked to me most; I suppose it was because she was in her setting, on her terms. She told me that she was from Kannapolis and had lived there all her life. She had never been married and did not have any children. She had worked for the mill in town but was laid off around 1962 and had not worked since. "I'm not crazy," May insisted. 7

"People think I am, but I'm perfectly normal." She had strong feelings about welfare and about taking money from other people. "I could work if I wanted to," she told me, "but I just don't feel like it. But I'm not going to take money from hard-working people, and I don't expect them to support me." May also believed that people should live in the simplest way possible, and I guess that's what she did.

8 On my last day in the store, I stopped by the Christian Supply on my way to work and bought May a new Bible. On the front, I had the words "Mrs. Lula May Johnston" embossed. When I got to the store, she was waiting for me out front.

Word Power

embossed decorated with raised, printed letters or designs

9 "You're running late, son," she said.

10 "I know," I replied. "I had to stop and get you a present."

11 "For me?" May asked as I handed her the package. She opened her gift and looked at the Bible. "Nobody's ever given me anything before," she said. Then she looked at Charlie (sitting, as he always was, in the child's seat of May's shopping cart) and added, "Our friend's leaving us, boy. Our friend's leaving us."

12 "It's my last day," I explained. "Well, I guess I'll see you around."

13 "Yep," May said. She leaned over and gave me a hug. I didn't realize a little woman could squeeze so hard. Finally, she let go and said, "You know, I was almost ready to get rid of Charlie."

14 "Why?" I asked.

15 "Well, you were my friend, and I didn't need Charlie anymore. I guess it's a good thing I kept him." May turned around and began walking away. "Magic dust and persimmon tips, those are the things that keep you fit," she whispered to herself. I watched May until she was out of sight, and that was the last time I saw her.

Thinking about the Reading

1. Brines states that the most memorable thing about May was her smell. How did she smell? Why do you think Brines chose to focus on that detail? What does May's smell suggest about her personality?
2. What do the three items in May's shopping cart reveal about her personality and beliefs?
3. In what ways does May differ from your idea of a typical homeless person? In what ways does she fit this stereotype?

*4. Brines seems to think of May as a wise person even though others might consider her crazy. What examples does he give of her wisdom? Do you consider May a wise woman? Why or why not?

Writing Practice

1. May claimed she could not live without "magic dust and persimmon tips," which she found in her heart (paragraph 4). What are two things that you cannot live without? Why?
2. Write a description of someone you consider to be eccentric. It might be someone you know or a character in a movie or story. Include specific details that show what the person looks like and what he or she says and does.
3. What effect do you think Justin's friendship with May had on him? What effect do you think their friendship had on May? (Some of these effects are stated in the essay, but others are left for you to figure out.)

CAN YOU IMAGINE?

Jared Esposito

Student writer Jared Esposito compares and contrasts life before and after cell phones and computers became an important part of our daily lives. He examines the positive and negative effects of these two inventions and comes to a conclusion that you may or may not agree with.

A few days ago, my grandmother talked to me about how much things have changed since she was a girl. "Can you imagine," she asked, "what life without television was like?" Of course I could not; I have grown up with television. Like people in my grandmother's generation, those in my generation have seen many changes during our lifetimes. And our children will find it difficult to imagine what life was like before cell phones and computers.

2 Ten years ago, the only people who had cell phones were people like doctors whose jobs required them to be on call twenty-four hours a day. Average people could not afford the high cost of cell phones, and they were impressed when they saw someone use these devices. If parents went out to a movie or a restaurant, they would have to call home several times during the evening to find out how their children were. If there was an emergency, the babysitter would have to call the theater or the restaurant and hope that the parents could be located. If a car broke down on the way home, the driver would have to hope that a police cruiser would come by or that another motorist would stop. If that did not happen, someone would have to hike to the nearest phone booth.

3 Now everyone seems to have a cell phone. These items are so inexpensive that many phone companies simply give them away if a customer signs up for service. Now people can be reached anywhere. If there is an emergency at home, a babysitter can get hold of the parents wherever they are. If someone has car trouble, all he or she has to do is get out a trusty cell phone and call the auto club or a gas station. Of course, the availability of cell phones has some drawbacks. The ringing of cell phones constantly interrupts movies, and restaurants are filled with people talking loudly on their cell phones. In fact, some restaurants have even put up signs asking patrons to turn their phones off when they enter. The biggest drawback of having a cell phone is that a person never can be completely out of reach. No matter where a person is—at the beach, at a ball game, or even at church—someone can call.

4 Much the same situation exists with computers. Only a few years ago, most people did not own computers. When someone wanted to write a letter, he or she had to type it or write it by hand, mail it, and then wait several days for it to arrive. If the writer wanted to take some words out or add a sentence, he or she would have to copy or type the letter over. The same was true for schoolwork. As every student knows, essays and reports have to go through several drafts. Before word processing, each draft had to be typed or hand written. Then, students would have to correct small mistakes in spelling or grammar with correction tape or Wite-Out. If students needed to look up a fact or find information for their papers, they would have to go to the library to use the card catalog or to look through periodical indexes.

Now almost everyone has access to a computer. People who do not 5
own computers can go to the public library or to a community center and use one. Some rest stops on the turnpike even have computers that patrons can use without cost. Email makes it possible for people to type and send letters in a matter of minutes. After a letter is finished, the spell checker and a grammar checker can identify mistakes, and the writer can correct them with a few keystrokes. Computers have also made schoolwork easier. Now students can write drafts of an essay or a report quickly and easily. Word-processing programs enable them to add and delete material and to move whole blocks of text. No longer do students have to type and retype material before they submit it. If students have to find information for their papers, they can get on the Internet and access an online encyclopedia, a library's online card catalog, or a magazine article.

Cell phones and computers have changed our world forever—for 6
better and for worse. They make it possible for us to communicate almost instantly over great distances. And by enabling us to write more efficiently, they make us more productive workers. Still, even with their obvious advantages, there are certain drawbacks. For example, cell phones have almost destroyed our privacy, and email has almost eliminated thoughtful writing and editing. These drawbacks have led me to conclude that although life might have been more difficult before cell phones and computers, in some ways it might also have been better.

Thinking about the Reading

*1. What are the advantages of cell phones? What are their disadvantages? Discuss the advantages and disadvantages mentioned in the essay as well as some from your own experiences and observations.

*2. How have computers made writing and researching for school easier? How have they made communication easier?

3. In the final paragraph, Esposito states his opinion about whether these inventions have, on the whole, made our lives better or worse. What is his conclusion? Tell why you agree or disagree with it.

4. How does Esposito organize his essay? How do the two paragraphs on cell phones differ? How do the two paragraphs on computers differ? Why do you think he organized his ideas the way he did?

Writing Practice

1. Write about how your life was different before and after one of the following: beginning college, the birth of a sibling or child, a move, a new responsibility, or a new hobby.
2. Write about two careers you are considering. What are their advantages and disadvantages?
3. What are the advantages and disadvantages of married life and single life? Consider your own experiences and the experiences of friends and family members.

ONE OF THE BAD GUYS?

Ray Hanania

Are all Arabs terrorists? Hollywood seems to think so. In this article, Arab-American writer Ray Hanania discusses the negative stereotyping of Arabs in movies. Hanania is a syndicated columnist and stand-up comedian who lives in Chicago.

1 As a child in the 1960s, I thought my relatives were famous. It seemed like they were in many Hollywood movies, often playing similar roles. OK. They weren't the headliners, but they did appear alongside stars like Paul Newman (*Exodus*), Sophia Loren (*Judith*), and Kirk Douglas (*Cast a Giant Shadow*). My "relatives" always played the "terrorists."

Word Power
wield to handle with ease and skill

2 As I grew older, though, I realized that those actors were not my relatives, at all. They just looked like them. They have that "terrorist" look, and so do I. I can safely assure you, though, I don't have the mannerisms. I'm tired of seeing my likeness wielding an AK-47, murdering innocent women and children, getting stomped by Arnold Schwarzenegger (*True Lies*), or Harrison Ford (*Indiana Jones and the Temple of Doom*), or Kurt Russell (*Executive Decision*), and now Bruce Willis (*The Siege*).

3 I'm Arab American. And for some reason, Hollywood seems to think it's OK to portray all Arabs—and all Muslims, for that matter—as the bad guys. I don't mean just bad. I mean *really* bad. It makes me so angry I want to get in my half-track with my 50-caliber howitzer that's parked in my two-Hummer garage, drive to the center of town and start shooting! I mean, isn't that what you've come to expect Arabs to do?

Word Power
ominous threatening

4 After I was honorably discharged from the U.S. Air Force in 1975, the FBI opened a file on me. It began with the ominous suggestion that I might be involved in "suspected" terrorist organizations, but the investigation concluded two years and twenty-three pages later that I was concerned only about improving the condition of my community. The investigation seemed based on the assumption that because I was an Arab, I must also be a potential terrorist. Most of the juicy text was blocked out with heavy, black Magic Markered lines, so it's hard to know for sure.

5 Hollywood movies are founded on the same assumption, that the Arab is the terrorist. I once thought movies were just entertainment, but they're much more. It's at the movies that the public learns about people like me. And it's also where I compare myself to the characters on the screen and wonder if there really is something wrong with me. How did my look suddenly become something so sinister? My eyes become even darker and more deep set? My accent heavier? I begin to question myself. Why is this person who looks like me so angry he wants to murder and harm innocent people? What is it that makes him wreak havoc and wanton suffering upon an innocent world?

Word Power
wreak havoc to bring about devastation

wanton cruel; merciless

6 Occasionally, there is an upside to being pegged as a terrorist. Once at Miami International Airport, a gaggle of people all wearing the same light gray jackets were following me around the terminal. Finally, introducing themselves as airport security, they directed me to a room where they rifled through my bags and grilled me about my travel history. They held up the embarrassing evidence of my terrorism. Wood carved heads. Goofy-looking hats. And dirty clothes.

When they finally realized I was just a tourist-trap junkie, they excused themselves. Usually, it takes about fifteen minutes before I am released from airport detention and I'm on my way. Meanwhile, the nonterrorist-looking commuters are left waiting in the long immigration lines, impatiently nudging luggage across the tile floor, complaining about the heat and delays. But the security officers always have a reason to stop me. At Miami, they said I looked like the suspect they were pursuing. And, they just happened to have a Polaroid picture of the "suspect." He wore a double-breasted, polyester leisure suit, with a wide-brimmed Panama hat. And he had olive skin, dark eyes, and those skinny little fingers that fit neatly around the trigger of a gun, like mine do. Naturally, I was very impressed. It must be difficult to get a terrorist to stop long enough to pose for a Polaroid picture. 7

Look, I'm realistic. I don't think we can erase all of Hollywood's stereotypes. But the movies seem fixated on the exaggerated bad side of Arabs. To Hollywood, the Arab is the wife-abuser who wants to buy Steve Martin's home in *Father of the Bride II.* Or the guy hanging from the missile in *True Lies* when Schwarzenegger pushes the launch button and says in his Austrian accent, "Yaw're fi-yard!" We Arabs murder innocent airline passengers in *Executive Decision* simply because it makes us feel good. 8

Even a company like Disney takes a shot at us, with these lyrics from the movie *Aladdin:* "Oh I come from a land, from a faraway place, where the caravan camels roam; Where they cut off your ear if they don't like your face; It's barbaric, but hey, it's home." (Disney responded to Arab Americans' complaints by changing the last line for the video release.) 9

Must every Arab portrayed in the movies be the villain? Why can't we be the hero just once? There are plenty of overlooked role models to choose from. The first heart-transplant surgeon is an Arab American, Michael DeBakey. Candy Lightner, who founded Mothers Against Drunk Drivers, is Arab, too. There were at least seventy-four Arab passengers aboard the *Titanic* when it sank. Half of them drowned. Director James Cameron had a good opportunity to highlight the human side of the Arab community. Instead, he chose to highlight a make-believe Irish wedding aboard the ship, rather than include one of the three Arab weddings that actually took place. 10

Arabs are everyday people. Doctors. Teachers. Football stars and team owners. Grocery-store clerks. Engineers. Elected officials. We're the mail carriers who deliver your mail. The nurses and emergency medical technicians who hold your hand through tragedy. The clerks who help you at the bank. 11

I'm not asking Hollywood to hate someone else. That would be wrong. But I'm asking Hollywood to be fair. Don't just show the bad. Show our good side, too. But, if that can't be done, I do have one last question: are you still mad about the Crusades?[1] 12

Thinking about the Reading

*1. This essay was written in 1998, three years before the terrorist attacks of September 11, 2001. If Hanania were writing today, how might his essay be different?

1. Wars undertaken by European Christians in the eleventh, twelfth, and thirteenth centuries to win what they considered the Holy Land from its Muslim rulers.

2. How does Hanania support his claim that Arabs are always portrayed in films as the "bad guys" (paragraph 3)?
3. List some examples of how Arabs are portrayed in recent films. Do your examples support Hanania's position?
*4. How does Hanania's own experience at the airport (paragraphs 6–7) support the position he takes in this essay? Is this anecdote convincing?

Writing Practice

1. Drawing on the list you made for question 3 above, write an essay in which you argue that since September 11, 2001, the portrayals of Arabs in films have (or have not) changed.
2. Choose a group—for example, people with disabilities, rural Americans, recent immigrants, the elderly, or overweight people—that you believe is portrayed negatively (or unrealistically) in films or on television. Write an essay in which you take the position that these groups need to be depicted more accurately and fairly.
3. Write a letter to a producer of a TV show or film you have seen recently. In your letter, offer examples of how members of a particular ethnic group are portrayed, and then suggest ways they could be portrayed in more positive terms.

AT THE HEART OF A HISTORIC MOVEMENT

John Hartmire

As executive director of the National Farmworker Ministry, John Hartmire's father worked closely with Cesar Chavez to fight for social justice for farmworkers. But his father's dedication to the cause meant that he was absent for most of Hartmire's childhood. In this essay, Hartmire discusses what it is like to make a personal sacrifice for a social cause.

When my friend's daughter asked me if I knew anything about the man her school was named after, I had to admit that I did. I told her that in California there are at least twenty-six other schools, seventeen streets, seven parks, and ten scholarships named after Cesar Chavez. Not only that, I said, I once hit a ground ball through his legs during a softball game, and I watched his two dogs corner my sister's rabbit and, quite literally, scare it to death. I used to curse his name to the sun gods while I marched through one sweltering valley or another knowing my friends were at the beach staring at Carrie Carbajal and her newest bikini. 1

During those years I wasn't always sure of how I felt about the man, but I did believe Cesar Chavez was larger than life. The impact he had on my family was at once enriching and debilitating. He was everywhere. Like smoke and cobwebs, he filled the corners of my family's life. We moved to California from New York in 1961 when my father was named executive director of the National Farmworker Ministry, and for the next thirty-plus years our lives were defined by Cesar and the United Farm Workers. 2

Word Power

debilitate to take away the strength

During those years my father was gone a lot, traveling with, or for, Cesar. I "understood" because the struggle to organize farmworkers into a viable union was the work of a lifetime, and people would constantly tell me how much they admired what Dad was doing. Hearing it made me proud. It also made me lonely. He organized the clergy to stand up for the union, went to jail defying court injunctions, and was gone from our house for days on end, coming home, my mother likes to say, only for clean underwear. It was my father who fed the small piece of bread to Cesar ending his historic twenty-five-day fast in 1968. It's no wonder Dad missed my first Little League home run. 3

Word Power

viable able to survive

The experience of growing up in the heart of a historic movement has long been the stuff of great discussions around our dinner table. The memories are both vibrant and difficult. There were times when Cesar and the union seemed to be more important to my father than I was, or my mother was, or my brothers and sister were. It is not an easy suspicion to grow up with, or to reconcile as an adult. 4

While my friends surfed, I was dragged to marches in the Coachella and San Joaquin valleys. I was taken out of school to attend union meetings and rallies that interested me even less than geometry class. I spent time in supermarket parking lots reluctantly passing out leaflets and urging shoppers not to buy nonunion grapes and lettuce. I used to miss Sunday-afternoon NFL telecasts to canvass neighborhoods with my father. Since my dad wanted his family to be a part of his life, I marched and slept and ate and played with Cesar Chavez's kids. When we grew older his son, Paul, and I would drink beer together and wonder out loud how our lives would have been different had our fathers been plumbers or bus drivers. 5

Word Power
orchestrate to arrange

Word Power
transcend to be greater than; to go beyond

But our fathers were fighting to do something that had never been done before. Their battle to secure basic rights for migrant workers evolved into a moral struggle that captured the nation's attention. I saw it all, from the union's grape strike in 1965, to the signing of the first contracts five years later, to the political power gained then lost because, for Cesar, running a union was never as natural as orchestrating a social movement. 6

My father and Cesar parted company four years before Chavez died in 1993. Chavez, sixty-six at the time of his death, father of eight, grandfather of twenty-seven, leader of thousands, a Hispanic icon who transcended race, left the world a better place than he found it. He did it with the help of a great many good people, and the sacrifice of their families, many of whom believed in his cause but didn't always understand what he was asking of, or taking from, them. 7

So as students here attend Cesar Chavez Elementary School, as families picnic in a Sacramento park named after him and public employees opt to take off March 31 in honor of his birthday, I try to remember Cesar Chavez for what he was—a quiet man, the father of friends, a man intricately bound with my family—and not what he took from my childhood. Namely, my father. I still wrestle with the cost of my father's commitment, understanding that social change does not come without sacrifice. I just wonder if the price has to be so damn high. 8

Do I truly know Cesar Chavez? I suppose not. He was like a boat being driven by some internal squall, a disturbance he himself didn't always understand, and that carried millions right along with him, some of us kicking and screaming. 9

Thinking about the Reading

1. When he was a child, why did Hartmire "curse [Cesar Chavez's] name to the sun gods" (paragraph 1)? Do you think he still feels any bitterness about his childhood? If so, at whom is this bitterness directed?
2. In paragraph 2, Hartmire says that Chavez was "larger than life. The impact he had on my family was at once enriching and debilitating. He was everywhere." What does he mean?

*3. In paragraph 5, Hartmire says that he and Paul Chavez used to try to imagine how their lives might have been different if their fathers had been "plumbers or bus drivers." How do you think their lives would have been different?

4. How has Hartmire's opinion of Chavez changed over the years? Has his opinion of his father also changed?

Writing Practice

1. What historical or political figure was "larger than life" for your family? Write an essay explaining the impact that this person had on you.
2. Who is your greatest living hero? Write an essay explaining this person's contributions to society. (If you like, you may write your essay as a recommendation for an award, addressing your remarks to the awards committee.)
3. If your middle school or high school was named after a person, write an article for the school newspaper in which you explain why this individual deserves (or does not deserve) this honor.

WHAT I DID FOR LOVE

Macarena del Rocío Hernández

Do you believe in fortune tellers, love potions, or psychic advisers? Journalist Macarena Hernández did not think she did until love made her change her mind. Hernández is a staff writer for the *San Antonio Express-News*.

I know what I will be serving at my wedding. My mother's neighbor Doña Ester García will make carne guisada, beef stew, for the main course. My uncle has volunteered one of his steers. I am wondering whether it should be a huge affair, à la Mexicana,[1] with a guest list including the mailman and distant relatives of my second cousin's inlaws. Or a simple, more Americanized ceremony, with only those by my side who have been part of my most recent life. I have some time to work out the details since I still don't have the groom. 1

I'm a twenty-five-year-old Mexican American whose relationships wilt faster than orchids in the Texas sun. And that, according to my aunts and cousins, makes me an old maid. 2

Never mind that I've spent the last seven years living and working in major cities throughout the United States where women tend to get married in their late twenties and early thirties. Whenever I come back home to La Joya, Texas, my family is quick to remind me that time is running out. My love life, or lack of it, is especially troubling to my aunts, most of whom have children who are at least seven years younger than I and already married. 3

I know about the chisme[2] that the aunts swap as they huddle over the kitchen table making tamales. 4

"She studies way too much. All that work can't be good for her head," says one as she spreads masa on a cornhusk and tops it with a spoonful of beef. 5

"Maybe she doesn't like men. You know, in San Francisco where she used to live, there are a lot of gay people," another tía[3] adds. 6

I suspect they also talk about me while they watch their favorite Spanish-language soap operas, overwrought stories that always involve a poor girl crying crocodile tears as she calls out, "Carlos José! No me dejes. Yo te amo." (Carlos José! Don't leave me. I love you.) 7

It was probably during one of those pain-filled telenovelas[4] that one of my tias had an epiphany. Something, she realized, must have happened to me during my childhood, some awful trauma that has made it impossible for me to keep a man. 8

Word Power

epiphany a sudden flash of insight

trauma an injury or wound, either physical or emotional

I'll admit I can scare men off. But I think it has more to do with growing up with four older brothers who rarely spoke to me unless they wanted a shirt ironed or dinner cooked. At an early age, I began to equate marriage with slavery. I couldn't see myself spending the rest of my life washing someone else's underwear. 9

My relatives view my attitude on the subject as a disease that seems to be getting worse. 10

It's no secret that my mother has been praying for years for a "good man who can take care of you." And if all that prayer hasn't helped, my Tía Nelly concluded, I must be cursed. 11

1. In the Mexican style.
2. Gossip.
3. Aunt.
4. Television soap operas.

She knew the perfect person to help me: a curandera, a healer who can cure a person of lovelessness just as easily as colic. 12

"I don't believe in it," my cousin said to me, "but maybe you should go." 13

I thought about it for a week. If I went, I'd be admitting that I have a problem. If I didn't, I might miss out on a cure. 14

> **Word Power**
> **anemic** weak; lacking vitality

I picked a Friday afternoon. I decked myself out in a short black dress and red lipstick so the curandera couldn't blame my anemic love life on the way I dressed. Tía Nelly and I drove thirty-five minutes to Rio Grande City and the curandera's storefront office. 15

I hid my truck in an alley so nobody I knew would see it. The store looked like a herb shop one might find on South Street in Philadelphia, except this one inhabited an old grocery. Inside were long aisles of neatly displayed candles, religious statuettes, soaps, and good luck charms. One wall offered packages of herbs and spices. 16

In Latino neighborhoods curanderas are considered not only healers, but also spiritual advisers. They are like doctors, psychiatrists, and priests rolled into one. 17

I am told my father's grandfather, Emeterio Chasco, was a curandero. He didn't charge his clients money; in exchange for banishing a fright, bad luck, or a rash, he'd receive chickens, boxes of fruit, and personal favors. 18

The only curandero I'd ever met was El Papi, one of my mother's younger cousins. A dark-skinned man who never married and lived with his parents in Mexico, El Papi had big crooked teeth that you saw even when he wasn't smiling. My mother doubted his spiritual powers, but people from nearby towns and ranches consulted with him in his bedroom, which was also the family living room. Nonetheless, I expected my curandera to be an older woman, with hands as worn and soft as my grandmother's. Her touch, I imagined, would be magical enough to cure anything. 19

> **Word Power**
> **vixen** a female fox; (slang) a tempting, sexy woman; can also mean a bad-tempered woman.

But this curandera greeted me wearing a tight purple shirt and black pants that hugged a killer figure—curves that the bottle-blond healer told me were the product of hours at the gym. She was a middle-aged vixen, not a grandmotherly adviser. A thoroughly modern healer who drives a white convertible and recently divorced her husband of more than twenty years. 20

She performed her consults in the area once designated "for employees only." For $20 she gave me a card reading that she said would give us both a better handle on mi problema.[5] She asked me to shuffle the tarot cards and then split the deck into three stacks. She instructed me to use my left hand to place the different piles back into one. I kept my left hand on the pile. She covered it with her left hand and prayed. Then she began to deal the cards. Her long, pearl-colored acrylic nails made clicking noises every time she placed one down, face up. She spread the cards out on her desk. "Your problem," she said, "is a sentimental one." 21

No one could hear our conversation, so I decided to be honest. "My aunt said maybe you could help me because I can't seem to find the right guy or even keep the bad ones I date." 22

"This is not logical. You are very pretty," she said, looking me straight in the eye. "Men are desgraciados [ingrates]. You can give everything except your heart, because they will hurt you." 23

After a few more minutes of reading my life in the cards, she looked at me as if to say: "This is more serious than I thought." 24

"There was a woman about five years ago, and her name starts with the letter *M*," she said. "There was money paid to keep men away from you, 25

5. My problem.

and it was probably done in Mexico because they will do anything over there."

But that was all she could tell me. I would, she said, have to come back the next morning so she could start doing some work on me. She asked for $48 to buy 40 candles that she'd burn while she prayed that night in hopes that everything we needed to know about the mysterious *M* would reveal itself. I would also need to pay $20 for a barrida, a cleansing ritual. 26

The next day the curandera was ten minutes late—she had just finished a two-hour workout. She said she had news for me. Her overnight mediation had revealed two more letters of the mystery woman's name: *A* and *R*. 27

"Do you know anyone whose name starts with *M-A-R*?" she asked. Half of the Latinas I know have names that start with *M-A-R*: Maria, Martina, Marisa, Marisela, Marielena, Marina, Marta, Margarita. 28

Well, she said, the woman in question now dyes her hair guerro, blond. That only disqualified half. 29

"Last night," she said, "I saw a small black-and-white photo, probably from a yearbook." 30

Then the curandera explained what was wrong. The evil MAR woman, she said, had loved someone I was dating and had paid a dark man from Mexico to curse me, to keep men from sticking around. 31

The curse, she said, could be removed for $275, and even if I opted to go somewhere else, she advised me to get help as soon as possible. I couldn't remember dating anyone within the last five years who was so special that another woman would pay to have him. But I told her she could give me a barrida. 32

That, she promised, would definitely make me feel better, but I still needed to have the curse removed. 33

For the barrida, she had me stand just outside her office, facing south, in the middle of a circle that looked as if it had been burned into the floor. She instructed me to stretch my arms over my head as if I were singing or praising the Lord at church. 34

She doused her hands with lavender-scented alcohol and touched my neck, arms, hands, and legs. She then began making the sign of the cross with a brown-shelled egg that she said had been laid by a black hen. The egg was cold. I couldn't help but wonder whether it had lost its magic while sitting in the refrigerator. 35

The curandera prayed, fast and in Spanish, imploring the bad spirits to leave. She then lighted a candle and walked around me, asking some invisible power to illuminate me. She put the candle down and crumbled some dried leaves around the circle and poured alcohol on them. She grabbed the candle and set the circle on fire. 36

Her praying was so fervent and so rapid that I could understand only a few phrases: "Give her a pure love," "send her a good man." Essentially, the same thing my mom had been asking for. 37

It was getting hot. The flames were inching closer to my toes and there was smoke. Just when I thought I might melt I heard her say: "Jump over the flame." I did. 38

For the next three days, she said, before I ate anything else I was to drink half a cup of water mixed with sugar followed by a single banana cut into slices and covered with honey. She sold me two $10 candles that I was supposed to light and pray to. 39

Then she calmly reminded me that I still had to come back to get the curse removed. 40

But I'd had enough. I had no intention of drinking sugar water, eating honey-coated slices of banana, or lighting candles. Maybe I was afraid to rely on some vague magic I didn't understand. 4

Or maybe I believed in it too much, and couldn't bear the thought that it might not work. 4

When you live squeezed between two cultures, two languages, you are often a walking contradiction. Sometimes there is little you can do to keep both worlds at peace. 4

> **Word Power**
>
> **contradiction** situation in which one element is inconsistent with another

For days after the barrida I thought about everything the curandera told me. I held on to the things I wanted to believe—that I was too pretty not to attract men, that I would eventually end up with a successful, good man. And weighed those I didn't—that unless I reversed the curse there was no hope. 4

I wondered why a modern woman like me should listen to a curandera, even a with-it one clad in spandex. And then I remembered the words of another curandero: El Papi. 4

I was in the fourth grade and we were visiting his family in Nuevo Leon. 4

He and I were standing in the middle of the woods and I was watching him break an egg over a pile of sticks he was about to set on fire. 4

"Can you make someone fall in love with someone else?" I asked. 4

He looked up. 4

"Yes. I can," he said. "But that wouldn't be true love. You can't force love. You just have to wait for it to happen." 5

Thinking about the Reading

1. How does Hernández's attitude toward being single at age twenty-five differ from her family's attitude toward her marital status? In what way does she seem to agree with them?
2. Why do you think the author describes her experience with the curandera in great detail? What do these details reveal about the curandera and her methods?
3. *Hernández describes herself as a "walking contradiction" (paragraph 43). What does she mean by this? Cite some examples from the article that reveal contradictions in her personality.
4. In what ways does Hernández poke fun at herself, her family, and the curandera?

Writing Practice

1. Hernández is embarrassed by her trip to the curandera. To make herself feel better about the experience, she describes it with humor. Write about an embarrassing situation you experienced. Use humor to describe the situation and your feelings at the time.
2. Are you a "walking contradiction" like Hernández? Most of us are, even if we do not live in two cultures. Do you sometimes think one way and then act a different way? Describe the ways in which you are a contradiction—for example, in your personality traits or beliefs.
3. Hernández presents several details that show the importance of love and marriage in her culture, such as the custom of huge weddings and the popularity of Spanish-language soap operas. Write about how love and marriage are viewed in your culture. What customs and celebrations show their importance?

BEFORE AIR CONDITIONING

Arthur Miller

Pulitzer Prize–winner Arthur Miller is considered one of America's greatest playwrights. His dramas *Death of a Salesman, All My Sons,* and *The Crucible* are classics of the modern theater. Here, Miller recalls his life in New York City during the days before air conditioning became common.

1 Exactly what year it was I can no longer recall—probably 1927 or '28—there was an extraordinarily hot September, which hung on even after school had started and we were back from our Rockaway Beach bungalow. Every window in New York was open, and on the streets venders manning little carts chopped ice and sprinkled colored sugar over mounds of it for a couple of pennies. We kids would jump onto the back steps of the slow-moving, horse-drawn ice wagons and steal a chip or two; the ice smelled vaguely of manure but cooled palm and tongue.

2 People on West 110th Street, where I lived, were a little too bourgeois to sit out on their fire escapes, but around the corner on 111th and farther uptown mattresses were put out as night fell, and whole families lay on those iron balconies in their underwear.

Word Power
bourgeois middle-class and proper in attitudes

3 Even through the nights, the pall of heat never broke. With a couple of other kids, I would go across 110th to the park and walk among the hundreds of people, singles and families, who slept on the grass, next to their big alarm clocks, which set up a mild cacophony of the seconds passing, one clock's ticks syncopating with another's. Babies cried in the darkness, men's deep voices murmured, and a woman let out an occasional high laugh beside the lake. I can recall only white people spread out on the grass; Harlem began above 116th Street then.

4 Later on, in the Depression thirties, the summers seemed even hotter. Out West, it was the time of the red sun and the dust storms, when whole desiccated farms blew away and sent the Okies,[1] whom Steinbeck immortalized, out on their desperate treks toward the Pacific. My father had a small coat factory on Thirty-ninth Street then, with about a dozen men working sewing machines. Just to watch them handling thick woolen winter coats in that heat was, for me, a torture. The cutters were on piecework, paid by the number of seams they finished, so their lunch break was short—fifteen or twenty minutes. They brought their own food: bunches of radishes, a tomato perhaps, cucumbers, and a jar of thick sour cream, which went into a bowl they kept under the machines. A small loaf of pumpernickel also materialized, which they tore apart and used as a spoon to scoop up the cream and vegetables.

Word Power
desiccated dried-up
immortalize to make famous forever
trek a difficult journey

5 The men sweated a lot in those lofts, and I remember one worker who had a peculiar way of dripping. He was a tiny fellow, who disdained scissors, and, at the end of a seam, always bit off the thread instead of cutting it, so that inch-long strands stuck to his lower lip, and by the end of the day he had a multicolored beard. His sweat poured onto those thread ends and dripped down onto the cloth, which he was constantly blotting with a rag.

1. Oklahoma farmers forced to abandon their farms during the dust storms of the 1930s; subject of the 1939 Pulitzer Prize–winning novel *The Grapes of Wrath* by John Steinbeck.

Word Power
physique the structure or form of a person's body

6 Given the heat, people smelled, of course, but some smelled a lot worse than others. One cutter in my father's shop was a horse in this respect, and my father, who normally had no sense of smell—no one understood why—claimed that he could smell this man and would address him only from a distance. In order to make as much money as possible, this fellow would start work at half past five in the morning and continue until midnight. He owned Bronx apartment houses and land in Florida and Jersey, and seemed half mad with greed. He had a powerful physique, a very straight spine, a tangle of hair, and a black shadow on his cheeks. He snorted like a horse as he pushed through the cutting machine, following his patterns through some eighteen layers of winter-coat material. One late afternoon, he blinked his eyes hard against the burning sweat as he held down the material with his left hand and pressed the vertical, razor-sharp reciprocating blade with his right. The blade sliced through his index finger at the second joint. Angrily refusing to go to the hospital, he ran tap water over the stump, wrapped his hand in a towel, and went right on cutting, snorting, and stinking. When the blood began to show through the towel's bunched layers, my father pulled the plug on the machine and ordered him to the hospital. But he was back at work the next morning, and worked right through the day and into the evening, as usual, piling up his apartment houses.

7 There were still elevated trains then, along Second, Third, Sixth, and Ninth Avenues, and many of the cars were wooden, with windows that opened. Broadway had open trolleys with no side walls, in which you at least caught the breeze, hot though it was, so that desperate people, unable to endure their apartments, would simply pay a nickel and ride around aimlessly for a couple of hours to cool off. As for Coney Island on weekends, block after block of beach was so jammed with people that it was barely possible to find a space to sit or to put down your book or your hot dog.

8 My first direct contact with an air conditioner came only in the sixties, when I was living in the Chelsea Hotel. The so-called management sent up a machine on casters, which rather aimlessly cooled and sometimes heated the air, relying, as it did, on pitchers of water that one had to pour into it. On the initial filling, it would spray water all over the room, so one had to face it toward the bathroom rather than the bed.

9 A South African gentleman once told me that New York in August was hotter than any place he knew in Africa, yet people here dressed for a northern city. He had wanted to wear shorts but feared that he would be arrested for indecent exposure.

10 High heat created irrational solutions: linen suits that collapsed into deep wrinkles when one bent an arm or a knee, and men's straw hats as stiff as matzohs,[2] which, like some kind of hard yellow flower, bloomed annually all over the city on a certain sacred date—June 1 or so. Those hats dug deep pink creases around men's foreheads, and the wrinkled suits, which were supposedly cooler, had to be pulled down and up and sideways to make room for the body within.

11 The city in summer floated in a daze that moved otherwise sensible people to repeat endlessly the brainless greeting "Hot enough for ya? Ha-ha!" It was like the final joke before the meltdown of the world in a pool of sweat.

2. Large, flat, crisp bread eaten during the Jewish holiday of Passover.

Thinking about the Reading

1. The opening paragraphs describe how poor people coped with extreme heat in the 1920s. Was Miller's family poor? Which details in the essay answer this question?
*2. Why do you suppose New York businessmen in the 1920s wore suits instead of cooler, more comfortable clothes? How has men's summer business wear changed since the days Miller writes about?
3. Why do you think Miller chose to focus on the man in his father's factory who smelled like a horse? How does Miller seem to feel about this man? Which details reveal his attitude?
4. Why do you think Miller decided to write about life before air conditioning? Does he accomplish his purpose?

Writing Practice

1. Write a description of a time when you or someone you know had to live without a modern convenience, such as a refrigerator, a telephone, or electricity. How did you (or the other person) cope? As an alternative, imagine a day in your life without one of these conveniences, and write about how your life would be affected.
2. Write a description of your workplace, focusing on the physical appearance, actions, and attitudes of one employee in particular.
3. Write a description of a time when you were physically uncomfortable—hot, cold, exhausted, or in pain or discomfort. What did you do to make yourself feel better?

THE LAST GENERATION TO LIVE ON THE EDGE

Robb Moretti

Is our culture becoming obsessed with protecting children from everyday life? Robb Moretti reminds us that there was a time when all that stood between us and danger was a coonskin cap.

Word Power
malign to make harmful statements about

My parents are part of what has been labeled the Greatest Generation. I hail from a great generation as well. That's because my peers and I, the oft-maligned baby boomers,[1] came before seat belts, bike helmets, and all things plastic protected children from the hazards of everyday life. We were the last Americans to grow up without a childproof safety net.

I know that many of today's protective gadgets prevent kids from getting seriously injured. Looking back, I sometimes wonder how my friends and I survived childhood at all. But I believe that we experienced a kind of freedom that children who came after us have not.

I was born in November 1954 and whisked from the hospital during a violent California rainstorm, not in a car seat but in my mother's arms. Since our car didn't have seat belts, we drove commando.

As a baby, I was tucked into my crib without a padded bumper guard or a machine that soothed me to sleep with amplified sounds of the ocean. Baby pictures show me smiling while I stuck my big head through the wooden bars. At night my mother swaddled me in warm pajamas—the non-flame-retardant kind.

Word Power
diligence attentive care

Once I could walk, I was free to roam around the house under the watchful eye of my parents. Unfortunately, their diligence couldn't prevent every mishap. My mom still tells the story of how I learned not to play with electricity by sticking my toy into an open light socket. When my parents needed peace and quiet, they didn't put me in front of the television to watch a "Baby Einstein" video; they plopped me in a chair to watch my mom do housework or cook.

My dad drove a monstrous Chrysler that had a rear window ledge large enough to provide a comfortable sleeping area during long drives. As a five-year-old, I loved lying on that ledge, staring at the sky or the stars while we roared down the new California freeways. I was a projectile object waiting to happen! Riding in the front didn't improve my odds much: whenever the car came to an abrupt stop, my mother or father would fling an arm across my chest to keep me from going airborne.

During my grade-school years, my mother would often leave my younger sister and me in the car, keys in the ignition and doors unlocked, while she went shopping. When we got home, I would run out to join my friends, with the only rule being to get home by dark. My parents weren't terrified if I was out of their sight. In fact, they enjoyed the silence.

Playing at the park was a high-risk adventure for my friends and me. The jungle gym was a heavy gray apparatus with metal bars, screws, and hooks. On a hot day the metallic surface of the sliding board would burn our behinds. A great afternoon at the park usually meant coming home with blisters on our hands, a bump or two on the melon, and the obligatory skinned knee.

1. The generation born between 1946 and 1964.

I rode my red Schwinn Stingray without wearing a bike helmet; my Davy Crockett cap protected me from serious head injury. Although I did not have the benefit of a crossing guard at the blind intersection I had to traverse to get to school, I was sure the snapping sound made by the baseball cards stuck in my spokes alerted the oncoming traffic to my presence. 9

Every school day my mother packed my Jetsons lunchbox with a tuna-fish sandwich, which we found out later often contained high levels of mercury and a dolphin or two. Also stuffed in my lunchbox was a pint of whole chocolate milk and a package of Hostess Twinkies or cupcakes. 10

Despite our high-fat, high-sugar diets, my friends and I were not out of shape. Maybe that was because we worked so hard in phys-ed class every day. Occasionally our teacher pushed us so far that some poor kid would throw up his lunch. 11

In the afternoons we all played in a school-sponsored baseball league. We didn't wear plastic batting helmets or cups, and we hit pitched balls instead of hitting off a plastic tee. Worst of all, we received trophies or medals only if our team won the championship. 12

Last February, Americans were captivated by the skeleton event at the 2002 Winter Olympics. But thirty-five years earlier, my junior-high friends and I had invented our own version of the sport. We'd roar down steep Bay Area streets on a flexible sled with wheels instead of runners. Like the Olympians, we held our chins just inches above the ground. You don't see kids today with two false front teeth nearly as often as you did in 1967. 13

We baby boomers may not have weathered the Depression or stormed the beaches at Normandy. But we were the last generation to live on the edge and, I believe, to have fun! 14

Thinking about the Reading

1. What examples does Moretti give to support his claim that his generation lived "on the edge" (paragraph 14)?
2. How were Moretti's childhood experiences different from those of today's children? How do you explain those differences?
3. Do you agree with Moretti that his life "on the edge" was worth the risk, or do you believe that the dangers of his generation's behavior outweighed the benefits?

*4. How were Moretti's childhood experiences like and unlike your own? Do you think he is correct in saying that his generation was "the last generation to live on the edge" (paragraph 14)?

Writing Practice

1. Explain in what sense you lived on the edge when you were a child—and in what sense you did not.
2. What risks do you experience as part of your adult life? Do you see these risks as necessary? Do you seek them out? Do you think you live on the edge?
3. Do you believe today's parents of young children are overprotective? Do you think children should be given fewer rules? Write a letter to the editor of a parenting magazine in which you support your position with examples from your own experience.

WHY WE NEED ANIMAL EXPERIMENTATION

Thuy Nguyen

Student writer Thuy Nguyen argues that animal experimentation is necessary to improve medical technology and thus to save human lives. Thuy develops her argument with three points. As you read this essay, note the specific examples she supplies to support these points.

With our advanced medical technology today, medicine has helped save 1
many lives. The advances in medical technology that have saved these lives, for the most part, have been developed from animal experimentation. However, some people have claimed that animal experimentation is cruel and should not be continued. In my opinion, because medical research is so dependent on it, animal experimentation should be continued. It provides preventive measures to protect humans against getting diseases, helps discover cures and treatments for diseases, and helps surgeons to perfect the surgical techniques that are needed to save human lives.

First of all, animal experimentation provides preventive measures to 2
protect humans from getting diseases. With the help of medical research on animals, scientists have found useful applications of vaccines to prevent many diseases. For example, the vaccines for polio, typhoid, diphtheria, tetanus, tuberculosis, measles, mumps, and rubella were all developed through animal experimentation. In addition, the principle of sterilization came out of Pasteur's[1] discovery, through animal experimentation, that microbes cause diseases. As a result, nowadays, medical professionals know that it is extremely important to sterilize medical tools such as gloves and syringes in order to keep them bacteria-free and to prevent patients from getting infections. Also, from experiments on rats, the connection between smoking and lung cancer was conclusively proved. This led many people to quit smoking and avoid getting cancer.

Word Power

sterilization the process of making something free of germs

microbe a germ

Besides leading to preventive measures, animal experimentation also 3
leads to the discovery of cures and treatments for many diseases. For instance, it has helped with the treatment of diabetic patients who are in need of insulin. Through experiments on cows and pigs, researchers have found the usefulness of cows' and pigs' insulin for treating diabetes. In addition, many drugs discovered through animal tests have been proven to cure ill patients. For example, a number of antibiotics, such as penicillin and sulfonamides, which were found from animal experimentation, help cure many infections. Also, many antihypertension medicines, which were developed in experiments on cats, help control blood pressure in hypertensive patients. Similarly, anticancer drugs were developed from tests on rats and dogs.

Word Power

hypertensive having high blood pressure

Besides providing preventive measures to protect humans from getting 4
diseases and helping discover cures and treatments for many diseases, animal experimentation also helps surgeons to perfect the surgical techniques needed to save human lives. Surgeons have always been searching for better techniques to make surgery safer and more effective for their patients. One good way to perfect these techniques is to practice them on animals. From experiments on cats, researchers have found suturing tech-

1. Louis Pasteur (1822–1895) was a French chemist.

niques for transplants. Similarly, techniques for open heart surgery were perfected through many years of animal experimentation. Animal research programs have also helped surgeons to refine their techniques for kidney dialysis needed by patients with kidney failure.

5 Animal experimentation should be continued because it provides preventive measures to protect humans against diseases, helps to discover cures and treatments for diseases, and helps surgeons to perfect their surgical techniques. Therefore, animal experimentation is vital for the medical research that saves human lives.

Word Power

suture to use fiber to close up wounds or to connect two parts of the body

Thinking about the Reading

1. What are the three points Thuy Nguyen makes to develop her argument that animal experimentation is essential to medical research?
2. What does the first paragraph of this essay accomplish? Where does Thuy first state each of her reasons for continuing animal experimentation? Where does she support each of these points? What does the last paragraph achieve?

*3. Are the examples Thuy presents convincing? Does she present enough support? Do any of the following elements appear in this essay?

- An explanation of what animal experimentation means
- Expert opinions on the subject of animal experimentation
- A response to possible arguments against Thuy's point of view

If not, how would the addition of these elements improve the essay?

*4. Do you agree with Thuy's position on animal experimentation? What objections do you have? Support your position with facts and examples from your reading and experience.

Writing Practice

1. Revise Thuy's essay to give it more personal appeal for the reader. For example, make some of the examples come alive with narratives about people who could be helped by animal experimentation.
2. Write an editorial that takes a position against the use of animal experimentation. Consider some of the following points made by opponents of animal experimentation:

   - The same medical results could be obtained by means other than animal experimentation.
   - Some animal experimentation is not necessary to medical research and could be eliminated.
   - Animal experimentation is not humane.

3. Choose an issue that is important to you, and write an essay supporting your position on that issue. Use facts and examples from your reading and experience to support your point of view.

HOW TO STOP A CAR WITH NO BRAKES

Joshua Piven and David Borgenicht

In this instructional essay from *The Worst-Case Scenario Handbook,* Joshua Piven and David Borgenicht explain how to avert catastrophe in a car with no brakes. Piven and Borgenicht are the authors of the best-selling book *The Worst-Case Scenario Handbook* (1999), whose success sparked a series of *Worst-Case Scenario* books as well as a reality television show.

1. Begin pumping the brake pedal and keep pumping it. You may be able to build up enough pressure in the braking system to slow down a bit, or even stop completely. If you have anti-lock brakes, you do not normally pump them—but if your brakes have failed, this may work.

2. Do not panic—relax and steer the car smoothly. Cars will often safely corner at speeds much higher than you realize or are used to driving. The rear of the car may slip; steer evenly, being careful not to over-correct.

3. Shift the car into the lowest gear possible and let the engine and transmission slow you down.

4. Pull the emergency brake—but not too hard. Pulling too hard on the emergency brake will cause the rear wheels to lock, and the car to spin around. Use even, constant pressure. In most cars, the emergency brake (also known as the hand brake or parking brake) is cable operated and serves as a fail-safe brake that should still work even when the rest of the braking system has failed. The car should slow down and, in combination with the lower gear, will eventually stop.

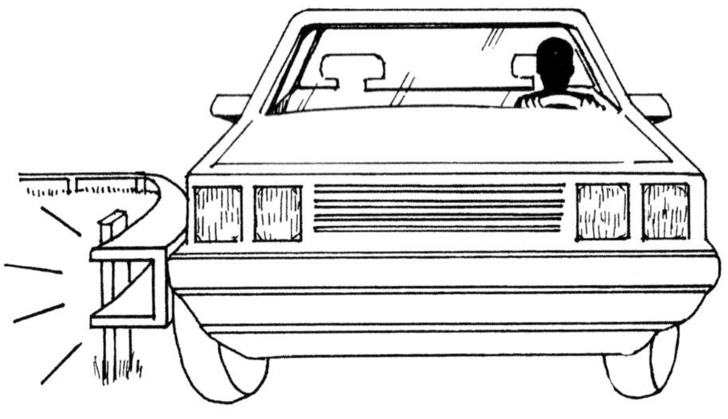

Sideswiping guardrails or rocks may help slow you down. Do this only at slower speeds.

5. If you are running out of room, try a "bootlegger's turn." Yank the emergency brake hard while turning the wheel a quarter turn in either direction—whichever is safer. This will make the car spin 180 degrees. If you were heading downhill, this spin will head you back uphill, allowing you to slow down.

6. If you have room, swerve the car back and forth across the road. Making hard turns at each side of the road will decrease your speed even more.

7. If you come up behind another car, use it to help you stop. Blow your horn, flash your lights, and try to get the driver's attention. If you hit

the car, be sure to hit it square, bumper to bumper, so you do not knock the other car off the road. This is an extremely dangerous maneuver: It works best if the vehicle in front of you is larger than yours—a bus or truck is ideal—and if both vehicles are traveling at similar speeds. You do not want to crash into a much slower-moving or stopped vehicle, however.

8. Look for something to help stop you. A flat or uphill road that intersects with the road you are on, a field, or a fence will slow you further but not stop you suddenly. Scraping the side of your car against a guardrail is another option. Avoid trees and wooden telephone poles: They do not yield as readily. 8

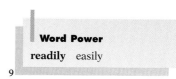

Word Power
readily easily

9. Do not attempt to sideswipe oncoming cars. 9

10. If none of the above steps has enabled you to stop and you are about to go over a cliff, try to hit something that will slow you down before you go over. This strategy will also leave a clue to others that someone has gone over the edge. But since very few cliffs are sheer drops, you may fall just several feet and then stop. 10

Word Power
sheer very steep; almost perpendicular

Thinking about the Reading

*1. Because the steps in the process that Piven and Borgenicht outline are numbered, they do not include transitions to indicate the order of the steps or the relationship between one step and the next. Can you suggest some transitional words and phrases that could be added?

2. What warnings and reminders do the writers include? Do you think they need additional cautions?

3. Do you think the picture on page 500 is necessary? Can you suggest other visuals that might be more effective?

*4. Do you think the writers should have omitted the last paragraph? Why or why not?

Writing Practice

1. Write an introduction and a conclusion for "How to Stop a Car with No Brakes." Then, select the most useful information in this essay, and use it to help you write a short article *in your own words* for a driver education manual.
2. List ten steps that would help readers survive a different difficult or dangerous situation. Then, expand the items on your list into an essay, adding an introduction and a conclusion.
3. Write an essay directed at an urban audience in which you explain a process that is familiar to residents of rural areas, or write an essay for a rural audience in which you explain a process that is familiar to city dwellers.

THE LITTLE PRETZEL LADY

Sara Price

For some children, adult responsibility comes early in life. Student writer Sara Price recounts her experience as a ten-year-old working a Saturday job with her brother. For three years, to help their financially strapped family, Sara and her brother sold pretzels in a local shopping center.

When I was ten years old, selling pretzels at the corner of a shopping center was not my favorite weekend activity. Unfortunately, however, I had no alternative. My father had recently been injured on the job, and we had been experiencing severe financial difficulties. His disability payments and my mother's salary were not enough to support four children and my grandparents. When my parents could not pay our monthly mortgage, the bank threatened to take our house.

Word Power

persist to continue to do something despite setbacks

Knowing we had to find jobs to help, my older brother and I asked the local soft pretzel dealer to give us work on Saturdays. At first he refused, saying we were too young. But we simply would not take no for an answer because our parents desperately needed financial help. When we persisted, the pretzel dealer agreed to let us start the next week. In return for his kindness, my brother and I agreed to work faithfully for the next three years.

On the first Saturday morning, my brother and I reported promptly to our positions in front of the Cool-Rite appliance shop at the Academy Plaza shopping center. When Tom, our dealer, arrived with three hundred pretzels, he set up the stand and gave us instructions to sell each pretzel for a quarter, and five for a dollar. Then, Tom wished us luck and said he would be back later to pick up the table and the money. The arrangement with him was that we would get one-third of the total sales.

On that first Saturday, after selling our three hundred pretzels, my brother and I earned ten dollars each. (We also received a two-dollar tip from a friendly man who bought fifteen pretzels.) Our first day was considered a good one because we sold out by 4 p.m. However, the days that followed were not always as smooth as the first. When the weather was bad, meaning rain or snow, sales decreased; there were times when we had to stay as late as 7 p.m. until the last pretzel was sold.

To my regular customers, I was the little pretzel lady. But to my classmates, I was the target of humiliation. My worst nightmare came true when they found out that I ran a pretzel stand. Many of the boys made fun of me by calling out nasty names and harassing me for free pretzels. It was extremely embarrassing to see them walk by and stare while I stood like a helpless beggar on the street. I came to dread weekends and hate the sight of pretzels. But I was determined not to give up because I had a family that needed support and a three-year promise to fulfill. With that in mind, I continued to work.

Although winter was the best season for sales, I especially disliked standing in the teeth-chattering cold. I still remember that stinging feeling when the harsh wind blew against my cheeks. In order to survive the hours of shivering, I usually wore two or three pairs of socks and extra-thick clothing. Many times, I felt like a lonesome, leafless tree rooted to one spot and unable to escape from the bitter cold of winter.

7 The worst incident of my pretzel career occurred when I was selling alone because my brother was sick. A pair of teenage boys came up to the stand, called me offensive names, and squirted mustard all over the pretzels. My instant reaction was total shock, and before I could do anything else, they quickly ran away. A few minutes later, I discarded the pretzels, desperately fighting back the tears. I felt helpless and angry because I could not understand their actions.

8 The three years seemed like forever, but finally they were over. Even though selling pretzels on the street was the worst job I ever had, I was grateful for it. The money I earned each Saturday accumulated over the three years and helped my family. Selling pretzels also taught me many important values, such as responsibility, teamwork, independence, and appreciation for hard-earned money. Today, as I pass the pretzel vendors on my way to school, I think of a time not too long ago when I was the little pretzel lady.

Word Power

offensive hurtful; disagreeable; unpleasant

accumulate to gather or pile up little by little

Thinking about the Reading

1. What emotions did you experience as you read "The Little Pretzel Lady"? Which incidents or statements caused these emotions?
2. Children are often cruel to one another. What do you think caused the cruelty that Sara Price experienced?
3. Sara says that she sometimes felt like "a lonesome, leafless tree rooted to one spot and unable to escape from the bitter cold of winter" (paragraph 6). Explain how this image suits Sara's situation.

*4. Do you think that Sara's experience as a "pretzel lady" was more hurtful than beneficial to her? Give reasons to support your answer.

Writing Practice

1. Write about a time in your childhood when you felt different from others and vulnerable to teasing or cruelty by other children.
2. Write about the "little pretzel lady" and her experiences from the point of view of a clerk in the Cool-Rite appliance shop who watches the two children sell pretzels every Saturday.
3. Write about an experience you had at work that made you like or dislike your job. Be sure to include details about the workplace, your job responsibilities, the other people involved in the situation, and any conversations that occurred.

SAY SOMETHING

Lucie Prinz

Lucie Prinz urges adults to lose their fear of teenagers and dare to "say something" when they encounter unacceptable behavior. Is she making a courageous moral statement, or is she encouraging meddling or even harassment? You be the judge.

I was sitting on the subway a few weeks ago when I looked up and saw a 1
baby, just a little less than a year old, swinging from the overhead bar. She was flanked by two young teenage girls who thought this was a great way to entertain their little sister. As the train began to move, I could visualize the baby flying across the car. Without really thinking, I said to the girls, "Hey, that's not a good idea. That baby is going to get hurt. You better sit down with her on the seat." The kids gave me one of those "Who do you think you are?" looks they reserve for meddling adults, but they took the baby off the bar and sat down.

I was suddenly struck by the silence in the subway car. The normal hum 2
of conversation had vanished. My fellow passengers, who had witnessed my encounter with the kids, were now engrossed in their newspapers and books or staring at something fascinating on the subway-tunnel wall. The car was not very crowded, and everyone had seen that endangered baby just as clearly as I had, but they had chosen not to get involved. Although most of them now avoided eye contact with me, a few treated me to the kind of disdain reserved for troublemakers. Could it be that my fellow passengers didn't care about that baby? Or were they just afraid to interfere?

We've all heard the old African saying "It takes a whole village to raise a child." Americans have adopted it, and I understand why. It expresses some things that we can all easily accept: family values, shared responsibility, community spirit. But do we really believe in it as a guiding principle for our lives? When we repeat it, are we pledging ourselves to carry out its imperative? I don't think so.

Word Power

imperative a command that must be obeyed

Americans are known for generosity. We're ready to rescue the suffering children of the world. We send food to Ethiopia after our television screens show us little kids with huge eyes and distended bellies. We help the victims of floods, and we fund agencies to take care of refugees and abandoned children. We are the nation that invented the poster child and the telethon. These nameless suffering children touch our hearts—but they do not touch our lives.

Word Power

plight an unfortunate or difficult situation

The same adults who are profoundly moved by the plight of children they will never know seem to be willing to ignore the children they encounter every day, even if it is obvious that these children are in trouble or that they need a little adult guidance. I've watched adults actually move away from children they see approaching. I'm not talking about hostile, swaggering gangs of teenage boys—although even some of them are just exhibiting the high that comes with that first surge of testosterone. I'm talking about the ordinary, harmless children we all come in contact with every day on the streets of our cities, towns, and, yes, villages.

I'm keeping score, counting the number of times I find myself the only person in a crowd who dares to interact with a child she doesn't know.

A few days after the swinging-baby incident I was waiting on a crowded subway platform when someone pushed me from behind. I turned to see three teenage girls, giggling, ebullient, and so eager to get on the train just pulling into the station that they were shoving. Again I reacted without thinking. "Stop pushing—we'll all get on," I said. After a few murmured remarks along the lines of "Get lost, lady," they stopped. So did the conversation around me. Eyes swiveled away. I felt a collective intake of breath. Disapproval hung in the air, but mainly I sensed fear.

8 Seconds later the train doors opened, and we all stepped in. The woman who dropped into the seat next to me said, "Wow, that was a brave thing to do." When I suggested that it was no such thing, she said, "Well, you can't be too careful these days." That's just it, I thought. You *can* be too careful.

9 In both these encounters I treated harmless children as if they were indeed harmless. They may have been foolish, thoughtless, rambunctious, rude, or annoying. But the only one in any danger was that baby swinging on the bar.

10 I live in a big city. I know that there are violent armed children, hopeless and desperate kids out there. There is no way that I can attack the serious urban problems we all hear about on the evening news. But I am convinced that I can contribute to the larger solutions by refusing to recoil from kids just because they are acting like kids. A lost child who encounters fear instead of concern is twice lost. By responding to these children we may begin to build a village where they will flourish and adults can live without fear.

Word Power

ebullient lively and enthusiastic

Word Power

rambunctious unruly; full of uncontrolled energy

Word Power

recoil to shrink away from something in fear or disapproval

Thinking about the Reading

*1. When Prinz confronted the girls who were endangering the baby, the other adults in the subway car reacted with fear or disapproval. Do you think these reactions are typical? Give examples from your own observations and experience to support your answer.

*2. What does Prinz mean when she writes, "The same adults who are profoundly moved by the plight of children they will never know seem to be willing to ignore the children they encounter every day" (paragraph 5)? Why might it be easier to help a child or teenager we will never meet personally?

3. What does the woman in the subway car mean when she says to Prinz, "You can't be too careful these days" (paragraph 8)? Do you agree with her or with Prinz, who believes that "you *can* be too careful"? Give reasons for your answer.

*4. Why does Prinz think that all adults should say something if they see children or teenagers behaving in an unacceptable way? Do you think this would make life better for the youngsters as well as for the adults?

Writing Practice

1. Write about a time when your childish actions were misinterpreted by an adult. Could a more understanding adult have made the situation better? Give examples to support your answer.
2. According to Prinz, most Americans agree with the idea that "It takes a whole village to raise a child" (paragraph 3). Write about how your town or neighborhood might help children and teenagers develop into responsible adults. Give at least two examples of how this might be accomplished.
3. Write about a time when you chose not to get involved in a situation you were witnessing. Explain your reasons for not getting involved, and tell how you would act in that situation today.

REALITY TV'S "HICK HUNT" AND THE APPALACHIAN TRUTH

Gerry Roll

In 2003, CBS began work on a new reality series billed as *The Real Beverly Hillbillies*. In this article, Gerry Roll tries to dispel the negative mythology surrounding Appalachian culture, a place she calls home. Roll lives in Hazard, Kentucky, and is executive director of Hazard Perry County Community Ministries.

CBS is scouring my Kentucky county for *The Real Beverly Hillbillies*. Evi- 1
dently, CBS's CEO Les Moonves thinks families who have struggled with poverty for generations and overcome obstacles for survival that would make most urban Americans cringe is good comedy. I am saddened by his assumption that anyone would think this is entertainment.

In the new world of reality TV, I guess you could call my life *The Real* 2
Green Acres. About twelve years ago, I moved from Palm Beach County, Florida, to Perry County, Kentucky. Unlike so many people before me, I didn't move here to save Appalachia. I moved here so Appalachia could save me. I came here to find a community of hard-working folks who cared not only about themselves but also about one another.

I came here to live in a place where a modest wage will support a mod- 3
est lifestyle. I came here so my children could go to a school where everybody knows everybody and the principal calls you at home when they aren't there. I came here to breathe clean air. I came looking for my own personal Camelot,[1] and I found it.

Appalachia, just like most of rural America, has all of the same mal- 4
adies you find in the city. There is homelessness, which occasionally appears similar to that in urban areas—people sleeping on the street, under the bridge, in the car. But rural homelessness here is more often hidden, experienced by families living in severely substandard housing; families doubled and tripled up so no one is left on their own to freeze.

There is hunger, sometimes experienced by children from homes with 5
no food or potable water. But mostly hunger is hidden, experienced by families whose wages are so low that an inordinate number of them survive on food stamps, gardening, and sharing. And there is drug abuse in Appalachia. Yes, some people sell meth or crack on Main Street, but more often, people overuse prescription drugs to combat depression and boredom.

> **Word Power**
> **potable** safe to drink

In recent years, the problems of rural America—particularly Appa- 6
lachia—have reached the radar screen for state and federal initiatives. These programs have recognized our problems and engaged us in finding solutions.

> **Word Power**
> **initiative** a new legislative measure

Now, just as quickly as rural America got the attention it deserved, the 7
much-needed initiatives are threatened by state and federal budget cuts. Just when we were gaining our momentum to truly be a part of a solution to poverty—not just for ourselves but by showing our entire nation what can happen with a true sense of community—we must waste precious time fighting backward media moguls who have obviously spent too much time watching TV.

> **Word Power**
> **mogul** a rich or powerful person

1. The legendary site of King Arthur's court; an idealized place.

The Beverly Hillbillies are fiction. What is real is the meaningful life and work that rural people who still live in a community with one another have. What is real is the responsibility we feel in Appalachia to take care of our own. What is real is the way we rally around a problem and work toward a solution together. What is real are the high moral standards of hardworking rural Americans. 8

We need good jobs and decent housing, just as the folks in the big cities do. As communities, we're working hard toward creative solutions to problems we have. People like Mr. Moonves need to understand that to build a strong nation, we have to build strong communities. That means letting yourself be touched by someone else's needs, not launching a "hick hunt" to take jabs at a mythical culture. Rural America is still holding on to one thing our urban counterparts lost long ago, that sense of community. Perhaps CBS should do a special about that. 9

Word Power

counterparts two items that closely resemble each other

Thinking about the Reading

1. Exactly what are Roll's objections to CBS's plans for a reality TV show set in Appalachia?
*2. In paragraph 2, Roll says, "I didn't move here to save Appalachia. I moved here so Appalachia could save me." What do you think she means?
3. According to Roll, what problems exist in Appalachia?
4. According to Roll, what is the difference between the reality of Appalachia and the fiction of the proposed series?

Writing Practice

1. Imagine that a TV network is about to film a reality series set in your community (or your school). Write a letter to a network executive in which you defend your community as Roll defends hers.
2. Do you see reality TV as harmless entertainment, or do you think it is a disturbing—or even dangerous—trend in TV programming? Use examples of current reality shows to support your position.
3. Write a proposal for a new reality show that would have a serious purpose and educational value. Where would you set this program? Who would participate? What lessons would you hope to communicate to viewers?

THE DOG ATE MY DISK, AND OTHER TALES OF WOE

Carolyn Foster Segal

> **Word Power**
> **woe** sadness

Carolyn Foster Segal, assistant professor of English at Cedar Crest College in Pennsylvania, has heard practically every student excuse for handing in late papers. In this humorous essay, she divides student excuses into categories. This article appeared in *The Chronicle of Higher Education,* a periodical for college teachers.

> **Word Power**
> **feline** (noun) a member of the cat family; (adjective) catlike

1 Taped to the door of my office is a cartoon that features a cat explaining to his feline teacher, "The dog ate my homework." It is intended as a gently humorous reminder to my students that I will not accept excuses for late work, and it, like the lengthy warning on my syllabus, has had absolutely no effect. With a show of energy and creativity that would be admirable if applied to the (missing) assignments in question, my students persist, week after week, semester after semester, year after year, in offering excuses about why their work is not ready. Those reasons fall into several broad categories: the family, the best friend, the evils of dorm life, the evils of technology, and the totally bizarre.

> **Word Power**
> **veracity** truthfulness

2 **The Family** The death of the grandfather/grandmother is, of course, the grandmother of all excuses. What heartless teacher would dare to question a student's grief or veracity? What heartless student would lie, wishing death on a revered family member, just to avoid a deadline? Creative students may win extra extensions (and days off) with a little careful planning and fuller plot development, as in the sequence of "My grandfather/grandmother is sick"; "Now my grandfather/grandmother is in the hospital"; and finally, "We could all see it coming—my grandfather/grandmother is dead."

> **Word Power**
> **conjure up** to bring to mind

3 Another favorite excuse is "the family emergency," which (always) goes like this: "There was an emergency at home, and I had to help my family." It's a lovely sentiment, one that conjures up images of Louisa May Alcott's little women rushing off with baskets of food and copies of *Pilgrim's Progress,* but I do not understand why anyone would turn to my most irresponsible students in times of trouble.

4 **The Best Friend** This heartwarming concern for others extends beyond the family to friends, as in, "My best friend was up all night and I had to (a) stay up with her in the dorm, (b) drive her to the hospital, or (c) drive to her college because (1) her boyfriend broke up with her, (2) she was throwing up blood [no one catches a cold anymore; everyone throws up blood], or (3) her grandfather/grandmother died."

> **Word Power**
> **adjunct** an instructor at a college or university who is not a permanent staff member; any temporary employee

5 At one private university where I worked as an adjunct, I heard an interesting spin that incorporated the motifs of both best friend and dead relative: "My best friend's mother killed herself." One has to admire the cleverness here: A mysterious woman in the prime of her life has allegedly committed suicide, and no professor can prove otherwise! And I admit I was moved, until finally I had to point out to my students that it was amazing how the simple act of my assigning a topic for a paper seemed to drive large numbers of otherwise happy and healthy middle-aged women to their deaths. I was careful to make that point during an off week, during which no deaths were reported.

6 **The Evils of Dorm Life** These stories are usually fairly predictable; almost always feature the evil roommate or hallmate, with my student in

the role of the innocent victim; and can be summed up as follows: My roommate, who is a horrible person, likes to party, and I, who am a good person, cannot concentrate on my work when he or she is partying. Variations include stories about the two people next door who were running around and crying loudly last night because (a) one of them had boyfriend/girlfriend problems; (b) one of them was throwing up blood; or (c) someone, somewhere, died. A friend of mine in graduate school had a student who claimed that his roommate attacked him with a hammer. That, in fact, was a true story; it came out in court when the bad roommate was tried for killing his grandfather.

The Evils of Technology The computer age has revolutionized the student story, inspiring almost as many new excuses as it has Internet businesses. Here are just a few electronically enhanced explanations: 7

- The computer wouldn't let me save my work.
- The printer wouldn't print.
- The printer wouldn't print this disk.
- The printer wouldn't give me time to proofread.
- The printer made a black line run through all my words, and I know you can't read this, but do you still want it, or wait, here, take my disk. File name? I don't know what you mean.
- I swear I attached it.
- It's my roommate's computer, and she usually helps me, but she had to go to the hospital because she was throwing up blood.
- I did write to the newsgroup, but all my messages came back to me.
- I just found out that all my other newsgroup messages came up under a diferent name. I just want you to know that its really me who wrote all those messages, you can tel which ones our mine because I didnt use the spelcheck! But it was yours truely :) Anyway, just in case you missed those messages or dont belief its my writting. I'll repeat what I sad: I thought the last movie we watched in clas was borring.

The Totally Bizarre I call the first story "The Pennsylvania Chain Saw Episode." A commuter student called to explain why she had missed my morning class. She had gotten up early so that she would be wide awake for class. Having a bit of extra time, she walked outside to see her neighbor, who was cutting some wood. She called out to him, and he waved back to her with the saw. Wouldn't you know it, the safety catch wasn't on or was broken, and the blade flew right out of the saw and across his lawn and over her fence and across her yard and severed a tendon in her right hand. So she was calling me from the hospital, where she was waiting for surgery. Luckily, she reassured me, she had remembered to bring her paper and a stamped envelope (in a plastic bag, to avoid bloodstains) along with her in the ambulance, and a nurse was mailing everything to me even as we spoke. 8

That wasn't her first absence. In fact, this student had missed most of the class meetings, and I had already recommended that she withdraw from the course. Now I suggested again that it might be best if she dropped the class. I didn't harp on the absences (what if even some of this story were true?). I did mention that she would need time to recuperate and that making up so much missed work might be difficult. "Oh, no," she said, "I can't drop this course. I had been planning to go on to medical school and become a surgeon, but since I won't be able to operate because 9

Word Power

harp on to repeat over and over again

of my accident, I'll have to major in English, and this course is more important than ever to me." She did come to the next class, wearing—as evidence of her recent trauma—a bedraggled Ace bandage on her left hand.

You may be thinking that nothing could top that excuse, but in fact I 10
have one more story, provided by the same student, who sent me a letter to explain why her final assignment would be late. While recuperating from her surgery, she had begun corresponding on the Internet with a man who lived in Germany. After a one-week, whirlwind Web romance, they had agreed to meet in Rome, to rendezvous (her phrase) at the papal Easter Mass. Regrettably, the time of her flight made it impossible for her to attend class, but she trusted that I—just this once—would accept late work if the pope wrote a note.

Word Power

rendezvous (verb) to meet at a prearranged place and time; (noun) a meeting of this kind

Thinking about the Reading

1. What categories of excuses does Segal identify? Can you think of others she does not mention?

*2. Sarcastic remarks mean the opposite of what they say and are usually meant to mock or poke fun at someone or something. In what ways does Segal use sarcasm? Give some examples.

*3. Do you think this essay is funny? Do you find it offensive in any way? Explain.

4. Would you be interested in reading a serious essay on Segal's topic? Why or why not?

Writing Practice

1. Write about the strangest excuse you have ever been given by someone for not doing something he or she was supposed to do. Tell about the circumstances of this excuse in a humorous manner.
2. Discuss one of the following topics (or a similar topic of your own choice):

   - Ways to turn down a date
   - Types of behavior by a baby, child, or pet
   - Types of students at your school

3. Write a letter to Carolyn Foster Segal explaining why your English paper will be late. Admit that you have read her essay about various categories of student excuses, but insist that *your* excuse is true.

THE COLORS

Gary Soto

The work of Mexican-American poet and short story writer Gary Soto is popular with children and adults alike. He often writes about his memories of growing up in Fresno, California, in the 1950s and 1960s. In *A Summer Life,* a book of short essays from which "The Colors" is taken, Soto describes the sights, sounds, smells, and textures of his childhood world.

Grandfather's favorite color was the green of dollar bills. On summer evenings he watered his lawn, the jet of water cooling his thumb from eight hours of stapling wooden crates at Sun Maid Raisin. He knew that his house, pink as it was, was worth money. He knew that if he kept the rose bushes throwing out buds of sweet flowers, the value of the house would increase. The fruit trees would grow and thicken with branches to feed his family and neighbor. 1

Grandmother was also fond of green but preferred the silver shine of coins that made her eyebrows jump up and down. She showed me a nickel slug from the county fair stamped: MILK IS GOOD. She could not read or write in Spanish or English and thought the coin was worth more than a brown child realized. I wanted to say that it was nothing. It could sparkle in the sun or make a nice necklace, but it was no rare coin. I drank my purple Kool-Aid, crunched spines of air trapped in the ice cubes, and made my eyebrows jump up and down like hers. 2

> **Word Power**
>
> **slug** a coin-shaped metal disk that has no monetary value

Yellow was her favorite color. Yellow roses floated in a bowl on the windowsill. The yellow sunshine clock hummed on the wall, and her yellow refrigerator, the first on the block, blended well with the floor, a speckled affair with some yellow but mostly black. From a top shelf of the hallway closet, she took down a shoe box of papers, including a single stock certificate from a sewing machine company. I looked closely at the yellowed paper and noted "one share" and the date "1939." It was now 1961, and even though I was young, nine at the time, I guessed that the stock was worth the memory of hope but little else. 3

> **Word Power**
>
> **speckled** spotted with dots of color

"When you marry, honey, I will give this to you," she said, shaking the paper at me. "You'll be a rich man." 4

My eyebrows jumped up and down, and I went outside to the backyard to play with my favorite color, mud. At my grandparents' house there were no toys, no pets, no TV in English, so when I stayed there I had to come up with things to do. I tried rolling summer-warmed oranges around the yard in a sort of bowling game in which I tried to knock over sparrows that had come in search of worms. But after twenty minutes of this I was bored. I did chin-ups on the clothesline pole, but that was sweaty work that bored me even more. 5

So I fashioned mud into two forts and a great wall on which I stuck flags of straw-like weeds. When the mud dried hard as a turtle, I pounded the hell out of the forts and wall, imagining that a Chinese war had come. I made bomb sounds and moaned for the dying. My thumb pressed a red ant, and I said, "Too bad." 6

Mud was a good color, and the purple of plums made my mouth water. Peaches did the same, and the arbor of greenish grapes that I spied in the neighbor's yard. Their German Shepherd, ears erect, spied me too, so I 7 couldn't climb the fence and help myself. But looking was almost like eating, and noon was near.

The brown of *frijoles*[1] was our favorite color as steam wavered in our 8
faces. Grandfather, who came home for lunch, left his shoes near the door, smothered his beans with a river of chile and scooped them with big rips of tortilla.[2] I ate with a fork and a tortilla, savoring little mouthfuls of beans with a trickle of chile. The clear color of water washed it all down, and the striped candy cane left over from Christmas sweetened the day. Grandfather, patting his stomach, smiled at me and turned on the radio to the Spanish station. For dessert, there was dark coffee and a powdered donut on a white plate. Grandmother sipped coffee and tore jelly-red sweetness from a footprint-sized Danish.[3]

While Grandfather played a game of solitaire, I fooled with the tooth- 9
picks in the wooden, pig-shaped holder, the only thing that resembled a toy in the house or yard. I swept the crumbs from the table and pinched the donut crumbs from Grandfather's plate. Grandmother did the dishes, ever mindful of the sweep of the sunshine clock. "Viejo,"[4] she said, "it's time."

I walked Grandfather to the front yard, where he stopped and said to 10
me, "A pink house is worth lot of money, m'ijo."[5] We both stood admiring the house, trimmed with flowers and a wrought-iron gate, a plastic flamingo standing one-legged in front of a geranium. This was home, the color of his life. We started up the block, me taking two steps for every one of his, and he said no one's lawn was as green as his. When we looked back, when Grandfather said I should go because it was time to work, Grandmother was at the front window beating the dusty windowsills with a dish towel, waving goodbye until later.

Thinking about the Reading

1. Circle all the color words in this essay. What do these words add to the memories of Soto's childhood?

*2. What do these characters' favorite colors suggest about them?

- Grandfather—green
- Grandmother—silver and yellow
- boy—mud brown

3. Why do you think Soto chose to describe the colors of the food at lunch rather than the smells or tastes?
4. In describing his grandfather's house, Soto says, "This was home, the color of his life" (paragraph 10). What do the colors in this essay suggest about the grandfather's life?

1. Beans.
2. A round, thin, flat cake of cornmeal or wheat, usually filled with meat, cheese, or other foods.
3. A large pastry containing a fruit or cheese filling.
4. Old man.
5. Shortened form of *mi hijo,* meaning "my boy" or "my son."

Writing Practice

1. Write a description of a meal, emphasizing the colors as well as the tastes and textures of each dish.
2. Write a description of a place, focusing on the colors. You might want to emphasize either the variety of colors in that place or the sameness of the colors.
3. Describe a memory you have of a grandparent or older person who was important to you when you were a child. Place the person in a setting that shows what the person's life was like, such as his or her home, work, or place of worship.

TAKE-OUT RESTAURANT

Kimsohn Tang

In this essay, student writer Kimsohn Tang examines the life of her Uncle Meng, the owner of a Chinese take-out restaurant. As Kim describes the stresses and risks that go with this demanding job, she asks whether the high income is worth the problems that Uncle Meng endures.

Word Power

profanity vulgar, abusive language

1 My Uncle Meng owns the New Phoenix Take-Out Restaurant at the corner of Main Street and Landfair Avenue in North Philadelphia, a dangerous place. Words of profanity and various kinds of graffiti are written on the wall outside his restaurant. On his windows are black bars just like those on the windows of prisons. Inside his take-out, bulletproof glass separates the customers' area from the workers' area. Every day, Uncle Meng works in his restaurant with his wife and a cook. He must prepare the food, carry it to the cooking area, take orders, run back and forth to get things, cook the food, and satisfy his customers. Although he earns a decent salary, his job not only takes him away from his family but is also stressful, hard, and dangerous.

Word Power

wholesaler a person who sells large amounts of merchandise to stores or individuals, who then resell it

marinate to let meat, fish, or vegetables soak in a sauce to make them more flavorful or tender

2 Uncle Meng works long hours, from 11 a.m. to midnight. He is constantly working. Even before he opens the restaurant, he has to prepare the food by getting the raw food from the wholesaler, marinating and putting bread crumbs on fifty pounds of chicken, coloring rice, making soup, and carrying heavy pots and pans of food to the cooking area. After he opens the take-out, the customers come in, and now Uncle Meng has to take orders; cook the food; put the food in containers, place sodas, drinks and food in bags; and hand the customers the bags through the little hole in the bulletproof glass. Throughout the day and into the night, Uncle Meng continues to work. Even at midnight, after the take-out is closed, his work is not finished because he has to clean up the place.

3 Because of his long working hours, Uncle Meng has little time to spend with his family, especially his two children, a sixteen-year-old daughter and a thirteen-year-old son. Most of his time is spent in his restaurant. The only time he is free is on Sunday, when the restaurant is closed; this is the only time he and his family actually spend together. On regular school days, if he has time, Uncle Meng brings his children to and from school; otherwise, his sister or one of his other relatives takes them. When his children get home, they stay in their apartment above the take-out and only come down once in a while. Because Uncle Meng is so busy, he does not even have time to help his children with their homework.

Word Power

pertaining to relating to or having to do with

4 Having little time to spend with his family is not the worst thing about his job; the stress from customers is even worse. Customers will yell out, "Man, where's my food? Why is it taking so long? I can't wait all day, you know!" Uncle Meng must have a lot of patience with the customers and not yell back at them. If the customers complain about getting different food from what they have ordered, Uncle Meng has to calm them down and make another dish for them. In addition, the customers are always asking for various things, such as more forks, spoons, or napkins, which is hard for Uncle Meng to handle. When a customer has a question pertaining to a dish on the menu, Uncle Meng also has to explain what ingredients are in the dish. He has to satisfy the customers and give them what they want, or else they will give him more trouble.

5 Uncle Meng's working conditions are the worst aspect of his job. Because the cooking area is always hot, Uncle Meng is never comfortable. The working area is also a dangerous place to be in; if he is not cautious while frying, he can get burns from the splattering oil. Lifting heavy pans while stir-frying, which requires a great amount of strength, causes Uncle Meng a lot of pain in his arms and wrists. In addition, because he has to stand on his feet all day and run all over the take-out to get food, he often gets pains in his legs. By the time the take-out is closed, Uncle Meng is always exhausted.

6 Uncle Meng works long hard hours at difficult, physical labor. Although the take-out brings in a lot of money, it is a stressful and risky environment. Money is worthless compared to family and health. Even though money can buy many things, it cannot buy strong family relationships or good health. Working in a take-out, therefore, is not a desirable job.

Thinking about the Reading

1. According to Tang, how do job stresses harm Uncle Meng's health? Give examples.
2. In what ways is Uncle Meng's job dangerous? Describe how both the working conditions at the restaurant and the neighborhood in which it is located are dangerous.
3. How does Uncle Meng's job affect his family life? Give examples.

*4. Why do you think Tang chose to write about her Uncle Meng? What does she think of her uncle's way of life?

Writing Practice

1. Imagine that you are Uncle Meng's teenage son or daughter. Write a letter to your father telling him how you feel about the sacrifices he is making by working at the restaurant.
2. Have you ever worked at a job that was stressful or dangerous? Give examples of the stresses and dangers and the effect they had on you. If you have never held a job that fits this description, write about a stressful or dangerous situation that you have experienced—or about a friend's or relative's job.
3. Tang states, "Money is worthless compared to family and health" (paragraph 6). Explain why you agree or disagree with this statement. Give examples from your own experience and observation of the world to support your position.

A "GOOD" AMERICAN CITIZEN

Linda S. Wallace

What is patriotism, and how should we demonstrate it? In this article, media consultant and former journalist Linda Wallace wades into the controversy surrounding the war in Iraq to explore the role of dissent in the American system of government.

Recently, I passed an antiwar protest in Center City Philadelphia, a mix 1
of young and old, office workers and students, patting drums to the rhythm of their rap. A moment later, a pickup truck filled with guys clad in bluejeans drove by, waving the American flag and yelling, "Go, America!" Passers-by cringed as they tensely viewed the scene and caught a glimpse of the hundred police officers monitoring the drama from across the street.

This "we versus we" conflict is uncomfortable. Even U.S. leaders seem 2
more focused on middle ground rather than finding ways to disagree more productively. But there is a critical conversation America has yet to have with itself. And with the ongoing dissension over the war with Iraq, it appears that now is the perfect time.

Definitions of what qualifies as national loyalty have always shifted as 3
American society has diversified and matured. A person who is viewed by many as a troublemaker, such as Dr. Martin Luther King Jr., just might end up an honored U.S. hero.

> **Word Power**
>
> **patriot** someone who loves and supports his or her country

So what defines a patriot, exactly? Is it a person who supports the gov- 4
ernment through right and wrong in a war or a crisis or the person who disagrees loudly and engages in lawful protest? Are those who push us all to conform and unite as one country the folks who most love this nation, or is it those who embrace differences and challenge fellow citizens' assumptions in order to reorder society and find hidden flaws?

There is no national handbook—at least not yet—that details how to 5
be a good American. Some would prefer a manual filled with "dos" and "don'ts" to point to and say, "I'm the real deal, and you are the pretender."

So it seems for the moment, each person is left to follow his or her own 6
set of personal rules regarding patriotism, even though those lists are bound to disagree. The first few rules on my own list are simple:

1. Vote in every federal, state, and local election even when you can't find one candidate you like.
2. Learn the names of elected officials, and email them periodically to offer insight. (Most of mine are white, and I am African American.)
3. Attend community or council meetings, and stay abreast of public policy and key issues by reading newspapers, listening to the radio, or watching the evening TV news.
4. Model the behavior you want to see in others: Put democratic principles into practice by challenging bias and discrimination in everyday life.

The next rules, which came with wisdom and experience, require a bit more effort and resolve:

5. Respect the rights of other Americans to disagree with you.
6. Accept that your point of view is not the only legitimate perspective.
7. Tolerate dissent.

7 As I watch American commentators condemn fellow citizens for expressing views contrary to the government, it saddens me. Some people see conformity and unity as building blocks of strength, but I tend to view them as indicators that fear or intimidation is stifling helpful dissent. I am like the CEO who prefers to identify the drawbacks before launching a new product rather than wait until after it hits the stores. The country that is able to identify the weakness of its own arguments, and make strategic adjustments, is more likely to win over its opponents.

> **Word Power**
> **dissent** a difference of opinion; a disagreement

8 Some Americans will look at these scenes of antiwar protesters standing off against those who support the war effort and shake their heads. They may see a nation in turmoil, but I see a country with the will and savvy to tolerate dissent. Those who think that the opinion of the majority is somehow sacred might wish to revisit history. Our Founding Fathers decided to create a republic instead of a democracy because many feared the majority would not, could not, rule without eventually becoming oppressive and unfair.

> **Word Power**
> **savvy** practical knowledge

9 Wisely, they opted for a republic, once described by John Adams as "an empire of laws, not of men." Therefore, the protection of the laws that safeguard liberty and free expression is more critical to us than any national consensus ever will be.

> **Word Power**
> **consensus** a position reached by group agreement

10 The law protects free speech, and those who seek to silence protesters in the name of patriotism might remember these words that Thomas Jefferson wrote in 1815:

> Difference of opinion leads to enquiry, and enquiry to truth; and that, I am sure, is the ultimate and sincere object of us both. We both value too much the freedom of opinion sanctioned by our Constitution, not to cherish its exercise even where in opposition to ourselves.

11 If we decide that sincere patriots are those who rally behind the government, then we have suppressed the law and sidestepped principles in order to gain a temporary accord. That's not only unpatriotic; it's downright dangerous.

Thinking about the Reading

1. What is the "critical conversation" that Wallace believes "America has yet to have with itself" (paragraph 2)?
*2. In paragraph 4, Wallace asks a series of questions. Answer those questions.
*3. How does Wallace define a patriot? Do you agree with her definition? Do you agree with all seven of her rules?
4. Why does Wallace begin her essay by describing an antiwar protest? How does she use this protest to support her position?

Writing Practice

1. Using the seven rules that Wallace lists in paragraph 6 as a starting point, write a pamphlet *in your own words* for middle-school students (or for new American citizens). Call your pamphlet "How to Be a Good American Citizen." (If you like, you may add rules of your own to Wallace's list.)

2. Choose one of Wallace's seven rules, and write an essay in which you use an incident you witnessed or experienced to illustrate the importance of the rule.
3. Choose an issue on which you and a friend or coworker strongly disagree. Interview the person whose position differs from yours, and then write an essay in which you support his or her position.

THE TRANSACTION

William Zinsser

William Zinsser has written many articles and books on improving writing and study skills. He has also had a long career as a professional newspaper and magazine writer, drama and film critic, and author of nonfiction books on subjects ranging from jazz to baseball. This excerpt is from his book *On Writing Well: An Informal Guide to Writing Nonfiction.*

Word Power

transaction an exchange or transfer of goods, services, or money; an exchange of thoughts and feelings

A school in Connecticut once held "a day devoted to the arts," and I was asked if I would come and talk about writing as a vocation. When I arrived I found that a second speaker had been invited—Dr. Brock (as I'll call him), a surgeon who had recently begun to write and had sold some stories to magazines. He was going to talk about writing as an avocation. That made us a panel, and we sat down to face a crowd of students, teachers, and parents, all eager to learn the secrets of our glamorous work. 1

Dr. Brock was dressed in a bright red jacket, looking vaguely bohemian, as authors are supposed to look, and the first question went to him. What was it like to be a writer? 2

He said it was tremendous fun. Coming home from an arduous day at the hospital, he would go straight to his yellow pad and write his tensions away. The words just flowed. It was easy. I then said that writing wasn't easy and it wasn't fun. It was hard and lonely, and the words seldom just flowed. 3

Next Dr. Brock was asked if it was important to rewrite. Absolutely not, he said. "Let it all hang out," he told us, and whatever form the sentences take will reflect the writer at his most natural. I then said that rewriting is the essence of writing. I pointed out that professional writers rewrite their sentences over and over and then rewrite what they have rewritten. 4

Word Power

vocation an occupation; regular employment

avocation a hobby or interest pursued for enjoyment rather than for monetary gain

arduous difficult and tiring; strenuous

"What do you do on days when it isn't going well?" Dr. Brock was asked. He said he just stopped writing and put the work aside for a day when it would go better. I then said that the professional writer must establish a daily schedule and stick to it. I said that writing is a craft, not an art, and that the man who runs away from his craft because he lacks inspiration is fooling himself. He is also going broke. 5

"What if you're feeling depressed or unhappy?" a student asked. "Won't that affect your writing?" 6

Probably it will, Dr. Brock replied. Go fishing. Take a walk. Probably it won't, I said. If your job is to write every day, you learn to do it like any other job. 7

A student asked if we found it useful to circulate in the literary world. Dr. Brock said he was greatly enjoying his new life as a man of letters, and he told several stories of being taken to lunch by his publisher and his agent at Manhattan restaurants where writers and editors gather. I said that professional writers are solitary drudges who seldom see other writers. 8

"Do you put symbolism in your writing?" a student asked me. 9

"Not if I can help it," I replied. I have an unbroken record of missing the deeper meaning in any story, play, or movie, and as for dance and mime, I have never had any idea of what is being conveyed. 10

"I *love* symbols!" Dr. Brock exclaimed, and he described with gusto the joys of weaving them through his work. 11

Word Power

symbolism the use of a symbol (something that stands for something else) in a work of art or literature

gusto an enthusiasm; a lively enjoyment

So the morning went, and it was a revelation to all of us. At the end Dr. Brock told me he was enormously interested in my answers—it had never occurred to him that writing could be hard. I told him I was just as interested in *his* answers—it had never occurred to me that writing could be easy. Maybe I should take up surgery on the side. 12

As for the students, anyone might think we left them bewildered. But in fact we probably gave them a broader glimpse of the writing process than if only one of us had talked. For there isn't any "right" way to do such personal work. There are all kinds of writers and all kinds of methods, and any method that helps you to say what you want to say is the right method for you. Some people write by day, others by night. Some people need silence, others turn on the radio. Some write by hand, some by word processor, some by talking into a tape recorder. Some people write their first draft in one long burst and then revise; others can't write the second paragraph until they have fiddled endlessly with the first. 13

But all of them are vulnerable and all of them are tense. They are driven by a compulsion to put some part of themselves on paper, and yet they don't just write what comes naturally. They sit down to commit an act of literature, and the self who emerges on paper is far stiffer than the person who sat down to write. The problem is to find the real man or woman behind all the tension. 14

Ultimately the product that any writer has to sell is not the subject being written about, but who he or she is. I often find myself reading with interest about a topic I never thought would interest me—some scientific quest, perhaps. What holds me is the enthusiasm of the writer for his field. How was he drawn into it? What emotional baggage did he bring along? How did it change his life? It's not necessary to want to spend a year alone at Walden Pond[1] to become deeply involved with a writer who did. 15

This is the personal transaction that's at the heart of good nonfiction writing. Out of it come two of the most important qualities that this book will go in search of: humanity and warmth. Good writing has an aliveness that keeps the reader reading from one paragraph to the next, and it's not a question of gimmicks to "personalize" the author. It's a question of using the English language in a way that will achieve the greatest strength and the least clutter. 16

Can such principles be taught? Maybe not. But most of them can be learned. 17

Thinking about the Reading

1. Why do you think Zinsser chose to use an interview format to compare and contrast his own writing methods and experiences with those of Dr. Brock?
2. What is Zinsser's purpose in comparing his views on the writing process with those of Dr. Brock? In what ways does he suggest that his work and methods are superior to those of the doctor? Contrast this attitude with his statement in paragraph 13 that "any method that helps you to say what you want to say is the right method for you."

1. The place where Henry David Thoreau (1817–1862), an American writer, naturalist, and political activist, lived for two years in a cabin he built himself. He wrote about the experience in his most famous book, *Walden*.

3. Zinsser claims that "rewriting is the essence of writing" (paragraph 4). Use your own experience to support or challenge this statement.
4. Zinsser states, "Ultimately the product that any writer has to sell is not the subject being written about, but who he or she is" (paragraph 15). The writer's ability to draw the reader into his subject is the "personal transaction" (paragraph 16) or exchange between two people that, according to Zinsser, makes writing come alive. Discuss any of the essays in Chapter 30 that you have read. Which of the essay topics did not really interest you until you were drawn in by the writer's personal view of the topic?

Writing Practice

1. Imagine that you have been asked some of the same questions as Zinsser and Dr. Brock—but about your own experience as a college student. Write your responses. Be sure to include answers to the following questions: What is it like to be a student? What do you do when schoolwork or classes are not going well? Does being depressed or unhappy affect your performance in the classroom? How?
2. In paragraph 13, Zinsser writes, "There are all kinds of writers and all kinds of methods." Describe the kind of writer you are. Do you find writing easy, as Dr. Brock does, or difficult, as Zinsser does? What methods do you use to come up with ideas or to get through a particularly difficult assignment? Do you use any of the methods that Zinsser describes in paragraph 13?
3. Zinsser claims that the most successful pieces of writing are produced when the writer really cares about his or her subject. Write about a topic that interests you—for example, a book, a sport, a famous person, a political opinion, or a religious belief. Why does this topic interest you? How has it affected your life?

APPENDIX

Building Word Power

Building a vocabulary is an important part of your education. Knowing what words mean and how to use them can help you become a better reader and a better writer. As you have worked your way through *Foundations First,* you have encountered one or more Word Power boxes in each chapter. At this point, you may know the meanings of many of these words, and you have probably used some of them in writing or speaking. By continuing to use these and other new words, you can further expand your vocabulary.

FOCUS **Using Context to Build Word Power**

You can often figure out what a word means by studying its **context**, the words that surround it. For example, consider the following paragraph:

> Do I truly know Cesar Chavez? I suppose not. He was like a boat driven by some internal squall, a disturbance he himself didn't always understand, and that carried millions along with him, some of us kicking and screaming. (John Hartmire, "At the Heart of a Historic Movement")

If you did not know the meaning of the word *squall* (a short, sudden windstorm), you might be able to figure it out by its context. For example, the paragraph as a whole compares Chavez to a boat, and the word *driven* suggests a force that blows the boat around. The appositive *disturbance* ("some internal squall, a disturbance . . .") makes it clear that a squall is a disturbance, and rest of the paragraph indicates that the disturbance was powerful enough to affect millions of people. So, even though the paragraph does not explicitly define a squall as a windstorm, the word's context suggests that a squall is a powerful disturbance.

One of the best ways to improve your vocabulary is to get into the habit of using a dictionary to help you understand what new words mean and how to use them in your writing. A **dictionary** is an alphabetical list of the words in a language. However, a good dictionary is more than just a collection of words. In addition to showing how to spell and pronounce a word and what its most common meanings are, a dictionary can give you a great deal of other information.

A typical dictionary entry begins with the **entry word**, the word being defined. This word is set in boldface type and divided into syllables by centered dots.

sneak•er

Following the entry word are a pronunciation guide and an abbreviation that identifies the word's **part of speech**—whether it is a noun (*n.*), a verb (*v.*), an adjective (*adj.*), or another kind of word. Next, the entry lists the word's meaning or meanings. (If a word has several meanings, the most common meaning usually comes first.)

sneak•er (snē′ker) *n.* A sports shoe usually made of canvas and having soft rubber soles. Also called *tennis shoe.*

Often a dictionary entry gives additional information. For example, it may note the word's origin in another language, show alternate spellings of the word, or supply plural forms of nouns or various tenses of verbs (if they are irregular). Some words are followed by **usage labels**, which tell readers that these words are used in particular academic disciplines, occupations, or areas of daily life. For example, in one dictionary the definition of *miniature golf* has the usage label *Games.* Usage labels can also tell you if a word is no longer in use (*archaic*) or if it is *obscene, informal,* or *slang.* (Such words are not appropriate for your college or on-the-job writing.)

Some dictionaries also include extensive notes in some entries. For example, a dictionary entry may list, explain, and illustrate a word's **synonyms**—other words that have similar meanings.

teach (tēch) *v.* **taught** (tôt), **teach•ing, teach•es.**—*tr.* **1.** To impart knowledge or skill to: *teaches children.* **2.** To provide knowledge of; instruct in: *teaches French.* **3.** To condition to a certain action or frame of mind: *teaching youngsters to be self-reliant.* **4.** To cause to learn by example or experience: *an accident that taught me a valuable lesson.* **5.** To advocate or preach: *teaches racial and religious tolerance.* **6.** To carry on instruction on a regular basis in: *taught high school for many years.*—*intr.* To give instruction, especially as an occupation. [Middle English *techen,* from Old English *tǣcan.* See **deik-** in Appendix.]

SYNONYMS: *teach, instruct, educate, train, school, discipline, drill.* These verbs mean to impart knowledge or skill. *Teach* is the most widely applicable: *teaching a child the alphabet; teaches political science. "We shouldn't teach great books; we should teach a love of reading"* (B. F. Skinner). *Instruct* usually suggests methodical teaching: *A graduate student instructed the freshmen in the rudiments of music theory. Educate* often implies formal instruction but especially stresses the development of innate capacities that leads to wide cultivation: *"All educated Americans, first or last, go to Europe"* (Ralph Waldo Emerson). *Train* suggests concentration on particular skills intended to fit a person for a desired role: *The young woman attends vocational school, where she is being trained as a computer technician. School* often implies an arduous learning process: *The violinist had been schooled to practice slowly to assure accurate intonation. Discipline* usually refers to the teaching of control, especially self-control: *The writer has disciplined himself to work between breakfast and lunch every day. Drill* implies rigorous instruction or training, often by repetition of a routine: *The French instructor drilled the students in irregular verbs.*

An entry may also provide **regional notes** to explain how a word is used in different areas of the United States.

♦**fry•ing pan** (frī′ing) *n.* A shallow, long-handled pan used for frying food. Also called ♦*fry pan,* ♦*skillet,* ♦*spider.*

♦***REGIONAL NOTE:*** The terms *frying pan* and *skillet* are now virtually interchangeable, but there was a time when they were so regional as to be distinct dialect markers. *Frying pan* and the shortened version *fry pan* were once New England terms; *frying pan* is now in general use. *Skillet* seems to have been confined to the Midland section of the country, including the Upper South. Its use is still concentrated there, but it is no longer used in that area alone, probably because of the national marketing of skillet dinner mixes. The term *spider,* orginally denoting a type of frying pan that had long legs to hold it up over the coals, spread from New England westward to the Upper Northern states and down the coast to the South Atlantic states. It is still well known in both these regions, although it is now considered old-fashioned.

A dictionary entry can also explain **word history**.

tax•i (tăk′sē) *n., pl.* **tax•is** or **tax•ies.** A taxicab.—**taxi** *v.* **tax•ied** (tăk′sēd), **tax•i•ing** or **tax•y•ing, tax•ies** or **tax•is** (tăk′sēz).—*intr.* **1.** To be transported by taxi. **2.** To move slowly on the ground or on the surface of the water before takeoff or after landing: *an airplane taxiing down the runway.*—*tr.* **1.** To transport (someone or something) by or as if by taxi: *taxied the children to dance class; taxi documents to a law office.* **2.** To cause (an aircraft) to taxi. [Short for TAXIMETER, or TAXICAB.]

WORD HISTORY: "Taxi" is much easier to yell into the traffic than *taximeter cabriolet,* the form from which *taxi* has ultimately been shortened. *Taximeter* comes from the French word *taximètre,* ultimately derived from Medieval Latin *taxāre,* "to tax," and the French combining form *-metre. Taximètre* orginally meant, as did its English companion, "a device for measuring distance traveled," but this device was soon adapted to measure waiting time and compute and indicate the fare as well. *Taximeter,* first recorded in English in 1898 (an earlier form *taxameter,* borrowed through French from German, was recorded in 1894), joined forces with *cab,* a shortening (1827) of *cabriolet,* "a two-wheeled, one-horse carriage." This word, first found in English in 1766, came from French *cabriolet,* of the same meaning, which in turn was derived from *cabriole,* "caper," because the vehicle moves along with a springing motion. *Cab,* the shortened form, was applied to other vehicles as well, including eventually public conveyances. Fitted with a taximeter, such a vehicle, first horse-drawn and then motorized, was known as a *taxameter cab* (1899), a *taximeter cab* (1907), and a *taxicab* (1907), among other names, including *taxi* (1907), a shortening of either *taximeter* or *taxicab.* Interestingly enough, the fullest form possible, *taximeter cabriolet,* is not recorded until 1959.

Finally, some dictionaries provide detailed **usage notes** that discuss changing or disputed uses of words or grammatical constructions.

sneak (snēk) *v.* **sneaked** also **snuck** (snŭk), **sneak•ing, sneaks.**—*intr.* **1.** To go or move in a quiet, stealthy way. **2.** To behave in a cowardly or servile manner.—*tr.* To move, give, take, or put in a quiet, stealthy manner: *sneak candy into one's mouth; sneaked a look at the grade sheet.*—**sneak** *n.* **1.** A person regarded as stealthy, cowardly, or underhanded. **2.** An instance of sneaking; a quiet, stealthy movement. **3.** *Informal.* A sneaker.—**sneak** *adj.* **1.** Carried out in a clandestine manner: *sneak preparations for war.* **2.** Perpetrated without warning: *a sneak attack by terrorists.* [Probably akin to Middle English *sniken,* to creep, from Old English *snīcan.*]

USAGE NOTE: *Snuck* is an Americanism first introduced in the 19th century as a nonstandard regional variant of *sneaked.* But widespread use of *snuck* has become more common with every generation. It is now used by educated speakers in all regions, and there is some evidence to suggest that it is more frequent among younger speakers than *sneaked* is. Formal written English is naturally and properly more conservative than other varieties, of course, and here *snuck* still meets with much resistance. Many writers and editors have a lingering unease about the form, particularly if they recall its nonstandard origins. In fact, our consolidated citations, exhibiting almost 10,000 instances of *sneaked* and *snuck,* indicate that *sneaked* is preferred by a factor of 7 to 2. And 67 percent of the Usage Panel disapproves of *snuck.* Nevertheless, in recent years *snuck* has been quietly establishing itself in formal writing. An electronic search of a wide range of reputable publications turns up hundreds of citations for *snuck,* not just in sports writing but in news columns and commentary: *"He ran up huge hotel bills and then snuck out without paying"* (George Stade). *"In the dressing room beforehand, while the NBC* *technician was making me up, Jesse Jackson snuck up behind me and began playfully powdering my face"* (Bruce Babbitt). *"Raisa Gorbachev snuck away yesterday afternoon for a 65-minute helter-skelter tour of San Francisco"* (San Francisco Chronicle). *"The Reagan administration snuck in some illegal military assistance before that"* (New Republic). Our citation files also contain a number of occurrences of *snuck* in serious fiction: *"He had snuck away from camp with a cabinmate"* (Anne Tyler). *"I ducked down behind the paperbacks and snuck out"* (Garrison Keillor).

The pages that follow list (in alphabetical order) and define all the words that appear in Word Power boxes in *Foundations First*. You can use this list as a minidictionary to help you incorporate these words into your written and spoken vocabulary.

Following the list are several pages on which you can create a personal vocabulary list, your own list of new words (and their definitions) that you encounter in your reading. Space has been provided for you to write an original sentence for each word so you can remember how it is used.

Finally, exercises at the end of this appendix will give you additional practice in using the Word Power feature in *Foundations First*.

1 Word Power

This alphabetical list includes all the words, along with their definitions, that appear in the Word Power boxes throughout *Foundations First*.

accumulate to gather or pile up little by little

adjunct an instructor at a college or university who is not a permanent staff member; any temporary employee

adrenaline a hormone in the body that produces a rush of energy and excitement in the face of danger

alienated emotionally withdrawn or unresponsive

altercation a quarrel

anemic weak; lacking vitality

annotate to make explanatory notes

anticipate to consider something before it happens and make necessary changes

apathetic feeling or showing a lack of interest

apathy a lack of interest

arduous difficult and tiring; strenuous

avocation a hobby or an interest pursued for enjoyment rather than for monetary gain

ballot a written or printed paper on which voters indicate their choices in an election

ban to forbid somebody from doing something

bourgeois middle-class and proper in attitudes

brawl a noisy quarrel or fight

classic something typical or traditional; something that has lasting importance or worth

commission to place an order for something

commotion a noisy disturbance

concoction a mixture of several ingredients

conjure up to bring to mind

consensus a position reached by group agreement

contemporary current; modern

contradiction a situation in which one element is inconsistent with another

controversial marked by controversy

controversy a dispute between sides holding different views

counterparts two items that closely resemble each other

crave to have a strong desire for something

debilitate to take away strength

demeanor a person's manner, appearance, or behavior

dependent relying on another for support

desiccated dried-up

dilemma a situation in which one must choose between two courses of action

diligence attentive care

display something considered attractive, interesting, or entertaining

dissent a difference of opinion; a disagreement

diverge to separate and go in different directions

ebullient lively and enthusiastic

eccentric having odd or whimsical ways; behaving in ways that are not usual or customary

embossed decorated with raised, printed letters or designs

envision to imagine

epiphany a sudden flash of insight

estranged separated from someone else by feelings of hostility or indifference

evaluate to examine something to judge its value, quality, or importance

facilitate to make something easier to do

feline (noun) a member of the cat family; (adjective) catlike

gender a person's sex

generation a group of individuals born and living at about the same time

genome a complete set of chromosomes and its associated genes; DNA

gusto an enthusiasm; a lively enjoyment

harp on to repeat over and over again

heritage something passed down from previous generations

highlight to mark the page to emphasize important details

hypertensive having high blood pressure

immigrant a person who leaves one country to permanently settle in another

immortalize to make famous forever

imperative a command that must be obeyed

improvise to make do with the tools or resources at hand

independent free from the influence or control of others

initiative a new legislative measure

institution a well-known person, place, or thing; something that has become associated with a particular place

lectern a stand or desk with a slanted top that supports a speaker's notes

lethal capable of killing

liability a financial and legal responsibility; a debt that must be paid

malign to make harmful statements about

marinate to let meat, fish, or vegetables soak in a sauce to make them more flavorful or tender

maroon to put ashore on a deserted island

masquerade (verb) to wear a mask or disguise; (noun) a costume party at which guests wear masks

mature full-grown

mellow to gain the wisdom and tolerance that are characteristic of maturity

memento a reminder of the past; a keepsake (the plural form is *mementos*)

memorabilia objects valued because of their link to historical events or culture

memorable worth remembering

microbe a germ

migrate to move from one area or region to another

missive a letter or message

mobility the movement of people from one social group, class, or level to another

mogul a rich or powerful person

monument a structure built as a memorial

multicultural of or relating to many cultures

naturalization the process of gaining citizenship

network to engage in informal communication for mutual help and support

newsworthy interesting enough to be worth reporting in the news

obligation a course of action demanded of a person by law or conscience

observer someone who watches attentively

obtain to get possession of something

offensive hurtful; disagreeable; unpleasant

ominous threatening

orchestrate to arrange

orient to adjust

orientation an adjustment to a new environment

ostracize to exclude from a group

parity an equality in power or value

patriot someone who loves and supports his or her country

persist to continue to do something despite setbacks

perspective a view or an outlook; the ability to see things as they are

pertain to to relate to or have to do with

physique the structure or form of a person's body

plight an unfortunate or difficult situation

potable safe to drink

priority a thing that deserves extra attention; an important or urgent goal

profanity vulgar, abusive language

prohibit to forbid

rambunctious unruly; full of uncontrolled energy

readily easily

recoil to shrink away from something in fear or disapproval

renaissance a rebirth or revival

rendezvous (verb) to meet at a prearranged place and time; (noun) a meeting of this kind

rigor a hardship or difficulty

role model a person who serves as a model of behavior for someone else to imitate

savvy practical knowledge

self-esteem a pride in oneself; self-respect

sheer steep; almost perpendicular

skepticism a doubtful or questioning attitude

slug a coin-shaped metal disk that has no monetary value

speckled spotted with dots of color

spectacle a public show or exhibition; an unusual sight

sporadic infrequent; happening from time to time

stark bare; harsh; grim

sterilization the process of making something free of germs

subsidize to give financial support to a project

surveillance the close observation of a person or a group of people, especially a person or group under suspicion

suture to use fiber to close up wounds or to connect two parts of the body

syllabus an outline or a summary of a course's main points (the plural form is *syllabi*)

symbol something that represents something else

symbolism the use of a symbol (something that stands for something else) in a work of art or literature

tradition a behavior or custom handed down from generation to generation

traditional relating to tradition

transaction an exchange or a transfer of goods, services, or money; an exchange of thoughts and feelings

transcend to be greater than; to go beyond

trauma an injury or wound, either physical or emotional

trek a difficult journey

unique one of a kind

vanity an excessive pride in one's appearance or achievements

vanity plate a license plate that can be customized for an extra charge

veracity truthfulness

viable able to survive

vixen a female fox; (slang) a tempting, sexy woman; can also mean a bad-tempered woman

vocation an occupation; regular employment

wanton cruel; merciless

wholesaler a person who sells large amounts of merchandise to stores or individuals, who then resell it

wield to handle with ease and skill

woe sadness

wreak havoc to bring about devastation

2 Your Personal Vocabulary List

On the pages that follow, keep a list of new words you come across in your reading. Write down a brief definition of each word, and then use it in a sentence.

Example

Word: memento Definition: a reminder of the past

Sentence: I kept a seashell as a memento of our vacation at the beach.

Word: ______ Definition: ______

Sentence: ______.

Word: ______ Definition: ______

Sentence: ______.

Word: ______ Definition: ______

Sentence: ______.

Word: ______ Definition: ______

Sentence: ______.

Word: ______ Definition: ______

Sentence: ______.

Word: ______ Definition: ______

Sentence: ______.

Word: ________________ Definition: ____________________________
____
Sentence: ____
____.

Word: ________________ Definition: ____________________________
____
Sentence: ____
____.

Word: ________________ Definition: ____________________________
____
Sentence: ____
____.

Word: ________________ Definition: ____________________________
____
Sentence: ____
____.

Word: ________________ Definition: ____________________________
____
Sentence: ____
____.

Word: ________________ Definition: ____________________________
____
Sentence: ____
____.

Word: ________________ Definition: ____________________________
____
Sentence: ____
____.

Word: ________________ Definition: ______________________________

____

Sentence: ____

____.

Word: ________________ Definition: ______________________________

____

Sentence: ____

____.

Word: ________________ Definition: ______________________________

____

Sentence: ____

____.

Word: ________________ Definition: ______________________________

____

Sentence: ____

____.

Word: ________________ Definition: ______________________________

____

Sentence: ____

____.

Word: ________________ Definition: ______________________________

____

Sentence: ____

____.

◆ PRACTICE 1

In the space next to each definition, write the word (from the list provided below) that best matches that definition. Check the Word Power list on pages 526–530 if necessary.

adrenaline	concoction	renaissance
annotate	immortalize	sterilization
arduous	liability	symbol
ballot	mature	transaction
bourgeois	orientation	viable
brawl	plight	vixen

1. ______________ an unfortunate or difficult situation
2. ______________ middle-class and proper in attitudes
3. ______________ full-grown
4. ______________ able to survive
5. ______________ a female fox; (slang) a tempting, sexy woman; can also mean a bad-tempered woman
6. ______________ a written or printed paper on which voters indicate their choices in an election
7. ______________ a mixture of several ingredients
8. ______________ to make explanatory notes
9. ______________ difficult and tiring; strenuous
10. ______________ a noisy quarrel or fight
11. ______________ an adjustment to a new environment
12. ______________ a hormone in the body that produces a rush of energy and excitement in the face of danger
13. ______________ to make famous forever
14. ______________ something that represents something else
15. ______________ a financial and legal responsibility; a debt that must be paid
16. ______________ the process of making something free of germs
17. ______________ an exchange or a transfer of goods, services, or money; an exchange of thoughts and feelings
18. ______________ a rebirth or revival

◆ PRACTICE 2

Fill in the blank in each of the following sentences with one of the words listed below. Check the definitions in the Word Power list on pages 526–530 if necessary.

accumulate	heritage	rambunctious
brawl	lethal	subsidize
concoction	malign	surveillance
conjure up	marinate	symbol
display	naturalization	tradition
eccentric	offensive	wield
embossed	orient	

1. We had to make a ______________ of cleansers before scrubbing the bathtub.
2. Our ______________ instructor came to class barefoot, wearing a bright Hawaiian shirt.
3. Other students sometimes ______________ the only girl who wears glasses.
4. The Puerto Rican Day parade participants displayed pride in their ______________.
5. Everyone at the ______________ ceremony carried American flags.
6. The band played at the Ritz, and their fancy costumes made an impressive ______________.
7. The bird in that poem is actually a(n) ______________ for freedom.
8. The strikers found the mayor's nasty comments______________.
9. Even the most common medications can be ______________ if you take too much of them.
10. Those songs ______________ memories of high school dances.
11. The hockey game soon became a noisy ______________ when the players started fighting.
12. The ______________ children ran around the room, throwing toys.
13. Once Ben had a chance to ______________ himself to his new office, he settled right in.
14. The tree surgeon showed us how to ______________ an ax with skill and precision.
15. The school agreed to ______________ our play and to provide refreshments during the intermission.
16. Having a Memorial Day barbecue is a ______________ in our family; we do it every year.

17. The bank robber had no idea he was under _______________ by hidden cameras.

18. Eric knows how to _______________ the meat in teriyaki sauce to make it taste better.

19. Maria sent out _______________ invitations for her wedding.

20. Passing this course is required for all English majors, so you should not let the assignments for your final portfolio _______________.

◆ PRACTICE 3

Use your dictionary to help you find synonyms for each of the following words.

1. altercation ____
____
2. arduous ____
____
3. classic ____
____
4. debilitate ____
____
5. epiphany ____
____
6. mature ____
____
7. memorable ____
____
8. microbe ____
____
9. newsworthy ____
____
10. offensive ____
____
11. parity ____
____

12. persist ______________________________

____

13. prohibit ______________________________

____

14. rigor ______________________________

____

15. spectacle ______________________________

____

16. sporadic ______________________________

____

17. stark ______________________________

____

18. vocation ______________________________

____

19. woe ______________________________

____

◆ COLLABORATIVE ACTIVITIES

1. Choose four words from the Word Power list on pages 526–530, and work with another student to write a paragraph that uses all of the words you chose. When you have finished your work, check the definitions to make sure you have used each word correctly.
2. *Composing original sentences* Write five original sentences using two of the following words in each sentence. Check the Word Power list on pages 526–530 if necessary.

alienated	migrate
anemic	physique
anticipate	recoil
apathy	self-esteem
ebullient	speckled
estranged	traditional
gusto	trek
improvise	veracity
memento	

Answers to Odd-Numbered Exercises

Chapter 9

◆ PRACTICE 9.1, page 156

Answers: **1.** Reality TV **3.** This show **5.** a man **7.** They **9.** Many viewers

◆ PRACTICE 9.4, page 158

Answers: **1.** P **3.** S **5.** S **7.** P **9.** S

◆ PRACTICE 9.5, page 159

Answers: **1.** the memorial; singular **3.** More than two and a half million people; plural **5.** Some visitors; plural **7.** One man; singular **9.** Spouses, children, parents, and friends; plural

◆ PRACTICE 9.6, page 160

Answers: **1.** Prepositional phrase: for many new businesses; subject: Internet **3.** Prepositional phrase: of a garage sale, collectibles show, and flea market; subject: eBay **5.** Prepositional phrase: of business managers; subject: founders **7.** Prepositional phrase: of antiques, cars, jewelry, DVDs, pet supplies, and many other things; subject: items **9.** Prepositional phrase: on eBay; subject: Buyers

◆ PRACTICE 9.7, page 161

Answers: **1.** traveled **3.** advertised **5.** packed; joined **7.** wrote **9.** understand

◆ PRACTICE 9.9, page 162

Answers: **1.** leave; action verb **3.** quit; action verb **5.** feels; linking verb **7.** are; linking verb **9.** appreciate; action verb

◆ PRACTICE 9.10, page 163

Answers: **1.** Subject: The night; linking verb: grew; descriptive word: cold **3.** Subject: George W. Bush; linking verb: became; descriptive phrase: the forty-third president of the United States **5.** Subject: Many people; linking verb: were; descriptive phrase: outraged at the mayor's announcement **7.** Subject: The fans; linking verb: appeared; descriptive phrase: upset by their team's defeat **9.** Subject: Charlie; linking verb: got; descriptive word: sick

◆ PRACTICE 9.11, page 164

Answers: **1.** Helping verb: may; verb: risk **3.** Helping verbs: has been; verb: thinking **5.** Helping verbs: could have; verb: been **7.** Helping verb: have; verb: wondered **9.** Helping verb: has; verb: loved

◆ PRACTICE 9.12, page 165

Answers: **1.** Helping verb: has; verb: become **3.** Verb: prefer **5.** Verb: need **7.** Verb: use **9.** Helping verb: can; verb: be

Chapter 10

◆ PRACTICE 10.1, page 169

Answers: **1.** [Speech is silver], *but* [silence is golden]. **3.** [The house was dark], *so* [he didn't ring the doorbell]. **5.** [They will not surrender], *and* [they will not agree to a cease-fire]. **7.** [She has lived in California for years], *yet* [she remembers her childhood in Kansas very clearly]. **9.** [Melody dropped French], *and* [then she added Italian].

◆ PRACTICE 10.2, page 171

Answers: **1.** but/yet **3.** and **5.** so **7.** so **9.** and

◆ PRACTICE 10.8, page 179

Answers: **1.** Every day, Americans use about 9.3 billion barrels of gasoline to power their cars and trucks; as a result, our environment is deteriorating. **3.** One of the newly designed cars is called a hybrid because it combines gasoline and electric power; consequently, this car uses less fuel and causes less pollution. **5.** The only emission from cars powered by hydrogen fuel cells is water; nevertheless, these cars create other problems. **7.** Some engineers believe that solar power is a good alternative fuel source; unfortunately, solar-powered cars are complicated to design. **9.** Most of these new types of cars have already been designed and tested; meanwhile, many other problems related to them have yet to be resolved.

◆ PRACTICE 10.9, page 180

Possible edits: **1.** Cutting paper into decorative designs is a popular form of folk art; in fact, it exists in different cultures around the world. **3.** The Mexican art of paper cutting, called *papel picado,* is very precise; consequently, small, sharp chisels and a hammer are used to cut the paper. **5.** The designs depend on the celebration; for example, illustrations might celebrate religious figures or christenings. **7.** To make the designs, artisans must first draw a pattern; subsequently, they lay the pattern on the tissue paper. **9.** With the entire design cut out, it is time to separate the layers; finally, the artists extend the banners and hang them on the walls or ceilings.

Chapter 11

◆ PRACTICE 11.1, page 188

Possible edits: **1.** Although **3.** Even if **5.** When **7.** unless **9.** Now that

◆ PRACTICE 11.3, page 190

Answers: **1.** While today's roller coasters are made of steel, the early ones were made of wood. **3.** Correct **5.** Today's steel coasters go faster and higher than earlier rides now that technology has improved coaster designs. **7.** The Dueling Dragons at Universal Studios in Orlando is unusual because it consists of two coasters—one named Fire, the other named Ice. **9.** Since it is 310 feet high, the Millenium Force in Sandusky, Ohio, uses elevator cables rather than the typical chain lift.

◆ PRACTICE 11.4, page 191

Possible edits: **1.** Although many Westerners rarely think about problems in Africa, the lack of money for medical supplies should concern everyone. **3.** When an outbreak of Ebola virus appeared in northern Uganda in 2000, doctors and nurses caring for Ebola patients lacked disinfectants and latex gloves. **5.** Because the Ebola virus makes a patient bleed profusely, medical workers without gloves face grave danger. **7.** The virus is named for the Ebola River in Zaire, where it first appeared in human beings. **9.** Even though a doctor and several nurses died of the Ebola virus, more than half of the patients survived.

◆ PRACTICE 11.6, page 193

Answers: **1.** Dependent Clause: *which* lasts five days; modifies: holiday **3.** Dependent Clause: *that* contain saffron, almonds, butter, and milk; modifies: cakes **5.** Dependent Clause: *that* represent banishing ignorance and darkness; modifies: candles **7.** Dependent Clause: *who* is said to have rescued sixteen thousand daughters of gods and saints from a demon king; modifies: Krishna **9.** Dependent Clause: *which* is associated with legends about mountains; modifies: day

◆ PRACTICE 11.7, page 195

Answers: **1.** Nonrestrictive. Working women, who have more career opportunities today than ever before, are successful in many fields. **3.** Nonrestrictive. After getting a position of power, which almost always involves supervising other employees, women may face additional problems. **5.** Restrictive. Workers admitted unhappiness with their female bosses on surveys that questioned both male and female employees. **7.** Restrictive; punctuation correct **9.** Restrictive. People who admire a tough attitude in a man may not like the same attitude in a woman.

◆ PRACTICE 11.8, page 196

Possible edits: **1.** In the nineteenth century, American whalers, who had very dangerous jobs, sailed around the world to hunt whales. **3.** Today, U.S. laws protect several species of whale that are considered to be in danger of extinction. **5.** Whale hunting is the focus of a disagreement between the United States and Japan, which have different ideas about whaling. **7.** Some of the whales killed in the Japanese hunt, which include minke whales, Bryde's whales, and sperm whales, are considered by the U.S. government to be endangered. **9.** The U.S. government argues that the Japanese whale hunt is not for research, but for businesses that want whale meat to sell to restaurants.

Chapter 12

◆ PRACTICE 12.2, page 203

Possible edits: **1.** With their cuddly teddy-bear looks, giant pandas are a favorite animal for people of all ages. **3.** Saving the panda has been a priority for wildlife conservation experts for decades, but it is not an easy task. **5.** Wilderness areas are increasingly rare in China, the giant panda's home. **7.** Some endangered wild animals have been saved by breeding programs in zoos, but panda-breeding programs have struggled. **9.** The cub, known as Hua Mei, was the first giant panda to be born outside of China. **11.** Now, wildlife conservationists hope that Bai Yun's success story will help them increase the numbers of giant pandas.

◆ PRACTICE 12.3, page 204

Possible answers: **1.** hot and steamy **3.** none **5.** dark and drab **7.** hot, dull scene **9.** none

◆ PRACTICE 12.6, page 207

Answers and possible edits: **1.** Protesters disrupted the World Trade Organization's meeting in Seattle in 1999. **3.** Some violent incidents happened in Seattle. **5.** Some of the protesters were interested mainly in protecting the environment. **7.** The Seattle protest was not an isolated event. **9.** Many young people are getting involved in these protests because they believe a global economy should help the poor as much as the wealthy.

◆ **PRACTICE 12.7, page 208**

Answers and possible edits: **1.** A few years ago, antibacterial cleaning products were introduced to the American market. **3.** The ads try to make people afraid of the germs in their homes. **5.** When the ads appeared, frightened people immediately began buying antibacterial soap to kill off the invisible germs. **7.** But new research suggests that antibacterial products may kill good germs. **9.** Scientists have warned that children who grow up in germ-free homes may get sick from normally harmless bacteria.

◆ **PRACTICE 12.8, page 209**

Answers and possible edits: **1.** Cliché: get up and go; Many Americans get their energy from a morning cup of coffee. **3.** Cliché: shake a stick at; In fact, there are more designer coffees than you can imagine. **5.** Cliché: melt in your mouth; Others have sweet, intense flavors that appeal to your sweet tooth, such as hazelnut, vanilla, and raspberry. **7.** Cliché: in a whirling blend of flavor; Some designer coffees even combine all three elements — exotic beans, strong flavors, and milk. **9.** Cliché: went out on a limb; In fact, Seattle, the home of the Starbucks chain, even took a chance and tried to tax designer coffees.

Chapter 13

◆ **PRACTICE 13.1, page 214**

Answers: **1.** sudden; unexpected; destructive **3.** lie down; take a nap **5.** expanded the parking lot; added a deli counter **7.** a bath; a bottle; a lullaby **9.** A beautiful voice; acting ability

◆ **PRACTICE 13.2, page 215**

Answers: **1.** Hundreds of people wanted to be on a game show that required them to live on an island, catch their own food, and have no contact with the outside world. **3.** Parallel **5.** The contestants held their breath underwater, rowed a canoe, and ate rats and caterpillars. **7.** Each week, the television audience saw one person win a contest and another person get voted off the island. **9.** Parallel

◆ **PRACTICE 13.3, page 217**

Answers: **1.** When orchids first became popular in the 1880s, the plants were dug up and collected from the wild. **3.** If the hunter found a rare species, he took every plant, causing harm to the environment and causing damage to the species. **5.** As a result, orchids have become both popular and inexpensive. **7.** Because of their natural habitat, orchids grown at home need bright light, moderate temperatures, and good air circulation. **9.** The single-footed orchid grows up from a single stem, and the many-footed orchid grows horizontally on several stems.

◆ **PRACTICE 13.5, page 218**

Answers: **1.** Each leaf is a miniature factory that uses water, carbon dioxide, and sunlight to make food. **3.** Also present in leaves are other chemicals that give the leaves their orange and yellow color. **5.** Throughout both the spring and summer, these beautiful colors are overshadowed by the green chlorophyll. **7.** Although too little rain can delay the arrival of fall, too much rain can make the colors dull. **9.** Warm, wet springs, moderately rainy summers, and clear, mild falls make the best leaf colors.

Chapter 14

◆ **PRACTICE 14.1, page 226**

Answers: **1.** Correct **3.** Correct **5.** Comma splice **7.** Comma splice **9.** Run-on

◆ **PRACTICE 14.2, page 228**

Possible edits: **1.** Flatbread is bread that is flat; usually, it does not contain yeast. **3.** The tortilla is a Mexican flatbread; tortillas are made of corn or wheat. **5.** Italians eat focaccia, but when they put cheese on a focaccia, it becomes a pizza. **7.** Indian cooking has several kinds of flatbreads, and all of them are delicious. **9.** Fifty years ago, most people ate only the flatbreads from their native land; today, flatbreads are becoming internationally popular.

◆ **PRACTICE 14.3, page 229**

Possible edits: **1.** Over the years, several hybrid fruits that have come to market have become popular with consumers. **3.** More recently, two more new hybrid fruits have been introduced which are called pluots and apriums. **5.** They are sweeter and juicier than plums because hybrids usually have higher sugar content than their parent fruits. **7.** Apriums, which have thin fuzz on their skins, are smaller than pluots. **9.** Both new fruits are good sources of vitamin A, which is essential for healthy skin.

◆ **PRACTICE 14.4, page 230**

Possible edits: **1.** Tex-Mex cuisine is a blend of foods and cooking styles. It combines the traditions of the Aztec, Toltec, and Maya with European and North American traditions. **3.** Before the arrival of the Spanish explorers, the Mexican diet was based on corn, which could be ground and made into tortillas, tamales, and flour. **5.** After the Spanish arrived, the cuisine changed. Rice, olives, beef, and various fruits were added to the corn dishes. **7.** Over time, Americans adopted Mexican foods, but they changed them. **9.** However, America's Tex-Mex cuisine kept the beans and peppers found in many Mexican dishes, and these continue to be a staple of Tex-Mex dishes.

Chapter 15

◆ PRACTICE 15.2, page 237

Answers: **1.** Fragment **3.** Correct **5.** Fragment **7.** Correct **9.** Fragment

Rewrite: According to some people who frequently use lip balm, this product is addictive. The purpose of lip balm is to keep the lips from getting chapped. Can people become dependent on lip balm? Some users say yes. However, the makers of lip balm strongly deny that it is addictive.

◆ PRACTICE 15.3, page 238

Answers: **1.** Correct **3.** Fragment **5.** Fragment **7.** Fragment **9.** Fragment

Rewrite: Hikers often wear bells to make noise on the trail, especially in areas populated by bears. Bears can hear very well but cannot see long distances. Sometimes, bears can be frightened by humans and attack them. However, a bear may hear a person coming and then is very likely to avoid the person. This is why experienced hikers never go hiking without bells.

◆ PRACTICE 15.5, page 241

Answers: **1.** Correct **3.** Correct **5.** Fragment **7.** Fragment **9.** Fragment **11.** Fragment

Rewrite: She is known to many for her marriage to fellow artist Diego Rivera, a mural painter. She is also famous for her many self-portraits. In these portraits, Kahlo is usually dressed up in colorful clothes. In her portraits, she is adorned with jewelry and flowers. The scenes that surround her are often exotic, with a dreamlike atmosphere. Kahlo's paintings express the reality of her own life, a life of great beauty and great pain.

◆ PRACTICE 15.6, page 242

Answers: **1.** Correct **3.** Fragment **5.** Correct **7.** Fragment **9.** Correct

Rewrite: It remains one of the largest eruptions in recorded history and one of the world's largest natural disasters. Nearly forty thousand people died in the resulting tsunamis, giant tidal waves reaching one hundred feet high. The force of the eruption caused shifts in climate around the world. Writer Simon Winchester researched this disaster. In 2003, he published a best-selling book, *Krakatoa: The Day the World Exploded.*

◆ PRACTICE 15.7, page 244

Answers and possible edits: **1.** My sister has forgotten the house where we used to live. **3.** The baby has been crying ever since you left. **5.** Vivian and her daughters have gone to the supermarket to pick up some groceries for dinner. **7.** Until yesterday, the choir had never sung a hymn that featured two soloists. **9.** More and more airplanes are flying over this neighborhood every day.

◆ PRACTICE 15.8, page 246

Answers: **1.** This young man has a very promising future. **3.** A box turtle was trying to find water. **5.** Most people think of themselves as good drivers. **7.** Frequent-flier miles can sometimes be traded for products as well as for airline tickets. **9.** She searched the crowd frantically.

Chapter 16

◆ PRACTICE 16.1, page 255

Answers: **1.** travel **3.** like **5.** plays **7.** takes **9.** records **11.** loves **13.** succeed **15.** provide

◆ PRACTICE 16.2, page 256

Answers: **1.** fear **3.** promises **5.** eat **7.** claim **9.** remain

◆ PRACTICE 16.3, page 257

Answers: **1.** is **3.** are **5.** is **7.** am **9.** are

◆ PRACTICE 16.4, page 258

Answers: **1.** have **3.** have **5.** have **7.** have **9.** has

◆ PRACTICE 16.5, page 258

Answers: **1.** do **3.** do **5.** does **7.** does **9.** do

◆ PRACTICE 16.6, page 259

Answers: **1.** is **3.** has, are **5.** does, has **7.** is **9.** does **11.** do, are **13.** do **15.** have **17.** does **19.** has

◆ PRACTICE 16.7, page 261

Answers: **1.** are **3.** work **5.** share **7.** make **9.** save

◆ PRACTICE 16.8, page 261

Answers: **1.** is **3.** have **5.** contains **7.** is **9.** costs

◆ PRACTICE 16.9, page 263

Answers: **1.** Prepositional phrase: of one of China's cities; subject: resident; verb: goes **3.** Prepositional phrase: with a huge, heavy frame; subject: bicycle; verb: has **5.** Prepositional phrase: of China; subject: economy; verb: is **7.** Prepositional phrase: with a long commute; subject: worker; verb: does **9.** Prepositional phrase: under age thirty; subject: people; verb: do

◆ PRACTICE 16.10, page 263

Answers: **1.** Prepositional phrase: of these plants; subject: roots; verb: go **3.** Prepositional phrase: on the night shift; subject: Firefighters; verb: take **5.** Prepositional phrase: with a hundred guests; subject: wedding; verb: costs **7.** Prepositional phrase: about chimpanzees; subject: book; verb: was **9.** Prepositional phrase: to this week's performances; subject: Tickets; verb: are

◆ PRACTICE 16.11, page 264

Answers: **1.** manage **3.** want **5.** wants **7.** risk **9.** think

◆ **PRACTICE 16.12, page 266**

Answers: **1.** Subject: program; verb: is **3.** Subject: dormitory; verb: is **5.** Subject: tests; verb: are **7.** Subject: people; verb: are **9.** Subject: student; verb: does

◆ **PRACTICE 16.13, page 266**

Answers: **1.** is **3.** are **5.** are **7.** are **9.** is

◆ **PRACTICE 16.14, page 267**

Answers: **1.** Subject: mother; verb: watches **3.** Subject: newscasters; verb: smile **5.** Subject: citizens; verb: need **7.** Subject: juice; verb: leaves **9.** Subject: panels; verb: charge

◆ **PRACTICE 16.15, page 268**

Answers: **1.** Subject: world; verb: depends **3.** Subject: People; verb: live **5.** Subject: simplicity, self-denial; verb: are **7.** Subject: lifestyle; verb: makes **9.** Subject: code; verb: is

Chapter 17

◆ **PRACTICE 17.1, page 274**

Answers: **1.** Verbs: ordered, takes; correction: *takes* becomes *took* **3.** Correct **5.** Correct **7.** Verbs: offered, tells; correction: *tells* becomes *told* **9.** Correct

◆ **PRACTICE 17.2, page 275**

Answers: **1.** Correct **3.** Lincoln needed 300,000 more men. **5.** For example, a rich man could pay a "commutation fee" that allowed him to pay someone else to fight so that he could stay home. **7.** On June 12, 1863, the first draftees were named, and soon mobs began to form. **9.** Correct

◆ **PRACTICE 17.3, page 276**

Answers: **1.** The students learned that they needed to use proper lab technique. **3.** I worked on an assembly line where I could not spend more than thirty seconds on each task. **5.** His boss told him that he had to be on time for work every day. **7.** Correct **9.** His brother said that he could find almost anything on the Internet.

◆ **PRACTICE 17.4, page 277**

Answers: **1.** Most of us hate these distracting ads because we have to stop whatever we are doing to get rid of them. **3.** If a person takes the time to read these ads, he or she often realizes the ads are random. **5.** People are getting fed up because they don't like to waste time with these ads. **7.** They are discovering that they can download free pop-up–blocking software. **9.** Over the next few years, companies may realize that they put themselves at a disadvantage by using pop-up advertising.

◆ **PRACTICE 17.5, page 278**

Answers: **1.** The lawyers discussed a settlement, but the defendant refused it. **3.** Roberto signed up for calculus, so he bought a new calculator. **5.** As the waves battered the beach, a gasping young man clutched a surfboard. **7.** When Brandon met Jane, he asked her for a date. **9.** Kathy mowed her grandfather's lawn, and she also did his yardwork.

◆ **PRACTICE 17.6, page 279**

Answers: **1.** Many people think that their landlord's insurance protects their personal property, but this insurance only covers the building itself. **3.** If the pizza delivery man trips on the carpet and breaks his leg, the tenant is responsible. **5.** Fortunately, most apartment insurance is inexpensive, and many companies offer reasonably priced policies.

Chapter 18

◆ **PRACTICE 18.1, page 285**

Answers: **1.** Present participle modifier: fearing for his life; modifies: soldier **3.** Present participle modifier: smiling professionally; modifies: winner **5.** Present participle modifier: Standing in the barbershop doorway; modifies: men **7.** Present participle modifier: ringing loudly at 2 a.m.; modifies: telephone **9.** Present participle modifier: blowing his whistle loudly in my ear; modifies: foreman

◆ **PRACTICE 18.2, page 286**

Answers: **1.** Present participle modifier: Appearing at picnics and other outdoor gatherings; modifies: yellow jackets **3.** Present participle modifier: causing allergic reactions in many people; modifies: stings **5.** Present participle modifier: Looking for food; modifies: females **7.** Present participle modifier: overflowing with trash; modifies: garbage can **9.** Present participle modifier: Pollinating flowers and eating other harmful insects; modifies: yellow jackets

◆ **PRACTICE 18.4, page 287**

Answers: **1.** Past participle modifier: Plastered with bumper stickers; modifies: car **3.** Past participle modifier: covered with mosquito bites; modifies: legs **5.** Past participle modifier: buried under two feet of snow; modifies: roof **7.** Past participle modifier: Shattered in its fall from the mantle; modifies: vase **9.** Past participle modifier: rejected by six publishers; modifies: book

◆ **PRACTICE 18.5, page 288**

Answers: **1.** Past participle modifier: committed in Fall River, Massachusetts; modifies: crime **3.** Past participle modifier: Horrified at the news of this murder; modifies: people **5.** Past participle modifier: changed repeatedly; modifies: story **7.** Past participle modifier: discussed in every home in town; modifies: motive

9. Past participle modifier: faced with a circumstantial case; modifies: jury

◆ **PRACTICE 18.7, page 290**

Possible answers: **1.** Hanging by one hand from the edge of the roof, he could not reach the fire escape. **3.** Frightened by the alligator, I almost turned over my canoe. **5.** Sitting on the dock in the bay, he caught many fish. **7.** Given a second chance, she ran out of luck. **9.** Feeling sick to her stomach, she was too far away to reach the bathroom in time.

◆ **PRACTICE 18.9, page 292**

Possible answers: **1.** The angry bull with a ring in its nose threw every rodeo rider. **3.** The bathroom door was quickly closed by Henry, blushing furiously. or: Blushing furiously, Henry quickly closed the bathroom door. **5.** A car kept in a garage is not likely to be damaged by rust. **7.** A bartender with long hair served strong drinks. **9.** A white limousine waited as the director, blowing kisses, emerged from the restaurant.

Chapter 19

◆ **PRACTICE 19.1, page 300**

Answers: **1.** Verb: sings; tense: present **3.** Verb: protested; tense: past **5.** Verb: cried; tense: past **7.** Verb: gurgled; tense: past **9.** Verb: pool; tense: present

◆ **PRACTICE 19.2, page 301**

Answers: **1.** qualified **3.** considered **5.** rejected **7.** remained **9.** tried

◆ **PRACTICE 19.3, page 302**

Answers: **1.** slept **3.** gave **5.** rose **7.** tore **9.** hurt

◆ **PRACTICE 19.4, page 303**

Answers: **1.** became **3.** found **5.** drew **7.** rose; fought **9.** said

◆ **PRACTICE 19.5, page 304**

Answers: **1.** were **3.** were **5.** was **7.** were **9.** was

◆ **PRACTICE 19.6, page 305**

Answers: **1.** Correct **3.** was **5.** Correct **7.** were **9.** were

◆ **PRACTICE 19.7, page 306**

Answers: **1.** would **3.** would **5.** could **7.** can **9.** could

◆ **PRACTICE 19.8, page 307**

Answers: **1.** can **3.** would **5.** can; could **7.** would **9.** will; would

Chapter 20

◆ **PRACTICE 20.1, page 312**

Answers: **1.** Present: agrees; past: agreed; past participle: agreed **3.** Present: drops; past: dropped; past participle: dropped **5.** Present: works; past: worked; past participle: worked **7.** Present: gargles; past: gargled; past participle: gargled **9.** Present: confuses; past: confused; past participle: confused

◆ **PRACTICE 20.2, page 313**

Answers: **1.** lived **3.** escaped **5.** helped **7.** inspired **9.** earned

◆ **PRACTICE 20.3, page 317**

Answers: **1.** Present: goes; past: went; past participle: gone **3.** Present: drinks; past: drank; past participle: drunk **5.** Present: feels; past: felt; past participle: felt **7.** Present: keeps; past: kept; past participle: kept **9.** Present: understands; past: understood; past participle: understood

◆ **PRACTICE 20.4, page 318**

Answers: **1.** made **3.** kept **5.** found **7.** been **9.** heard

◆ **PRACTICE 20.5, page 319**

Answers: **1.** become **3.** caught **5.** shown **7.** Correct; correct **9.** given

◆ **PRACTICE 20.6, page 320**

Answers: **1.** has been **3.** have chosen **5.** has caused **7.** have led **9.** had become

◆ **PRACTICE 20.7, page 321**

Answers: **1.** have enjoyed **3.** played **5.** saw; have never seen **7.** have ever had; has ever thrown **9.** moved

◆ **PRACTICE 20.8, page 322**

Answers: **1.** was; received **3.** have continued **5.** has become **7.** have gotten **9.** have celebrated

◆ **PRACTICE 20.9, page 323**

Answers: **1.** had become **3.** had marketed **5.** had been **7.** have used **9.** have developed

◆ **PRACTICE 20.10, page 324**

Answers: **1.** had done; hoped **3.** ran **5.** had planned; made **7.** spent **9.** had arrived **11.** had shown; proved

◆ **PRACTICE 20.11, page 325**

Answers: **1.** abandoned **3.** unconcerned **5.** injured **7.** rescued **9.** swamped

◆ **PRACTICE 20.12, page 326**

Answers: **1.** made **3.** registered **5.** worn **7.** sworn **9.** cut **11.** paved **13.** sworn **15.** registered **17.** hidden **19.** defeated

◆ **PRACTICE 20.13, page 327**

Answers: **1.** Past participle: injured. The injured quarterback played for the rest of the quarter. **3.** Past participle: dried. Rafika put the dried figs in a dish. **5.** Past participle: pointed. The baby stared at his pointed beard for several minutes. **7.** Past participle: burned. He put his burned fingers in his mouth. **9.** Past participle: expected. The students did not give the expected answers.

Chapter 21

◆ **PRACTICE 21.1, page 332**

Answers: **1.** holiday (common); year (common); spirits (common); dead (common) **3.** holiday (common); Aztecs (proper); ritual (common) **5.** people (common); Day of the Dead (proper); regions (common) **7.** Mexico City (proper); residents (common); festival (common); town (common); skeletons (common); skulls (common) **9.** places (common); tourists (common); celebration (common)

◆ **PRACTICE 21.2, page 334**

Possible answers: **1.** class **3.** class; hours **5.** people; problem **7.** solution **9.** voice; sound

◆ **PRACTICE 21.3, page 334**

Answers: **1.** obstetrician **3.** options **5.** years; correct **7.** woman **9.** Correct; countries

◆ **PRACTICE 21.4, page 336**

Answers: **1.** ladies-in-waiting (irregular) **3.** potatoes **5.** benches **7.** calendars **9.** highways **11.** cheeses **13.** enemies (irregular) **15.** calves (irregular) **17.** taxes **19.** stomachs

◆ **PRACTICE 21.5, page 337**

Answers: **1.** He became famous in many countries for directing the martial arts scenes in *The Matrix* and *Crouching Tiger, Hidden Dragon.* **3.** He has also done action scenes for several other movies. **5.** In the 1960s, he started his career, working alongside many other novice actors and stuntmen in movies and television. **7.** As a director, Yuen proved he had a talent for developing exciting stories that were full of comedy as well as action. **9.** For instance, Yuen will often have performers use ordinary objects, such as brushes or robe sleeves, to represent knives and other weapons.

Chapter 22

◆ **PRACTICE 22.1, page 342**

Answers: **1.** She (singular) **3.** We (plural) **5.** it (singular) **7.** he (singular) **9.** we (plural)

◆ **PRACTICE 22.2, page 343**

Answers: **1.** Antecedent: woman; pronoun: she **3.** Antecedent: hitchhiker; pronoun: his **5.** Antecedent: lawyers; pronoun: they **7.** Antecedent: Esteban; pronoun: he **9.** Antecedent: Fries; pronoun: they

◆ **PRACTICE 22.3, page 343**

Answers: **1.** it **3.** it **5.** they **7.** it **9.** they

◆ **PRACTICE 22.4, page 344**

Answers: **1.** Antecedent: schools; pronoun: they **3.** Antecedent: parents; pronoun: their **5.** Antecedent: schools; pronoun: their **7.** Antecedent: Williams; pronoun: his **9.** Antecedent: programs; pronoun: they

◆ **PRACTICE 22.5, page 345**

Answers: **1.** Compound antecedent: power and intelligence; connecting word: and; pronoun: their **3.** Compound antecedent: power and position; connecting word: and; pronoun: them **5.** Compound antecedent: movies and television; connecting word: and; pronoun: their **7.** Compound antecedent: *Chicago* and *Bringing Down the House;* connecting word: and; pronoun: their **9.** Compound antecedent: skills and talents; connecting word: and; pronoun: they

◆ **PRACTICE 22.6, page 346**

Answers: **1.** Correct **3.** Correct **5.** Correct **7.** them **9.** its

◆ **PRACTICE 22.7, page 348**

Answers: **1.** Indefinite pronoun antecedent: Everyone; pronoun: his or her **3.** Indefinite pronoun antecedent: anyone; pronoun: his or her **5.** Indefinite pronoun antecedent: few; pronoun: their **7.** Indefinite pronoun antecedent: Each; pronoun: her **9.** Indefinite pronoun antecedent: Either; pronoun: her **11.** Indefinite pronoun antecedent: no one; pronoun: his or her **13.** Indefinite pronoun antecedent: anybody; pronoun: his or her **15.** Indefinite pronoun antecedent: someone; pronoun: his or her

◆ **PRACTICE 22.8, page 350**

Answers: **1.** Pronoun: his or her; antecedent: Everyone **3.** Pronoun: their; antecedent: few **5.** Pronoun: he or she; antecedent: each **7.** Pronoun: her; antecedent: either **9.** Pronoun: their; antecedent: Many

◆ **PRACTICE 22.9, page 350**

Possible edits: **1.** Someone left his or her key in the lock. **3.** All the people on the platform missed their train. **5.** All the telemarketers hated making their calls at dinnertime. **7.** Anyone would love to give this toy to his or her children. **9.** All of the students must email their essays to the professor. **11.** Has anybody in this neighborhood lost his or her dog? **13.** Someone hung up without leaving his or her name on the answering machine. **15.** The voters thought the candidate was charming, but they did not want to vote for him.

◆ **PRACTICE 22.10, page 352**

Answers: **1.** Antecedent: pack (collective); pronoun: its **3.** Antecedent: officers; pronoun: their **5.** Antecedent: gang (collective); pronoun: its **7.** Antecedent: class (collective); pronoun: its **9.** Antecedent: jury (collective); pronoun: its

◆ **PRACTICE 22.11, page 352**

Answers: **1.** Correct; their **3.** his or her **5.** their **7.** Correct **9.** their

◆ **PRACTICE 22.12, page 354**

Answers: **1.** Canada has many sparsely populated areas. **3.** The video game that I bought broke almost immediately. **5.** Her granddaughter lives in another state. **7.** These apples were damaged in the hailstorm. **9.** The acrobat almost fell off the tightrope.

◆ **PRACTICE 22.13, page 356**

Answers: **1.** He: subjective; his: possessive **3.** I: subjective; my: possessive **5.** mine: possessive; yours: possessive **7.** me: objective; her: objective **9.** Their: possessive; we: subjective; them: objective; our: possessive

◆ **PRACTICE 22.14, page 357**

Answers: **1.** him: indirect object **3.** us: direct object **5.** him: direct object **7.** you: indirect object **9.** me: indirect object

◆ **PRACTICE 22.15, page 358**

Answers: **1.** him **3.** him; me **5.** She **7.** They; I **9.** they

◆ **PRACTICE 22.16, page 360**

Answers: **1.** he [is] **3.** I [eat] **5.** [it frightens] me **7.** [it costs] us **9.** [he pays] her

◆ **PRACTICE 22.17, page 361**

Answers: **1.** who **3.** who **5.** who **7.** who **9.** who

◆ **PRACTICE 22.18, page 362**

Answers: **1.** herself **3.** itself **5.** myself **7.** yourself [or yourselves] **9.** themselves

Chapter 23

◆ **PRACTICE 23.1, page 368**

Answers: **1.** The group called Rock Bottom Remainders is made up entirely of famous authors. **3.** They play to raise money for charity, and they sometimes make big fools of themselves in the process. **5.** Usually, she wears more modest clothes. **7.** The Rock Bottom Remainders' rare concerts take place only once or twice a year. **9.** Of course, nobody thinks that the authors are talented musicians.

◆ **PRACTICE 23.2, page 369**

Answers: **1.** The subway train screeched noisily into the station. **3.** Entering passengers struggled bravely to get through the narrow doors. **5.** I stood jammed uncomfortably in the middle of the car, praying I'd be able to wriggle out quickly when I reached my stop.

◆ **PRACTICE 23.3, page 370**

Answers: **1.** nearly **3.** differently **5.** freely **7.** widely **9.** really **11.** regularly

◆ **PRACTICE 23.4, page 371**

Answers: **1.** well **3.** good **5.** good **7.** good **9.** well **11.** well **13.** well

◆ **PRACTICE 23.5, page 373**

Answers: **1.** stronger **3.** more quickly **5.** neater **7.** fairer **9.** younger **11.** bluer **13.** easier **15.** more useful **17.** harder **19.** deeper

◆ **PRACTICE 23.6, page 374**

Answers: **1.** strongest **3.** most quickly **5.** neatest **7.** fairest **9.** youngest **11.** bluest **13.** easiest **15.** most useful **17.** hardest **19.** deepest

◆ **PRACTICE 23.7, page 374**

Answers: **1.** more durable **3.** more clearly **5.** more freely **7.** poorer **9.** more favorably

◆ **PRACTICE 23.8, page 375**

Answers: **1.** craziest **3.** tiniest **5.** most necessary **7.** greatest **9.** most surprising

◆ **PRACTICE 23.9, page 376**

Answers: **1.** best **3.** worse **5.** best **7.** better **9.** better

◆ **PRACTICE 23.10, page 377**

Answers: **1.** That **3.** this **5.** This **7.** those **9.** this

Chapter 24

◆ **PRACTICE 24.1, page 383**

Answers: **1.** It will rain all day tomorrow. **3.** Javier studied so that he could become an American citizen. **5.** Sofia watched television programs for children when she was learning English. **7.** She waited until she was sure they were gone. **9.** After Jean scored the winning goal, he went out to celebrate with his friends.

◆ **PRACTICE 24.2, page 385**

Answers: **1.** The old woman sells candles in the shop downstairs. **3.** Dmitri rides his bicycle ten miles every day. **5.** My neighbor watches my daughter in the evenings. **7.** My job starts at six o'clock in the morning. **9.** The best thing in my life is that my family is together again. or: I feel lucky that my family is back together again.

◆ **PRACTICE 24.3, page 386**

Answers: **1.** toddlers; children **3.** teenagers; interests; hobbies **5.** sports **7.** twins; tricks; people **9.** outfits; girls; outfits

◆ **PRACTICE 24.4, page 388**

Answers: **1.** Noncount **3.** Noncount **5.** Count; beaches **7.** Noncount **9.** Noncount

◆ **PRACTICE 24.5, page 390**

Answers: **1.** Each **3.** much **5.** A few **7.** a little **9.** Few

◆ **PRACTICE 24.6, page 393**

Answers: **1.** The **3.** a; a **5.** The; a **7.** a; blank **9.** an; blank **11.** the; the

◆ **PRACTICE 24.7, page 394**

Answers: **1.** Question: Are the sparrows searching for winter food? Negative statement: The sparrows are not searching for winter food. **3.** Question: Did I answer her email immediately? Negative statement: I did not answer her email immediately. **5.** Question: Did the porcupine attack my dog? Negative statement: The porcupine did not attack my dog. **7.** Question: Did Gunnar see the robbery at the convenience store? Negative statement: Gunnar did not see the robbery at the convenience store. **9.** Question: Is he working on the problem right now? Negative statement: He is not working on the problem right now.

◆ **PRACTICE 24.8, page 397**

Answers: **1.** Verb: has been studying. Correct **3.** Verb: is understanding. He understands the movements of planets and stars. **5.** Verb: is working. Correct **7.** Verb: is hating. He hates the boring work there. **9.** Verb: is earning. Correct

◆ **PRACTICE 24.9, page 398**

Answers: **1.** a pleasant old family tradition **3.** Anita's four pampered poodles **5.** both my annoying sisters **7.** a delightful outdoor wedding celebration **9.** a wonderful chocolate birthday cake

◆ **PRACTICE 24.10, page 401**

Answers: **1.** from **3.** in; in **5.** with **7.** of; in **9.** in; of **11.** to; in; for

◆ **PRACTICE 24.11, page 403**

Answers: **1.** Correct **3.** Correct **5.** When the friend gave it back to her, Juanita was relieved to find that it had very few mistakes. **7.** Correct **9.** She mailed them off to her prospective employers.

Chapter 25

◆ **PRACTICE 25.1, page 412**

Answers: **1.** The intersection was crowded with buses, cars, and trucks. **3.** Correct **5.** A good marriage requires patience, honesty, and hard work. **7.** Correct **9.** The kitchen is to the left, the guest room is upstairs, and the pool is out back.

◆ **PRACTICE 25.2, page 413**

Answers: **1.** At the end of the game, the bus took the team home. **3.** After the holiday season, many stores take inventory. **5.** Racing against the clock, Silvio finished the corporate earnings report. **7.** Often feared, bats are actually helpful creatures. **9.** Without access to telephones, more than half the world's population depends on face-to-face communication.

◆ **PRACTICE 25.3, page 415**

Answers: **1.** Bill, how did you do on the test? **3.** Correct **5.** When you give your speech, Jeanne, be sure to speak clearly. **7.** The party, consequently, was a disaster. **9.** Don't forget the key to the cabin, Amber. **11.** Furthermore, the team had lost its best defensive player. **13.** What do you suggest we do for Zach, Dr. Chen? **15.** Besides, genetics is the next medical frontier.

◆ **PRACTICE 25.4, page 415**

Answers: **1.** For example, Tiger Woods is an exceptional golf player. **3.** His golf game, consequently, is difficult to beat. **5.** Correct **7.** His success, moreover, has come at a young age. **9.** There may, finally, be no one to challenge him on the golf course.

◆ **PRACTICE 25.6, page 416**

Answers: **1.** My mother, Sandra Thomas, used to work for the city. **3.** The convention is in Chicago, my hometown. **5.** The world's tallest mountain, Mount Everest, is in Nepal. **7.** Aloe, a common houseplant, has medicinal value. **9.** Elvis Presley, a white singer, was influenced by African American music.

◆ **PRACTICE 25.8, page 420**

Answers: **1.** Correct **3.** The camera, which is automatic, often breaks. **5.** Correct **7.** Rafael, who finishes work at 5:30, met Carla for dinner at 7:00. **9.** Gray wolves, which many ranchers dislike, are making a comeback in the West.

◆ **PRACTICE 25.9, page 421**

Answers: **1.** Correct **3.** Correct **5.** The women, who call themselves the Weavers Society, needed customers for their work. **7.** A company that sells satellite telephones donated some phones to the weavers. **9.** The weavers, who could find no customers in their own village, soon sold many of their hammocks to customers in other regions.

◆ **PRACTICE 25.10, page 421**

Answers: **1.** Correct **3.** Having escaped from Europe, which was occupied by the Nazis, these athletes put their skills to use. **5.** They trained in the Colorado mountains for three years, which gave them plenty of time to prepare.

7. The battle that eventually earned them fame and respect was the result of their successful sneak attack on the German forces on Italy's Mt. Belvedere. **9.** Aspen and Vail, which are now two of the most popular ski resorts in the country, were founded by veterans of this division.

◆ PRACTICE 25.12, page 424

Answers: **1.** Alaska is a rugged state, and its population is small. **3.** Although many people live in Alaska's cities, many others live in small villages. **5.** Correct **7.** Correct **9.** Correct

◆ PRACTICE 25.13, page 425

Answers: **1.** Atif is from Lahore, Pakistan. **3.** Their first home was at 2122 Kent Avenue, Brooklyn, New York. **5.** They wanted to move to Boston, Massachusetts, where Atif's cousins lived. **7.** Their new address was 14 Arden Street, Allston, Massachusetts. **9.** Correct

Chapter 26

◆ PRACTICE 26.1, page 430

Answers: **1.** This means that students from low-income families who can't pay for school can still get a college education. **3.** The college wants only students who wouldn't otherwise be able to afford to attend a four-year college. **5.** Berea has made itself unique in other ways as well, in ways that other schools haven't. **7.** It's not unusual for Berea students to spend many hours every week volunteering in their Appalachian community. **9.** This school offers a rare opportunity in an age where income tends to determine who's eligible for college and who isn't.

◆ PRACTICE 26.2, page 431

Answers: **1.** In many homes, television isn't a luxury, it's a necessity. **3.** They'll argue that there's plenty of high-quality programming on television. **5.** They're designed to appeal to as many people as possible. **7.** The average American doesn't read nearly as much as he or she watches television. **9.** Fifty years ago, people couldn't have imagined how attached we'd become to our television sets.

◆ PRACTICE 26.3, page 432

Answers: **1.** the shop's owner **3.** the neighbor's cat **5.** Indira's cell phone **7.** Chris's sister **9.** the class's opinion

◆ PRACTICE 26.4, page 433

Answers: **1.** the travelers' bags **3.** the women's faces **5.** the ministers' car **7.** the Huangs' apartment **9.** the lawyers' first meeting

◆ PRACTICE 26.6, page 434

Answers: **1.** New York's **3.** Correct; father's **5.** Harold Lee's; correct **7.** family's; Chinatown's **9.** agency's; Arthur's

◆ PRACTICE 26.7, page 435

Answers: **1.** its **3.** it's **5.** its **7.** you're **9.** it's

◆ PRACTICE 26.8, page 435

Answers: **1.** lovers' **3.** It's; correct **5.** its; correct **7.** Who's **9.** Correct; residents'; your

Chapter 27

◆ PRACTICE 27.1, page 442

Answers: **1.** The Ojibwa are the largest Native American group in North America. **3.** The Ojibwa made maple syrup that was something like the syrup sold in Shoprite or Safeway. **5.** A century before the Revolutionary War, Europeans traveled west and met the native peoples who lived there. **7.** The American Indian Movement is an organization that calls attention to unfair treaties, such as the Treaty of 1854. **9.** In November 2000, LaDuke ran for vice president on the Green Party ticket.

◆ PRACTICE 27.3, page 445

Answers: **1.** "These clothes are too small for me," Sue said. "These clothes," Sue said, "are too small for me." **3.** "The exam should not be too difficult," the instructor said. "The exam," the instructor said, "should not be too difficult." **5.** "Tell all the truth but tell it slant," the poet Emily Dickinson wrote. "Tell all the truth," the poet Emily Dickinson wrote, "but tell it slant."

◆ PRACTICE 27.4, page 446

Answers: **1.** Identifying tag: Dorothy Parker said. Dorothy Parker said, "The cure for boredom is curiosity." **3.** Identifying tag: Patrice asked. "Why does it always rain on my birthday?" Patrice asked. **5.** Identifying tag: Rebecca insisted. "If you lose this tape," Rebecca insisted, "I'll never lend you anything again." **7.** Identifying tag: the instructor was saying. When I walked in, the instructor was saying, "Please be sure to arrive on time." **9.** Identifying tag: Kurt Vonnegut observed. "High school," Kurt Vonnegut observed, "is closer to the core of the American experience than anything I can think of."

◆ PRACTICE 27.6, page 449

Answers: **1.** The show *A Prairie Home Companion* has been on public radio for many years. **3.** Did you see the article "Chocolate: A Sweet Life after Bitter Start" in Wednesday's *New York Times*? **5.** The song "And All That Jazz" was written for the musical *Chicago*. **7.** The textbook *Foundations First* includes the chapter "Understanding Mechanics." **9.** After studying Shakespeare's play *Hamlet,* we will read John Milton's book-length poem *Paradise Lost*.

◆ PRACTICE 27.7, page 450

Answers: **1.** Lucy's favorite novel is *For Whom the Bell Tolls*. **3.** Recent television cartoons created for adults include *The Simpsons* and *King of the Hill*. **5.** The articles "Stream of Consciousness" and "School's Out" in *Wired* magazine focus on new technology.

Chapter 28

◆ PRACTICE 28.1, page 456

Answers: **1.** Correct; achieve **3.** Neither; correct **5.** Correct; correct **7.** society; correct **9.** relieve; correct

◆ PRACTICE 28.2, page 457

Answers: **1.** uneasy **3.** overcook **5.** unwind **7.** underpay **9.** prewar

◆ PRACTICE 28.3, page 458

Answers: **1.** adorable **3.** judgment **5.** whistled **7.** truly **9.** insurance **11.** senseless **13.** noticeable **15.** amusement **17.** imagination **19.** microscopic

◆ PRACTICE 28.4, page 459

Answers: **1.** trying **3.** noisily **5.** destroyed **7.** dryness **9.** tinier **11.** busily **13.** replied **15.** thirtyish **17.** joyful **19.** daily

◆ PRACTICE 28.5, page 460

Answers: **1.** shopper **3.** preferred **5.** climbed **7.** fairest **9.** beginning **11.** written **13.** appealing **15.** existing **17.** runner **19.** trapper

Chapter 29

◆ PRACTICE 29.1, page 464

Answers: **1.** Correct; correct **3.** affect; correct **5.** Correct; correct; correct **7.** By; already **9.** Correct; correct

◆ PRACTICE 29.2, page 465

Answers: **1.** conscious **3.** It's; hear **5.** Every day; its **7.** every day; correct **9.** conscious; its

◆ PRACTICE 29.3, page 467

Answers: **1.** laid; correct **3.** past; mind **5.** lose **7.** lie; correct **9.** Correct; lie

◆ PRACTICE 29.4, page 469

Answers: **1.** Correct; rise **3.** plain; correct **5.** quiet; sit **7.** Correct; correct **9.** Correct; principal

◆ PRACTICE 29.5, page 470

Answers: **1.** used; their **3.** through; correct; their **5.** Correct; correct **7.** Correct; their **9.** Correct; too

◆ PRACTICE 29.6, page 472

Answers: **1.** Who's; correct **3.** You're; your **5.** Were; correct **7.** you're; correct **9.** Whose; where

Appendix

◆ PRACTICE 1, page 533

Answers: **1.** plight **3.** mature **5.** vixen **7.** concoction **9.** arduous **11.** orientation **13.** immortalize **15.** liability **17.** transaction

◆ PRACTICE 2, page 534

Answers: **1.** concoction **3.** malign **5.** naturalization **7.** symbol **9.** lethal **11.** brawl **13.** orient **15.** subsidize **17.** surveillance **19.** embossed

Acknowledgments

Picture acknowledgments

3, S. Zuckerman/Old School Photo; 21, Gary Conner/Index Stock Imagery, Inc.; 22, ©2001, Tropicana Products, Inc. Courtesy, Frankel; 23, The Metropolitan Museum of Art, Catharine Lorillard Wolfe Collection, Wolfe Fund, 1906. (06.1234) Photograph © 1995, The Metropolitan Museum of Art; 39, Michael Bryant/*Philadelphia Inquirer*; 55, Michael Newman/PhotoEdit Inc.; 67, Bob Daemmrich Photography, Inc.; 84, Rudi Von Briel/Index Stock Imagery, Inc.; 101, AP/Wide World Photos; 102 (top), Robert E. Klein/AP/Wide World Photos; 102 (bottom), David McGlynn/Getty Images; 104, Bettmann/CORBIS; 137, Lou Requena/AP/Wide World Photos; 150, Ghislain & Marie David de Lossy/Getty Images; 155, Tony Freeman/PhotoEdit Inc.; 166 (top), AP/Wide World Photos; 166 (bottom), Library of Congress; 168, SuperStock; 182, Jeff Greenberg/PhotoEdit Inc.; 183 (top), Bob Daemmrich/The Image Works; 183 (bottom), David Young-Wolff/PhotoEdit Inc.; 186, David Zelick/Getty Images; 198 (top), Jeff Greenberg/PhotoEdit Inc.; 198 (bottom), Tony Anderson/Getty Images; 199, David Young-Wolff/PhotoEdit Inc.; 201, Judy Gelles/Stock, Boston, LLC; 210, Robert W. Ginn/PhotoEdit Inc.; 211 (top), Steve Dunwell/Index Stock Imagery, Inc.; 211 (bottom), Bob Sacha/IPN/Aurora Photos; 213, Charles Gupton/Corbis Stock Market; 220, Bettmann/CORBIS; 221, Bettmann/CORBIS; 225, Scott Houston/CORBIS Sygma; 233, The Kobal Collection; 235, Joe Raedle/Getty Images; 251, Myrleen Ferguson Cate/PhotoEdit Inc.; 252, Chris Rogers/Index Stock Imagery, Inc.; 254, John Elk III/Stock, Boston, LLC; 270 (top), Alan Schein Photography/CORBIS; 270 (bottom), Tony Freeman/PhotoEdit Inc.; 273, Syracuse Newspapers/John Barry/The Image Works; 281, Stu Forster/Getty Images; 282, Mike Powell/Getty Images; 284, Mitch Diamond/Index Stock Imagery, Inc.; 295 (top), Felicia Martinez/PhotoEdit Inc.; 295 (bottom), Felicia Martinez/PhotoEdit Inc.; 299, Time Life Photos/Getty Images; 309 (top), Stapleton Collection/Bridgeman Art Library International; 309 (bottom), Index Stock Imagery, Inc.; 309 (center), Denver Public Library, Western History Collection, X-33607; 311, Frank Rossotto/Corbis Stock Market; 329, BOONDOCKS © 2004 Aaron McGruder. Dist. By UNIVERSAL PRESS SYNDICATE. Reprinted with permission. All rights reserved.; 331, Syracuse Newspapers/The Image Works; 338, James Marshall/The Image Works; 341, CORBIS; 364, David Young-Wolff/PhotoEdit Inc.; 365, Scholastic Studio 10/Index Stock Imagery, Inc.; 367, Bob Daemmrich/The Image Works; 379, CORBIS; 382, Bob Daemmrich/The Image Works; 405, Library of Congress; 405, Library of Congress; 405, Library of Congress; 405, Library of Congress; 411, Dan Loh/AP/Wide World Photos; 427, Bettmann/CORBIS; 427, Bettmann/CORBIS; 429, Grantpix/Photo Researchers, Inc.; 437, Spencer Grant/PhotoEdit Inc.; 438, Volvox/Index Stock Imagery, Inc.; 440, Photofest; 451 (top), Hulton | Archive Photos/Getty Images; 451 (bottom), Kevin Winter/Getty Images; 453, Tom McCarthy/Corbis Stock Market; 461 (top), Jeff Dunn/Index Stock Imagery, Inc.; 461 (bottom), Bob Daemmrich/The Image Works; 463, George B. Jones III/Photo Researchers, Inc.; 473, Seth Perlman/AP/Wide World Photos.

Text acknowledgments

Kiku Adatto. "Trigger-Happy Birthday." From *The New York Times Magazine,* May 14, 2004. Copyright © 2004 by The New York Times Company, Inc. Reprinted with the permission of the publisher.

American Heritage Dictionary of the English Language, Third Edition. Entries "teach," "frying pan," tax," "sneak." Copyright © 1996 by Houghton Mifflin Company. Reprinted by permission from *The American Heritage Dictionary of the English Language,* Third Edition.

Ray Hanania. "One of the Bad Guys." From *Newsweek,* November 2, 1998. Copyright © 1998 Newsweek, Inc. All rights reserved. Reprinted by permission.

John Hartmire. "At the Heart of the Historic Movement." From *Newsweek,* July 24, 2000. Copyright © 2000 Newsweek, Inc. All rights reserved. Reprinted by permission.

Macarena del Rocío Hernández. "What I Did for Love." From the *Philadelphia Inquirer Magazine,* July 2, 2000. Copyright © 2000 by Philadelphia Newspapers, Inc. Reprinted by permission.

Don H. Hockenbury and Sandra K. Hockenbury. "Attribution." From *Psychology 2/e* by Don H. Hockenbury and Sandra K. Hockenbury. Copyright © 1997, 1999 by Worth Publishers. Used with permission.

Arthur Miller. "Before Air Conditioning." From *The New Yorker.* Copyright © 1998 by Arthur Miller. Reprinted by permission of the author.

Robb Moretti. "The Last Generation to Live on the Edge." From *Newsweek,* August 5, 2002. Copyright © 2002 Newsweek, Inc. All rights reserved. Reprinted by permission.

Joshua Piven and David Borgenicht. "How to Stop a Car with No Brakes." From *Worst Case Scenario Survial Handbook™: Travel.* Copyright © 2001 by Quirk Productions, Inc. Used with permission of Chronicle Books LLC, San Francisco.

Lucie Prinz. "Say Something." From *The Atlantic Monthly,* October 1996. Copyright © 1996 by Lucie Prinz. Reprinted by permission of the author.

Gerry Roll. "Reality TV's 'Hick Hunt' and the Appalachian Truth." From *The Christian Science Monitor,* February 7, 2003. Copyright © 2003 by Gerry Roll. Reprinted by permission of the author.

Carolyn Foster Segal. "The Dog Ate My Disk, and Other Tales of Woe." From *The Chronicle of Higher Education,* August 11, 2000. Reprinted with the permission of the author.

Susan Snyder and Kristin E. Holmes. "Philadelphia Students Get a Scholarship Guarantee." From *Philadelphia Inquirer,* October 1, 2003. Copyright © 2003 by the Philadelphia Newspapers, Inc. Reprinted by permission of the publisher.

Gary Soto. "The Colors." From *A Summer Life* by Gary Soto. Copyright © 1990 by the University Press of New England. Reprinted with the permission of the University Press of New England via Copyright Clearance Center.

Linda S. Wallace. "A 'Good' American Citizen." From *The Christian Science Monitor,* April 1, 2003. Copyright © 2003 by Linda S. Wallace. Reprinted by permission of the author.

William Zinsser. "The Transaction." From *On Writing Well: An Informal Guide to Writing Nonfiction, 6th edition* by William Zinsser. Copyright © 1976, 1980, 1985, 1988, 1990, 1994, 1998 by William Zinsser. Reprinted with the permission of the author.

Index

Note: Numbers in **bold** type indicate pages where terms are defined.

Index of Rhetorical Patterns